SQUADRON A
A HISTORY OF ITS FIRST FIFTY YEARS
1889-1939

To Jonathan
With warm regards,
Harry Collins
4/12/15

MAJOR GENERAL CHARLES F. ROE

SQUADRON A

A History of Its

First Fifty Years

1889–1939

Association of
Ex-Members of Squadron A
Reprinted by Squadron A Association

DEDICATED TO

SQUADRON A AND THE ACTIVE ORGANIZATION

HERITAGE BOOKS
2010

HERITAGE BOOKS
AN IMPRINT OF HERITAGE BOOKS, INC.

Books, CDs, and more—Worldwide

For our listing of thousands of titles see our website
at
www.HeritageBooks.com

A Facsimile Reprint
Published 2010 by
HERITAGE BOOKS, INC.
Publishing Division
100 Railroad Ave. #104
Westminster, Maryland 21157

Copyright © 1939 Association of
Ex-Members of Squadron A, Incorporated

— Publisher's Notice —
In reprints such as this, it is often not possible to remove blemishes from the original. We feel the contents of this book warrant its reissue despite these blemishes and hope you will agree and read it with pleasure.

International Standard Book Numbers
Paperbound: 978-0-7884-3503-4
Clothbound: 978-0-7884-8363-9

COMPILERS AND EDITORS

HERBERT BARRY, *Chairman*
CARLETON S. COOKE
KNOWLTON DURHAM
RODMAN GILDER
FREDERICK P. KEPPEL
RONALD C. LEE
PHILIP J. MCCOOK

COMMITTEE ON ILLUSTRATIONS

HENRY STUART OTTO, *Chairman*
FRANCIS O. NOBLE
AUGUSTUS D. SHEPARD
FRANK TINSLEY

PUBLICATION COMMITTEE

EDWARD OLMSTED, *Chairman*
GEORGE P. BRETT
EDWARD P. HAMILTON
HENRY STUART OTTO
FREDERICK A. VIETOR

The names of members who have contributed papers included in this volume are given in the Table of Contents.

CONTENTS

	PAGE
Preliminary Statement by the Compilers	xi

A Picturesque Civilian Group That Preceded Troop A

The New York Hussars, Also Called Dragoons (Oliver B. Bridgman)	3

1889–1911
The Era of Charles F. Roe; and That of His Successors Avery D. Andrews and Oliver B. Bridgman

The Troop Comes into Being and Develops	17
A Trooper's Diary of the First Five Years (William R. Browning)	17
The Armory Training	28
Athletics and the Annual Games	31
Sundry Activities and Amusements	35
The Cadet Corps (S. Sidney Haight)	39
Small Arms Practice and Competitions	41
Camps of Instruction, Practice Marches, and Tactical Exercises	47
The Manassas Maneuvers, 1904 (Eliot Tuckerman)	53
The Massachusetts Maneuvers, 1909 (Noel Bleecker Fox)	70
Strike Duty	77
Buffalo, 1892 (Walter W. Price)	81
Brooklyn, 1895 (Frederic R. Coudert)	85
Croton, 1900 (Abel I. Smith)	89
Escort Duty, Parades, and Reviews	94
The Year of the Spanish-American War (Avery D. Andrews)	103
Volunteer Troop A in the Spanish-American War (Frederic R. Coudert)	110

CONTENTS

1912–1918
The Period in Which Major William R. Wright Commanded

	PAGE
The Years 1912–1918: Including Reorganization and Changes of Name; the Connecticut Maneuvers; the Mexican Border Service; the Entry into Federal Service for the World War; and the Change to the Machine Gun Battalion (William R. Wright)	129
The Mexican Border Service (Knowlton Durham)	158

The Depot Troop—Later, Squadron A, New York Guard

The Depot Units: Organization and Development, 1916–1917 (Latham G. Reed)	169
The Depot Troop, the Depot Squadron, and Squadron A, New York Guard: A Short Interlude, 1918 (Herbert Barry)	177
Squadron A Cavalry, New York Guard: Carrying On and Fulfillment, 1918–1919 (Alfred Wendt)	180

1917–1919
The World War Period

The Roll of Honor	187
The Roll of Service	189
The 105th Machine Gun Battalion (Narrative by Knowlton Durham, Kenneth Gardner, Stanton Whitney, Robert R. Molyneux, L. Horatio Biglow, and John Reynolds)	190

1919–1939
Squadron A Again Becomes Part of the National Guard

The Squadron from July 1919 to December 1932 (N. Hillyer Egleston)	255
The Squadron of Today (Frederick A. Vietor)	262
Squadron A in the Army Maneuvers, August 13–27, 1939—A Supplement to the History of the First Fifty Years (Frederick A. Vietor)	269

CONTENTS

Additional Papers

	PAGE
Address upon Dedication of Memorial Tablet to General Roe (Herbert Barry)	283
Chronology of Squadron A	286
The Armory	309
The Association of Ex-Members of Squadron A	313
Riding in the Squadron (Carleton S. Cook)	319
Reminiscences (John D. Kilpatrick)	325
Verses and Songs of the Squadron	333
List of Former and Present Members of Squadron A	355

PRELIMINARY STATEMENT BY THE COMPILERS

The fortunes of above half the world, for want of a record, stir not from their place and vanish without duration.—MONTAIGNE

Two interesting volumes have been published dealing with portions of the career of Squadron A. The first was the story of Volunteer Troop A in the Spanish War—1898. The second was the story of the 105th Machine Gun Battalion and of individual ex-members in the Great War—1917, 1918. Both were issued by the parent organization. The present work does not attempt to supersede these earlier ones, but to supplement them, and to cover a wider field and longer periods.

The publication of this history commemorates the fiftieth anniversary of the mustering of Troop A into the National Guard of the State of New York, on April 2, 1889. The central figure on that day was Charles F. Roe, a former lieutenant of cavalry in the United States Army, who was graduated at West Point in 1868. He had resigned from the army in 1888 and gone into business in New York City, and was a friend of the military artist Rufus F. Zogbaum. It was Zogbaum, who after attending a drill at Dickel's Riding Academy upon the invitation of the provisional commander of the embryo troop (known as Hussars or Dragoons) brought about the introduction of this Regular Cavalry Officer who, as Zogbaum said, was "homesick for the cavalry."

Roe became the moving spirit in developing the organization, which he commanded from its inception until his resignation, in 1898, to take charge of the entire National Guard of the state. He held the warm affection as well as the highest respect of all the members of the command throughout his lifetime. His own feeling for the squadron is indicated in the communication of February 11, 1898, which accompanied his separation from Squadron A:

PRELIMINARY STATEMENT

HEADQUARTERS
OF THE DIVISION OF NATIONAL GUARD
NEW YORK, February 11th, 1898.

I hereby relinquish command of Squadron A by reason of being promoted to the position of Major General Commanding the Division of the National Guard of the State of New York; but in so doing, it is with extreme official and personal regret at leaving the Squadron. I wish to have it distinctly understood that the splendid way in which the members of Troop A and Squadron A have responded to military duty and have worked with me to build up a successful cavalry organization has more than enhanced my military reputation, and is the real cause of my being advanced to the very honorable position of Major General.

Although my direct touch with the Squadron is severed, my personal and official interest will ever continue. It is my wish to each and every member to keep up the esprit de corps and continue to keep the organization what it is for all time.

CHAS. F. ROE
Major General

The history of the troop and the squadron divides naturally into several periods. The first covers the inception and joyous early years of the original Troop A; the birth of the squadron and its sturdy growth and colorful development under Major Roe; the year of the Spanish-American War; and a period of nearly two decades during which the command devolved upon officers trained in its own ranks. This period culminated in Federal service on the Mexican border.

Following this, came the troop's dedication to the grim, drab, and exhausting realities of service in the World War, with full and effective performance of every assigned undertaking.

The latest period followed the return of the squadron to its place in the peace-time system of national defense, in which it has continuously functioned as an outstanding, distinguished unit of highest discipline, efficiency, and morale.

The compilers of this record had the good fortune to find available some papers already written covering portions of the picture. Three of the authors, Bridgman, Wright, and Wendt, are no longer with us. It is a matter of regret that there is no paper by General Roe—other than a brief chronology of the first five years—and no history by General Bridgman of the period during which he was in command. The official records of Troop A and of Squadron A prior to the World War have apparently disappeared; and some of the story—particularly the general narrative from 1889 to 1912—is therefore built in part on the memories of those who took part, supplemented by such contemporary papers as have been preserved by individuals.

General Avery D. Andrews, who, as major, commanded the squadron in 1898, has written a paper covering that period, which contains some hitherto unpublished data of peculiar historic interest; also Major Wright wrote a narrative of the years 1912–1918, during which he was in command. Service in aid of civil authority, the Spanish War Volunteer Troop, the maneuvers at Manassas and later in Massachusetts, and the activities on the Mexican border are dealt with in separate papers by individual members. The Depot Squadron—afterwards Squadron A, New York Guard—is the subject of papers by its three commanding officers. This unique organization carried on when the squadron was at the border, and later when it entered Federal service for the World War. Through this state guard unit, Squadron A, N.G.N.Y., was revived and continued after the war.

In the World War the history of Squadron A includes its service as the unit constituting the 105th Machine Gun Battalion, 27th Division; also the Federal service in other units of men and officers who had been members of the squadron. The history published in 1923, entitled "Squadron A in the Great War, 1917–1918," contains an impressive recital entitled "Roll of Service," and in this will be found the names of approximately 600 commissioned officers. The quality of its membership is also indicated by the fact that more than 115 officers and enlisted men whose service began in Squadron A were awarded decorations or citations, or both. This roll of service was compiled from replies to questionnaires, but as many were unanswered, the record is necessarily incomplete. In the narrative written by Major Wright and included in this volume, he said: "Our one comparatively small organization furnished over 750 officers"; and in a circular issued by Major Egleston in 1919 the number is placed at more than 800.

For the saga of the Machine Gun Battalion there is an introductory paper by Major Knowlton Durham, its adjutant, and a concise recital by Colonel Kenneth Gardner, who, as major, commanded it in combat in France. Following this are descriptive papers by other members of the battalion.

For the two decades following the World War, papers have been secured from General N. Hillyer Egleston, who was in command as major until 1932, and Major Frederick A. Vietor, who has been in command since that time. These complete the word picture of the history of the first fifty years of the life of our organization.

There have been many anniversaries on which the birth of the troop has been celebrated; probably the most elaborate was the twenty-fifth, in April, 1914. It is described in the narrative by Major Wright.

That celebration came prior to the firing of the first shot in the World War. The next five years culminated in that great struggle in which our organization and its former members held to and justified the ideals of Squadron A and lived up to its motto, *"Boutez en avant."* In the years succeeding that epoch the squadron has continued to provide a school for officers, an exceptional body of organized and highly trained cavalrymen, and a body of citizen soldiery upon whom in any military emergency the country can depend.

The Ex-Members are proud of the outfit in its present embodiment as well as in its earlier phases. They expect that in the future the Ex-Members of each succeeding year will contribute to a continuing and ever inspiring tradition.

APOLOGIA

In this compilation some errors and omissions will doubtless be discovered; also there are some unavoidable repetitions. It is hoped that they will be considered with indulgence.

As to the quotations preceding papers contributed by individuals, criticisms must be borne by the compilers. The writers of these papers are not responsible for them.

A PICTURESQUE CIVILIAN GROUP
THAT PRECEDED TROOP A

THIS highly decorative group of uniformed horsemen first made the headlines in 1884 as a feature of a political parade, and with varying uniforms and varying fortunes continued to April 2, 1889. A musical composition was dedicated to it as the "First Hussars," and it was also called the "First New York Hussars," and still later the "First Dragoons." Long after most of those who had played their parts in the civilian organization had passed away, General Oliver B. Bridgman in an address at the annual meeting of the Ex-Members' Association in 1933 vividly pictured this almost prehistoric period, and upon request wrote out and signed the narrative which we now present. It gave the initial impulse to the compiling of this history, and but for his death a few months later, he would doubtless have written a narrative of later events.

THE NEW YORK HUSSARS, ALSO CALLED DRAGOONS

> When I first put this uniform on,
> I said, as I looked in the glass,
> "It's one to a million
> That any civilian
> My figure and form will surpass."
> —W. S. Gilbert, "Patience"

My Former Fellow Troopers:

You do not know how it warms the cockles of the heart of your former "Old Man" to have so many here with him tonight. When I was much younger, it pleased me immensely to be so called, but when I look around this room, and realize that I probably am *The* Old Man, I do not know that the appellation gives me the same thrill as formerly. However, let us turn to the subject before us.

It was suggested a short time ago that possibly it might be interesting to you to know, or, knowing it, might care to again go over the circumstance which led up to the birth of our present full-grown and robust Squadron A. And I, probably being the *oldest inhabitant*, was asked to tell the story.

We all know that in the construction of any building there is an immense amount of work done before it is even visible, and the great majority of people simply look at the finished product, without ever giving a thought to all that was done to make it possible.

So now I am going to ask you to look backwards with me, for over forty-eight years—No wonder I am well named.

I can assure you the infant was not carried and gently laid down by the proverbial stork, but came after many, many months of genuine hard labor.

During the Blaine-Cleveland presidential campaign in the summer of 1884, a mounted political club was formed which made quite a hit—especially when the mounts refused to be frightened by the "rockets' red glare" and the torches of the paraders; at any rate it was the most picturesque part of the parades. After the election, the campaign ended. No reason then existed for the club to continue; but there were a few who felt that in some manner, possibly as a riding club, they might keep together. At any rate it was early in 1885 that a few who had taken part in the political battle got together to talk over the matter. It was decided to form a very exclusive troop of cavalry. Then the trouble began. Meetings were held at various times and places, when, if there were sixteen or eighteen present, there were about the same number of ideas presented as to how things should be done; but eventually the name New York Hussars was decided on, and Horace J. Brooks, a veteran of the 7th Regiment of this city, was elected captain. A uniform was adopted which, as I remember seeing it, consisted of a very dark blue, almost black, tunic with black braid and yellow piping, long trousers of the same color with a narrow yellow stripe, and a cap to correspond; but those who availed themselves of the privilege of purchasing it were few. The reasons given were such as: "I wasn't present when it was adopted and don't like it anyway"; "I am not going to get one as I am not sure the organization will go on, and anyway I don't know whether I shall stay in."

Drills, or rather rides, were held during the early part of 1885 in Dickel's Riding Academy, 130 West Fifty-sixth Street, with as many present as could find it convenient to attend—the total membership was then about eighteen. During the early summer of 1885, Captain Brooks decided that several, who were not really keen for the strict military work necessary for admittance to the Guard, should resign. Early in the fall, a reorganization took place and new blood entered into it; and at a meeting called for the purpose, Thomas Manning was elected captain, Herbert H. Balch, first lieutenant, and Douglas Green (the father of our Douglas Green), second lieutenant.

Drills were again begun in Dickel's, and continued weekly during the winter and spring of 1886, although I will say they occasionally took the form of meetings and discussions. In that year the martial spirit in me, which had been slumbering since I was a cadet in the Albany Military Academy, was aroused, especially when I realized it was to be in connection with the mounted work. I was assured by Seymour Hyde and Louis Whiton, who invited me to join, that it was a great privilege; and at my first drill, when there were sixteen present, including the officers, I was greatly thrilled.

About this time—the fall of 1886—one of our members, Edward Sanford, submitted a uniform, which was made in London to fit him and was the fatigue uniform of the 10th Hussars. It consisted of a dark blue tight-fitting mess jacket, with yellow pipings and olivettes; long trousers of the same color, with a double row of yellow stripes; round forage cap with broad yellow band and heavily braided in yellow on top; white enameled leather saber slings; and baldric with black patent leather box with gilt bursting bomb—I remember that Dan Winslow, a member, upon being asked by a young woman what the box was for, replied, "To carry candied violets and rose leaves"—black patent leather or highly polished shoes, with gilt box spurs and white gloves. Mr. Sanford stated that as this organization was distinctly different from any other, it should have a uniform which was entirely distinct, and this would be; and also it must be made in England—it would be too ordinary to have it made here. His idea was adopted with much enthusiasm. The cost without baldric, saber slings, etc., was about fifty dollars, and it required about a month, after measurements were taken and sent to London, for the outfit to be delivered here. The full dress of the 10th Hussars was approved but, as I recall it, was not purchased except by the three officers and was worn but once or twice. The cost was two hundred and fifty dollars.

When I received my uniform from London I took it downtown to a firm of military tailors, then in existence, who duplicated it for thirty dollars and delivered it in ten days. Thereafter, they were purchased here—needless to say to Mr. Sanford's great disgust.

After we had all been properly adorned, it was decided to change the name—and we became "The First Hussars." At one of our frequent meetings I was made a corporal, which delayed my returning home until about one A.M. When I proclaimed the glad news to my wife, she replied, "That's fine; but don't ever be made a lieutenant, for then you will never come home." I should add we had very few members at the time, which may have had something to do with the promotion.

In the fall of 1886 an item appeared in one of the daily papers which stated: "The Independent Hussars of this city are still in existence. They have never yet offered any public excuse for being in that condition, and what they look like and what they can do are a good deal of a mystery."

About this time we found living here in the city a former U.S. Cavalry sergeant whom we engaged to serve as janitor or armorer of our quarters at Dickel's. He also acted as drillmaster for the mounted work. Hardly any necessity for telling you it was Frank

L. Aber, later familiarly known as "Buck" Aber. For the benefit of those who for one reason or another could not find it convenient to attend the regularly ordered drills, a squad drill was held at five o'clock —anything so as not to interfere in any way with social engagements of the members. I recollect at one of these afternoon drills, when there were four present, I was in the gallery where there were a number of young men and women who had been riding in the ring and were waiting to see the "drill."

Aber saw one man rising to the trot, which was not allowed at that time. He called out in no uncertain tone, "Mr. Wynkoop, will you sit tight to your saddle, the ladies don't want to see your backside." *He did.* Needless to say, great pleasure was evident in the gallery. I should like to say that Gerardus Wynkoop was one of the most popular of our members. A little later, in riding in line across the ring, from west to east, one of the members—who was a good cross-country rider and a first-rate fellow but very much of an Anglomaniac and couldn't take cavalry work seriously—really a "Do as you please" man, so that he was not a particular favorite of Aber's—was on a horse which stopped short directly in front of the large mirror on the east wall; and he went over the horse's head to the tanbark, an experience not hugely enjoyed by him, as some friends were among the spectators, but it added much to Aber's pleasure, for he said in no uncertain tones: "Well, only what might be expected. The horse looked in the looking-glass, saw what was on his back, and that settled it."

Later in the fall of 1886, feeling the dignity of a real troop, a brilliant idea took possession of some mind—I believe Mr. Balch's—and most formal invitations, on our elaborate and very attractive letter paper, to become an "honorary member of the First Hussars of New York" were sent to

>   General Wm. Tecumseh Sherman
>   Major General John M. Schofield
>   Major General Daniel Butterfield
>   Major General T. W. Crawford, and
>   Brigadier General Henry L. Burnett

all of the U.S. Army.

All of them, in most appreciative terms, accepted—I might add here that none of them had ever seen the hussars.

Early in 1887 it was felt that an honest-to-goodness military event should take place; and to that end formal invitations, with the names of our honorary members suitably engraved thereon, were sent out to witness the drill and attend the reception after—all of Dickel's Academy being given over to the hussars that evening.

We had a most representative assemblage, which included many men who were prominent in military life and were interested in the ambition of the members to make themselves cavalrymen. Well—I will tell you how the evening started. The troop, consisting of twenty-four men, lined up at the south side of the ring. Halpin, who was first sergeant, had called the roll and was just about to count fours, when the gate of the ring was opened, and a figure appeared on horseback—never was one arrayed like this. It was a member of the uniform committee who had decided that this was the time to launch something new in the way of uniforms. And he certainly did. For he had on the regulation mess jacket with white baldric, saber slings, etc., breeches and boots, white gauntlets, and a *white helmet* with a gilt spike and gilt chin strap. An audible murmur was heard among the assembled audience, and one remark was quite distinct, "Ah, there is the captain, now it will begin." With this addition, we had four types of uniform—Louis O'Donohue was in the first one adopted by the New York Hussars; the officers, Captain Manning, Lieutenants Balch and Green, were in the full dress—and I will say looked mighty well for they, as I have said, were the only ones who had secured it—the rest of us, in our regular outfit. The affair was really very creditable; the men were all good riders and had excellent mounts.

One daily paper afterwards said:

A brilliant assemblage of ladies and gentlemen witnessed the evolutions of the *Club*—24 men being in line at one time. Late in the evening there was a display of the precision acquired in the evolutions of a drill by bugle. A portion of Cappa's 7th Regiment Band was present, and played a march composed by Mr. Cappa—dedicated to the First Hussars. A standard of Colors was presented by some ladies interested in the organization.

The "standard of colors" was the red silk guidon with gold "H. I.," which I had the honor of carrying as guidon sergeant. It seemed to me the staff was about the size of a tent pole, but everything was done big in those days, and without a socket it had to be balanced on the top of the hooded stirrup. It is now, as you know, in our trophy room. Being now on the map, we decided to have a banquet at Delmonico's—held in March, 1887—at which time we had as our honored guest General Sherman, and invited representatives from the Philadelphia City Troop, Boston Lancers, Governor's Horse Guards from Connecticut, and various organizations here, among them the "Old Guard." It was a very colorful affair, all being in uniform. General Sherman responded to the toast "Our Guests," and mentioned that Gerardus Wynkoop's great-grandfather was his first captain.

I tell these things to show how everything was done to popularize the organization.

A short time after, it was found that there were several in whom the idea had taken root that the proper thing, in order to be very exclusive, was to make it an independent troop, have attractive quarters, much as a club, and only condescend to appear in public when we served as escort to some prominent civil or military person, and we should not be put in the position of ordinary soldiers to be ordered at any time by the state authorities. It would have been a good deal after the style of that play of some time ago called "The Milk White Flag" which had one scene of a luxuriously fitted clubroom; at different times individuals would enter, go to a locker, don an elaborate uniform coat and cap, sit at a table, strike a bell, order a highball which was served by a negro attendant; as soon as this was accomplished, *coats* were changed and the *soldier* departed.

You may imagine this was like a wet blanket to those of us who had been working hard with the sole idea of enlistment in the Guard. After the first shock, it was decided to hold an unheralded meeting of such at my home, and take proper, or possibly improper, steps to elect to office at the meeting then about due only those who were absolutely in accord with becoming national guardsmen. This was done, and a complete slate made up; in fact, some of the present-day political affairs have nothing on us.

We had moved our headquarters to Durland's Riding Academy, Broadway and Sixtieth Street, just at this time, for with thirty men on our roll we naturally felt it necessary to have a larger drill space. We held the regular meeting there, and everything had been so carefully arranged that those who had the idea of the independent affair were left entirely out of the picture and the following were elected:

Captain H. H. Balch
First Lieutenant Henry S. Iselin
Second Lieutenant Francis Halpin
Assistant Surgeon Thomas H. Allen, M.D.
Chaplain Revd. D. Parker Morgan, D.D.
First Sergeant Oliver B. Bridgman
Second Sergeant A. J. Manning
Third Sergeant Henry W. Williams
Fourth Sergeant Charles E. Schuyler
Fifth Sergeant Howard G. Badgeley

I should like to call your attention to Article X of the by-laws adopted. It imposed all sorts of fines (but I am free to admit I am not at all certain they were always collected): absence from drill—officers, $2.00, non-coms and privates, $1.00; *leaving room at any meeting without permission,* $1.00. Immediately after this meeting we had several resignations, which as you may imagine were promptly accepted. And I will say that among them there were those whom we disliked very much to lose, but as they were not in accord with the general idea, it was necessary to accept their resignations.

The only parade the hussars ever made was with a troop of thirty men in March, 1888, when Captain Balch on March 21st issued "General Order 24" which read:

You are ordered to report for duty, in full uniform, at headquarters on Saturday morning March 24th at 8:45 sharp to escort Lt. General Philip H. Sheridan and Major General Daniel Butterfield, U.S.A., on the occasion of the obsequies of General José Antonio Paez.

By order of Captain H. H. Balch

O. B. BRIDGMAN
1st Sergeant

The remains of General Paez, which had been here some time, were taken by a naval ship to Venezuela. I don't know whether this was done in order to give us a chance to parade, but at any rate it was our first and only public appearance. The next day, one newspaper speaking of the parade said, "General Sheridan's carriage was followed by some polo club." Such was glory; but another spoke highly, as follows: "The First New York Hussars attracted much attention by their fine appearance, their handsome black and yellow uniforms and magnificent horses. The company as it appeared yesterday numbered twenty-five men." It did, too, after we had dressed Aber up in one of our uniforms so as to complete a four.

It was a very cold blustering day, with light snow on the ground, so that, as we had no overcoats, we put newspapers underneath our tunics; but pride did a great deal towards keeping us warm.

It was soon after this that Captain Balch recommended that the first captain, Horace J. Brooks, be invited to come back and assume command—it being Balch's idea that he would have more influence in getting our admission to the Guard. This was done, and Balch became first lieutenant, Iselin, second lieutenant, and Halpin became a sergeant again.

In the fall of 1888, twelve of us had the nerve to enter the National Horse Show in Madison Square Garden, then at Madison Avenue and Twenty-sixth Street, in connection with a military event in which a platoon from the Philadelphia Troop entered. In the head-cutting contest, the Philadelphians naturally beat us on points, but we received very complimentary words in the papers.

Later in the fall, a man, accompanied by Mr. Zogbaum, the well known military artist, came to one of our drills and afterwards several of us were introduced to Lieutenant Charles F. Roe, who had recently come to New York, after twenty years in the U.S. Army, including his four years at West Point—and all of the sixteen years, I might add, were in the cavalry. He had resigned in order to look after some personal affairs here. He told us that he saw we had the foundation of a first-class troop; and with that in mind a committee of us waited on him and asked him to come as first lieutenant, Balch again reducing himself to the ranks. He accepted, and very soon after that Captain Brooks, realizing that we now had a professional cavalryman who could put the troop in proper form, very generously and gracefully resigned, and Captain Roe assumed command; with Balch and Iselin again lieutenants. From there, as you may imagine, things took on a very different aspect, all realizing that a cavalryman of long experience was at the head. In a short time, at his suggestion, our name was again changed—luckily a court order was not necessary every time this was done—this time to the "First Dragoons."

In January, 1889, we returned to Dickel's, as they made changes there which gave us larger space for meeting room, officers' rooms, and lockers.

During that winter we had a troop drill and reception which showed the large number in the audience that we at last had a real troop; and the enthusiasm of the forty-odd men in the organization extended to those outside, and people generally realized that the long and earnest work of those of us who had determined to carry on was close to its goal.

Those who had questioned, now came to applaud. The drills and instruction continued through that winter, during which time I had the joy of being very close to Captain Roe. As first sergeant, I was with him almost daily, and not only did I, as did every one who knew him, have the greatest admiration for him, but I grew to have the deepest affection for him.

Drill being a purely voluntary affair, absentees were more frequent than later on; so it had been the duty of the Top Sergeant to call upon each absentee within a day or two and paint in glowing colors what an interesting evening he had missed, and to endeavor to exact a promise for attendance the next week.

Through that winter, however, the attendance was very perceptibly better, the enthusiasm of the Captain being instilled into each man— so much so that Captain Roe, feeling that the requisite number of fifty-one men would be available, made application for "mustering in" to the National Guard; and the order was issued by Governor David B. Hill through the Adjutant General, Josiah Porter, for that ceremony to take place on April 2, 1889. On March 27th the following was issued:

FIRST N.Y. DRAGOONS

Circular   N.Y., March 27, 1889

Drill as usual next Friday evening at 7:45. Weather permitting, Troop will go out on the road.

The Adjutant General of the State having appointed next Tuesday April 2nd for the "Mustering In" of the Troop, every member of the said Troop is hereby directed to be present at Dickel's, 130 West 56th Street, at 8 P.M. sharp, on Tuesday April 2nd. If any man who received this order finds that he cannot be present at that time and place he will notify 1st Sergt. Bridgman, 103 Franklin Street, to that effect immediately. Unless there are 51 members present April 2nd the Troop will not be mustered into the State Guard.

By Order   CHARLES F. ROE
Captain Commanding Troop

OLIVER B. BRIDGMAN
1st Sergeant

On the afternoon of April 2nd, Captain Roe had been at my office for some time, going over a report I had for him, after checking up with each man, which showed that we would be short two men of the number required. As he left me, he said: "Well, Bridgman, if we don't have the fifty-one men on hand tonight we will be out of luck. See what you can do."

In going uptown, racking my brain as to how to produce those two men, I remembered two brothers who lived in East Fortieth Street, Jared and Alfred Baldwin, and hied me there, finding them both at home—then about 5:30 o'clock. After a long talk in which I endeavored to instill in their minds and hearts the glory attached to becoming a cavalryman, Alfred decided he would take the chance; but Jared thought it better that only one should do so, and he was therefore counted out.

At the appointed hour all were present, but we were still shy one man. Where to get him was a question, until we espied in Dickel's ring one man, who was riding with several others, and who was a splendid fellow and fine rider; so we got hold of him and told him we wanted him to come upstairs and be a soldier. After hearing what it was all about he consented; and, believe me, there was great rejoicing when Robert L. Lee appeared, for he saved the day and became one of our most enthusiastic troopers. When I called the roll for General McEwan, the Assistant Adjutant General (who was the mustering officer), it seemed to me like a regiment, never having had so many together before—fifty-three men. After each man had been mustered, Charles F. Roe was commissioned captain by the Governor, and Oliver B. Bridgman, lieutenant.

So by eleven o'clock that night, April 2, 1889, there was born a new infant in the National Guard, christened Troop A, N.G.S.N.Y.; and I might add, it was the beginning of the cavalry arm of the state, which at present writing boasts two full regiments, the 101st and 121st. On April 5, 1889, Captain Roe issued his first order, appointing the non-coms.

The original order was typewritten on an ordinary piece of paper by Aber. I have it here now and will give it to the chairman of the house committee for preservation.

So, hoping it has not wearied you and that you will realize a little of the many months of real hard work done to bring it about, I leave with you the record of the conception and birth of Troop A, now our beloved Squadron A.

OLIVER B. BRIDGMAN

Ex-Members' Association of Squadron A
Annual Meeting, Squadron A Armory
    Monday, January 16, 1933

1889–1911
THE ERA OF CHARLES F. ROE
AND THAT OF HIS SUCCESSORS
AVERY D. ANDREWS AND OLIVER B. BRIDGMAN

THE earlier years of Troop A were filled with enthusiasm and achievement. It was a period of swift growth in efficiency and prestige, of associations and friendships that endured; a part of our lives, the memories of which recall vivid life and action.

First of all were the years from April 2, 1889, when Troop A became a military unit and part of the National Guard of New York State, to 1898, when Major Charles F. Roe relinquished immediate command to take control of the entire New York National Guard, with the rank of major general.

Avery D. Andrews succeeded Roe as major of the squadron and held the position during most of the year 1898. Oliver B. Bridgman succeeded Andrews, and held command until 1912, when he too was called to other duties and higher rank. The end of this period was practically contemporaneous with the retirement of General Roe from active service and with the abolishment of the cherished designation of Squadron A by the military Solons at Albany—the first of a series of name changes that has served to confuse the identity of troop units with their predecessors. In a broad sense, 1911 was the end of an era.

THE TROOP COMES INTO BEING AND DEVELOPS

> In the days when earth was young.
> —MACKAY
>
> Ten good soldiers wisely led
> Will beat a hundred without a head.
> —THOMPSON, "Euripides"

DURING the first twelve years of its existence, Troop A, and later Squadron A, responded to calls for armed service in the suppression of domestic disorder on three occasions: in 1892 at Buffalo; in 1895 at Brooklyn; and in 1900 at Croton Dam. In 1898 it provided a troop, designated as Volunteer Troop A, which served in the war with Spain.

Its record of military service then and later is one of which all the members may be proud. Its high efficiency was developed in the years of enthusiastic and intelligent training prior to the World War, preparing hundreds of men qualified to act as officers elsewhere after leaving this cavalry command. It is here attempted to outline the development of the organization and its members for the aim of a military unit.

A TROOPER'S DIARY OF THE FIRST FIVE YEARS

The brief diary entries made by William R. Browning, one of the original members of Troop A, have a peculiar piquancy. They show the lure of the cavalry, the misgivings with which he took the plunge, and the satisfaction and pride which replaced the doubts. There is a triumphant note in his entry of the first ride on April 5, 1889: "Did not lose any men this time."

1889

Thursday, March 14th. I saw the dragoons ride in the evening.
Friday, March 22nd. Rode in the first dragoons at Dickel's.[1] We expect to be mustered in tonight, and think possibly I made a mistake to belong.
Friday, March 29th. Rode out nearly to Grant's tomb with the first dragoons. Enjoy riding with them, and think I can stand it for five years if we are mustered in next Tuesday.

---
[1] The reference to "Dickel's" is to Dickel's Riding Academy located at 130 West Fifty-sixth Street.

Tuesday, April 2nd. Was entered as a first dragoon and hope I will not regret it for five years.

Friday, April 5th. Rode up Riverside Drive with the first dragoons. We had about forty-eight on the drill, and did not lose any men this time.

Friday, April 12th. The drill as usual at Dickel's, and I was late as usual. We practiced riding without stirrups. Rather rough on some.

Wednesday, April 17th. Drilled with the troop at the armory on Forty-fifth Street and Broadway.[2] We went through some very odd calisthenics.

Monday, April 29th. Went to the store and did not witness the naval parade. Escorted the President with Troop A from City Hall to Mr. Morton's house in the afternoon.

Tuesday, April 30th. The ball last night was a great affair. I arrived home half-past three, and had to ride all day. The drill of Troop A continues during May on every Wednesday. We will have to parade Decoration Day.

Wednesday, May 15th. Drilled with the troop at the armory, Forty-fifth Street and Broadway. We had to stand for two hours in one place, while we went through evolutions with the saber and carbine.

Wednesday, May 22nd. We have seventy-one members in the troop now, and four or five proposed—a very rapid increase.

Thursday, May 30th. Paraded with the troop in the morning.

Wednesday, June 5th. Meeting of the troop at the armory. Elected eight new men. Adopted a set of by-laws. Have now eighty men in the troop.

Thursday, October 17th. Government inspection of Troop A at Forty-fifth Street and Broadway. Passed through very favorably, I think.

Tuesday, October 29th. Drilled at Dickel's preparatory for parade tomorrow.

Wednesday, October 30th. Did not go downtown as the parade took up the whole day.

Friday, November 22nd. Troop drill. Had intended going home immediately afterwards, but changed my mind till nearly two o'clock.

Friday, December 6th. Had no drill this evening, I am sorry to say.

Friday, December 20th. Drilled with the troop. Practised riding two on one horse, etc.

1890

Friday, January 10th. Had a rather fatiguing troop drill, because I felt tired anyway before I went up there. The Captain practised us in cutting off heads perched on poles.

[2] The "armory on Forty-fifth Street and Broadway" is the former armory of the 12th Regiment, N.G.N.Y. It is probable that Captain Roe found his new command quite untrained in dismounted drill and promptly made the men acquainted with it.

DRILL OF HUSSARS
TENT PEGGING

A CHARGING HUSSAR IN FULL-DRESS UNIFORM
(*From a program of one of the games*)

Monday, March 31st. The troop goes to the Casino in a body next Wednesday to celebrate anniversary.

1891

Thursday, Feb. 19th. Did not go downtown. Spent 1½ hours in dental chair in morning and paraded in General Sherman's funeral from 12 to 6:30 P.M.

Friday, Feb. 20th. Went to the troop; about the same drill as usual. Willie Ficken, who fired his revolver through the roof at the last opportunity, tried the floor tonight with better success. [The revolver drill consisted of holding the revolver pointed upwards and bringing it down, pulling the trigger when on line target; the following week, of holding it pointing to the floor and bringing it up and firing it when muzzle was in line with target.] The first week he made a hole in the roof, of sufficient size to see light through it, and the second week he broke a lot of plaster from the ceiling over Austen Colgate's clothes. Fortunately they were not occupied.

Friday, April 3rd. Rode with the troop. Will have extra drills during April.

Wednesday, May 6th. Took part in inspection of Troop A at Claremont Park. Left Dickel's at four o'clock and got back about eight. The gray horse was pretty well used up.

Tuesday, June 23rd. Was summoned before a delinquency court of the troop to account for absences, so took dinner at Athletic Club. Did not get back till 11 P.M.

1892

Friday, Jan. 8th. Went to the troop this evening. This was our first drill in three weeks, as the last two Fridays were Christmas and New Years. Have commenced pistol practice in the armory. I shot tonight and made two out of a possible fifty, I think. I will not shoot again for three weeks; on every third Friday. Have missed three drills thus far this year out of thirteen, so my average is not bad.

Friday, Jan. 15th. Drilled with the troop. Rather a harder drill than usual as we had considerable bareback riding, but still I enjoyed it. The troop will give a reception in February.

Friday, Jan. 22nd. Went to the troop. Had quite a drill.

Friday, Jan. 29th. Went to the troop this evening. We had rather a hard drill with wrestling and pursuing, as last time. Quite a good many men are dropping out of the troop and new ones filling their places. Lee Hunting, Hunter, Baldwin are already gone, and I think some others will soon follow if they do not attend more regularly.

Friday, Feb. 6th. Did not have so hard a drill as we had a melee instead of wrestling and pursuing. It was quite cold in the ring before we got warmed up by drilling.

Tuesday, Feb. 16th. Went to the delinquency court at the drill this evening. We watched the men drill after it was over. I was called up for field day and one drill, but to my surprise I was excused from the former, the fine for which is $5.00. Was fined $1.00 for drill. It was raining on field day and I had rheumatism, but no discharge certificate to vouch for it.

Friday, Feb. 19th. Went to the troop in the evening. This is my ninth drill in succession. Have been more regular of late. It was also my night for shooting with the pistol, but succeeded in making nothing. They are very hard to shoot with, as the charge is so heavy, they kick abominably and it is almost impossible to hold them steady. The melee that we have been having the last few Fridays is quite exciting. Was whacked on the wrist quite bad this evening with one of the sticks.

Friday, Mar. 4th. Went to the troop. My horse acted very badly in the shooting as he kept rearing with me most of the time.

Friday, Mar. 11th. Went to the troop. We came near killing two of the fellows tonight—think we will do so yet. Holly's horse slipped and fell with him, and also another fellow whose name I do not know. Holly was pretty badly shaken up but not damaged seriously in any way. The Captain gave out an invitation to the troop from the gentlemen's riding club to come over some night this month and give an exhibition drill and partake of a collation.

Friday, Mar. 18th. Went to the troop. Did not have as hard a drill as usual as there was a great deal of platoon business.

Friday, Mar. 25th. Went to the troop tonight as usual. It was a preliminary for inspection of the 27th and full dress. Think it will improve our appearance. The troop has decided to drill during April as usual. The dinner comes off April 1st, but hardly expect to be present. Today was the first touch we have had of real spring.

Have missed but four drills so far and Van Cortlandt Park—a much better record than last year.

Friday, Apr. 1st. Had rather a hard drill and had a severe tussle in the wrestling with Dr. Clayborne. Have decided to go to Brooklyn with the troop on April 12th and drill over there. Did not care much about that, but the Captain asked me personally and I thought I had better go. The troop dance comes off tomorrow night, but I am not going.

Friday, April 8th. Drilled with the troop. Was feeling rather miserable when I went up and first class when I came back, so presume the exercise did me good. Am going to ride John in Brooklyn. Hope he behaves himself properly. It was raining quite hard tonight.

Friday, May 27th. Expect to go to Creedmoor tomorrow. Hope we have a clear day.

Saturday, May 28th. Took the eight o'clock boat at Thirty-fourth Street Ferry for Creedmoor. Made nineteen points at 100 yards, and fifteen at 200. At 300 yards could not get enough points to qualify until the fifth trial, when just made twelve, making my score twenty-seven, and letting me through some hard shooting on volleys at a canvas with black soldiers painted on it; by the time we were through, my shoulders were pretty lame from the firing. It was a perfect day, and we had no rain. Got home by seven P.M.

Monday, May 30th. Paraded in the morning. Was pretty well wet before the parade commenced, waiting in Fifty-fourth Street. Had a rather poor horse from Dickel's.

Thursday, Aug. 18th. Received a telegram about 2:30 to report at the armory at 6 P.M. Went up there on time and the Captain said if he did not receive any word by 6:30 he would dismiss us and we should report next evening. We were dismissed but scarcely got outside of the building when a telegram came ordering us to Buffalo that night. There were about sixty men present. I obtained leave of the Captain to stop over the next day at Milford and to come on Friday. The troop got off by 2 o'clock that night. Took the morning train for Milford, arrived there about 12 o'clock, and left again on the 9:20 P.M. for Buffalo where I arrived at seven o'clock next morning. Had great trouble finding the troop as I did not know enough to go to headquarters, and I tramped all over the railroads. Finally went to headquarters and found they were at a suburb called Black Rock for the day, though stationed at the stockyards. I was among the first of the men who did not come up with the troop to arrive this morning (Sat. Aug. 20th)—finally found them at Black Rock as stated. Our quarters in the stockyards are quite comfortable as we have hay to sleep on, and about fifty cots have been made of plain deal boards that, when covered with hay, make very comfortable beds. I have fortunately got one. The living is very poor, mainly owing to Hurry's desire to send in a small item of expense. I think the fellows kick at it a good deal.

Sunday, Aug. 21st. Was on guard duty tonight, and nearly froze in the baggage car where the guard had to sleep during their four hours' off as I left my overcoat in the barn, and when I came on at 12:30 it was too late to get it. Everything was quiet during the night. We simply guard around over our own quarters and do not attempt to guard the whole of the stockyards, as they cover fully seventy-five acres. There are guards all day on the outside of them in front and on the railway tracks behind us, so our guard duty really does not amount to much. The troop was ordered out today as an escort to General Porter.

Went with the troop to the Lake Shore Road on Lake Erie and was stationed there two hours at a time all day. Did not see anybody that looked like a striker, and nearly went to sleep on my feet. Left there about four o'clock and got back to the Yards by six. We ate a graded combination of fire, apples and cake, and drank Sarsaparilla and pop that was bought of small boys throughout the day. The boys were quite honest, and brought back what you sent them for with the change, even if the amount was a dollar or more. The majority of the troop went in swimming, but did not feel like it myself.

Tuesday, Aug. 23rd. Had no orders this morning, so the fellows had a ram's fight which was quite interesting and also a bull fight in the morning which latter I did not see. There scarcely seems to be any reason for so many troops here, though the railroads around Buffalo are very much spread out and cover many square miles so that the chance for a few strikers to do damage is large. The trouble originated with the Erie Road; when the ten-hour-a-day law passed it paid the men by the hour instead of the day and graded the pay so it would be about the same as before. There are only about 500 strikers altogether. Took dinner with Colby and Goadby at the Iroquois Hotel after a good swim in Lake Erie.

Wednesday, August 24th. Was rather nervous going home last night as the switchmen of the D. L. & W. went out today and there is trouble reported for tomorrow. Was stationed at the D. L. & W. yards all day. They are in a very low neighborhood, but we had no trouble, contrary to expectations. The Road has been preparing for the strike and was all ready to fill the places of the switchmen who went out. Asked permission of the Captain to go home tonight, which was granted. Took dinner at the Iroquois and later the 11:40 P.M. train on the Central Road for New York. Woolsey went down with me. It rained hard all night. I would have been on guard.

Friday, Oct. 7th. Troop drilled dismounted this evening, it was the first drill of the season. The Captain divided us into squads, each squad under its respective sergeant. I was under Throop and he did not understand much more about the tactics than the men he was instructing. The Captain drilled us afterwards for a short time. Did not get home until nearly 10:30. Am going to try and start off with a clean record of drills this year.

October 10th. 400th anniversary of Columbus. Was up at the armory at 7 A.M. Was assigned No. 3 on right of Third Platoon. Went to New York Hotel where we waited for Grand Marshal McMahon and some of his aides, and escorted them down to the Battery where we only waited a few minutes before starting on the parade. It was noon when we passed our house on Fifth Avenue and Forty-fifth Street. Father had built a stand and decorated the house with flags. Arrived at Dickel's at one. Had some lunch at Athletic Club with Arthur Goadby, and then went home. The Essex and Philadelphia troops had not come by three o'clock. The evening parade did not amount to much.

October 14th. Drilled with the troop. We are going to Chicago after all, as it seems Governor Flower was away when we were notified we would not be requested to go. On his return he was quite angry about it and determined we should go.

December 16th. Friday. Drilled with troop. Succeeded in dismounting Clayborne in the wrestling and also picked up hat from the ground.

1893

January 13th. Went to troop. Had a hard drill, as we were practicing for the games on February 17th.

February 10th. Had the usual drill. Except no head cutting with sabers, as the practice for games next Friday occupied the time.

February 24th. Drilled with the troop. Commenced with pistols with blank cartridges. Troop going to Washington in March for the inauguration.

March 17th. Drilled with troop. Had pistol firing. There is some doubt of our drilling in April, and hope we do not.

April 7th. Had a hard drill and firing with carbine and pistol, the former was mostly dismounted.

April 21st. Drilled with troop dismounted. Carbine firing in ring. I did a very careless thing which might have been serious. I brought mine to a carry loaded, without uncocking it. The result was it went off very close to my ear and also to my neighbor's. My ear has rung ever since, and I am not sure I escaped scot-free. Captain Roe said great carelessness on the part of someone.

April 28th. Had to go to armory at 8:15 this morning to take part with the troop in the Naval parade show. We led the parade as escort to Governor Flower. Got to City Hall 2 P.M. and waited there an hour and a half while the Governor reviewed the parade. Was not able to see it as we were stationed in center of park on the sidewalk. Got home about 4 P.M.

October 27th. Went to the troop inspection this evening, full attendance. The troop has had three drills thus far and a field day at Van Cortlandt Park—all of which I missed.

December 22nd. Drilled with troop: absent two Fridays. We are practicing for the games in January. Wrestled with Dr. Jacobus and managed to get him off, or rather he pulled himself off.

1894

Friday, Jan. 12. Drilled with troop. I entered for the wrestling, potato race, and double mounting with Grace, in the games which are to take place February 16th.
January 26th. Drilled with troop. Practiced for games.
February 16th. Troop games this evening. Entered four events. Was second in double mounting.
March 9th. Drilled with troop. Drill was better than a week ago though it was somewhat slow as it always is when the Captain is not present. The officers have not much experience, and their voice is not inspiring.
Tuesday, April 10th. Did not go to the drill as I intended to ask for my discharge papers. Am sorry to leave, but do not want to give the time to the drills, so think I had better leave. It was five years ago since I joined and am quite glad I did.

The foregoing excerpts—which omit many items of routine attendance—cover the five-year enlistment of one of the original members. They present the experience and impressions of the enlisted man, and picture the early stages in the moulding of a care-free group of young men of fine qualities into an efficient military body.

Captain Roe guided and led his men; he did not drive them. His example stimulated, and he developed interest and enthusiasm. He encouraged efficiency and did not criticize harshly; his discipline was light but effective. He was rewarded with affection and the highest respect—and these gave to his wishes even greater force than a command. The succeeding years demonstrated the wisdom and success of his policy. At the outset the whole troop was in effect a recruit squad and the non-coms had no more knowledge and experience than the other enlisted men.

At the beginning of the drill season in October, 1892, and following the tour of strike duty at Buffalo, the diary states, "The Captain divided us into squads, each squad under its respective sergeant." This seems to have initiated the organization by squads and the vesting of responsibility in the non-coms. Private Browning found his squad leader—a sergeant—rather inadequate as such: "I was under Throop and he did not understand much more about the tactics than the men he was instructing." Probably the same might have been said of others; but the non-coms were quick to meet duties and responsibilities, and before the end of Browning's enlistment the picture was transformed. The chevrons became the outward mark of experience, ability, and soldierly qualities.

Captain Roe had two ex-regulars as paid employees of the troop. Sergeant Aber, known to us as "Buck" and previously employed by the Hussars, had the job of armorer and was also very useful in the early days in imparting elementary military instruction to the recruits. He had an entertaining flow of barrack-room conversation, and his loyalty to and affection for the organization were unbounded. A trooper who got his telegraphic notice in Virginia to report for the Buffalo strike duty found Aber alone in the armory, eager to assist in any way but quite desolated at being left behind. He was universally liked and will always be remembered with affection. Sergeant Braithwaite was the trumpeter—and a very efficient one. The capable trumpeters that were developed in the regular membership had the benefit of a good example.

The earlier civilian Hussars had been spectacular almost to the point of being theatrical; with varied and brilliant uniforms and a reputation for lavish outlay. Troop A, newly arrived in April, 1889, changed from fine feathers to the plain uniforms of the army; but it was not born to blush unseen. The creating of an actual cavalry troop in New York City—a bona fide military unit of the New York National Guard—captured popular interest. It was this, and not bright uniforms, that made for the troop's success. Doubtless public interest was whetted by newspaper comments from time to time upon the social standing of the members and the reputed wealth of some of them. The wealth was overestimated, but the social standing was a fact, and the standards for admission were rigorously maintained throughout the years. The requirements of the committee on admissions included those of an élite club—and more. The candidates had to be formally proposed and seconded, to appear in person before the committee, and have letters from at least three members of the organization in addition to the proposer and seconder. They were elected by the entire organization at a formal meeting called upon printed notice to the members. It may be said that a member in good standing of Squadron A was eligible to membership in any social club in New York.

When Prince Henry of Prussia was the guest of the city in 1902, Rush Duer as one of the troopers in his escort rode alongside the carriage of the royal guest and Admiral "Bob" Evans. Rush heard H.R.H. inquire, "What is this cavalry organization that forms our escort?" Evans replied: "Oh, that's Squadron A of New York; they are all millionaires."

The unique position of Troop A and of Squadron A was due to this quality of the enlisted personnel. The troopers gave full loyalty and respect to their officers in every military capacity—there was no let-down of discipline; but out of uniform the rank carried no precedence. Officers and enlisted men met on the same footing of equality that existed in civil life. The eminence attained by former enlisted men in professional careers, finance, business, and other activities is common knowledge. In this city today we have Justice McCook of the New York Supreme Court and Judge Goddard of the Federal Bench; both served as enlisted men. In Washington five Cabinet officers served in our organization as enlisted men, and four of these never wore the officer's uniform in the squadron. New Jersey has today a Senator and a member of Congress who formerly served as enlisted men. These are only illustrations. A list of those who achieved distinction in civil life and were never officers in the organization would be impressive, but unnecessary for this narrative. Nevertheless, in seeking the source of the vigor and the success of our organization an appreciation of these facts is important.

The service uniform of Troop A in its early days was similar to that of the cavalry of the Civil War: dark blue forage cap; dark blue blouse or tunic, with brass buttons; trousers of lighter blue, with a yellow stripe for non-commissioned officers; and heavy boots, with the leg cut higher in the front than in the rear. The officer's uniform was much the same, except that it bore the rank insignia on shoulder straps and had a wider stripe on the trousers. For dress uniform there was a helmet surmounted by a spike which carried a long horsehair plume—a menacing-looking piece of equipment. The full-dress tunic was not impressive, being also dark blue, with short tails and yellow piping. The overcoat, of a lighter blue, was the most favored feature; it was double-breasted and had a cape, with a yellow lining, extending below the elbows and buttoning in front. The cape could be—and usually was—thrown back and held in that position by two buttons; then the yellow lining was quite resplendent. The campaign hat was adopted in the first few years; and the gray flannel shirt with yellow silk handkerchief knotted about the throat, as well as canvas leggins and gray leather gauntlets, became a very useful and practical part of the service uniform. The present olive drab service uniform appeared much later.

The hussar uniform for full dress was adopted in May, 1896, after various unsuccessful attempts to find a type on which the members could agree. Such matters were left democratically to the choice of the members. In presenting a proposed dress uniform, Captain Roe would have one made for himself of the suggested pattern, and then exhibit it in person (or on person) for the suffrages of the troop. Thus arrived the short, gay, hussar tunic of pale blue with black braid decoration and cavalry yellow facings, the black astrakhan busby, with cavalry yellow cloth top overhanging on the side, gilt insignia in front and erect black horsehair pompon (yellow for officers), the black leather baldric with brass mountings and insignia-mounted cartridge box, and other features of the full-dress uniform.

REVEILLE.

THE ARMORY TRAINING

"Let us now praise famous men"—
Men of little showing—
For their work continueth,
And their work continueth,
Broad and deep continueth,
　　Greater than their knowing!
　　　　　　　　—Rudyard Kipling

The spectacular appearances of the troop and later the squadron in public functions were interesting and useful in many ways; but the real activities were the constant, steady work—enthusiastically performed—in developing a genuine, practical military body.

The troopers received instruction from Captain Roe; that what he taught was also embodied in printed form did not dawn upon most of the members until several years later, and then the memorizing of that little yellow-covered book was a constant occupation.

From the outset, the drills in Dickel's riding ring became progressively more comprehensive. Riding without stirrups and bareback riding, bareback wrestling, and taking hurdles bareback were featured; as were the low reach from the saddle at the gallop and dismounting and mounting bareback as the horse took the hurdles. Tent pegging with saber, *tierce à tête,* and "head cutting" were practised for proficiency in the arme blanche.

An entertaining feature was the melee, a mounted combat with single stick, in which groups sometimes as large as platoons were opposed to one another. The combatants wore fencing helmets and masks with padding extending over the neck and shoulders; and on the top of each helmet was attached a plume of tissue paper, with different colors for the respective groups engaged. These groups lined up and, at a signal, went for one another, beating at every hostile plume until one side or the other was stripped of the last colored shred. It was warm, exciting, and entertaining, for men and horses often stopped blows intended for the plumes, and the air was filled with fragments of colored paper.

In 1896 the Squadron A Cavalry Institute was organized to develop and expand the range of military knowledge of the members. The feature of the first meeting on April 24th was a lecture by Baron George de St. Mart on the battles of Rezonville and Gravelotte. For the following year a comprehensive course was arranged. In a scrapbook kept by Corporal E. C. Parish a post card received in the following year touches on this as well as on a different activity.

DEAR SIR:

Owing to the meeting of the Cavalry Institute at nine o'clock Major Roe wishes the roughriding squad to fall in promptly at eight o'clock, Saturday. Drill from 8 to 9 P.M.

Respectfully,

ALFRED WENDT,
Sec. Athletic Com[ee].

The nature of the armory work is illustrated in a circular issued by Major Andrews on December 28, 1898:

The troop drill will be varied from time to time with sabre exercises, mounted exercises, wrestling, double mounting, fencing mounted, melee, cutting at heads, etc. One squad will be sent to the target range as usual.

The annual inspection and muster was a practical and serious occasion. The members were assembled in formation and inspected, and the property assigned to each was rigorously inspected, as were also the properties of the organization and the books and records. An occasional trooper might have a valet to look after his clothes in private life, and the great majority with no valet might be careless at home, but the trooper was held personally accountable for his uniform and equipment, and the annual inspections were preceded by unit inspections that were little less exacting. One of the squadron's most renowned humorists, John D. Kilpatrick, who after later and long service as a major and lieutenant colonel in the regular army is now retired, gives an entertaining sketch of an inspection of his former troop.

"Going back to the 'dear dead days beyond recall' a picture comes to my mind that must not be overlooked. It was the occasion of an annual inspection of the armory by Major Louis Greer, at that time inspector general on the staff of General Roe, then commanding general of the National Guard of New York. It was in the afternoon. Herbert Barry was captain of Troop 3, Monty [H. P. Alan Montgomery] was quartermaster sergeant, and Jimmy McTiernan was the factotum and doer-of-all-the-work of the Third Troop. Get the picture: the locker doors open, full wide, each locker with complete equipment perfectly dressed by Jimmy; Greer, very military, first, then next to him Herbert Barry, then Monty, then Jimmy; Louis starting in at the first locker, observing closely the top shelf down to the second shelf and to where the uniforms neatly hung on the hangers and on to the bottom with its boots, shoes, and leggins; Greer very stiff, taking one step to the right followed in cadence by Barry, Monty, and Jimmy. Nothing said until about the tenth or fifteenth locker when Greer remarked, 'Captain Barry, what do you use on your leather—it seems to be in good condition?' Captain Barry to Sergeant Montgomery, 'Sergeant Montgomery, what do we use on our leather?' Monty in a stage whisper to Jimmy, 'Jimmy, what do we use on our leather?' Reply: 'Fahairrey soap, sorr.' Monty, 'Fairy soap, Captain Barry.' Barry to Greer, 'Fairy soap, sir.' That was all right for about ten more lockers; then Greer noticed the absence of a service uniform in a locker. 'Captain Barry, there seems to be a uniform lacking in this locker. Where is it?' Captain Barry to Sergeant Montgomery, 'Where is the uniform in this locker?' Monty, in a loud whisper, 'Where is the uniform in this locker, Jimmy?' Jimmy, in a loud whisper, 'It's on your back, sorr.'"

ATHLETICS AND THE ANNUAL GAMES

> And witch the world with noble horsemanship.
> —Shakespeare, "Henry IV"

AT AN early period, competitive exhibitions were introduced and the "annual games," first held in 1891, became a yearly sporting and social event, in which boxes, stands, and galleries were filled with spectators. The colorful programs were illustrated with drawings and photographs, and frequently contained data of troop and squadron history. In these competitions rivalry was keen, since each successful competitor represented a victory for his troop. The individual trophies were merely pewter cups, many of which, however, are still cherished for the associations and memories that they recall.

The organization of these exhibitions was taken seriously, and was handled by a number of committees, the membership of which (with the exception of the squadron commander, who was *ex officio* a member of the committee on athletics) was composed entirely of enlisted personnel.

The selection of events for the games was usually made about two months in advance, and so large were the entry lists that it became necessary to hold preliminaries on the respective troop drill nights and, later, semi-final contests, in order to leave a suitable number of contenders for the night of the finals.

The games held in March, 1899, are illustrative. The program gives the following list of events.

1. Double riding—one mounting behind the other
2. Low reach at gallop, picking up handkerchief
3. Head cutting—with hurdle
4. Dog tent drill
5. Novelty race
6. Team wrestling
7. Potato race
8. Cossack drill
9. Double pursuit
10. Melee

All the events with the exception of 4 and 8 were competitive.

A circular had announced that the annual mounted games would be held at the armory on March 7, 1899. The events were listed and notice was given for the running off of the preliminaries and the semi-finals.

Governor Theodore Roosevelt, however, wished to be present, and as he could not attend on the evening of March 7th, the date was changed at his request to March 10th. This was the subject of another circular issued under date of February 3, 1899:

> Notice is hereby given that by reason of the particular desire of Governor Roosevelt to be present at the games, the date thereof has been changed from March 7th to March 10, 1899, at which time the Governor has signified his intention to be present.

The day of the games was almost coincident with the tenth anniversary of the mustering in of Troop A; and virtually marked the conclusion of the first decade of the existence of the organization. The following is a list of the competitors. All were from the enlisted personnel.

FIRST SERGEANT
    Edward L. Patterson

COMMISSARY SERGEANT
    Arthur F. Brown
    J. N. Sterns, Jr.

QUARTERMASTER SERGEANT
    Frederick W. Cheesebrough

GUIDON SERGEANT
    Arthur J. Slade
    William J. Wallace
    William R. Wright

SERGEANT
    Francis C. Huntington
    E. Norman Nichols
    Edward C. Parish
    Henry M. Ward
    Alfred Wendt

CORPORAL
    George B. Agnew
    Robert W. Bush
    James G. Clark, Jr.
    William D. Judson
    George S. Ledyard
    Emlen T. Littell
    Stowe Phelps
    Theodore Sedgwick
    Howard C. Smith
    Merritt H. Smith
    Wilson F. Smith
    George DeWitt Williamson

HOSPITAL STEWARD
    Russell Bellamy

ARTIFICER
    Robert C. Barclay
    Alfred W. Booraem
    Frank S. Rollins

PRIVATES

William C. Adams
Cornelius R. Agnew

Robert P, Barry, Jr.
Putnam Bates

PRIVATES (*Cont'd.*)

Frederick Becker
James H. Brookfield
Edward M. Cary
Julian I. Chamberlain
Everett Colby
Arthur Corlies
Harward W. Cram
James M. A. Darrach
Lamont Dominick
George E. Fahys
Henry J. Fisher
Rector K. Fox
Louis V. Froment
Richard P. Goldsborough
John H. D. Grannis
James W. Hall
Joseph C. D. Hitch
Henry E. Holt
Philetus H. Holt
Leonard S. R. Hopkins
Leonard S. Horner
John T. Kelly
Walter S. Kencys
Charles H. Kerner, Jr.
James T. Kilbreth
John David Lannon
John W. Loveland
Francis B. McAnerny
William D. Moore
Franklin B. Morse
James O. Nichols
Edward Olmsted
Ezra P. Prentice
Reginald W. Pressprich
Albert W. Putnam
Irving E. Raymond
George O. Redington
Wolcott P. Robbins
Francis L. Slade
Augustus C. Smith
Philip T. Stillman
Henry L. Stimson
James G. P. Stokes
David Stuart
Howard A. Taylor
James T. Terry
Benjamin B. Tilt
Frank D. Veiller
Oscar M. Von Bernuth
Alexander L. Ward
Robert D. White
Hans W. Zinsser

It was a successful exhibition, and it had a special popular appeal by reason of the presence of the Governor, Commander-in-Chief of the armed forces of the state. The *Sun* of March 11, 1899, stated:

A large crowd, including Governor Roosevelt and his staff in full uniform, attended the ninth annual mounted games of Squadron A at the Armory, Madison Avenue and Ninety-fourth Street, last night.

The interest of the squadron in the games is shown in part by the fact that more than eighty men entered as competitors—and a number in two or more events. Of course the number competing was greatly reduced after the preliminaries and semi-finals had been run off.

Of the competitors, twenty-five had served in the Spanish War, and a nearly equal number served in the World War, twenty years later. Indeed, a number of those whose names appear as contestants served in both the Spanish-American War and the World War.[1] The spirit and zeal for service which were developed in Squadron A are illustrated in the games of 1899.

In June of the same year, while in camp at Peekskill, the exhibition of field sports included:

Hurdle race	Tent pegging
Potato race	Low reach at gallop
Head cutting	Novelty race

In the winter of 1900-1901, and again in the following winter, there was, in addition to the annual games, an earlier exhibition, called the Morse Cup competition. It was largely attended by the public, and one of the features was:

Mounting over hurdles. Two men and two horses, blanket and surcingle. Near horse to be led by rider on off horse around the ring over hurdle at each side of ring. Rider of near horse to dismount and mount over near horse on off horse, faced to the rear while taking hurdles. Twice around the ring.

In the earlier years, when there was only one troop, dividing the troop into platoons afforded healthy and friendly rivalry. These platoons developed vigorous activities and each strove to excel the others in drill, horsemanship, athletic prowess, and, later, in carbine and pistol proficiency. Thus the foundation for friendly but active inter-troop competition originated with the platoons.

[1] On page 111 is given the full roster of the Spanish War Volunteer Troop, together with the names of those who served with other organizations in that war.

PYRAMID RIDING
MOUNTED CHARGE AT PEEKSKILL

TOUR OF DUTY DURING BROOKLYN STRIKE, 1895

MEN IN STREET   MOUNTED SQUAD
         LIVING QUARTERS

SUNDRY ACTIVITIES AND AMUSEMENTS

> They are soldiers,
> Witty, courteous, liberal, full of spirit.
> —SHAKESPEARE, "Henry VI"

> The brazen throat of war had ceased to roar;
> All now was turn'd to jollity and game,
> To luxury and riot, feast and dance.
> —MILTON, "Paradise Lost"

THE platoons, and later the troops, showed their pride and solidarity by having dinners and reunions—sometimes with an elaborate menu, original drawings, and songs. The scrapbooks of this era bring reminders of many social interests that were incident to the bond of membership in Squadron A.

One memory is the gathering in the canteen after drill, with beer and sandwiches supplied from a common fund, and Chick Childs at the piano indefatigably playing ragtime and accompanying the songs.

The annual dinners of the squadron were well planned, well attended, and never dull. There were no formal speeches, but members of an earlier day will remember, among other choice recitals, those of Lloyd Garrison (including "Odd Fellows Hall," later sung by Joe Hunt); Joe Frelinghuysen's story of the Rev. Dr. Snigglefritz; and in later years John Kilpatrick's famous "Walla Walla Horse" and other strange beasts, as well as his series of inventions such as golf balls produced by a hitherto unthought-of method. And stories and recitals by Jimmy Terry and others gave these occasions a zest and gaiety that we did not perhaps then fully appreciate; it seemed a matter of course.

Habitually as captain, and later as major, and frequently as major general, Roe took part in the social events of the squadron. His songs, rendered in a rich, deep baritone, became celebrated, and the chorus to "Ten Thousand Miles Away" will rouse the memories of those who joined in, and were a part of that era:

> So blow, ye winds, hi-o!
> A-roving I will go;
> I'll stay no more on England's shore.
> Then let the breezes play-i-ay.
> I'm off by the morning train
> To cross the raging main;
> For I'm on the rove to my own true love,
> Ten thousand miles away!

Another, "The Revelry of Death," will be remembered for its melodramatic note beginning: "We meet 'neath the sounding rafters." There was a fine swing to its chorus, of which the first line was: "Then stand to your glasses steady."

"Home, Boys, Home" brought its fine marching chorus back from Puerto Rico; and "My Beautiful Irish Maid", sung by Bill Cammann in his clear tenor, had a haunting melody in its chorus.

Other songs, some original and many unprintable, acquired popularity on the march and in camp as well as at reunions: for example, "Cav-al-ree," to the tune of "Tam-man-ee," and "Christmas on the Island."

From such information as is available to the compilers of this book, the tendency to Rabelaisian verse among the élite and virtuous troopers of the early days may still be found in the equally élite and virtuous troopers of the present generation.[1]

The spirit of the troopers was such that something of interest was constantly being evolved. The Squadron A Polo Club was organized in the spring of 1900, and the following year it played matches at

[1] In the appendix is printed a partial collection of printable verses originating in the squadron.

Great Neck and at Saratoga, both of which were lost; and a match at Rumson, which was won. In October, 1901, the club was dissolved and the sport was taken over by the squadron organization.

In 1902, through the cooperation of the park authorities, stimulated by the indefatigable and effective efforts of J. Osgood Nichols, the squadron acquired a unique plant at Van Cortlandt Park, with three playing fields, stables for fifty ponies, and a clubhouse that had been a private mansion before it was acquired by the city. The squadron players numbered seventy-five or more, and probably more players of low efficiency enjoyed the game there than at any other known place. There were many practice and inter-troop matches, of which no record remains; but good players and teams were developed, and matches were played with outside teams, including two with West Point (both won by the squadron) and others, unchronicled, with Lakewood, Rockaway, Rumson, and Westchester. In 1903 the squadron played with West Point, Yale, and neighboring clubs. In 1904 the team was especially successful, defeating West Point, Great Neck, Rumson, Staten Island, Princeton, and Albany. In 1905 it won eleven out of twenty games; and its most notable victory was at Newport, where it met and defeated the team of the Westchester Club, which had an aggregate of thirty goals' handicap, while the aggregate handicap of the squadron team was only eight.

The Squadron A Club was organized September 1, 1911, and secured a clubhouse on the northeast corner of Ninety-third Street and Madison Avenue, just one block from the armory. It operated with great success and prosperity up to the time the squadron was called into service in the World War, and its McAllen Auxiliary in 1916 won fame. It also had an important part in aiding the reestablishment of the squadron as a unit in the National Guard after the war.

The squadron farm at New City, New York, was purchased in 1914 and developed into a successful feature for the squadron. It still functions and is more fully considered in the narrative of Major Wright and that of the post-war activities.

An ambitious and successful enterprise was the Squadron A coach, which ran on regular schedule from the Plaza Hotel to Van Cortlandt Park on polo days. The turnout was meticulously correct in all details: the four horses, the driver in gray top hat, with the long whiplash caught in a thong, the guard with the horn, and the coach itself with passengers inside and above. A picture of this coach, as well as several photographs, hangs in the ex-members' rooms in the armory.

Throughout this era, groups of troopers found life more full when they took their amusements together. In the days before the troop had its own stable and horses, groups rode bicycles to various points, in one instance as far as Mendham, New Jersey, where Seymour Cromwell was host. Later, horses replaced bicycles, and mounted groups rode together, with Woodmansten Inn as a frequent objective. In a still later period Squadron A "horse marines" earned considerable, if not flattering, reputation and, after divers exploits along the shores of the Sound, transferred activities to Great South Bay.

The combination of Jimmy Terry and Laurie Lee ensured laughter. On one occasion a member of the party had a chill, and his companions put him to bed with an extra blanket over him. There were several beds in the room, and toward the end of a long evening other horse marines drifted in. Finally, Jimmy Terry arrived; but all the blankets not on the invalid had been taken by the others. Jimmy undressed leisurely, commenting to himself from time to time on the unblanketed condition of his bed. Finally the invalid felt a slight tug at the bed-covers. Looking up, he saw Jimmy gently pulling away the upper blanket.

"Take it, Jimmy," he said. "I don't need it now."

Jimmy expostulated: "No, no, old man—go to sleep, go to sleep."

Just as the invalid was dozing off, he felt another gentle pull at the blanket. There was Jimmy again.

"Say, Jimmy, take the blanket. I really don't need it."

"No—no, far—far be it from me to—to take a blanket from a sick friend—when he's awake."

MESS.

THE CADET CORPS

Those things which they will use when men.—DIOGENES

THE Cadet Corps was a familiar feature to those who served in the first decade of Troop A and Squadron A. Frederic R. Coudert, who, as an outside activity, took part in drilling and training the cadets, wrote: "Many a pleasant hour I passed with them, when as a very youthful National Guardsman I had the privilege of drilling these young boys."

The career of the cadets presented a picturesque feature, and they took a firm hold on the affections of some of those who participated, as is shown in the following narrative written by C. Sidney Haight, retired Colonel of Cavalry, U.S.A. He was one of the original members of the Cadet Corps, and later enlisted in Squadron A in 1895.

"Inspired by the Seventh Regiment's successful sponsoring of the 'Knickerbocker Greys,' Sergeant Jacobus and several other old Troop A men got together in the fall of 1892 about thirty boys between the ages of fifteen and seventeen and organized them under the official designation of the Squadron A Cadet Corps. Robert M. Maclay, a brother of Sergeant Alfred B. Maclay of the original Troop A, was appointed a first lieutenant and its commander. A later roster carried the name of Private Ulysses S. Grant, 2nd.

"Uniformed in a dark blue blouse with yellow facings, dark blue breeches with yellow stripes, a dark blue, Civil War style forage cap, black boots and brass spurs, black belt, and armed with carbine and saber, the corps when mounted presented a very snappy and martial appearance.

"As Squadron A was then drilling in Dickel's Riding Academy in West Fifty-sixth Street, the cadets, as did the squadron, used the Academy horses. Each cadet was assessed about fifty dollars for horse hire and other expenses. Saddles and other horse equipment were furnished by the squadron.

"Drills were held one night each week during the winter under the direction of Sergeant Jacobus, Corporal Vermilye, and other troopers. Lieutenants Coudert and Frelinghuysen took a particular interest in the boys, and Major Roe always reviewed them before their annual games. Besides close order drills, both mounted and dismounted, there were competitions for cups and ribbons, in bareback and rough-riding, wrestling, jumping, tent pegging, and mounted melee with wire helmets and paper plumes. At least once during the nine years of their existence, joint games were held with the squadron.

"On Decoration Day and at various other times the cadets paraded mounted with the squadron. They made an excellent appearance and often won the commendation of military officers and the press. Their esprit de corps was very high. The corps was disbanded in 1901, when the growing popularity of boarding schools made recruiting difficult.

"Those of us who were cadets look back upon our two or three years in the corps as among the happiest of our boyhood. We learned the value of discipline, at the time in our lives when it made a lasting impression; and we benefited from the really strenuous physical training. We also learned how to stick on a horse, even if we did not become expert horsemen.

"Too much praise cannot be given to the members of the old troop and squadron who gave their time and energies to recruiting and drilling the corps. Those cadets who were guests of Lieutenant Joe Frelinghuysen in 1899 and 1900 at his place in New Jersey will never forget his many courtesies to them, or the evening campfire and the realistic night alarm. The corps marched mounted to and from Somerville and camped for three days on his grounds. In 1901 Lieutenant Marcellus of the squadron took the boys off on a similar camping trip. Who can say that the corps did not justify its existence, especially to its own members. Long live its ever pleasant memory!"

SMALL ARMS PRACTICE AND COMPETITIONS

> He knocks out a bull's-eye every time he shoots.
> —GILDER, Squadron Ditty

IN ADDITION to mounted and dismounted drills and mounted gymnastics, small arms practice became an important feature in the training of the troop and squadron. Before the Squadron A Armory was ready for occupancy, facilities were limited and there was little opportunity for carbine and pistol practice except when the organization was ordered to the range at Creedmoor, Long Island, on a single day each year. The armory when completed in 1895 provided a pistol and carbine range, and later extensive use of the Creedmoor range was afforded. With these opportunities the squadron made rifle and pistol shooting a major feature of training.

In any attempt to sketch the history of Squadron A of the old days, the rifle range at Creedmoor deserves attention. It had already become historic as the scene of international rifle matches. In 1892 it was owned by the state and used as the official rifle range in this section. It had well equipped ranges for distances up to 1,000 yards. In the early years, Troop A, like all other National Guard units, had an official tour of duty at the range of only one day each year. The carbine was of the Remington pattern, an early vintage of breech-loading rifle, with short barrel, large bore—possibly .50-caliber—black powder, short-range, and with a tremendous kick. It is fondly remembered by some as an arm of precision, but by others as anything *but*. The ranges at which the practice was had were one, two, and three hundred yards, and at the top distance most of the troopers found it a matter of speculation whether they could get on the target. In course of time they got the Springfield carbine—still with black powder, but with better and longer trajectory; and in 1903 the Krag-Jorgensen .30-caliber with smokeless powder.

From about 1896 the range facilities were increased and troopers individually and in groups could use them on the days of supplementary practice, which included most of the Saturdays in the summer and fall. Competition became keen, and each troop worked to surpass the others in the number who qualified as sharpshooters and experts. Also teams were organized for competition in the carbine matches held at Sea Girt, New Jersey, as well as at Creedmoor; and the results were creditable.

In the scrapbook of an ex-member, Sergeant G. DeWitt Williamson, are found some of the published orders of that period. General Orders No. 14, of June 5, 1903, dealing with indoor shooting recites that during the season of 1902–1903 a revolver match was won by the Troop 2 team, and a carbine match won by the Troop 3 team; both matches being shot in the armory. There was also a revolver match between teams from Squadron A and the 1st Naval Battalion won by the Squadron A team, and a revolver match with Light Battery A, Massachusetts National Guard, which was won by the latter.

In the following year, the indoor matches with other organizations were all won by the squadron, including a match between the Troop 2 revolver team and the 2nd Field Battery. It is interesting to note that the artillery team was headed by "1st Lieut. J. P. O'Ryan," who made the top score of his team. He later headed the 27th Division.

As to shooting on the Creedmoor and Sea Girt ranges in those same years, General Orders No. 6, of March 26, 1904, reads in part as follows:

The results obtained in the Department of Small Arms Practice are herewith published for the information of the Squadron, and the Commanding Officer notes with pleasure the increased interest that has been taken by the members of the Squadron in this duty.

The increase in the number of Distinguished Experts, Experts and Sharpshooters is especially gratifying.

For the first time prizes for the highest figures of merit have been awarded in the organizations attached to Headquarters, and it is a source of great pride that all these have been taken by the Squadron.

At Sea Girt, New Jersey, the Revolver Team won the trophy offered by the National Rifle Association, defeating teams representing Massachusetts, Pennsylvania, New Jersey and the District of Columbia.

In the Carbine Match two teams were entered but secured only fifth and sixth places respectively.

First Lieutenant Sayre won the Military Revolver championship of the United States for the fourth consecutive time.

Sergeant Frank Outerbridge, Troop II, was awarded the medal of the National Rifle Association for the highest score in 15 consecutive shots at 100 yards, 200 yards and 300 yards on the day of general practice at Creedmoor.

The name of Sergeant G. deW. Williamson is to be inscribed on the Gould Cup for the highest score and the highest average at Creedmoor.

In the next following year the published order stated:

It is a source of great pride that all the prizes for the highest figures of merit awarded in the organizations attached to Headquarters have again been taken by the Squadron.

The headquarters match at Creedmoor was won by the Squadron.

At Sea Girt, New Jersey, the Revolver Team won for the second time the trophy offered by the National Rifle Association. It was also victorious at Creedmoor.

In the Carbine Match at Sea Girt the team secured second place.

The Squadron was represented on the State team by First Lieutenant Sayre, who secured second place in the National revolver match at Fort Riley. He also won the squadded revolver match at Sea Girt and was second in the Military Revolver Championship at Creedmoor; First Lieutenant M. H. Smith being third.

The name of R. W. G. Welling is to be inscribed on the Gould Cup for the highest score at Creedmoor and that of Thomas Le Boutillier, second, for the highest average.

The medal offered by the National Rifle Association of America for the best score at 200, 300 and 500 yards was won by First Lieutenant R. H. Sayre, with a score of 61.

In other years also the squadron did well in carbine matches. From incomplete data available it appears that in the six years from 1900 to 1905 it won first place on three occasions: 1900, 1902 and 1905.

In the Creedmoor days every man was expected to qualify in the shorter ranges with the title of marksman. And repeated individual effort—sometimes reinforced by considerable urging—resulted in nearly all the members of a troop qualifying as sharpshooters at the 500 to 600-yard ranges. These results were the fruit of fine esprit de corps and the persistent effort applied to the excellent facilities afforded.

The zeal in this matter was humorously illustrated on one occasion when a conscientious corporal, Richard Welling, succeeded in getting all of his squad qualified save Theodore Douglas Robinson who, though a fine horseman, didn't like the shooting and was unresponsive to his corporal's urging. Welling, however, had been a classmate of Theodore Roosevelt, then President of the United States, and the recalcitrant member of Welling's squad was a nephew of the President; so the Corporal invoked the aid of the President, and the Commander-in-Chief telegraphed a direction to the trooper—who then indignantly but successfully qualified. Under a later administration he became Assistant Secretary of the Navy.

Welling himself made highest score in this year and his name was placed on the Gould Cup.

In one of the issues of the Seventh Regiment *Gazette* is the following comment upon the activities of one of the troops of Squadron A during the Creedmoor season of 1904:

Three distinguished experts, twenty-eight experts, fifty-one sharpshooters, and, of course, all the marksmen that the law allows, shows hard work by every man, and especially by I. R. P. Williamson, who is now resting in South Carolina after his labors. The giddy height of distinguished expert was attained by 1st Lieut. Phelps, Sergt. Williamson and Artificer Welling. The experts in addition to those are Capt. Barry, 2d Lieut. Wright, 1st Sergt. Bush, Guidon Sergt. Booraem, Sergt. Cary, Corpls. Watson, Newell, Sheldon and Choate, and Pvts. Bayne, Camp, Dana, Douglas, Dyer, Geer, Henderson, Howe, Hoxie, Jevons, Le Boutillier, Lee, Marvin, Montgomery, Valpy and Whitney. Following the usual custom, no common or garden sharpshooter any longer gets his name inscribed on the roll of fame, as it is expected that all will qualify as such.

The Creedmoor range no longer exists. The growth of New York City and the encroachment of the built-up areas caused its abandonment as a rifle range, and the property is now a portion of Queens Village. Today there are no such facilities for developing expert riflemen, and no such proficiency as was then achieved can be looked for.

In a printed report, dated December 15, 1908, Lieutenant Reginald H. Sayre says:

On account of the closing of Creedmoor Rifle Range practice has been confined to such as could be secured at Sea Girt, N.J., by the courtesy of the New Jersey authorities. This has made it most difficult for men to attend practice—not only on account of the great loss of time and incident expenses, but also from the necessary curtailment of the number of days allowed for practice. In consequence the number of qualifications is less than for many years past.

The report contains a table showing the results of individual practice during the fourteen years from 1895 to 1908. It shows some interesting contrasts: the number of sharpshooters and experts in 1897 and in 1907, respectively; also the number in 1908 after the Creedmoor range was closed.

	1897	1907	1908
Experts	13	182	51
Sharpshooters	39	213	97
Marksmen	246	265	238
Strength at inspection	243	250	248

It is significant that in both 1897 and 1907 the number of marksmen exceeded the total strength. This is explained by the fact that practically 100 per cent qualified as marksmen, and the number included new members who qualified as well as some whose service ended during that summer. In 1908, however, the number of marksmen was not equal to the actual strength.

At the Creedmoor range various organizations, including Squadron A, had simple clubhouses erected where supplies and equipment could be kept and where occasionally men would pass the night on cots and so get some early morning practice. A picture of this clubhouse erected in 1903 hangs in the trophy room of the Ex-Members' Association.

Captain Reginald H. Sayre, our inspector of small arms practice, will always be remembered. His zeal was untiring and his efficiency remarkable. The cabinet in the Ex-Members' Room containing the extraordinary collection of trophies won by "Reggie" Sayre gives a vivid illustration of his individual achievements.

In 1909 the *New York Press* on March 28 said:

> The members of Squadron A are famous shots with the rifle or the revolver. In a big glass case in the Armory are fifteen massive cups and a revolver trophy as evidence of their prowess. The latter is a perpetual revolver team challenge trophy presented by the National Rifle Association. The contest first started in 1903, and Squadron A has kept the trophy ever since. It is competed for annually. Squadron A's highest score was 987 out of a possible 1,000. . . . Among the other prizes that the Squadron has carried off is

a cup that it won from the marksmen of the West Point United States Military Academy.

How vivid is the memory of those days at Creedmoor with lunch at the canteen, rye whisky served from teapots in teacups, and Lieutenant Colonel Nathaniel B. Thurston ("Peggy" Thurston), state inspector of small arms practice, riding fiercely up and down behind the firing line on his little black pony.

The bareback drills and other mounted exercises in the armory, together with the intensive efforts in rifle and pistol practice, largely achieved the object of developing soldiers with the basic qualities of cavalrymen—"men who can ride and shoot."

COMMENCE FIRING.

CAMPS OF INSTRUCTION, PRACTICE MARCHES, AND TACTICAL EXERCISES

> The ranks and squadrons and right form of war.
> —SHAKESPEARE, "Julius Caesar"

> They feed us and break us and handle and groom,
> And give us good riders and plenty of room,
> And launch us in column of squadrons and see
> The way of the War-horse to "Bonnie Dundee!"
> —KIPLING, "Cavalry Horses"

IN JULY, 1890, the troop was assigned to a week's tour of duty at the camp of instruction, Peekskill, New York. The journey to and from the camp was made in marches of two days, each way. The troop traveled mounted, accompanied by its wagons and impedimenta, camping overnight en route and cooking its meals at these camps. This tour of duty was repeated in 1892, 1894 and 1896. In 1898 activities in connection with the Spanish War Troop prevented the customary tour of duty at camp, but in the following year this service was resumed, with spectacular additions.

On Friday, June 2, 1899, the squadron under command of Major Bridgman and accompanied by Commander-in-Chief Governor Theodore Roosevelt, Major General Charles F. Roe, commanding the National Guard of the state, Brigadier General Avery D. Andrews, Adjutant General, S.N.Y., Lieutenant Colonel Lee, representing the British army, and members of the Governor's and Major General's staffs started on the march to the camp of instruction at Peekskill. Camps were established on Friday night at Van Cortlandt Park and on Saturday at Sing Sing.

Very naturally, this three-day march aroused much public interest, and the newspapers featured it at length. The *New York Times* of June 3, 1899, describing the start from the armory, noted that the advance guard rode three blocks ahead of the main body, "led by the Governor" accompanied by the officers; following the three troops, "the non-commissioned staff, hospital corps, and wagon train brought up the rear."

All the men wore campaign hats, gray shirts, gauntlets, blue breeches with yellow stripes, and boots. Some of them had yellow handkerchiefs twisted about their necks.

After the three days of marching and the two nights in temporary camps en route, the *New York Times* reported Governor Roosevelt as saying in regard to the march:

I am of course extremely pleased with Squadron A. I regard its being here in camp as of infinitely less importance than the journey up here and the practice away from the camp. . . . It doesn't teach the men as much to live in tents with floors as it does to be out on the march and pitch their own tents and live in the open. . . .

The interest of the former Lieutenant Colonel of "Roosevelt's Rough Riders" in the personnel of the squadron was further indicated upon his departure. A newspaper dispatch from Peekskill dated June 5, 1899, said:

After parade last night Governor Roosevelt told Major Bridgman that he would like to meet the men of the Squadron, upon hearing which the three troops turned out and went to the Governor's tent, where he shook hands with all of them expressing to each, in a few pleasant words, his appreciation of their work.

In the years 1901, 1904 and 1906 the squadron again performed tours of duty at the Peekskill camp; but in later years it attended there only for rifle practice.

These camps at Peekskill were of a pattern that had become conventional. The camp was shared with infantry units and the men were quartered two each in white canvas wall tents, with board floors; and there was a large supply of colored servants available and very generally employed. The picket line was on the farther side of the drill field, and this involved the lugging of equipment over considerable territory but restricted the attentions of the flies. (The old *U.S. Cavalry Manual* contained a diagram designating the proper layout of a cavalry camp, and prescribed for the picket line and latrines a position directly in rear of the kitchens, which made very easy the travel of the flies from one place to another. Scientific attention resulted in radical changes after the Spanish War.) The mess hall was commodious, and the cooking and service were provided by caterers. The rules as to dressing the tents were minute and rigid, one requirement being that each blanket be folded in a certain artificial prescribed manner, and the policing of the streets and surroundings of the tents were regulated most minutely—everything must be very spick and span.

The day began with reveille and the morning gun as the colors were raised, followed by the martial music of the band. During this the trooper got himself awake and ready to fall in for roll-call. A full day's work followed: mounted drill, stables, etc., and troopers and officers also received instruction in the precise ceremonies of guard mounting and of evening parade and review, as well as in guard duty. But there was time for amusement also, which sometimes took the form of competitive mounted games and even horse races on the flat and a steeplechase. The evenings were for recreation until taps.

The relations of the cavalrymen with the infantry were cordial, but mounted staff officers who knew little of horses were not admired. The stable sergeants and their assistants, generally designated artificers, were a hardy, individualistic, free-spoken lot and particularly disliked providing horses and service for such butterflies. They sometimes gave them mounts that were equally individualistic. One of these took control of the situation, and after two or three rounds of the parade ground, at a run and quite against its rider's desire, stopped short at the picket line in front of a pile of stable litter into which the rider catapulted. As he struggled up, an artificer, standing rigidly at attention, saluted and asked, "Any orders, sir?" It made the day for the stable guard.

Any reference to these tours of duty at the Peekskill camp will bring back many reminiscences that there is not space to narrate here. The spirited dash of Dreier's horse at the end of a charge—up the hill and back to the ranks in a leap that startled the observers—is still a current topic where men of that era gather together; also the sportive effort of two prominent troopers to "run the guard," and the disciplinary consequences that followed.

Jimmy Terry had a fund of humor that, together with his stammer, made him an historic character; and it is narrated that once he had tough going as a recruit in bridling his horse—the beast kept his teeth closed and lifted his head high, and Jimmy couldn't get him to take the bit. After futile efforts, Jimmy stepped back, looked at the horse with aversion, and said: "D-d-damn you; s-s-say 'A-a-ah!'"

Supplementing these tours of duty the troops received some practical experience in marching, camping, and providing food, by marching mounted to and from Peekskill accompanied by their wagon train, making camp for the night en route.

The wagon train was somewhat of a problem, for the wagons were heavily loaded and the hills so steep that some teams would be unable to reach the crest. It was necessary to halt and double up the teams. After getting the wagons over separately with the extra power, the teams would be returned to their respective places in the column and the march would proceed. In 1904, Commissary Sergeant Ezra P. Prentice and his Troop Commander developed a device by which the horses of some of the mounted detail accompanying the train could be equipped with Dutch collars and rope traces hooked to the lead traces and so give added hauling power. It was not a substitute for a properly equipped team, but it was intended to and did supply useful auxiliary power. In 1915, the attempt to use it as a substitute was not a success.

In the early years it was the custom on these marches to proceed almost entirely at a walk, with but few intermissions. This was extremely tiresome and fatiguing to both horses and men. Later, the system of alternating walking and trotting with ten minute halts each hour resulted in covering the ground in much less time; and men and horses arrived in much better condition.

The squadron also had tours of duty in 1908 and 1910 at Pine Camp, New York, and in 1915 at Fishkill Plains, New York, and on these occasions the transportation was by rail.

Early one morning at Pine Plains in 1908, the squadron rode out of camp, proceeded at a walk about half a mile, halted in a road hidden by trees, and stayed right there until mid-afternoon (when the day's maneuvers were over), without so much as loosening cinches. Returning to camp, Corporal P. J. McCook, a veteran of the Spanish War, remarked to his squad, whose members had expressed disgust and acute boredom: "That's just like real war—the most realistic day we have had yet."

In 1897, from October 8th to 11th, the squadron installed its first separate camp at Van Cortlandt Park and, during the period in which Major Bridgman was in command, this was repeated in 1902, 1905 and 1907.

SQUADRON A

Under Bridgman's successor, Major Wright, similar camps at Van Cortlandt Park were established in 1912, 1913 and 1915. The 1912 camp was honored by a visit from President William H. Taft and Major General O'Ryan. Camps for separate units were established in 1915 at Van Cortlandt Park and at the squadron farm.[1]

In addition to these tours of duty at fixed camps, Troop A, and later Squadron A, participated in field exercises with other units.

In 1890 it took part in a field day with the First Brigade in Van Cortlandt Park.

In 1891 it took part in a field day and tactical exercises with other units at Prospect Park, Brooklyn.

In the same year a detail joined Troop A of Washington, D.C., on a practice march through Maryland and Virginia. It was an interesting and useful expedition, the troopers were received with great cordiality by the local population, and at some halts a demonstration was staged by the community with speeches and refreshments. On one occasion the refreshment included what appeared to be claret punch served in tubs, from which the troopers filled their mess cups. It was most agreeable to taste, but it had an unexpected potency because whisky was an ingredient instead of water! After taking it, the laziest trooper became fired with enthusiasm to put up tents or dig the ditches around them; and the high, uncut hay was found liberally sprinkled with sleeping natives.

In 1894 the squadron took part with the First Brigade, in field-day exercises at Van Cortlandt Park.

In 1897, while in camp at Van Cortlandt Park, it took part in field maneuvers of the First Brigade. These were the subject of an article in *Harper's* under the title, "An American Army Manoeuvre."

In retrospect, these earlier "field days" and tactical exercises seem more in the nature of "sham battles," for employment of a holding force and a maneuvering mass was then hardly developed, and frontal attack was a preponderant feature. This was also largely due to the effort to condense a problem of attack and defense into a single day's time, with a maximum expenditure of blank cartridges.

At a later period maneuvers were conducted on a much larger scale. The first was held in 1904 and known as the Manassas maneuvers.

[1] The events subsequent to 1911 are dealt with in the paper by Major Wright, see p. 129.

The Massachusetts maneuvers in 1909 and the Connecticut maneuvers in 1912 were the most impressive.

In 1915 a mobilization with field exercises was had at Van Cortlandt Park with other units of the 1st and 2nd Brigades, but it occupied only one day.[2]

[2] This and the Connecticut maneuvers are described in the paper written by Major Wright, p. 119.

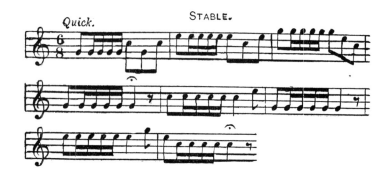

THE MANASSAS MANEUVERS, 1904

> You may go in haste
> And indulge your taste
>   For the fascinating rattle
>   Of a complicated battle,
> For the rum-tum-tum
> Of the military drum
>   And the guns that go boom! boom!
>   —W. S. GILBERT, "Princess Ida"

THE forces employed at Manassas were larger and the time given to the problems of maneuvers was more adequate than on earlier occasions. The customary Fourth of July expenditure of ammunition and undetermined claims of victory by both sides, however, marked the conclusion. One educational feature was the withdrawal of the attacking force and its return to the original camp some eight or ten miles to the rear; many of the infantry units were completely disorganized, and the individual men drifted back without formation, without officers, and with no attempt at discipline. The flight of the routed Union Army over this same terrain in the 1860's was perhaps paralleled, though here the retiring force claimed victory. Such experiences had great value in showing up defects and bringing about steps to insure against repetition.

John Kilpatrick's reminiscences, printed in this volume, give some entertaining incidents of the expedition.[1]

The narrative by Eliot Tuckerman was written for the most part shortly after the maneuvers, with an appended conclusion written some thirty-four years later. It gives the enlisted man's viewpoint of the operations during that week, and one of the present compilers has written the following comment:

"Trooper Tuckerman's chief contribution is the charm of youthful energy and enthusiasm and the realism that goes with frank current comment; most of his story is in the language of his original diary.

[1] See p. 327.

Since the United States—unless our policies radically change—in crises must depend for the bulk of its forces (outside the Regular Army, National Guard, and Marine Corps) upon relatively untrained material, knowledge of how such material *has felt and will feel* when plunged suddenly and for the first time into the primitive conditions of field service is valuable. The author gives the military student, professional or amateur, the inside information which can come only from a private soldier with an open and intelligent mind.

"From many another standpoint the diary possesses peculiar interest. For example, the 'Sergeant Stimson' mentioned so frequently as tent-mate and patrol commander was to become Secretary of War and Secretary of State.

"Certain reactions are noteworthy: the vigilance and cooperativeness of the best type of regular officer (he seems not to have encountered the other kind); the snootiness of the cavalry toward the infantry, plodding miserably through thick dust in tropic heat; the importance of sanitation, moderation in the use of drinking water, care by officers and N.C.O.'s of men and animals; the dangerous fiasco in personal contact of armed masses during the final stages of maneuver; the disorganization which follows recall and demobilization; the advantages and disadvantages to military efficiency of the ineradicable American democracy even under arms.

"Certain conditions favorable to the members of this composite troop, in comparison with their National Guard comrades on both sides in the Manassas maneuvers, appear as we go along. They were better trained than most, and so better able to endure the hardships of the brief campaign. They were more comfortable than most, being blessed with the services of Charlie and Louis Muller as farriers and of two hired cooks; last, but not least, they possessed an ample troop fund to supply luxuries."

NARRATIVE OF ELIOT TUCKERMAN

Pursuant to the provisions of the "Dick Bill," the army authorities called for troops from the eastern states to take part in maneuvers to be held on the ground where the battles of Bull Run were fought in the Civil War.

New York, among other troops, sent a squadron of cavalry under command of Major Bridgman (Lieutenant Stowe Phelps, adjutant; Lieutenant M. de M. Marsellus, quartermaster; Lieutenant G. B. Agnew, commissary; and Sergeant Major Whitney), with two troops, Troop A from New York City (made up from the three troops of Squadron A by volunteers) and Troop C of Brooklyn.

Troop A was under command of Captain Howard G. Badgley (Troop 2) with First Lieutenant Merritt H. Smith (Troop 1) and Second Lieutenant Wm. R. Wright (Troop 3). The enlisted men included eight sergeants, eight corporals, three artificers, and a trumpeter, together with forty-five privates—in all, three officers and sixty-five enlisted men.

A preliminary meeting to organize was held at the armory, and preliminary drills with instruction in pitching shelter tents and guard mounting and formation of advanced guard were given. On Friday, September 2nd, we left by troop train with tourist sleepers and horse cars, after riding to the terminus.

September 3rd we arrived at the siding near the cavalry camp at Maneuver Camp 1 near Manassas, Virginia, about noon, led our horses from the cars, reported with a detail to Sergeant Stimson, and put up our squadron headquarters' tents. The heat was very oppressive and the only way we could keep going was by frequently wetting our heads and shoulders at the faucets, with one of which each troop street was supplied.

The entire campsite had been very carefully laid out by the engineer corps of the army. Wells had been driven, pumping stations established, and abundant good water supplied and distributed. Our troop was encamped next to Troop A, Connecticut, and then came eight troops of the 15th U.S. Cavalry from Fort Myer, Virginia, and Fort Ethan Allen, Vermont. Troop C of Brooklyn was on our other side. During the inspection of the regular cavalry that first evening, two regulars fainted from the heat and were carried from the field on stretchers by the hospital corps.

Corporal Putnam, as senior corporal, had the first Sibley next the First Sergeant. In it were Sergeant Stimson, Corporals Putnam and Cram, Privates Stone, Smith, Robinson, Libby, Tuckerman, Pool, Coleman, Powers, and Godley.

Sunday, September 4th. The troops, tired by the exertions of the day before in the unusual heat, had a quiet day; morning and afternoon stables and mess being the only calls. Two infantry regiments came in on their way to camp from the trains. It was a great sight. The men were swinging along through the dark, singing songs and whistling marches. One regiment came from Florida, one from Maine. We passed by the sidings whence they had come and saw the hospital corps gathering in the few who, lying by the side of the cars that had brought them, were starting their experiences on stretchers.

Monday, September 5th. The regimental trumpeters sounded to the Standard about eight o'clock, and we left in column of fours to take our place as a squadron of the regiment with Troop C under Major Bridgman. We rode a mile or two to a large clearing—part field, part cleared woodland with the stumps of trees still projecting—and there had a stiff regimental drill: eight troops of the 15th Cavalry, Troops A and C of New York. The drill lasted till about noon, when our troop was ordered to report to Major Hoppin who was to command us during the maneuvers, and Troop C went with another squadron of regular cavalry. Major Bridgman was given a squadron consisting of the Connecticut troop and one troop of regulars.

Major Hoppin's squadron included Troops L, M, and N of the 15th Cavalry and our Troop A of New York. He divided us up, placing one platoon with each of the regular troops. We then all moved off and rode some miles out into the country and had practice in forming outposts. Mine was in touch with the outpost of one of the regular troops on our left and posted in an orchard and near a farm. I was told to put my sentry on the roof of the barn, and to dismount the whole squad.

There was a white flag with a black cross on it flying in the orchard, which meant forbidden ground; that is, troops must not enter it. Lieutenant Smith told the people in the house that we had done no harm, which was true, and would do none, and they gladly assented to our occupation. No sight of the enemy that day.

We returned to camp, some three or four miles, at a smart pace, arriving about 2:30 P.M., when mess tasted pretty good. I had not expected a ride of six and one-half hours and had worn khaki breeches and no underdrawers, and so took the precaution to have a good bath and to put on thick breeches at once.

On returning to our street I was surprised to see everybody on the *qui vive,* rolling packs and preparing for the field. I found that we had been ordered to start almost at once to begin our campaign for the capture of Thoroughfare Gap, by our Blue forces.

At 5:30 P.M. we moved out, taking bed blanket, shelter half, nose bag, poncho, and saddle bags—also all arms. Wore blue shirts and blue blouses, and heavy olive drab breeches. About eight o'clock in the pitch darkness we passed C Troop of Brooklyn and some regulars, turned off the Gainesville road on which we had been traveling, and prepared to bivouac.

We were ordered to tie our horses anywhere in the woods thereabout where we could find them without difficulty, and to unsaddle them, and, if we wanted, to pitch shelter tents. The wagon came up with coffee and the evening mess and grain for the horses. Just as I was preparing to unsaddle, I heard Sergeant Stimson call for me and for Coleman and Godley, and found we were to follow him and establish a Cossack post. We rode out into the darkness in single file on the Gainesville road, Stimson and then myself and then Godley and Coleman, and soon overtook two mounted men who I found later were Captain Badgley and Trumpeter Braithwaite. We rode about a mile till halted by a sentry. Captain Badgley answered that we were an officers' patrol, and advanced and had a talk with the officer in charge of the outpost; then we all turned back and, after riding about a quarter of a mile, turned up a road leading to our (then) right hand. We went about a hundred yards to a fork where our road met another coming from the same Gainesville road, and here the Captain ordered Stimson to establish our post, and he returned to his troop with his orderly. Stimson, Coleman, Godley, and I dismounted and took the rolls off our tired horses and loosened the girths, tying them to trees. Coleman went on guard, and the rest of us lay down under the stars to get such rest as we could. We rolled ourselves in bed blankets and lay on shelter tents with our arms beside us. Godley relieved Coleman, and about a half-hour after midnight I relieved Godley. The man on guard was posted about thirty to fifty feet up the road from the rest of the guard, and sat in the shade of a bush.

Tuesday, September 6th. Soon after I came on guard, the first shots of the campaign were heard far off; an occasional one, two, or three signifying that some patrol of our force (the Blues) or of the Browns had run into an outpost. We all had another turn on guard; this time those not guarding rolled their packs as their time to go on again drew near, and put them on the saddles. The firing had gotten quite close, and at one time we thought the post on the Gainesville road had been attacked and we should all have to skip for it. Our plan was that in case of an attack we should all try to repel it and that Stimson after firing his five shots would put for our "support" in case the enemy's numbers were too great for us to handle. He was the sergeant and also had the fleetest mount (his thoroughbred Fanny). It began to grow light about 4:30, and soon after—while I was on post, sitting behind a stump and looking down the road—I saw a trooper coming along at a hand canter. He was dressed in brown khaki; I whistled to Stimson, who was close beside me, and told him one of 'em was coming and asked if he wanted to challenge him. He said he did; and when the man was about thirty to forty feet away he halted him and dismounted him; that is, ordered "Halt! Dismount! Advance to be recognized! Surrender!" The regular (for he was a private of the 7th Cavalry) obeyed promptly, for two of us had him covered and it would have been dangerous to have a wad hit him at that distance. He was pretty disgusted to be captured by the "milish." After about half an hour some of the support came up under Lieutenant Wright, and I was ordered to draw pistol and take the prisoner in. I ordered him to precede me and rode up the Gainesville road to where our troop had bivouacked at raise pistol, and to my huge amusement and joy made my prisoner walk, trot, and gallop at will. As I approached camp I heard a roar of laughter, "It's Tuck, with a prisoner," and could hardly restrain my own amusement sufficiently to report to the Captain that Sergeant Stimson had sent me in with the prisoner. The Captain told me to hand him over to Captain Putnam, who was already in charge of another prisoner of the 7th Cavalry captured by our men. I was then ordered to return to my post, and rode back whence I had just come to find that the whole post had been moved down the wood road about a quarter of a mile to a place where several roads met in the scrub-oak wood.

This post, of about fifteen men under Lieutenant Wright and Sergeant Stimson, was in touch with a post of regulars further out on its left and acted as the support to two Cossack posts, consisting of three men each under a corporal, which had been pushed out about fifty yards on two wood roads towards the enemy. Our whole cavalry was acting as a screen to watch the left flank of our army and protect it from flanking movements before the infantry support could be brought up. Our post was all dismounted, the horses being held by two or three men in the thickets, while the rest of us not on the Cossack posts were hidden behind trees and watching approaches by the various paths. Lieutenant Wright and Sergeant Stimson were constantly going with one or two men to patrol the posts and keep touch with the neighboring posts of regulars.

Every little while lively firing was heard to the front and left as advanced parties of the Brown cavalry ran into some post or patrol of our force. I was watching on one of the bypaths, finding it very difficult to keep my eyes open—as I had at eleven o'clock been without a wink of sleep for thirty hours or much of anything to eat for twenty hours; but the lack of sleep was what was most difficult to bear. At about eleven I was called in to take my turn at holding horses and was soon fast asleep, holding five or six horses who were quietly standing saddled in the bushes. While I slept, a native from a neighboring house came along with pies for sale, which one of our men bought; and my share, I was afterwards told, was half a pie (a southern pie is not much thicker than brown paper). As I was asleep they put the half-pie in my mouth and left me. About noon (I had been asleep about an hour) I was awakened by someone kicking me. I blundered to my feet, found the pie, and was told to take the horses further into the woods as we were being attacked by Brown cavalry. I staggered along drunk with want of sleep and not in the least heeding the brisk firing that was going on about me. I was now put on lookout again behind a stump, so got no more chance to sleep. Later in the afternoon the Brown cavalry captured the regular post on our left and, in an attack on Butler Wright's Cossack post, captured Talbot—one of the three privates—as he was trying to mount his horse. The others got back to our support, which drove the enemy back.

About three o'clock Sergeant Stimson told me to tighten up my girths and go with him.

We rode to our right past the post of regulars to the Gainesville pike where we found the troop with Captain Badgley, in the woods near by. The column was formed and marched back down the Gainesville pike to where the troop had bivouacked the night before, and we all watered our horses in some muddy water holes, about a quarter of a mile beyond in the woods. Returning, we unsaddled, and I gave Duncan a thorough cleaning till he shone. He had a nice quiet place away from the other horses and ate his oats with a good appetite.

I turned in about eight, and knew no more till I felt a strong pull on my feet and was told to turn out quick and saddle up as we were soon to start. It was 11 P.M. We had slept three hours! but no three hours' sleep had ever seemed so good. I felt as fresh as could be. We rolled our bed blankets in our shelter tents and then saddled up, put on our rolls and arms in the darkness, and by 11:30 were ready. We all got a cup of coffee and two hard tacks as rations for the day, and one to eat for breakfast. Sharp at twelve (midnight) we got the order to move, and soon found that we were in line of troops (all the cavalry except two or three troops which I afterward learned were left to watch the left flank) being moved around to the right flank of our army.

Wednesday, September 7th. I shall never forget that night march. It was one of the most beautiful sights of the campaign. We moved at a walk, keeping well closed up as it was very dark. Starting at twelve, we got to our position between three and four A.M. Every little while we would pass a regiment bivouacked in a field by the roadside. You could see the sentries and the glow of the campfires and men sleeping around them.

After marching about three hours we all thought we were in the enemy's country (that is, we privates did), and fully expected to be attacked any minute. After a while we turned off the road and the order came back, "Single file, keep closed up and pass the word back." Then it was great fun. Now a trot, now a short gallop, and then walk again—and so dark that you had to keep closed up to follow the man ahead in the many turns and twists made by the column. Finally, we came out on some high fields and there were fires going; we were dismounted and gladly got near a fire or helped to make another, for it was very cold. It was still black night with the stars shining. At a neighboring fire a knot of officers, some of them umpires with white caps or helmets, and some non-combatants with white brassard on the left arm, were looking at the maps of the country. Our troop and the regulars were all mixed up round the fire, lying down and holding our horses—who were glad of a chance to rest after the long ride. As the first light of dawn began to appear we mounted and formed column. We moved perhaps a quarter of a mile and then got the command, "Prepare to fight on foot—Action left." I was riding number four, and so was a horse-holder. Sergeant Stimson gave me his Fanny as well, so I had my hands full with five horses to manage. After a little the men came back and we started again. We rode in and out of fields in column and up and down hill, now fording a little brook, now jumping a low fence, and now running to catch up. It was a beautiful sight in the early morning light. Once we heard a shot, and a rider in brown—an officer—jumped a fence into an open field and started across. A fusillade began, and had the bullets been real, he must have died a thousand deaths. He kept on, and a troop of cavalry rushed out and surrounded him. He was an officer of the 7th U.S. Cavalry who, seeing that he was surrounded, wanted a lark, and had it.

We got the order "Fight on foot," and again mounted and proceeded through some half-cut oak woods, when the order to fight on foot came again, this time in earnest. Our troop deployed and went into action in great form—as well as any of the regulars, I thought. Troop after troop was deployed; they charged across an open field into thick woods and were lost to sight by us horse-holders. It must have been about six o'clock then. After about an hour we got the order to take the led horses into the field where they had charged. We had to jump a low fence—or rather, the bottom rail of the fence; the other rails lay about in confusion. Fanny on my left hand was a thoroughbred and wanted to waste no time over the fence. Hal Learned was riding a polo pony, a little broncho; it was number two in the four, the second horse from me, between Bill Putnam's and Charlie Coleman's. As we jumped the rail, the broncho set his little feet out and refused to go over, and Fanny, with a shy, came round and I had to hold her so she swung round in front of the others. It took all my patience and what experience I had had to straighten the horses out; but I did, and got them all safely over and back into line. We now had a tiresome wait. About an hour in this field, and then all moved back where we had come from.

The firing in the woods continued heavy, and occasionally the artillery would take part. Some of the men dismounted and slept, but I sat it out, now on one horse and now on another so that Duncan might have a little rest. About noon we got another order to move the led horses and this time heard the recall sound, and soon our tired fellows came out of the woods. They had enjoyed the deployment and first rush, but said that, after the first, the fight degenerated into a farce. Men were firing at each other at point blank range and shouting that they were dead. After a little they began to drop asleep, and Sergeant Stimson told me afterwards that our Captain called his attention to the fact that practically his whole command was asleep with firing going on all around it. I did not close my eyes all this time, but sat it out on the horses in the broiling sun.

We now mounted up and started for home. Smith had gotten an ear of green fodder corn and thrown it in the ashes the night before, and it was about half-roasted. He gave me a third of it and I ate it with joy. On the road, when we had finally straightened out on our march home, a man came along with pies. Several men bought pies as they passed; one or two straggled and bought pies, as I did unthinkingly, only to get called down hard by Lieutenant Wright, who was riding at the rear of the troop. I am glad to say I did not retort or get mad, and left the pie, though I was pretty hungry.

The march home was about ten miles. The road was deep with dust, so that when we moved at a trot the man in front was lost to sight; only the horse's tail showed. We passed infantry by the roadside when one could not see the men through the dust. They suffered from it much more than we did. Some of the infantry commands marched home in good order, keeping their formation, but there were a great many stragglers. Now and again a pale chap stretched out by the side of the road, dead beat. Sometimes two or three had laid out their blankets and gone to sleep, or were having a little bivouac. Some troops, however, were still gamely marching, singing, and whistling to keep up their pluck. As we were nearing camp, a train came along with ordinary flat cars black with men. Even the engine was covered with soldiers wherever they could get a foothold.

We got in to camp about five o'clock. I cleaned Duncan with great care at once, as he had had a very tiresome trip. I then started to get a bath and, to my disgust, found that there was no water in the showers. There was a faucet near the bath tent, so I went back to the troop street and got a pail, meaning to have a bath out of that. When I got back with the pail, the water had given out also in the faucet. By this time I was mad and, on my way to the troop street for a pail of water, went to the headquarters' mess tent, asked for Captain Badgley, and told him that there was no water and what I thought of it (using I am glad to say, no profanity, and perfectly respectful language). I returned again to the bath tent and had a good pail bath, and, refreshed, went back to the street only to find that we were to be ordered out on the second campaign at 11 P.M. It was then 6 P.M. I had been up sixty-one hours and had slept four during that time.

I simply lost my temper and expressed myself in most unparliamentary language. My feeling was that I could do it if necessary, but what was the use? We were there for instruction. Well, I would get my evening mess anyway. As a great treat the commissary had procured a lot of the best porterhouse steak and had, besides, potatoes, coffee with milk, delicious ice cream from Washington, and watermelon. To my utter disgust, I found that the steak had all been eaten up—every bit! Again I was angry. I finally filled up on scrambled eggs and bacon and bread, with plenty of ice cream and watermelon to top off with, and, after a cigar, turned in at seven with the delightful knowledge that General Corbin, finding the exhausted condition of most of the troops, had ordered that they be allowed to sleep till five. Poor Walter Libby, who had been laid up with diarrhoea, had moved out of the tent. He slept next to me, so I had all the room I wanted and was feeling so fine when I was waked up at five on Thursday, September 8th, that I had to jump up and dance a cancan for pure joy.

I was ordered to report at 8:30 A.M. at the head of the street as one of the detail to Division Headquarters as guard. Our troop sent seven troopers, Troop C, seven, and Troop A of Connecticut, six; the whole under the command of Sergeant Kelly of the 15th Cavalry. Of course we took, besides our arms, bed blankets and shelter halves on the cantle roll, blouses and ponchos on the pummel, saddle bags, and canteen and cup. The orders to our troop called for us to send two feeds for each horse to headquarters. The order also said: "Each man will receive one day's rations." Captain Badgley read this to mean that we would be fed at headquarters. It really meant that we should take our rations with us. We were given each, one bread-and-butter sandwich as a precaution, and I sneaked two hard tacks. I also found a lemon and had a piece of chocolate. All came in well in the end. I got Vic Froment to let me fill my nosebag even, though he had sent feed ahead for me, and I took it on my saddle.

Promptly at 8:30 we started and trotted over to Division Headquarters, where Sergeant Kelly halted and dismounted us, and reported. While he was reporting, General Grant and his staff came along with the Division flag, and Sergeant Kelly mounted us and we marched out behind the staff. We moved along the Sudley's Springs road which passes the Division Headquarters of our permanent camp and took a westerly course to Stone House, where Division Headquarters for the day was established. On the way we passed a great many infantry regiments marching out to take their position in line. Some cheered the General lustily, and many had witticisms to address to the cavalry guard as it passed. Some wanted to ride and some to deride. We passed Texas, Georgia, and Connecticut troops—to my certain remembrance—and a Virginia battery.

Arrived at Stone House, the guard was posted in a field diagonally across from the post office, which is next to Stone House of historic association. This house stands facing the "Warrenton Pike," which leads from Warrenton through Centerville on to Alexandria and Washington, and at a place where the pike is cut by the road from Manassas Junction to Sudley's Springs. This famous corner was the center of both Bull Run fights. One end of Stone House was shot away in the war, but has been rebuilt.

The sun baked down on the little lot, and, surrounded as we were by higher land, there was not a breath of air. It was, however, good fun to watch the troops coming up the Sudley's Springs road from camp and turning up the Warrenton Pike round our corner, and to see the different methods the officers used in keeping the men up to the hard work in the dusty hot roads. The Texans went by with a rush, all shouting and singing.

After about an hour, an officer came galloping over from Stone House and sang out to the Sergeant that he wanted a man with a good horse to follow him. Porter Stone volunteered and so did I, and as Duncan shone with careful grooming, he took me. He told me to take off my saber and packs, and hustle after him. Everybody turned to, and we had the horse stripped of saddle bags, cantle roll, saber and canteen and cup in a jiffy. The officer galloped up the road to Sudley's Springs with me at his heels. We turned off to the left and went through a field, and I took down some bars for him, and put 'em up again, and we went on in a roundabout way to Sudley's Springs, where we forded Bull Run and rode on up to Sudley Mansion.

The government had tested all the water about in the region open to the maneuvers, and had posted up signs—"Good Water" or "Bad Water"—wherever there was water to be had. Sudley's Springs was labeled "Good Water," and there was a line of thirsty infantrymen waiting to fill their canteens. Sometimes one would come along with a dozen canteens for himself and friends. Major Hoppin, our C.O., said that after thirty years in the service he had found it was better for a man to drink nothing from the time he started in the morning till he got through at night. The average man, especially in the infantry, had not gotten to that state of hardihood, however, as he seemed to run by water power—he called on his canteen so regularly. Of course the dustiness of the roads made thirst greater. The dust in most places was from two to three inches thick on the pike—pulverized red dust which soon made a blue shirt look gray.

When we got up to Sudley Mansion which stands on a hill above the springs we rode into a field and dismounted. I held the officer's horse while he had a look about him with his glass. He showed me where we were on the map, and told me that it was to be nearly the extreme right of our army. Just then a young Engineer Captain rode up and inquired if we had seen his wagon, which we reported as being just below the springs with his company. He was laying the field telegraphic communication to headquarters. The telegraph followed the wire fence where that was possible, and was hardly distinguishable from the fence, which protected it in many cases.

We were looking for General Bliss, whom we expected to find thereabout. As he was not, we retraced our steps to the springs and, fording the run, turned off to our right and mounted the higher land beyond. On the hill we met more engineers laying the field telegraph, and the officer in command directed us to where General Bliss was and said, by that time, he should be in telegraphic communication with Division Headquarters. We rode on as directed and passed some of the 14th N.Y., who were pretty tired, and lying by the roadside. We passed one poor fellow shaking from head to foot with a chill. The two companions who were looking out for him begged us to get a doctor; said they had tried to get one to come to him but he would not. Lieutenant Mowry—for so I learned my officer was named (he was in command of I Troop, 15th Cavalry)—told them to go back to the surgeon and report the condition of the man.

We went on, and at a fork of the road Lieutenant Mowry turned off and spoke to an officer—I judged a colonel in the regular army—who said he was going along. His orderly mounted up after him and rode along with me. The Colonel soon turned off into a field and, finding he had some instructions to give, told us to go on, which we did. An ambulance nearly broke down the field telegraph by careless driving, and Lieutenant Mowry spoke to the drivers and sent an engineer private, whom we found sitting by the side of the road, to watch the wire and see that the hospital corps did it no damage. I noticed especially the workman-like way in which the regular officers kept their eyes open for all such little things and worked together. My Lieutenant watched everything. For example, we started back to Stone House at a gallop but came down to a slower pace, as he had taken particular note of the condition of my mount and saw that he was very tired.

On the piazza of Stone House General Grant with one or two officers was seated smoking a cigar. Aides like Lieutenant Mowry returned from time to time with reports, and then went to the end of the piazza or sat on the grass in the yard of the house, talking. The Warrenton Pike runs directly in front of the gate to the house, and across the pike an open field slopes down to Young's Branch. On the grassy bank across the road a dozen or so orderlies, mostly regular cavalrymen, were seated holding horses—their own and their officers'. Occasionally an officer would ride up and his orderly would join our number, or one would come out of the gate and be met by his orderly with his horse.

During the afternoon one or two infantry regiments passed on the pike, and two or three long wagon trains. Towards dusk a company of regular engineers came to a halt in the field where we were, and in about ten minutes had pitched their camp, set up their dog tents, and were making themselves as comfortable as a regular can. By now we wished the General would get a move on and let us get to our own camping place before night set in. Lieutenant Mowry came out and called for one of the volunteer cavalrymen, and Porter Stone (he with Keyes Winter had been given my rolls and equipment by Sergeant Kelly to look after, and had dropped out of the sergeant's guard when they rode by, and waited at headquarters with me) stepped up and was directed to take a message to General Bliss. He rode off; and soon after it got dark and the word came to move, the General with his orderlies and his Division flag moved down the pike towards Centerville. We took our place as guard and marched at a walk down the pike, across Young's Branch and Stone Bridge, famous in the first battle of Bull Run, to Bull Run Post Office, where General Grant was to make his headquarters for the night.

Of course it was pitch-black night when we arrived. The headquarters' tents were all up, and we turned off to the right about fifty yards from them to where around two campfires we found all the rest of the guard assembled. Sergeant Kelly told us to tie our horses to the fence as best we could and remember where they were, and to keep our equipments together where we could get them easily if necessary. He got some hay for me. I was much amused at the raving of an Irish corporal of the regulars, whose appearance, with fierce moustache, was enough to convince you he would eat you on the slightest provocation. He declared that we had all his hay, and went storming and swearing about, but neither Sergeant Kelly nor anybody else paid any attention to him. I got a good big feed of oats for my horse, but as he was too tired to eat them, I let him pick at the hay and I put the oats where he could easily get them, and they were all gone by morning.

At the first gray light of the 9th of September, Friday, we were all awake and up, and I breakfasted on coffee which I had bought and now heated in my cup on the fire, and some crackers. I then saddled up and put on my rolls and equipment. Sergeant Kelly called for six men to take down the Division Headquarters' tents, and I jumped into it with five others, all but one being A Troop men. We took down all General Grant's tents and rolled and tied them up, and then loaded them on wagons. General Grant and his Adjutant General stood by looking on. Before we began, the A.G. told us to each take a cup of hot coffee, which we gladly did. We then attacked the tents. Sergeant Kelly would tell four men to loosen guys and pull the pins, he and I then grabbed the poles and lowered the tents and rolled them up, tying them with two of the guys. When we got through, the Adjutant General said: "I want you New York cavalrymen to know that we appreciate the way you have done your work. It won't be forgotten"—or words to that effect.

We returned to our horses, and an officer came over and told Sergeant Kelly he wanted four men with good horses right away, and that one must have a pencil. I had no pencil but was ready, and Sergeant Kelly let me go when I applied for the chance. The other three were Porter Stone, Tom Britton, and a Connecticut Troop A man who everybody thought was the one with a pencil. We all rode after our officer whose uniform showed him to be a first lieutenant of the 12th U.S. Infantry. He told us later that his name was Merrill. We rode in single file at first toward the west, and then turned south through the wood. We found we were to ride as far as we could down the left flank of our army and, if attacked, we were to scatter, take cover and get back as best we could to report to General Grant what we had seen. I luckily had a map of the country which an engineer sergeant had given me at headquarters the day before. It was like the kind all the officers carried, and whenever Lieutenant Merrill pulled out his map, I pulled out mine and found where he thought we were. I also had a small pocket compass which I had thought might prove handy, and did subsequently use.

We heard infantry fire soon after we started—at first light, and later heavier and heavier—accompanied with some artillery now and again. We then would stop and listen. Occasionally one of us would dismount to open a gate or take down some bars, always being careful to shut the gate or replace the bars. We passed cattle grazing, Lieutenant Merrill remarking that there could be no force of the enemy in that direction, they were so quiet. We forded Cub Run, and later Flat Run, and came to Bull Run at a place where there was a good chance of getting across fairly dry.

Thirty-four Years Later

I will try to finish this account from memory.

I remember being given a short written note to headquarters by Lieutenant Merrill with orders to deliver it as quickly as possible. I rode back to the bridge across Bull Run and, seeing a notice posted to the effect that the bridge was supposed to have been blown up, forded the stream and proceeded. As I went along, the firing in the direction to which I was going increased in volume and the engagement was evidently in progress.

I finally reached General Grant's headquarters in the field just as the show was about over and I delivered my message to the Staff Adjutant and was told the war was over and I was to return to my command.

I have a dim recollection of getting back to our squadron, and breaking camp, and standing in line to sign receipts for federal pay (which was not given out); the only money I remember earning as a soldier.

I remember sleeping in a cornfield without blankets or other luxuries, loading our equipment on the cars, and finally sleeping again on the floor of a freight car between stacks of kit bags and duffle; but anyway sleeping—the one thing that seemed at that time like joy.

My old horse Duncan had had the best care I could give him, but he was very thin and tired, and so shad-bellied that it was hard to keep the girth from slipping back. I remember that I said he had lost sixty pounds on the trip; but how I knew that, I have forgotten.

The rest is a blur today. My chief memory is of intense desire to sleep; a longing so great that it would not be denied. We were so tired we ached.

The army found that it had tried to do too much in too short a time and that raw troops could not stand it. We, in the troop, were in far better training for the work than most of the infantry regiments. It did us no harm and is, even at this day, a very pleasant memory.

THE MASSACHUSETTS MANEUVERS

They ride upon horses, set in array as men for war.—Jeremiah 6:23

THESE maneuvers were carried out in 1909, five years after those at Manassas and five years before the World War. The New York National Guard supplied a large part of the troops of the "Red" army, and Squadron A was combined with cavalry from New Jersey, Connecticut, and a squadron of the 10th U.S. Cavalry, as a provisional regiment under command of Major Bridgman. The personnel, however, which would be appropriate for the headquarters of a cavalry regiment was not supplied, and the duties involved in the special work which fell upon the adjutant, First Lieutenant George E. Fahys, were difficult and exhausting. In addition to the mass of office work, the reports rendered daily to General Leonard Wood, chief umpire, often miles away and late at night, made him at the end of the campaign a candidate for a forty-eight-hour sleep. The experienced war-correspondent Richard Harding Davis, who "carried" these maneuvers, attempted to explain to the public the vital necessity of such training.

Upon the troops being assembled at New Bedford on Saturday, August 14th, General Wood, who was not only chief umpire but also in supreme command, issued a statement as to the assumed situation. It read:

On August 10th, immediately following an unexpected severance of diplomatic relations, war was declared between a strong European Power (Red) and the United States (Blue).

On August 11th the (Blue) North Atlantic battleship fleet, after a severe engagement with a superior (Red) fleet off the Maine coast, was defeated and scattered. Remnants of the crippled (Blue) fleet took refuge in Portland and Portsmouth harbors, and are now blockaded by the victorious Red fleet. Command of the North Atlantic Ocean has been secured by the Reds.

On August 12th a portion of the victorious Red fleet left the Maine coast to report to General Bliss, commanding the First Division, First Corps, Red Army, designated for operations in the Boston district. If the enemy is to be kept out of Boston by the Blue forces, under command of General William A. Pew, stationed in that city, a line of nearly twenty-three miles must be protected against the invading army.

The advance of the Red forces was pushed vigorously despite heavy rains during part of the period, and the cavalry was used continuously and effectively. The newspapers published extensive and often conflicting reports of the operations and stressed the activity and importance of the cavalry. One news item stated that Lieutenant Alfred Wendt of Squadron A, with two troopers, captured and brought in twenty-two prisoners of the Blue forces—which perhaps inspired the marvelous single-handed exploits of Sergeant Yorke in the World War.

At the period of these maneuvers the mounted forces were still supreme in mobility and speed. Motorized units had not been developed and there were no motorcycles for scouting or messenger service, nor was there radio communication; armored cars and tanks had not been invented, and military airplanes were unknown or in an experimental stage. Even the machine gun and the magazine rifle were novelties and not a part of standard equipment. The army mule was still the basic motive power of the wagon trains, and the operations in the field were based upon conditions not very different from those of the Civil War era.

The narrative of Noel Bleecker Fox gives an interesting illustration of the experiences and the viewpoint of the individual trooper.

NARRATIVE OF NOEL BLEECKER FOX

For one week commencing August 14, 1909, the squadron participated in maneuvers of the kind where we bivouacked at a different place each night and rode by day on saddles heavily packed with blanket rolls, saddle bags, canteens, and other equipment.

In those days only one camp every two years was considered required, and since these maneuvers came between the camps of 1908 and 1910 our attendance was not large. The four troops of the squadron were condensed into three by adding a squad of Fourth Troop men to each of the other three troops. The Essex Troop of New Jersey was joined to us to make a squadron of four troops. That squadron and a squadron and machine gun platoon from the Tenth U.S.

Cavalry (negro) formed a provisional regiment which Major Bridgman commanded.

The situation assumed an invading Red division landed from transports at New Bedford and marched north with the mission of capturing Boston, which was defended by the Blue division of Massachusetts militia, commanded by Major General William A. Pew. The Red division was under command of a regular, Brigadier General Tasker H. Bliss, who in the World War became chief of staff. It had infantry brigades from the National Guard of New York, Connecticut, and the District of Columbia, field artillery from New York and Connecticut, the cavalry already mentioned, and other troops. The opposing sides wore wide cotton hatbands of their respective colors while the umpires wore white ones. One amusing result of this alignment of states was the intensely partisan favor of the local inhabitants for the Blues, which made it difficult for our patrols to get information from them.

Our provisional squadron was among troops sailing from New York on the old steamboat *Pilgrim,* which had been retired after many years of service on the Fall River Line. Guards were established as on a transport. The troops aboard were more numerous than the berths, and the remainder slept on mattresses on the floor. On debarking at New Bedford we saddled, loaded wagons, and marched to Rochester for our first bivouac. The next morning the war was on.

The maneuver area extended from the Rhode Island line to Cape Cod Bay. In defending this wide front General Pew stretched his line too thin. The Red army camped the first night in the form of a crescent with the points to the enemy. Our squadron formed the east point and the negro squadron the west one. On the first day of combat General Bliss attacked suddenly with cavalry and some infantry on the west to attract attention there, while the rest of the infantry shifted behind us on the east. Our squadron was immediately sent forward in many small patrols to locate the enemy and to conceal the infantry in our rear.

It was this efficient use of cavalry patrols that made the squadron men enjoy the Massachusetts maneuvers more than others. The New York infantry did not like them so well, as the rapid advance made the marches long and some units trudged along dusty roads for a couple of days before getting the excitement of battle. From the first morning of combat our cavalry patrols were continually coming in contact with the infantry patrols, outposts, and advance guards of the Blues. They had much less cavalry than we, and they must have kept what they had on their west flank as it never opposed us.

The Boston Cadets and some other Massachusetts infantry organizations had numerous men mounted on bicycles, and attempted to use them as patrols in place of cavalry. They carried their rifles either on their backs or strapped to the bicycles and in either case could not fire when mounted, while we were well supplied with blank cartridges for our revolvers and on meeting them had great fun firing at them as we tried to gallop them down. If they were on one of the few hard roads they would get away, but most of the roads were sandy and we often captured them.

Prisoners were held until the close of fighting for the day, when they were free to try to find their regiments. Once a patrol took a rifle from a prisoner and failed to guard it sufficiently to prevent its appropriation as a souvenir by some one of the inhabitants who came in crowds to see the excitement and were always getting in our way. That incident resulted in a correspondence lasting all the next winter, in which a Massachusetts regiment sought to make the squadron pay for the lost rifle.

One of our patrols which located an enemy position took cover mounted among thick shrubbery while trying to estimate the enemy's strength. Suddenly an automobile passed us, full of high ranking officers wearing blue hatbands. We galloped out and called on them to surrender, meanwhile firing our pistols at closer range than regulations allowed. The firing stampeded the horses of a farm wagon which almost blocked their road, but before we could surround them they squeezed past it and escaped. Our disappointment at losing them was greatly increased the next day when we learned that the Governor of Massachusetts was in the car at the time.

That night we bivouacked at Rock Station with the First Troop half a mile in advance as an outpost and with Lieutenant Wendt's platoon still further to the front. One squad was out to one side as a flank guard and had to be fed in the morning by sending out a mounted trooper carrying a pail of hot oatmeal and several canteens of coffee.

A hard rain came down as our squadron took the road and advanced against the enemy position located the day before at the small village of Middleboro Green just east of Middleboro. Part of the Eighth Massachusetts held a line along a rise of ground past the front of a typical white New England church. We dismounted to fight on foot and worked our way around their flank through the cover of a field of standing corn. The rain poured on us as we waded through the mud, and by the time the umpires decided that the position was ours we were so wet through that our toes splashed in the water which filled our shoes.

That action being over, we sought shelter from the rain by crowding into the long line of horsesheds behind the church. We were not looking for any further fighting in that weather, but after we had rested under cover for half an hour or more there was a sudden outburst of firing, and great confusion prevailed as the officers tried to form their troops dismounted for immediate action. It seems that a company of the Eighth Massachusetts had come to join the other companies which it supposed were still at the church. We were so well concealed by the horsesheds that they did not see us until they almost reached us. Fortunately we outnumbered them and soon brought them in as prisoners. A humorous drawing of this incident is framed in our armory.

On the arrival of the hour for ending the day's combat, we picketed our horses in the rain and proceeded to encamp in the horsesheds, hanging our pup tents across the front of the sheds to keep out the rain. Our officers enjoyed the greater shelter of the Sunday school room behind the church, while a few of the men chose to sleep on discarded pews in the basement. This ended our only day of bad weather.

The next two days saw larger forces joined in a series of general engagements, each of which was northeast of the previous one, as the Reds tried to work around the Blue flank and the Blues shifted further east to prevent it. Each time, the Red cavalry would make a wide sweep around the Blue flank to be stopped at some point north of the previous line. They would then dismount and hold a line until the infantry arrived to relieve them. The cavalry would then mount up, withdraw to the rear, ride rapidly east, and repeat the operation. Our squadron had the fun of leading most of these flanking operations.

We were in such a fight at Plympton, but on the following morning when the opposing armies met at Bryantville and the Blues succeeded in repulsing the Reds, we were some distance away and could barely hear the firing. We rode to the east and held a road by which the

Red infantry withdrew from Bryantville, passed behind us, and continued to march north.

At Pembroke we were guarding the left flank of the infantry column when a patrol from the First Troop was sent out to locate the approaching enemy. It ran into the Sixth Massachusetts and sent back a messenger, but the rest of the patrol was captured. Our squadron and the squadron of the Tenth Cavalry dismounted and repulsed the Blue attack while the squadron men who were prisoners sat on a stone wall, holding their horses and watching to see how a squadron battle looked from behind the enemy line.

Finally came the biggest battle of all—at Hanover Four Corners. When it started we were south of it guarding the long wagon train. Instead of halting until the action was over, the wagon train continued to move north right through the village which was held by the Reds. We were astonished to find that instead of facing north as in previous actions the Red battle line faced west, leaving open the main road leading northward to Boston. Amid the noise of battle our squadron left the wagon train which was passing through the village just behind the artillery batteries in action. We took up the gallop along the road to the north and were thrilled to see from the road signs that we were at last between the enemy and Boston. But we could not understand why we were hurrying away from the battle. About two miles north of Hanover Four Corners we turned sharp left on a reverse fork and rode back toward the noise of gunfire, except that this time we were in the rear of the enemy's north flank. On reaching the church at Hanover Center we dismounted and took a position facing south on high ground overlooking the smoke of battle in the distance.

The hour for ending operations arrived and as we made camp we anticipated excitement on the resumption of fighting the next day. For unless the enemy could dislodge us the entire Red army could pass behind us and have a clear road to Boston with only rear-guard actions to fight. Great was our disappointment that evening to learn that the maneuvers had been declared over and that nothing remained for us to do but to go home. The next day after a long march to South Braintree we spent the afternoon in the freight yards loading horses and wagons on a train. The train took us to Fall River and in the evening we embarked again on the old *Pilgrim*. Its wornout engines took that night and most of the next day in reaching New York, but by late afternoon we were back in our armory.

The infantry was tired out with its long marches, but I think the squadron men who took part in the Massachusetts maneuvers will vote them the most interesting and instructive of our summer camps.

STRIKE DUTY

When we assumed the soldier, we did not lay aside the civilian.
—GEORGE WASHINGTON

DURING the years before 1916, and exclusive of the participation of the representative Volunteer Troop A in the Spanish War, the activities of Troop A and Squadron A most tinged with the quality of operations against hostile forces were those when called out to aid the civil authorities to suppress disorders. There were three occasions. The first was in Buffalo at the time of the railroad strike of August, 1892; the second was in Brooklyn at the time of the trolley strike in January, 1895; the third was at Croton Dam at the time the strike threatened the city water supply in April, 1900. Each of these is the subject of a separate paper.

The call for duty at Buffalo in 1892 found the troop ready. Said *The Rider and Driver* of March 17, 1900:

It is a remarkable circumstance to the credit of the Troop that whereas orders were not received until 7 P.M., all but six men were on board a special train at 1 A.M., six hours later. . . . Of the six men not on the train, one was in California and two in Europe. The three remaining delinquents turned up at Buffalo the next day, and one of those who had gone to Europe, Coudert, received a cable message informing him of the Troop's going to Buffalo, and immediately returned to America, arriving home on the same day that the Troop got back.

There was only one day between the 19th and the 25th when the Troop was not on duty. During that time the men slept in a stock barn, bathed in the horse troughs, and ate the food cooked by Commissary Gilford Hurry, now Lieutenant Colonel and a Commissary on General Roe's staff.

This is quoted as a comment from an outside source, but the paper of our fellow-member Walter W. Price gives a more intimate view, and the diary of William H. Browning[1] also gives a personal experience.

[1] See p. 21.

The next instance of riot duty occurred in January, when the streets were glazed with ice. On the night when the troop was assembled details were sent out collecting horses—partly from the horse-car stables—until day was breaking. The horses as collected were brought to temporary quarters at Fifth Avenue and Ninetieth Street; and when the troopers saddled up and started for the ferry, it was found that many of the horses were smooth-shod and slithered about hopelessly and helplessly on the icy pavements. Arrived in Brooklyn, however, they were soon reshod, and thereafter the service given was all that could be asked. Captain Roe's report to the Adjutant General as to the service in suppressing disorder included commendations of a number of individuals and concluded with this tribute:

The entire Troop accepted every discomfort without complaint, behaved in the most gallant manner, and are worthy of the name of true soldiers. If there are any better soldiers I have never seen them.

This service immediately preceded and possibly resulted in the transformation of Troop A into Squadron A.

Two incidents not included in the narrative of Lieutenant Coudert illustrate unexpected phases of this service.

The strikers devised an ingenious method of cutting trolley wires by laying one end of a length of iron pipe against the trolley rail and dropping the other end against the wire carrying the current. The resulting short circuit was accompanied by a blinding flash and loud detonation; and as the loose ends of wire swung to the ground, they created lesser pyrotechnic displays and menaced with electrocution anyone who might come into contact with them. On night duty escorting the repair gangs, this was a spectacular and not insignificant hazard.

On one occasion a detachment under Sergeant Badgley was sent out to where disorder had been reported. Arriving there, he estimated the situation as serious and detailed a trooper to ride back to headquarters, about a mile away, and ask for reinforcements. The trooper trotted off on his mission, but when he had gone about halfway he saw ahead of him a large packing case on the trolley tracks and a crowd filling the avenue. To try to detour might lead him to worse conditions and he might also lose his way. To go back would be cowardly. The only course, he thought, was to cut his way through if possible or perish honorably. So he drew his saber and spurred his horse to a gallop directly toward the crowd. The result was as successful as it was unexpected. The crowd was actually much more curious than hostile, and it made for the sidewalks as the menacing rider approached with great clatter of hoofs. The street was automatically cleared; and sensing the situation, the trooper pulled up his horse and rode to the packing case, which though large was empty; he executed "return saber," and reaching down took hold of the case, which with a little lifting was easily carried by the horse to a point clear of the tracks. The trooper, now very bold, said in a loud, stern voice that anybody who attempted more obstruction would be severely dealt with, and continued his journey at a dignified trot. When reinforcements passed that point later, the packing case had not been moved and the crowd had disappeared.

As to the service at Croton Dam the program of the annual games held February 26, 1901, said:

The event of Squadron history of the past year was the trip to Croton—the "Italian" or "Two Weeks' War," as it has been known. On Sunday night, April 16th, we received our orders to start the next morning, and Monday evening we were camping at Ardsley. During the night a drizzle began, which grew to a rain of large proportions and seemed to last for a period slightly shorter than the reign of the late Queen. About the middle of the following day we camped on a hill above the Croton Dam in a field of mud dotted with fine large stones.

The works about the dam which we guarded spread across the valley and up both its slopes, and the non-striking workmen who needed protection lived at considerable distances apart, so that for a week the Squadron had its full share of duties to perform and more wet night-work to do than some of the members thought essential to their comfort. But the Major General told us, at a little reception we gave to the Seventh Regiment and Troop C, that we had done our work well, and that was a satisfaction that drowned in the waters of Lethe the memory of a good deal of water in our clothes. . . .

On Saturday, the 24th, two troops went home, one troop remaining with Troop C from Brooklyn on the other side of the valley, until the end of the week. . . .

The work done on this occasion was not on city streets as in the previous riot duty, but in a country area with broken terrain, and with the camp adjacent to woods and underbrush, in which its line of sentries, armed with loaded carbines, was posted at night. In making a round of inspection one night, the officer of the guard was challenged by a sentry some distance to the left, and immediately afterward by another sentry some distance away to his right; neither was visible to him in the darkness.

First Sentry: Halt! Who goes there?
Officer: Officer of the guard.
First Sentry: Advance, officer of the guard, and be recognized. [*The officer starts toward the first sentry.*]
Second Sentry: Halt! Who goes there?
Officer: Officer of the guard. [*The officer continues toward the first sentry.*]
Second Sentry: Halt! or I fire.

The manual of guard duty did not seem to provide for this situation.

Another incident narrated runs as follows: Charles E. Merrill, Jr., hailed a fellow-trooper, the artist and architect Walter B. Chambers, who was doing valiant but unaccustomed work with a manure pitchfork on the picket line at Croton Dam, and Chambers said, "I'll never love another country!"

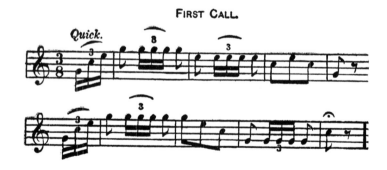

First Call.

THE BUFFALO STRIKE, 1892

Walter W. Price

> Hark! the shrill trumpet sounds; to horse, away!
> —COLLEY CIBBER, "Richard III"

NEW YORK was a smaller place in those days than it is today, both from the standpoint of the state and from the standpoint of the city, and for about three days prior to the calling out of the troop, rumors were flying all around.

To the best of my recollection, on Thursday, August 18th, in the morning, we received orders to report at Dickel's Riding Academy for active duty. Like all soldiers called for the first time, we were deeply impressed with the seriousness of the mission upon which we were to be sent.

At six o'clock sharp in the evening the order was given to prepare to mount. At 6:10 we were all lined up on the south side of Fifty-sixth Street, and by 6:15 the order was given to form fours and march. We started for the old Thirtieth Street station of the New York Central Railroad. There we found a state of suppressed excitement, for the only men who were serving the railroad were those who were regarded as "scabs." Without assistance and under the penetrating eye of General Roe, those amateur soldiers quickly led the one hundred and six horses into the places assigned them in freight cars. At 12:30 A.M. we started in passenger cars, each filled to the limit, on our trip to Buffalo. The officers and non-commissioned officers occupied a car by themselves. That, of course, with the exception of certain details of non-commissioned officers, made possible an environment of jollity. It was an evening of great hilarity.

We reached Buffalo the next day at about noon, and for a long time were held in the freight yards. At about one o'clock word came that we were assigned to the cattle barns of the New York Central Railroad—barns in which cattle were held when they were assembled for reshipment. The railroads in those days handled matters in a much more primitive fashion than they do today. It was a strange habitation for these men, and I never will forget the impression which Captain Roe made upon me by his quick grasp of the situation; he assigned squads to various places in the barn, so that at six o'clock the troop had its horses safely tied up and quietly munching hay in the stalls, and the troopers commanded by their various non-commissioned officers under direct orders from Captain Roe had found places in a great barn with some hay for improvised beds.

The situation was very tense with sympathy for the strikers in many quarters; conscious of that sympathy, they became very aggressive under the direction of their leaders. Our first experience came early on the morning following our arrival, when a group of twenty troopers were detailed to suppress disorder which had developed on the tracks about three-quarters of a mile from where we were bivouacked.

The hearts of the troopers beat faster when Captain Roe halted them in line mounted and gave the commands: "Raise pistol. With ball cartridge, Load." That certainly sounded like practical application of law enforcement *vi et armis;* and Captain Roe was calm and businesslike about it. "Return pistol." And back they went into the holsters—and remained there. Perhaps Captain Roe realized that his position sitting his horse in front of the line involved more jeopardy than that of the strikers—with at least one trooper in the line who, from nervousness or inexperience, had shot a hole through the ceiling on one drill night, and through the floor on another; but if so, he did not show it.

To the best of my recollection we were in Buffalo from August 19th to August 25th—seven days—and that trip saw about as much active duty as any group of soldiers could have that was confronted with a similar situation. Sometimes we were detailed as a troop to points where disorder developed. Sometimes we were detailed in squads or platoons; but in every instance, as a result of Captain Roe's training, the troop acquitted itself admirably, even though at times it was confronted with small groups or mobs of strikers who would throw sticks and stones, poke at the horses and run away; at no time was a command given to charge upon those men, but by a forceful attitude the strikers were soon brought to a realization that so far could they go and no further.

One of the incidents which comes to my mind is when we were

CAPTAIN ROE IN TOUR OF DUTY DURING BUFFALO STRIKE, 1891
TROOPERS AT WATER TROUGH IN BUFFALO STOCKYARDS, 1891

CROTON DAM CAMP IN COURSE OF TOUR OF DUTY DURING STRIKE, 1900
CHANGING THE GUARD, TOUR OF DUTY DURING CROTON DAM STRIKE, 1900

lined up as a troop and a striker came to one of our troopers, Geer—a great athlete and one of the best amateur boxers this country has ever produced—and attempted to hit him with a stick. Quick as a flash, Geer was on his feet. He threw down his hat and said to the striker: "You are too much of a coward to fight in the open, but if you are not, I will give you all you want." That virtually ended the incident.

The patrolling, and the show of force that awed potential troublemakers, was conducted with such skill and appreciation of how military force should be used in support of the civil authority, that no actual clash occurred. The result was a tribute to the ability of the Troop Commander and to the efficiency of his command.

During a large part of the time spent at Buffalo the troop was held waiting in readiness to respond to any call. As time went by the individual members explored the stockyards and found among the livestock considerable numbers of sheep and rams. A series of battles resulted—apparently not chronicled in the military reports or in the press. Enterprising troopers got rams from different groups and put them by twos in unoccupied pens. The rams faced each other, backed off, and came together in head-on collision; then backed off again and repeated the charge until one was knocked over or had enough; whereupon another pair of combatants was brought in. It was a merry game until an official of the stockyards had the sport outlawed.

Troops were summoned to Buffalo from different parts of the state. Gradually, the strikers recognized the determination of the military authorities to maintain order at all hazards; and on the evening of the 25th, order had been restored to the point where we were told that we were to start for home. We stopped en route at the old Poughkeepsie railroad station, which had an eating house on the main floor that was famous. Never shall I forget the excitement created by those one hundred and six men as they marched en masse into that room and surrounded the counters three deep, consuming every vestige of provisions that the house contained.

We arrived at Thirtieth Street, New York City, the morning of August 26th, and our march from the station up Tenth Avenue and through Fifty-sixth Street to the armory revealed the interest which the people of New York had in this new form of cavalry unit which Captain Roe had brought into existence.

As I look back, I often think that this first taste of military service had much to do with the splendid record which the troop made later, not only in the Brooklyn riots and the Croton riots, but in the Spanish-American War, on the Mexican border, and in the World War—in which the members served in 1917. In every one of these services Troop A and Squadron A were inspired by the splendid spirit and character of that great soldier and gentleman, Major General Charles F. Roe.

THE BROOKLYN STRIKE, 1895

Frederic R. Coudert

> Half a block,
> Half a block,
> Half a block forward.
>
> —Squadron Ballad

In a forgotten drawer of an office desk the other day, I came across an old brass bell about the size of a child's fist. It gave out a strident and unmelodious sound when shaken. Engraven on its unattractive brass exterior were the words, "Trolley Riots, January 20–29, 1895," with the crossed sabers of Troop A insignia and my name, Frederic R. Coudert, Jr. The origin of this priceless souvenir is as follows:

Jeannot & Scheibler's jewelry factory across the street from the Brooklyn trolley yard where we were stationed was closed down and we were allowed to use it in daytime to wash up and warm ourselves. The superintendent of the trolley company presented us with bells formerly used on the collars of the horses in the pre-trolley-car era, and as several factory workers came in the daytime and sat at their benches reading newspapers, they engraved our names and the date on the bells for want of something to do. Several of the workmen had been in the Franco-Prussian War and seemed to enjoy seeing soldiers again.

This is my memento of the once stirring event which we sometimes called the "Brooklyn Campaign." I remember vividly the evening of January 20th when between the hours of nine and ten a uniformed trooper knocked at my door and notified me that Captain Roe had demanded my immediate presence in uniform at the armory for strike service. For some days previous we had heard of the difficulties in Brooklyn: the tie-up of the trolley service, the disorder spread by trolley-car employees and their sympathizers, and the apparent impotence of the police to restore order.

At the temporary armory we found our comrades and a few horses commandeered from livery stables. As a non-commissioned officer, I was detailed with some six men to bring some twenty horses from Dickel's Riding Academy in Fifty-sixth Street as quickly as possible. We found the horses, equipped merely with halters and watering bridles, assembled in the ring. Each man mounted a horse and led three or four others, and so we marched over to and up silent Fifth Avenue somewhere near midnight. The ground was covered with frozen snow, and a number of horses were not sharp-shod. Every few blocks a horse would slip, fall, and usually pull down two or three other horses with him, and sometimes a rider also. To the stray observers or to the few who poked their heads out into the wintry cold, it must have been a curious sight—men and horses strewn along Fifth Avenue in apparently inexplicable confusion. Why no legs, either of men or of horses, were broken in the struggle, I do not know.

Stretched upon the floor or on a few cots, the men slept until daylight, and then were aroused by the thrilling tones of bugles sounding "Boots and saddles." As I recollect, some work on sharp-shoeing the horses had been done during the night, and so, despite the snowy streets, the troop was able to get under way in the early morning and move toward the Brooklyn Bridge.

We reached Thompson Street trolley yard (which had been horsecar stables)—a musty, underground place—where we were to lodge through nine days of bitter cold and very inclement weather.

A guard formation was immediately organized and small patrols were sent out through the streets to protect property and, if necessary, individuals, from lawless violence or other forms of riot. Somewhat to the disappointment, I think, of our thirst for adventure, the strikers turned out to be a rather mild-mannered lot who did little more than stand in the side streets and make grimaces and utter uncomplimentary sounds. Occasionally, a little group would form on the street, but when the non-commissioned officers gave the order to trot and we went toward it with drawn saber, the incipient opposition scurried to the four winds. The question of the efficiency of cavalry on icy streets was settled the first day, when a mounted trooper pursued a hoodlum through the door of a saloon, brought him out, and turned him over to a policeman. The policeman told him to "beat it," and then congratulated the trooper. The electric repair men, who were enjoying double pay, insisted that troopers rather than infantry be sent to guard them.

Our greatest danger came from the weather, the poor accommodations, and the necessity of cooking in very dirty and ill-kept streets. One day after things had dried up and quantities of dust were floating in the winter breezes, a great caldron of stew was being brewed by the commissary-sergeant and his assistant in the middle of a side street next to the trolley barn. One particularly mild-mannered recruit of perhaps eighteen remarked: "Sergeant, this stew is filled with grit and dirt!" Said old Sergeant Hurry, with counterfeited grimness, "Don't you know, my boy, that you must eat your peck of dirt before you die?" "But, Sergeant," replied the rookie, "I hate to eat it all at once!"

Exposure to constant cold and wet made some of the men very uncomfortable, but resulted in no serious illness. Saddle blankets under the canvas covers hardly kept our horses from freezing, and the water pipes in the car barn froze one night even though the water had been left running.

After we had been at the trolley barn for a few days, we heard that the strikers were assembling a great body of men at Maspeth, and might march from there to the trolley stables, to give a demonstration of their strength. At the call of the bugle we saddled and bridled with suppressed excitement and marched off with Captain Roe (as always, at the head) and finally, after a long march, reached the then distant goal of Maspeth.

We found a few hundred men assembled in a field; and in near-by houses windows were opened and people were peering out with mingled curiosity and animosity. We were ordered to dismount and look to "girths and saddles." Our excitement rose to a high pitch and we wondered if we should have to charge the mob; but apparently the assembly had no desire to be charged. In those days the terror created by the horse was considerable, and as our column moved toward the crowd at a walk, then at a trot, the mob melted away, contenting themselves with a few jeers. I think one or two boys were hit lightly, and one slightly cut in the face. There was no more bloodshed than that, at what we subsequently called the "Battle of Maspeth."

I do remember that there were weary hours of guard duty and waiting about in the trolley stables. We organized classes in the saber and in the various drills for those who volunteered for the exercise. The service was quite strenuous. Some of us did not have our boots off for several days, partly because of the cold and wet, partly because of our inability to get them off, and partly because some of us "non-coms" were on duty a great part of the time, sleeping when we could, very soundly, upon a hard floor softened only by a little straw.

I believe that it was the presence of the National Guard units along the Brooklyn trolley lines that led in a few days to the termination of the strike.

We returned to the armory after eight days of this duty, feeling that we were really tried soldiers and ready to face any emergency. Most of us, if not all, thoroughly enjoyed the experience.

STRIKE DUTY AT CROTON DAM, 1900
Abel I. Smith

> Arms on armor clashing bray'd . . .
> . . . dire was the noise
> Of conflict.
> —MILTON, "Paradise Lost"

THE Croton Dam is situated about three miles from the town of Croton on the Hudson River, two miles below the old Croton reservoir. In 1900 the dam was being built to enlarge the old reservoir that supplied water to New York City. The contractors were Brouchard & Coleman. The stone for the construction of the dam was supplied from a stone quarry seven miles above the dam, connected by a small railroad which brought the stone from the quarry to the dam.

On April 2, 1900, two hundred men employed in the quarry went out on strike without warning, and the next day, April 3rd, five hundred more working on the dam—teamsters, drillers, etc.—were notified that there would be no work until the stone could be secured from the quarry. The men were striking for an increase in their daily wage from $1.25 to $1.50. Sheriff Molloy, of Westchester County, sent a number of deputies to the dam to preserve order, and on Saturday the strikers charged the deputies with stones and clubs. On the 12th, the strikers and contractors held a conference to see if an agreement could be reached; the conference failed. On Saturday the 14th, the headlines of the daily papers read:

STRIKERS AND DEPUTY SHERIFFS READY TO FIGHT

700 swarthy strikers lined up against Westchester posse of 150. Croton Dam in possession of armed rioters. Trouble is looked for today and fears are expressed that strikers may use dynamite of which they have plenty.

On the same day General Roe wired Governor Theodore Roosevelt as follows:

Sheriff of Westchester County has called for the Fourth Separate Company of Yonkers, and the Eleventh Separate Company of Mt. Vernon to assist him against the strikers at Croton Dam. They go tomorrow to be on hand Monday morning. I will be in touch with the situation and request authority to send more troops from here if the Sheriff makes requisition.

To which Governor Roosevelt replied:

I hereby authorize you instantly to order out whatever troops are required to restore and preserve order.

General Roe immediately ordered out the Fourth Separate Company of Yonkers and the Eleventh Separate Company of Mt. Vernon. On the following day, Sunday April 15th, Sergeant Douglas of Mt. Vernon was shot and killed, and on that date the papers stated that troops might be used to quell the riots.

On this date, the 16th, the leader of the strikers—Rotella—announced that the strikers would fight, that only a small portion of them were armed at the time, but they would be armed within a day or so.

On Sunday night, April 15th, about midnight, Sergeant Alfred Wendt of Troop I, Squadron A, called at my house and directed me to report at the armory at 6 A.M., Monday the 16th, for strike duty at Croton. One can easily imagine what my feelings were, after having read the newspaper articles for the week previous, to be starting for duty in what one of the newspapers described as the "Valley of Death." However, I did get to the armory, in fear and trembling, at about six o'clock.

When I arrived there was considerable confusion. Men were hurrying around and breakfast was being served. We all worked like Trojans to get into our uniforms, to get the equipment in shape and the wagons packed to make a prompt start. Twenty rounds of ball cartridge were issued per man and, if you had any misgivings before arriving at the armory, this was the finishing touch. Considerable delay at the start was due to the impossibility of getting, in so short a time, a sufficient number of horses good enough to stand the journey.

The *New York Times* of Tuesday, April 17th, said:

There was a crowd of over 1000 men, women and small boys gathered about the Armory; the whole neighborhood was excited with the warlike preparations, and patriotism ran high; one youthful enthusiast gave vent to cheers; there has not been such excitement since the war [Spanish-American];

a number of the troopers were visited by relatives and friends, male and female, and the leavetakings were in some cases tearful, in others smiling, and in others exceedingly affectionate. Everyone wanted to know where Cornell Dam was, what the estimated force of the enemy was, and other similar questions. Many sisters and sweethearts brought little dainties and sweetmeats with which the loved one might regale himself far from the city market.

"Boots and saddles" was sounded at 11:10, on April 16th, and we started in the rain on our way to Croton Dam to make camp at the Cyrus Field Judson property at Ardsley. When the squadron got to Dyckman Street and Kingsbridge Road the horse ridden by Major Oliver B. Bridgman (who was in command) slipped and fell, and the Major was thrown and fractured his leg. The hospital corps immediately took him in the ambulance to the hospital and then rejoined us.

When Major Bridgman could no longer continue, Captain Badgley became acting major and took us through the entire strike duty. We reached Ardsley that night, and made camp in the pouring rain. The heavy rain ran off our ponchos directly into our high leather boots, so that when we reached camp our boots were so full of water we dared not take them off for fear we could not get them on again. After a most unpleasant night we were ready to start at six o'clock for our destination.

I well remember the enthusiasm at breakfast when Frederick Kernochan arrived. He was in Norfolk, Virginia, when he saw in the papers that the squadron had been ordered out; he immediately took the train to New York, got to the armory at eleven o'clock that night, saddled, and rode all night to Ardsley. We finally reached our destination on the west side of the dam about three o'clock in the afternoon. One battalion of the Seventh Regiment was ordered out the day after we were, and it had gone to Croton by train and was camped on the east end of the dam. It rained night and day Monday, Tuesday, and Wednesday; and it was not until Thursday that any sunshine appeared to cheer up the bedraggled muddy men of the squadron. I have never seen anything worse: the horses had tramped around the picket line, ruled over by Quartermaster Freddy Cheeseborough's "Crab" and my own "Buster"; and the rain made the troop streets just a quagmire which in due course was generously carried into the Sibley tents quartering ten men. Thursday afternoon I succeeded in getting the hospital corps to pull off my boots. They did this most cheerfully, filled them with hot oats, and dried them out. And Harry Day gave me a drink of Wonder Rye.

I had been assigned to Sergeant Craig Havemeyer, troop commissary, and continued as his assistant until he left for New York, when I carried on his work with the assistance of Private Colby M. Chester. I have always suspected that Chester's training as assistant commissary at Croton really qualified him for his later job as president of General Foods. On Tuesday, after we arrived, pickets were immediately put out and there was some promiscuous shooting at phantom strikers, for General Roe had issued orders to the guard to shoot at anybody who did not answer the challenge. A guard was put around the village, just to the northwest of us, occupied by the Italian strikers.

On April 19th, Wednesday, we were all called out and directed a search of the strikers' houses, General Roe personally conducting this maneuver. All were gone through and anything in possession of the strikers that could be used as a weapon, defensive or offensive, was confiscated.

That same afternoon under an armed guard, work was commenced on the dam. At the suggestion of General Roe, Sheriff Molloy secured warrants for the arrest of thirty ringleaders of the strikers. After this the Croton Dam strike became back-page news for the newspapers. However, for us who were on duty there, it was far from back-page news. We had the daily grind of cleaning our horses, guard duty, and general camp policing. By Friday so many pieces of equipment were missing and others acquired from Heaven knows where, that the troops were assembled and each man had to state what equipment and parts of uniforms he had which did not belong to him. Wonderful as it may seem our Artificer Jim Terry did not have one single piece of uniform or equipment which bore his number—and yet he was fully equipped.

However, when the sun came out we had some delightful warm spring days. The brook adjacent to the camp was finally tabooed for bathing purposes on the ground that it was contaminated, and we could only use the water there for washing our clothes. Along about Thursday friends came up from New York and brought us a few things, including foods, which were most acceptable. Kelly Prentice, who was lieutenant commissary, fed us in great shape, even to securing fresh shad from Croton Point, which were most delicious. My experience as a fisherman stood me in good stead, for in selecting the fish for Troop I mess, I thought I was extremely brilliant in picking all roe shad; but I subsequently learned that all shad for all troops were roe shad, which pricked my conceit no little bit. At the end of the week the members of the squadron were asked who would volunteer to form a provisional troop to stay an additional week. I remained as acting commissary sergeant of this troop, and was ably assisted by dear old J. Willett (Billy) Hall.

Lieutenant Prentice sent for me before he left to explain the intricacies of making out a food requisition. After he had given me volumes of manuals and forms by the score, to feed the troop on twenty-seven cents a day per man (all of which were so much Greek to me), he then turned and said: "Give them the best you can buy and don't bother about the expense."

On Tuesday the 24th, the remaining men left for New York, in command of Captain Badgley. Little of interest occurred during the stay of the provisional troop under the command of Captain Cammann. There was a lot of policing to be done; in the camps left by the other troops much straw bedding was burned, and as many a shell had fallen into the straw from the belts of the troopers there was much excitement as these shells kept popping off at frequent intervals. One day as a great treat I served succotash. A trooper coming down the line asked for corn without the beans and became highly indignant when Bill Hall remarked: "My God, what will they ask for next!"

A large party was given on Saturday the 21st to the Seventh Regiment. We had a big bonfire and a grand singing fest.

On Monday, the 30th, "Boots and saddles" was sounded and we pulled out of Croton for New York. We reached Ardsley about eleven o'clock for lunch and arrived at the armory about 7:30 that night, where a hot shower and store clothes were indeed welcome.

GOVERNOR ROOSEVELT, MAJ-GEN. ROE. MAJ. LEE (BRITISH ARMY) ADJT-GEN. ANDREWS

ESCORT DUTY, PARADES, AND REVIEWS

> Pomp and circumstance of glorious war
> —SHAKESPEARE, "Othello"

> Man is a military animal,
> Glories in gunpowder, and loves parade.
> —P. J. BAILEY, "Festus"

IN PUBLIC ceremonies cavalry is always impressive and spectacular, and even the mounted civilian outfit that preceded Troop A was greeted with enthusiasm. After it became a military body, Troop A was much employed in such decorative service, with resulting applause and wide publicity. The same month in which it was mustered into the New York National Guard saw it twice performing escort duty. First it escorted the President of the United States, Benjamin Harrison, on April 29th, when he came to New York to attend the centennial celebration of George Washington's inauguration. On the following day it rode as escort to Governor Hill in the parade. The *New York Herald* commented:

It consisted of fifty well mounted men in the State service uniform with yellow trimmings. The troop was under the command of Captain Charles F. Roe and acted as escort to the Governor.

In the following month it escorted the Brigade Commander in the Memorial Day parade. In the same year it again acted as escort; on this occasion, October 30, 1889, to General William Tecumseh Sherman at the laying of the cornerstone of the Soldiers' and Sailors' Arch, in Prospect Park. Less than a year and a half later, on February 19, 1891, the troop participated in escorting the remains of General Sherman in impressive funeral ceremonies. On October 8th of that year the troop was escort to Governor Hill of New York and Governor Abbott of New Jersey at ceremonies at Van Cortlandt Park.

On April 27, 1892, at the laying of the cornerstone of Grant's tomb, the troop again was escort to President Harrison. The following is quoted from the *New York Tribune*, April 28, 1892:

> The effect was heightened at 12:30 P.M., when Troop A, Capt. C. F. Roe commanding, came dashing down the avenue, and at the command "On right into line", wheeled into line which extended all along the front of the hotel. The cavalrymen were in full uniform with helmets and flowing plumes and side arms, and were further equipped with carbines and pistols, as they were to have a review and inspection by General McGrath immediately after the ceremonies. They were a splendid-looking escort for the President. . . . There was also the mounted band of the troop of twenty pieces, which took up its position at Twenty-Sixth Street. The military men waited for the appearance of the President's carriage, and the crowd stood admiring the brilliant troop. . . . The ceremonies began soon after 2 P.M., when the President's party arrived at the tomb. General Horace Porter and Grenville M. Dodge and Henry W. Cannon called for the party at the Fifth Avenue Hotel, and, escorted by Troop A, the carriages drove to Riverside Park.

In October of the same year the troop journeyed to Chicago, where it escorted Vice President Levi P. Morton and Governor Roswell P. Flower at the World's Fair. A news dispatch printed in the *New York Herald* of October 22nd indicated the appreciation of Troop A:

> The bugle call aroused the members of Troop A of New York from their tents this morning before the dawn had broken, and before eight o'clock the cavalrymen from New York had groomed their horses, eaten their breakfast and started out in full uniform for Chicago. . . . The Governor and his escort received rousing cheers all along the long line of march. . . . Later, Governor Flower and his staff visited the camp. He made a speech to the troop complimenting it on the readiness with which the members left their business to respond to his call to Buffalo. The Governor and staff partook heartily of the soldiers' dinner of soup and beans and departed amid rousing cheers. Tomorrow the troop will escort the Governor in the dedication of the New York State Building.

Another publication commented:

When a detail of twenty-four men under Lieut. Oliver B. Bridgman escorted Chauncey M. Depew to his boat, the Doctor said he was better pleased with their escort than by his having been invited to make the oration at the dedicatory ceremonies.

In 1893 the troop was called on for escort duty on six occasions; the first was the inauguration of President Grover Cleveland—the troop again acting as escort to Governor Flower of New York and taking part in the ceremonies at Washington.

The growing social and military prestige of the organization brought it before the public with increasing frequency. Indeed, it might be said that during this period it became the custom in New York City to express public esteem for holders of high office and for foreigners of distinction by honoring them with the spectacular cavalry escort of Troop A—later Squadron A.

The *New York Press* on March 28, 1899, said in part:

Squadron A always acts as the escort of the Governor of New York State at the Presidential inaugurals at Washington. In its ten years' history it has been the escort of more dignitaries and distinguished personages than any other military organization. . . . In fact, whenever a highly distinguished foreign personage or a President of the United States comes to New York on an official visit, it is Squadron A that always turns out as his escort. But this organization's activities have not been entirely along such peaceful and picturesque lines. Whenever there has been war or riot, Squadron A has taken eager part. . . .

During the first two decades following that momentous mustering in on April 2, 1889, Troop A and its successor Squadron A acted as escort on more than forty occasions, and on eleven of these the service was at a distant point, involving entraining of horses and equipment as well as men, and covering from two to seven days. In addition to the expeditions to Chicago and to Washington, functions in other cities during the first two decades included trips to Atlanta in November, 1895, Buffalo, 1901, St. Louis, 1903, and Norfolk (for the Jamestown tricentennial ceremonies) in 1907. There were also a number of trips to Albany and Washington, and one to Trenton.

The squadron acted as escort not only to presidents and vice presidents, but also to governors and mayors when other historic and commemorative events were celebrated; to military officers of high rank officiating on other occasions; to foreign visitors of distinction, among them the Duke of Veragua in April, 1893, and the Infanta Eulalia in the following month; to the Chinese viceroy, Li Hung Chang, in 1896; and to Prince Henry of Prussia, in February and March, 1902—the last, covering seven separate occasions. All of these honored foreign visitors represented reigning dynasties that later suffered extinction, while the squadron continued to flourish. The French guests of the nation in May, 1902, were likewise escorted by the squadron.

Contemporary comments on these events are interesting:

Under the heading, "The Duke at the City Hall," the *New York Tribune,* April 19, 1893, said:

With flags waving, banners streaming, bands playing and crowds looking on, the Duke of Veragua was conducted from the Waldorf Hotel yesternoon to the City Hall. The cavalcade, though short, was a brilliant one. Troop A, the crack cavalry organization of the State, acted as honorary escort, and made a splendid appearance, with its fine uniforms, polished trappings and handsome horses. It was exactly one o'clock when the blast of the bugles announced the arrival of Troop A at the Waldorf. The Troop A Band, mounted, struck up a Spanish air when the signal was given to march.

The *Sun,* May 26, 1893, lifted the organization into the headlines:

WELCOME TO DONA EULALIA

Escorted to the station in Washington by U.S. Troops, and to her Hotel in New York by Troop A.

For the Chinese viceroy, four troops of the Sixth U.S. Cavalry were detailed as escort and bodyguard; but when the Viceroy came to New York, the city could not let him escape without the special distinction of escort by Squadron A. "About one o'clock the Viceroy, escorted by Troop A, went to the Merchants' Club in Leonard Street, where he was entertained at luncheon," said the *New York Tribune,* September 2, 1896. "First of all came a squad of mounted policemen, and then two troops of Squadron A, headed by their band. After the carriages came two more troops. The troops were in command of Captain Bridgman."

On the expedition to Atlanta in 1895, when the train bearing the squadron with its horses and its mounted band (then civilian though uniformed) approached Atlanta, it was met by a welcoming delegation which came aboard a few miles out of the city. The delegation entered the train at the rear where Major Roe and his staff were quartered; and the band in a forward car, having observed the arrival of the Atlantans, endeavored to show appreciation by striking up, in honor of the occasion, "Marching Through Georgia." As the strains of the hated Yankee song were wafted back, an orderly raced forward through the train with the order from the embarrassed Major to STOP. Explanations and apologies restored the *entente cordiale*.

This Atlanta expedition was described in *The Rider and Driver*, from which the following is quoted:

> This trip was made on a special train of passenger and horse cars, the Squadron acting as escort to Mayor Strong, on the occasion of the Industrial Exposition in Atlanta. During the stay in Atlanta the Squadron held mounted athletic games, to which the citizens were invited. . . . A barbecue was given in honor of the Squadron by the Governor's Horse Guards, at the Exposition grounds, on November 25, after which a silk banner, a duplicate of the Horse Guard's colors, was presented to Major Roe, on behalf of the Atlanta organization, by Col. John Milledge, who commanded a battery in Gen. Lee's army and afterward organized the Guards. Col. Milledge was at the time a white-haired ex-Confederate, and he made an eloquent and patriotic speech in presenting the colors.
>
> . . . Immediately afterward Squadron A rallied upon the colors which had been presented to them, and, with their band playing "Dixie," marched across the grounds to a field where the Squadron proposed to entertain the people with athletic contests. . . . Two or three dozen of the best riders in Squadron A took part in the games. Thousands of people gathered in and about the field to see them. Before the sports began, Sergeant Barry and a private astonished the spectators by riding their horses bareback down a steep incline of 40 or 50 wooden steps which led from the Exposition grounds into the field.

A notable occasion was the escorting of President William McKinley when he attended the dedication of the Grant monument in April, 1897. The new full-dress uniform was here worn for the first time. A local newspaper in an advance report stated:

> The great demonstration begins promptly at 9:20 o'clock, when the President and Vice President and all the City's official guests, including the Cabinet, the justices of the Supreme Court, the Diplomatic Corps, and Grant family, will leave the Fifth Avenue Hotel in carriages, and, escorted by Troop A, will proceed to the tomb.

SQUADRON A ACTING AS ESCORT TO VICE PRESIDENT ROOSEVELT AT INAUGURAL CEREMONIES, MARCH 4, 1901

SQUADRON A ACTING AS ESCORT TO PRESIDENT ROOSEVELT AT INAUGURAL CEREMONIES, MARCH 4, 1905

CHURCH PARADE
SQUADRON A AS ESCORT TO GOVERNOR HUGHES IN HUDSON-FULTON PARADE,
SEPTEMBER 30, 1909

The newspaper scribe was not up-to-date as to the name of the outfit, but a later article corrected his error and showed a picture of the Presidential party and the squadron.

The *Sun*, April 28, 1897, reported:

On the east side of Fifth Avenue, extending from 26th Street to 23rd, was the long light blue and yellow line of Squadron A, the President's personal escort. Back of it was a crowd that covered almost a third of the square. . . . There was nothing in the whole mounted display which excelled our own Squadron A in neatness and general appearance.

Squadron A also escorted Admiral George Dewey, who was accompanied by Governor Theodore Roosevelt, in the Dewey parade, 1899. On this occasion the duties were somewhat extensive and exacting, as commented in the *New York Times* on October 8, 1899:

The Squadron during the Dewey parade had double honors, being the escort for Admiral Dewey and also for Governor Roosevelt; and in such capacity covered more ground and was longer on duty than any other organization.

Another newspaper remarked that "the troops as they passed got an ovation all the length of the successive stands that bordered Madison Square."

The following is quoted from squadron orders:

Orders No. 102. Pursuant to Special Orders H.Q., N.G.N.Y., Squadron A will escort Admiral Dewey on Saturday, September 30th, from the landing to the City Hall and afterwards to the boat.

"Boots and saddles" will be sounded at 4.30 A.M.; assembly at 5:00 and Adjutant's call at 5:15. . . .

The Commissary will have breakfast ready at the Armory at 4:00 A.M.

At the inauguration of Theodore Roosevelt as vice president, March 4, 1901, the squadron was his escort, and the comments of the *Washington Post* include:

Squadron A of New York, the crack military organization which had been selected as an especial military escort, clattered up N Street from Connecticut Avenue, and took its place along the curb opposite the Cowles house. . . .

This command with its mounted band, its gorgeous uniforms, and fine mounts was possibly the handsomest and most picturesque in appearance of any in the column.

Later in the same year, the squadron escorted Governor Benjamin B. Odell, Jr., and Major General Charles F. Roe at the Pan-American Exposition, Buffalo, New York. While there, the midway was visited by the troopers almost en masse, and when off duty officers and men in full-dress uniforms might have been seen riding camels instead of horses. On one occasion, as the time approached for evening parade, the enlisted men were cautioned to get back to camp and saddle up, but the officers lingered, since orderlies would get their horses ready. At the last minute they mounted rickshaws and proceeded in a spirited race to the parade ground. On the way the Adjutant's call was heard, and they knew that their absence was putting the C.O. in a state of mind. The rickshaw coolies were urged to higher speed, but, as they drew near, the troops could be seen marching to their positions under command of the first sergeants. This was proper; but all officers, and captains in particular, should be there mounted and in place to receive them when the sergeants reported. At the last minute the rickshaws arrived, the officers leaped out and mounted, rode into position —and fulfilled their responsibility by a narrow margin. The Major frowned disapproval, but, technically, the day was saved.

Governor Odell, upon returning from this expedition, expressed his appreciation of the squadron in the following letter:

ALBANY, October 23, 1901

Major Oliver B. Bridgman
217 West 45th Street
New York

MY DEAR MAJOR:

Since my return from Buffalo I have had occasion to review the many incidents which contributed to make my visit so enjoyable and the New York Day so successful. I desire to thank you for the efficient escort furnished by your command and take this occasion to compliment you upon the splendid showing made by Squadron 'A'.

Very truly yours,

B. B. ODELL, JR.

Of many other interesting and brilliant functions of this nature, only two more will be noted.

In 1902 the squadron was again escort to Theodore Roosevelt, then President, at the installation of Nicholas Murray Butler, as president of Columbia University; also when Theodore Roosevelt in 1905 was

SQUADRON A

inaugurated as President, the squadron formed part of his escort. The *New York Tribune* of March 5, 1905, reported:

> The journey of the President from the White House was the occasion for impressive enthusiasm. He was accompanied by his chosen escort, Squadron A of the National Guard of New York, a platoon of Rough Riders composed of thirty picked comrades of his old command, etc.

These outdoor parades and escort duties by no means covered all ceremonies of a full-dress nature. During the twenty years following the acquisition of the armory, a review was a feature of almost every year, and in some years two or more reviews were held. The names of the respective reviewing officers, with the year of the review, are as follows:

Year	Month	Day	Reviewing Officer
1897	Apr.	20	Major Charles F. Roe
1898	Mar.	17	Major Charles F. Roe
1899	Jan.	5	Brigadier General Avery D. Andrews, A.G.
1900	Jan.	17	Brigadier General Hoffman, A.G.
1901	Sept.	18	Paraded at armory for Memorial Services, President McKinley
1902	Dec.	22	Colonel A. L. Miller, U.S.A.
1904	Jan.	21	Major General Corbin, U.S.A.
1905	Jan.	17	Major George M. McClellan
1906	Jan.	16	Colonel Daniel Appleton, 7th Regiment
1906	Nov.	26	Brigadier General Nelson E. Henry, A.G.
1907	Feb.	20	Lieutenant Colonel Robert L. Howze, U.S.A.
1908	Jan.	3	Colonel Hugh L. Scott, U.S.A.
1908	Feb.	26	Major General Charles F. Roe
1908	Apr.	29	Colonel Edwin F. Glenn, U.S.A.
1909	Feb.	27	Major General Leonard Wood, U.S.A.
1909	Apr.	20	Major General Charles F. Roe
1909	Dec.	22	Lieutenant Colonel F. W. Libby, U.S.A.
1910	Dec.	14	Brigadier General William Verbeck, A.G.
1911	Mar.	25	Governor John A. Dix
1911	Dec.	6	Honorable H. L. Stimson, Secretary of War
1913	Jan.	24	Major General Thomas H. Barry
1913	May	2	Major General John F. O'Ryan
1914	Apr.	20	Major General Charles F. Roe
1915	May	8	Colonel Daniel Appleton, 7th Regiment
1915	Nov.	26	Brigadier General George R. Dyer, 1st Brigade

The annual Church Parade is a function begun in 1890 and continued to the present time. The members—now accompanied by ex-members—assemble in dress uniform and march dismounted to the Church of the Heavenly Rest, where the service is conducted by the Chaplain of the organization, who has always been also the rector of that church. In the early years, Rev. D. Parker Morgan was the chaplain. He was succeeded by Rev. Herbert Shipman, who during the war became senior chaplain of the A.E.F. and later was suffragan bishop of New York. His successor is Rev. Henry Darlington.

FULL DRESS.

THE YEAR OF THE SPANISH-AMERICAN WAR

Brigadier General Avery D. Andrews, General Staff
Late Assistant Chief of Staff, G-1, Headquarters, American Expeditionary Force

> My soul's in arms, and eager for the fray.
> —CIBBER, "Richard III"

THE year 1898 was an eventful and important one in the history of Squadron A. Early in that year the legislature adopted a new military code, replacing an antiquated system of administration which had been in force for many years. The new code was designed to eliminate politics from the administration of the National Guard, to properly distinguish between the functions of the line and the staff, and to give the state a modern and efficient military organization suited to the requirements of active service. Instead of several independent brigades and smaller units reporting direct to the Adjutant General and virtually under his command, the entire National Guard of the state was organized into a single unit, in effect a division, but not so called, under the command of a major general with a suitable divisional staff.

This part of the new code went into effect at once with the result that Major Roe was, on February 11, 1898, commissioned a major general and assigned to the command of the National Guard. Thus the squadron lost the services of the distinguished soldier whose wide experience, demonstrated ability, and many soldierly qualities had developed a small group of enthusiastic horsemen into a highly efficient military organization, and one who, by his kindly charm of heart and soul, had endeared himself to every member of the squadron. Roe's promotion was an irreparable loss to the squadron, but a great gain to the entire National Guard of the state. A few weeks later, on March 17, 1898, the writer, who had served several years as engineer officer of the 1st Brigade on the staff of Brigadier General Louis Fitzgerald, was chosen to command the squadron, vice Roe, and formally assumed command on March 23rd.

My first social duty as commanding officer of the squadron was to preside at its anniversary dinner, a very happy occasion at which the chief event was the presentation to General Roe of a superb loving cup in recognition of his long and distinguished services with the squadron. About this time the rumblings of war with Spain had been intensified by the destruction of the *Maine* in the harbor of Havana, and demands for intervention in Cuba became more insistent. War was in the air, and naturally was the subject of great interest and discussion in the squadron. Drills were speeded up, equipment overhauled, and all hoped and expected that the squadron would be among the first units called into active service. During this waiting period an order was issued by General Roe directing commanding officers of all units to report the number of men in their commands who would enter the service of the United States as volunteers, for service either at home or abroad. I immediately called a meeting of the squadron and within twenty-four hours was able to telegraph General Roe that the squadron volunteered its services to a man, for either foreign or domestic service.

Among the many letters which I received congratulating me upon my appointment as major of the squadron was one which concluded as follows:

It is certainly a fine command, and it begins to look as though you would have an opportunity to try them in the field. . . . If we all go to Cuba we may have occasion there to renew old times. Consider me an applicant for a captaincy in your squadron upon the occurrence of a vacancy.

That letter was dated, West Point, April 6, 1898, and was signed, "John J. Pershing," then a lieutenant of cavalry on duty at the U.S. Military Academy as an instructor in tactics. But unfortunately there was no vacancy to offer the future General of the Armies of the United States.[1]

During this period I was frequently in Washington serving as voluntary aid to my former chief, Lieutenant General John M. Schofield, Retired, who, when war became imminent, had been called to Washington by President McKinley as his confidential military adviser. The President frequently invited to the White House, on Sunday evenings, a few of his intimate friends and advisers, and it happened that I accompanied General Schofield to the White House on the Sunday evening immediately preceding the call for troops. The squadron was well known to the President and had acted as his escort on some recent occasion. In the most cordial manner the President congratulated me upon my selection to the command of such a splendid body of troops, and then, to my surprise and delight, said that the squadron under my command would be included in the first call for troops. Beyond any question the kindly McKinley believed and meant what he then said; but politics, and particularly Ohio politics, was dominant in the War Department. There was no General Staff in those days, and no Newton D. Baker as Secretary of War. A few days later when the first mobilization orders were issued, the state was called on for only two troops of cavalry, and Squadron A was allowed only one of these; while two troops, which did not then exist even on paper, were called for from the State of Ohio. Instead of reducing the squadron to a single troop, it could easily, with its splendid personnel, have been expanded to a regiment; in which case a field officer's commission would certainly have been offered to the cavalry lieutenant who later commanded the American Expeditionary Force.

With the call for one troop instead of the entire squadron, we were at once faced with a real problem. All three troops wanted to serve, and no one of them would give way to the others. Instead of a few possible vacancies here and there, there was a great surplus of fine personnel. A meeting of the squadron was called at the armory on April 27th, when it was announced by the commanding officer that a composite troop would be organized, made up from selected personnel of the three troops, each troop to contribute one-third. The troop commanders lined up their men and explained the situation, saying, "All

[1] It is gratifying to know that General Pershing is, however, a part of the association of members of Squadron A, having been elected to honorary membership; and his graceful letter of acceptance as well as the letter quoted by General Andrews are among the records of the Association.

men who desire to volunteer, step two paces to the front"; and in each troop the entire line stepped to the front.

I emphasized to the meeting the serious side of war service, and urged that volunteers be limited to those who were free from family or other obligations at home. Finally near sunrise, after much sifting, sorting, and arguing, the roster of Troop A, New York Volunteers, was completed with the following commissioned officers: Captain Howard G. Badgley, First Lieutenant Frederic R. Coudert, Jr., Second Lieutenant Joseph S. Frelinghuysen, First Lieutenant Medwin Leale, Medical Officer, and a full complement of non-commissioned officers and privates. A few days later, on May 2nd, the troop was ordered to Camp Black, near Garden City, and there mustered into the service of the United States.

Many members of the squadron who were excluded from Troop A volunteered in other branches of the service and served with distinction. The failure of the government to avail itself fully of the services of the finest body of cavalry in the country outside the regular army was a bitter disappointment to the entire squadron and to its commanding officer. Possibly as slight compensation for the loss of my fine command, I was at once given a commission as lieutenant colonel of volunteers and ordered to report to Major General James H. Wilson at Camp Thomas, near Chickamauga, Tennessee. I did not, therefore, serve with the squadron again until shortly before the return of Troop A from Puerto Rico, when, having secured my discharge from the volunteers, I returned to New York and resumed command of the squadron. Meanwhile the squadron maintained its three-troop organization and usual high efficiency and morale under the command of its senior captain, Oliver B. Bridgman. The history of the squadron during this period, as well as that of Troop A, can best be written by those who served with these units and are familiar with their records.

But briefly, after three weeks at Camp Black, the troop entrained for Camp Alger, near Washington. Late in July it entrained for Newport News and thence by transport to Puerto Rico, where it arrived in the early days of August and went into camp at Ponce. Here the troop participated in the activities of the Army of Occupation and returned to New York in September.

During these months of Troop A's official and physical separation from the parent squadron, its ties with the home organization were unbroken. More than twenty-five per cent of its enlisted personnel received commissions in other organizations, and these vacancies, as well as all others, were promptly filled from the ranks of the squadron at home.

The many friends of Troop A, the city officials, and the general public were proud of its war service and determined to give it a cordial and enthusiastic welcome upon its return. Plans for its reception were quickly made and ample funds were provided for all purposes, including decorations and substantial refreshments at the armory. The troop arrived in New York from Puerto Rico on Saturday, September 10th, on the transport *Mississippi*. Men and horses disembarked in Jersey City and were ferried to the foot of Cortlandt Street where they formed ranks in field uniform and equipment. Here they were met by a reception committee and the squadron, in full dress, presenting a marked contrast to the bronzed and bearded troopers in their somewhat worse-for-wear field uniform.

On account of delays in disembarking the horses, it was late in the afternoon before the troops could be formed for the march to the armory. Cortlandt Street and vicinity were filled with crowds who had waited for hours to be among the first to welcome the returning troopers. Their very first greeting came from a gray-haired Irish woman who had fought nearly all day to maintain her position of advantage on the curb, and who upon seeing the troopers exclaimed, "God bless them, ain't they dirty!"

To which the nearest trooper replied, "God bless you, you're dead right!"

The column was finally formed as follows: platoon of mounted police; the squadron band of 35 pieces, mounted; Major Avery D. Andrews, commanding; Troop 1, Captain Oliver B. Bridgman; Troop 3, Captain Latham G. Reed; Troop A, New York Volunteers; carriages and ambulances for convalescent and sick troopers; Troop 2, Lieutenant George B. Robbins; platoon of mounted police. The line of march was Cortlandt Street Ferry to the Battery, up Broadway to Waverly Place, up Fifth Avenue to Ninety-fourth Street, to armory. At the City Hall the column was reviewed by Mayor Van Wyck and city officials. Enthusiastic crowds lined the streets, cheering the returning troopers, and were apparently intrigued by their unshaven, rough and ready appearance in such marked contrast to the immaculate appearance of their escort in the blue hussar full dress. It was dusk when we reached Madison Square and well after dark when we arrived at the armory. The armory (decorated with flags inside and out) and surrounding streets were packed with relatives and friends who had waited for hours to greet the troopers. In a short time the troop was mustered out of the United States service, and the squadron resumed its normal status and duties. After being mustered out of the Federal service some members resumed service with the squadron, bringing with them the valuable training and experience of their war service. Among these veterans whose subsequent services were of special value to the squadron, particular mention must be made of Corporal William R. Wright who ten years later became captain of his original troop, and who in 1912 became major, commanding the squadron. In this capacity he, with great distinction, commanded the squadron when it entered the Federal service on the Mexican border, and again in the World War.

The election of Theodore Roosevelt as governor in November, 1898, was an event of outstanding importance to the National Guard. Probably no governor in the history of the state was more keenly interested in the National Guard than he, or better qualified to administer its affairs. In his speech of acceptance on October 4th he said:

"The National Guard must be raised to the highest standard of efficiency; it has amply proved its courage and its patriotism, and we are bound to see that soldiers so brave and willing are properly armed and handled on the best possible system."

Some of the provisions of the new military code which had been adopted earlier in the year 1898 did not become effective until January 1, 1899, when Governor Roosevelt took office. Among these provisions was the reorganization of the Governor's staff, which in the course of years had grown to fantastic proportions and in 1898 consisted of one major general, ten brigadier generals, twenty-eight colonels, twelve lieutenant colonels and six majors, a total of fifty-seven commissioned officers. These were now to be replaced by one adjutant general with the rank of brigadier general and a few assistants, one military secretary, and several aides-de-camp, the majority of whom were junior National Guard or Naval Reserve officers, detailed temporarily for duty with the Governor when needed.

And thus it happened, for the second time within a year, that the Governor of the state selected the commanding officer of Squadron A for promotion, when, in December, 1898, Governor elect Roosevelt announced my selection as adjutant general, thus completing the staff reorganization contemplated by the new military code. It was with the greatest possible reluctance and regret that I thus severed my brief command of the squadron; but the opportunities for important service as chief of staff to Governor Roosevelt were too great to be declined. No officer could desire a finer command than the squadron. Its roster contained the very best of America's young manhood, and its record during the many years since I relinquished command has amply justified the high esteem in which it always has been held.

After my last drill in the armory I was presented with a beautiful loving cup which now adorns my library, and which will always remain one of my most prized possessions. The squadron went to Albany and served as the governor's escort during the inaugural ceremonies. It attended the inaugural ball on New Year's eve and remained under my command until my appointment as adjutant general became effective on New Year's day. The squadron returned to New York under the command of its senior captain, Oliver B. Bridgman, who shortly thereafter was promoted to be major commanding; a position which he held with distinction for many years. My last appearance with the squadron was at a formal review in my honor, only a few days after relinquishing my fine command.

VOLUNTEER TROOP A IN THE SPANISH-AMERICAN WAR

It wasn't much of a war, but it was all the war there was.
—Theodore Roosevelt.

The Spanish War service of Volunteer Troop A, composed of volunteers from the three troops of the squadron, was the first contact of Squadron A with actual warfare. There was much competition for service in the troop, which functioned efficiently in all it was called on to do. Its organization, service and demobilization occurred within seven months in 1898. An excellent illustrated account, with papers by various members of the troop, was published in 1899, in book form, under the title, "The History of Troop A, New York Cavalry, U.S.V." It is a source of satisfaction that the squadron contributed efficiently, although in a minor way, to the land campaign of a war that is famous for its almost tragic amateurishness.

One incident, which appeared in the public press, might be added. While en route to Puerto Rico on the transport, the troop had suffered severely both from overcrowding and at times from lack of water supply. It was a typical example of faulty staff administration at Washington; the troop was, however, more fortunate than some, in not going hungry.

When the time approached for the troops to return, Senator Platt sent the following to the Adjutant General:

HON. H. C. CORBIN, ADJUTANT GENERAL, U.S.A.
Washington

Please see that Troops A and C New York Volunteer Cavalry about to embark on return voyage from Ponce are not overcrowded and are supplied with abundance of water.

T. C. Platt

The reply read:

Adjutant General's Office
Washington, August 26

Hon. T. C. Platt:
Manhattan Beach Hotel, Long Island.

Will give instructions that A and C Troops are not crowded on return voyage. Pray tell me when they took to water.

H. C. Corbin, *Adjutant General*

Although there is no written record of the following anecdote, it sounds realistic. While on the outward voyage, many troopers, seeking escape from the congestion, slept on deck, where there was a quantity of baled hay. One evening Jimmy Terry's carbine disappeared; it seemed the roll of the ship had probably carried it overboard. Fortunately he did not accompany it. Upon reflection he decided that as nothing could be done about it, there was no occasion to disturb the officers with a report of the loss. On arrival at Ponce, the troop was drawn up and inspected in very rigid military fashion by Lieutenant Frelinghuysen. We all remember the formality of seizing the carbine abruptly, upending it to look through the barrel, and jamming it back into the hands of the trooper. When Lieutenant Frelinghuysen reached Jimmy Terry in the line, there was no carbine to seize, and he said in impressive tones: "Terry, where is your carbine?" Terry's hand came up in salute, and he said: "Lieutenant, that—that is—the question."

The roster of the troop, with the names of those who served in other organizations, is here presented.

ROSTER

Troop A, New York Cavalry

U.S.V., 1898

Captain Howard G. Badgley
1st Lieut. Frederic R. Coudert, Jr.
2nd Lieut. Joseph F. Frelinghuysen
1st Lieut. Medwin Leale, M.C.
1st Sergeant A. Rene Moen
Q.M. Sergeant Francis D. Bowne

Sergeant William C. Camman
*Sergeant Edward L. Patterson
*Sergeant Alfred B. Maclay
Sergeant Stowe Phelps

Sergeant Robert Emmet
*Sergeant Charles E. Pellew
Sergeant Henry M. Ward
Sergeant E. Mortimer Ward

Sergeant Seymour L. Cromwell

*Corporal Edwin C. Hoyt
*Corporal C. Sidney Haight
*Corporal G. Beekman Hoppin
Corporal J. Langdon Erving
Corporal Francis C. Huntington
Corporal William J. Wallace

Corporal Henry I. Riker
Corporal William R. Wright
Corporal Benjamin W. Leigh
Corporal John H. Iselin
Corporal Irving Ruland
Corporal Arthur F. Brown

SQUADRON A

Lance Cpl. Ernest A. Thomson
Lance Cpl. Henry S. Satterlee
Trumpeter Albert E. Braithwaite
Trumpeter Howard S. Kerner
Farrier Charles W. Muller
Farrier Frank W. Bird
Saddler Frederick W. Becker
Wagoner James Glynn

PRIVATES

George T. Adee
Harold Barclay
Robert C. Barclay
Robert P. Barry, Jr.
Henry Batcheller
Ross C. Bayne
James A. G. Beales
William M. Benjamin
James G. Benkard
Arthur M. Blake
S. Rowe Bradley, Jr.
*J. C. Breckenridge
Howard K. Brown
John M. Bruce
Henry B. Cannon
Charles F. Carusi
John D. Chapman
Herbert H. Childs
James G. Clark
Lewis A. Conner
Robert W. Conrow
Edward V. Cox
George W. Coyne
William M. Crombie
William B. Crowell
Victor N. Cushman
*James M. A. Darrach
William W. Drake
Lyman T. Dyer
T. Addis Emmet, Jr.
Henry J. Fisher
*Nathan M. Flower

Charles Fuller
Louis P. Gillespie
Arthur J. Goadby
H. D. Grannis
Sherman R. Hall
*Francis B. Harrison
William W. Heaton
Horace L. Henry
*Charles R. Hickox
Philip R. M. Hildreth
John S. Hill
Fritz W. Hoeninghaus
Henry E. Holt
*Edwin O. Holter
Leonard S. Horner
Charles A. Hutchinson
Charles H. Kerner, Jr.
Philip Kearny
Herbert Killips
Arthur S. Knudsen
John D. Lannon
*Townsend Lawrence
George S. Ledyard
F. Lawrence Lee
Arthur M. Line
Emlen T. Little
George J. Little
Arthur H. Lockett
John W. Loveland
Richard F. Manning
Robert T. McGusty
*McKee D. McKee

James B. McKinlay
Robert D. Mills
Franklin B. Morse
Vernon Munroe
J. Osgood Nichols
Frank R. Outerbridge
Henry W. Perry
Reginald K. Pierce
Thomas H. Pierson
Amos R. E. Pinchot
*Frank L. Polk
Walter W. Price
Samuel L. Quinby
George O. Redington
*Allen A. Robbins

Thomas Slidell
Letchworth Smith
Francis K. Stevens
Leland S. Stillman
James T. Terry
Robert F. Troescher
Langdon B. Valentine
Edgar W. Van Vleck
Frank D. Veiller
Gustavus S. Wallace
*Ervin Wardman
Karl Webb
Richard Wharton
*William S. Whitehead
*William Williams

The men whose names are marked with an asterisk left the troop to accept commissions in other branches of the service. In addition, three members—Harold Barclay, Charles A. Hutchinson, and Walter W. Price—were transferred to different units in the Federal service. Other members of the squadron, who were not members of Volunteer Troop A, but served elsewhere in the army, were:

> J. Herbert Claiborne, Captain, 9th N.Y., Volunteer Infantry
> R. E. Dwight, Battery A, Pennsylvania Volunteer Artillery
> G. M. Ives, 1st U.S. Volunteer Cavalry (Rough Riders)
> H. S. Kip, First Lieutenant, 9th N.Y., Volunteer Cavalry
> F. H. North, 1st U.S. Volunteer Cavalry (Rough Riders)
> Ashley Pond, Jr., U.S. Navy
> Merritt H. Smith, Captain, U.S. Volunteer Engineers

NARRATIVE OF FREDERIC R. COUDERT

Malbrouck s'en va-t-en guerre, . . .
Ne ai quand reviendra.
—Ancient ballad

ON JUNE 1, 1898, after Volunteer Troop A had reached Camp Alger, Captain Howard G. Badgley was taken ill. His illness was diagnosed by Dr. M. Leale as typhoid fever and he was, therefore, taken to Fort Myer Hospital. We did not see him again until the troop returned to

New York in September. The command of the troop consequently devolved upon me.

Troops A and C, gathered together at the bottom of the hill upon which the Camp Alger headquarters was established, were formed into a temporary squadron by command of Major General Bertram C. Graham. The command naturally devolved upon Captain Clayton, while I was appointed acting adjutant—fulfilling the duties of that position in addition to those of troop commander. Captain Clayton, a West Point graduate, had been a regular army officer. He came from Alabama, I believe, and had a very deliberate manner and a drawling voice. He understood military matters thoroughly and was a careful, hard-working officer. He was entirely impartial as between the two troops, which he commanded until we reached Puerto Rico. When the Great War came along, he immediately sought service, went to France, and there lost his life by an enemy shell.

Second Lieutenant Joseph S. Frelinghuysen was appointed ordnance officer for the temporary squadron. Owing to his ceaseless efforts, both troops were completely equipped before leaving the country. The much-desired Krag-Jorgensen carbines were received and issued just before our departure for Camp Alger. The Squadron Commander also appointed a board for the purchase of horses for the two troops, as well as for the headquarters of the Second Army Corps. Lieutenant Frelinghuysen served upon this board and was assisted by Sergeant Debevoise of Troop C—that most expert judge of horseflesh, who subsequently commanded a regiment during the World War, and who has long been famous as a judge in the National Horse Show. For about three weeks this commission explored the surrounding Virginia country and, after considerable difficulty, completed the necessary quota of horses. They were on the whole excellent mounts and the best horses the troop had up to that time.

Despite extremely hot weather in June and July, there were two drills daily in the school of the troop and in the school of the squadron. Men and horses developed real efficiency and learned to charge over long distances at full gallop, stirrup to stirrup. We fancied that war was still to be conducted in that simple fashion. Indeed, tactics had changed little since the time of Frederick II of Prussia, and not at all since the War Between the States.

We did, however, spend a great deal of time in practising extended order and ground-scouting movements. The cavalry was still assumed

COVER PICTURE ON PROGRAM OF A PLATOON DINNER SHORTLY AFTER STRIKE DUTY IN BROOKLYN, 1895

CAMP ALGER, 1898
UNLOADING HORSES, PORTO RICO, 1898

to be the eyes of the army, and through the valleys and over the hills of the North Virginia country we practised reconnoitering, and the service of security and information as laid down in the military manuals. Mounted drills were also held in the school of theoretical instruction carried on by the Troop Commander. In addition, there was plenty of guard duty, and seven orderlies were furnished every day for headquarters.

In addition to the usual army ration, we were able to purchase fresh vegetables, milk, etc., with the troop fund raised for that purpose. There was at the time much newspaper discussion of tainted beef. Fortunately, the troop had little experience with this poisonous ration. Some of it did appear on the return trip from Puerto Rico on the S.S. *Mississippi*, but I think it was detected in time and not used, so that no cases of serious illness were attributable to it. It is fair to say that from the arrival of the troop at Camp Alger to its return to New York, neither men nor horses were ever short of food, although cooking facilities on the transports were almost nil.

The most interesting work during these "dog days" at Camp Alger was the practise marches, which on two occasions extended over several days and were very valuable in indurating both men and horses. Once we visited the field of First Manassas, or Bull Run, and had an opportunity to study the story of that confused and disorderly battle.

We greatly enjoyed these marches through the beautiful Virginia country, and over the historic battlefields. I remember occasions on which we were joined around the evening campfire by some old men who had fought in the Confederate Army and had been members of the famous Mosby Rangers.

Once I stopped at a house and asked the old farmer sitting on the porch for permission to camp in his field, where there was a well and plenty of grass for the horses. He looked me over for quite a time and slowly withdrawing his corncob pipe from his mouth, remarked: "Well, Captain, I reckon you're Federal soldiers, and the last time I see that blue uniform I was a-shootin' at it a-back of that rock down the road; but I suppose it's all over now and ye can have the field." Upon this generous invitation we picketed the weary horses and established ourselves for a quiet night bivouacked in the open. During the evening, our host, accompanied by half a dozen other men, joined us at the campfire. As some of our men were able to offer them refreshment, even more stimulating than coffee, we heard interesting stories of

Mosby and his raids, and of how that cavalry leader had kept 100,000 Federal troops busy along those roads guarding transports. It seems that some of them worked all day as perfectly peaceful farmers and then went to the rendezvous at night to surprise the Federal patrols and interfere with the communications of the army.

Among other instructive experiences was that of practising with horses and men in crossing streams and canals. Some marches were eighteen miles—a fair achievement with new horses and the heat.

Health as well as morale were greatly improved by these marches, because the men were growing very impatient of the delay in getting to the front, and tiring of the routine of drill. They heard of the exploits of the Rough Riders in Cuba and their military ambition was stirred to the uttermost. During the stay at Camp Alger, twenty-two of our men were commissioned and transferred to other commands. Their places were taken by others sent from New York; many being recruits who had received little military instruction.

A few days before leaving Camp Alger, the troop purchased (through contributions made by some friends of the organization) two machine guns, which were placed in charge of Sergeant E. M. Ward. While on the *Massachusetts* we practised with these guns, and the non-commissioned officers in charge familiarized themselves with their working. They were to be carried on mule back and would, had necessity arisen, have proved most useful.

There was some sickness during our stay at Camp Alger, and a number of men were furloughed and taken to hospitals in New York because the doctor believed that they had typhoid fever. Fortunately, they all recovered, but none did so in time to return and serve again with the troop.

A curious incident, indicating the lack of sanitary understanding then existing in the army, occurred from my having let the men go on furloughs. I was summoned to headquarters to interview General Graham, a very handsome white-haired gentleman, of rather courtly but, at times, severe manner, who had served with distinction in the Civil War. He asked me whether, when I had furloughed the men, I had been aware that they were ill. I told him that I had, and for that reason had allowed them to leave the camp. He said that I should have reported them sick and sent them to the camp hospital. In all frankness I had to reply that I avoided doing so because I was convinced that I was saving their lives by sending them to fine hospitals rather than to the military hospital at Alger, of which I had had some experience. When questioned as to whether in doing this I had been aware that I was violating regulations, I was forced to admit that the regulations did not weigh on my mind as against the lives of my men, for I knew that in no event would they be fit to fight for their country, and I could not see any ground for believing that their country would be benefited by their dying in a very inadequate hospital at Camp Alger. I thought for a moment that the General meant to discipline me, but he was evidently impressed by my earnestness in wishing to save the lives of my comrades and friends, and finally offered me a cigar and suggested we talk of other things.

If I had had any doubts before this about military hospitals, they would have been completely resolved by my own experience. Imprudently galloping an ex-polo pony—equipped with only a halter—down a road, I was run away with; and pony and I crashed into an army wagon, hurting my knees and other portions of my anatomy. I was picked up and carried to the army hospital, and woke up to find myself in a tent pitched in the open under a broiling sun among men lying about on cots with open mouths filled with flies and receiving no adequate care or attention. Crippled as I was, I managed to get out from under the tent-flap and crawl back to my own tent a quarter of a mile away, and thus avoided reporting on the sick list.

The most notable feature of the camps was the extraordinary ignorance of what we consider in these days elementary sanitation. On another occasion, the same Major General, intent upon carrying out regulations and maintaining the discipline of the army, threatened me with a court-martial for having removed the sinks from their proximity to the mess as prescribed by the then existing military regulations. I protested that I believed the flies carried disease from one place to another, but this highbrow notion of mine seemed to him the silly fancy of a mere civilian. Again I narrowly escaped trial for insubordination.

Our troop will remember vividly the midnight of July 23 when orders were received to leave in the morning for Newport News, there to await transportation to Puerto Rico. Never, I think, was a bugle sound more gladly heard than the "Boots and saddles" which took the troop from the dust and mud and routine of Camp Alger and suggested a career of military glory in the sun-kissed isles of the Caribbean. All unnecessary equipment was put away and we marched to the train at Falls Church, where we waited until nearly evening. We arrived at

Newport News on the following day and camped close to the beach where the men bathed in the lovely surf. During the next three days only strictly necessary work was done. The horses were gently exercised, and the men rested up.

On the afternoon of July 27th, we were ordered to embark upon the transport *Massachusetts;* "Boots and saddles" was sounded and the troop arrived at the transport, some two miles distant, within an hour and ten minutes after the order had been received. The horses were placed upon the transport, and we found we were the first to arrive. Apparently Troop C and our troop were the only cavalry expected to sail. This should have given us plenty of room and the trip could have been comparatively sanitary and not wholly uncomfortable. But during the night there was a great tumult, and three Pennsylvania troops arrived, crowding themselves and their horses into whatever small space was left, and greatly cramping everybody. Because of the excessive number, the quarters, for both men and horses, were hopelessly crowded. I learned afterwards from a troop commander that upon receiving no word to embark upon the *Massachusetts,* he had requested the General be awakened in the middle of the night in order that he might obtain permission to put the troop abroad. The Chief of Staff, apparently dismayed at the possible effect upon the General's temper of such an awakening, told him to get on board with his three troops and do the best he could.

We were fortunate in not meeting with a major disaster resulting from this overcrowding, on a small vessel, of one thousand men and the accompanying horses and mules. Additional discomfort was experienced because of defective pumps; water, quite muddy in appearance, came in small quantities and ran only a part of the day.

On the third day, the piston-rod broke and the water had to be brought in tanks and buckets—the men standing in line and passing the buckets. After a day or two of this wearisome occupation, the pumps were at least partly repaired, but the cry "Water, water" was heard for days. Fortunately, the weather was superb and the overladen transport had no occasion to battle with the seas. In order, however, that excitement might not be wholly absent, the vessel was on fire at least once a day. In between the great piles of hay some of the men found convenient nooks to smoke and sleep, which accounted for these daily occurrences. During inspection one day, I awoke a man who having gone to sleep with a pipe in his mouth had set a bale of hay on fire. Since he had spread the fire to himself and the rest of the ship, I promptly had him arrested and imprisoned for violation of orders. However, at dinner, it turned out that he was one of the cook's mess, so a superior officer had him released so as not to interfere with culinary operations.

We were greatly handicapped by lack of discipline among the men attached to the hospital and signal corps and they contributed little or nothing to the general policing of the ship.

On August 3rd the ship entered the port of Ponce, but ran upon a reef at the entrance to the harbor. I was informed that General Brooks had expected the vessel to go on to Guarica, where he had expected our troop to take part at once in outpost duty to rid him of some actual or expected trouble from Spanish cavalry.

The vessel stayed on the reef and, as there did not seem to be any danger of her sinking, the troop remained on board overnight. The next day the sea was quite rough and it was impossible to bring the lighters alongside to land the horses. By evening, the sea seemed to be still rougher and it was feared that the *Massachusetts* might break up. An order was then received to send the men off the ship. The *Prairie*, containing some of the naval volunteer units, was close by and its Commander offered to take our men aboard for the night. They managed to board the *Prairie* from a lighter and were comfortably quartered; and went ashore the next day. Unloading the horses, owing to the inadequacy of the lighters, was very slow, and not without considerable risk; the kicking animals were held by manpower over the side and deposited in the lighter which was being agitated by the sea. Finally, this slow and primitive process was completed, the last horse landed, and Troop A had the honor of being the first organization to reach shore with men, horses, and stores. Special credit should be given to Lieutenant Frelinghuysen for the ability and energy he showed in superintending and expediting this work; and to Sergeant E. M. Ward who cared for the horses and attended to the duties of getting them into the lighters. Although the work was accomplished at a time of intense heat and attended with a great shortage of water, not one animal was lost.

It is interesting to look back upon that trip on the *Massachusetts* and contrast it with the superb transportation methods employed during the Great War. Never have I witnessed a more archaic exhibition. On the *Massachusetts* three officers claimed command—one a colonel of the regular army who thought he should give orders in all matters directly affecting troops; one a volunteer quartermaster, who declared that his authority extended to all government property, including horses and mules and the ship itself as government owned or controlled; and finally, the ship's captain, who seemed in despair and to be powerless when he found so much of his authority disputed. Once I was called into a discussion when the three were claiming jurisdiction over the water supply on the ship. It was one of the most grotesque performances that I ever witnessed, and an impressive example of the hopeless unpreparedness of America in 1898 for military action.

On reaching shore, the men camped in the church square at Port Ponce under the eaves of the beautiful old cathedral—the cathedral which later became the subject of an important litigation in the Supreme Court of the United States involving the ultimate title to church property in that newly-annexed United States territory.

An order came from General Nelson A. Miles—who had been appointed general-in-chief in 1895 and was now in command of the expeditionary force that took Puerto Rico—attaching Troop A to his headquarters, and I was ordered to report to Captain C. B. Hoppin, of Troop B, 2nd Cavalry. At his direction we camped in the field next to his troop near a small river and a good grazing field for the horses.

Several detachments were sent out before the termination of hostilities. Lieutenant Frelinghuysen took out one on August 10th and did not return to the troop until August 25th. This detail had rather a difficult and interesting time. It proceeded over very bad mountain trails to Utuado. Apparently some Spanish troops had evacuated the town shortly before the arrival of Frelinghuysen's detachment. It was expected, however, that they would return and attack the town, and there would be some trouble with the inhabitants; but nothing occurred. On August 12th notice came of the armistice. On the 14th, orders were received from General Henry to proceed to Ciales with a flag of truce, notify the Spanish officers there of the protocol, and gain information regarding the charge by the natives that the Spanish soldiers had murdered fifty women and children. The detachment marched through Jeaululie Arribo, some twenty miles, and was greeted by great crowds bearing American flags and throwing flowers. Some citizens insisted upon our dismounting and accepting their hospitality. The detachment, however, prudently declined and proceeded toward

Ciales. There were all sorts of rumors about every kind of outrage by returning Spanish troops, but no confirmation was ever forthcoming.

On reaching Ciales Spanish soldiers appeared, advancing with rifles on their shoulders and apparently intending to fire. They halted and our men advanced nearer. We called to them to put down their guns, and asked to see the commanding officer. They said he was not in town; but Lieutenant Frelinghuysen insisted and finally the officer came from around the corner, accompanied by two others. He turned out to be Puerto Rican born, but apparently a loyal Spanish subject, and in command of a company of Guardia Civil. Frelinghuysen in his report of this incident says:

We asked Ladesma if he had been notified of the protocol. He said, "No." We then asked him if the people had been murdered as stated by the people fleeing from the city. He said, "No," that parties (armed Porto Ricans) had entered the town and raised the American flag. When his company returned, they resisted, and a battle ensued. When asked if any one had been killed, he said, "No." When asked if the people could reenter the town, he said, "Yes." When asked if he would protect them, he shrugged his shoulders. It was evident that the slightest show of force would have brought on a contest, and I cannot say too much for the coolness of the men in my detachment. They behaved like soldiers in the face of death in an ambuscade. During the heated argument which followed, an orderly dashed up and handed the Spanish officer a dispatch which was a notification from Captain General Macias to Ladesma, of the protocol. No further action was taken by Lieutenant Preston, bearing the dispatches, so we withdrew. In withdrawing, a guard was left at the turn in the road, and he reported several squads of Spanish that came out from under the underbrush when we left. Some of the men reported seeing Spanish soldiers in the trees on each side of the road, covering us with their rifles. I did not observe them, however. This company of Guardia Civil was armed with Remington rifles, and I think we could have successfully resisted it had we had the proper cover and not been exposed, as we had the Krag-Jorgensen carbine—a much more effective weapon. We rode fifteen miles to the camp of the night before. Total miles made during the day, thirty.

This detachment proceeded to various Spanish towns, where it had similar experiences. On August 24th it left Adjuntas and proceeded to Utuado, where orders were received from General Miles to rejoin our command preparatory to going home. In Lieutenant Frelinghuysen's report regarding this expedition, in which men and horses had traveled two hundred and forty-nine miles between August 11th and 25th, he says:

> I cannot say too much of the excellent behavior of the men during this tour of duty. Many of the marches were on exceedingly hard trails, the roads being sometimes almost impassable, made so by the heavy rains during the middle of the day.

During the late night of the 11th, an order was received to assemble the troop at once and explore the mountains about Ponce. Firing had been heard and it was supposed that Spanish bands were contemplating a night attack. As the troop was about to assemble, however, the order was countermanded, the firing having proved to be the result of a fracas sometimes indulged in by the natives.

On August 9th General Miles had informed me that the troop would leave Ponce to move up to the Spanish lines, where there were three excellent mule pack trains. I at once managed to obtain one of these with five mule wagons, and the command was in excellent condition. Shortly after this, General Miles informed me that he might leave for the front at any moment and would take the troop with him.

I went to headquarters to get final orders to move out toward Aibonito, where the Spaniards were strongly entrenched. (General Miles had said that he would send us as advance guard to draw Spanish fire and disclose their position.) While waiting, I heard a telegraphic tick-tack and assumed that important news was arriving from Washington. When this had finally ceased, some one came out and said that Spain had asked for an armistice and that it had been accepted by Washington. Hostilities had come to an end. The troop thus found itself still at Ponce with the exception of the detachment sent out with Lieutenant Frelinghuysen, and a small detachment of four men and one Colt machine gun sent out under Sergeant Seymour Cromwell, attached to Captain Hoppin and his troop, who had been ordered to join General Henry's command.

As we had expected to move at any moment, the men did not make a permanent camp, but had been sleeping in shelter tents. Now that the armistice had come, wall tents were put up and a comfortable camp established. The men were able to bathe in the river. Several times a week the troop, mounted bareback, marched to the sea where the men swam the horses; and short rides were made to various points of interest about Ponce in order to keep horses and men in condition.

On August 16th the troop was ordered to accompany General Miles to the outposts opposite the Spanish lines, where firing had ceased upon the announcement of the armistice. We proceeded along this magnificent macadamized road winding through the mountains. I rode behind General Miles and realized what a hard rider he was, for we hardly drew rein and trotted the greater portion of the distance to Coamo, where we arrived at four o'clock in the afternoon. I heard Captain Hoppin, who served with him in his last Indian campaign, remark that "General Miles is a great man-hunter."

We made camp a little beyond Coamo, and remained there over the next day, during which time the men had the opportunity of seeing the American and Spanish outposts. The Spanish forces were posted on the razorback mountains in front of Aibonito, seemingly a very strong, almost impregnable, position. We returned with the General to Ponce the next day. No halt was made, and again we trotted nearly all the distance, arriving in the afternoon about four-thirty with men and horses in good condition despite the tropic heat.

Notwithstanding the armistice, there were some incidental experiences of interest. At midnight on August 22nd, I received the following order:

COMMANDING OFFICER, Troop A, N.Y. Cavalry. Sir: Send officer and twenty-five men at once to Santa Isabella. Arrest all rioters and all participants, or those guilty of arson. Report at once. By command of MAJOR GENERAL WILSON.

There being only some thirty men in camp, "Boots and saddles" was sounded at once, and at 12:30 A.M. the column moved out proceeding along the Guayamo road to Santa Isabella. It was a dark night, and the road was full of ruts owing to constant rain. We trotted along at about six miles an hour and arrived in the vicinity of Santa Isabella at about 3:30. Every precaution was taken by sending out scouts to reconnoiter and ascertain the condition of affairs. To our surprise, the town was quietly sleeping and our column entered. Seeing no evidences of disorder or arson, I hurried to the house of the alcalde, where I learned (as well as from some of the chief citizens) that there had been no rioting or arson in the town. One of the signal-corps men attached to General Wilson's command had volunteered to accompany us, and had brought telegraph instruments. I telegraphed to General Wilson at Ponce and received the following reply:

Much obliged for the promptitude and efficiency of your action. Return at your leisure and report to me in person.

The alcalde gave us a good breakfast. We arrived in camp in the late afternoon. At this time of the year the heat was excessive. There was constant heavy rain and many of the men began to suffer from malaria and fever generally; flies and other insects were intolerable. Under these circumstances, there were no drills; all the rides were taken in the morning to exercise the horses. Military service, especially because of lack of sanitation, was of an arduous and painful character. Even the men who were not ill felt greatly debilitated by the climate. We were therefore much relieved when, on September 3rd, the troop was ordered to board the transport *Mississippi*. Sergeant Ward and ten men volunteered to take care of the horses, provided they were taken with us on the transport, and I therefore declined the permission of the Quartermaster to turn in the horses to his department at Ponce.

The *Mississippi* was not overloaded and the embarkation took place without difficulty. The weather was fine and the return trip pleasant and free from unusual incident. On September 10th, the transport having arrived at New York, Captain Howard G. Badgley assumed command.

The troop marched to the armory; but as I had been taken with a violent attack of typhoid aboard the transport, I was unable, to my very great regret, to share in the triumphal reception accorded us.

Subsequent to the armistice, the main concern of the officers of the troop was the matter of health, because of tropical conditions and the various diseases that prevailed in Puerto Rico. We obtained permission to rent a small house in the town which, by authority of the medical officers in one of the medical forces, was equipped as a hospital. All our sick men were nursed there with every possible attention to be obtained under existing conditions, and those who were seriously ill were sent home as quickly as possible. It was partly because of the direction and able and active cooperation of Assistant Surgeon Medwin Leale, of our troop, that no men of the command died. My impression is that our health record was equal to, or perhaps better than, any command that served in Puerto Rico; and the friends of the troop made liberal gifts to aid us in caring for the sick.

We were fortunate in having a body of most zealous and able non-commissioned officers. As I look back through the vista of some forty years, I feel that the record of Troop A, United States Volunteers, in this comparatively insignificant war—yet one fraught with highly important consequences—is one of which our organization may well be proud. That little troop, composed of men unaccustomed to military discipline under wartime conditions, acquitted itself in full accord with the high standards set up by our admired and beloved first Commander, Charles F. Roe.

1912–1918

THE PERIOD IN WHICH MAJOR WILLIAM R. WRIGHT
COMMANDED

THE YEARS 1912–1918

William R. Wright

The only good histories are those that have been written by the persons themselves who commanded in the affairs whereof they write.—MONTAIGNE

REORGANIZATION AND CHANGES

THE 1st New York Cavalry was formed December 28, 1911, by the consolidation of Squadron A, Squadron C, Troop B of Albany, and Troop D of Syracuse. Major Oliver B. Bridgman of Squadron A was made colonel, and Major Paul Debevoise of Squadron C, lieutenant colonel.

Troops 1, 2, 3 and 4 of Squadron A became Troops A, E, F and G of the new regiment and were commanded respectively by Captains Arthur F. Townsend, Frank R. Outerbridge, William R. Wright, and Edward Olmsted. Our U.S. Army instructor was Captain Lincoln C. Andrews.

As officers were elected at that time, an election to fill the position of major, made vacant by the promotion of Major Bridgman, was ordered to be held on January 17th, and after a spirited but entirely friendly contest resulted in the choice of Captain William R. Wright by a majority of one vote over Captain Townsend.

The new Major appointed Thomas B. Clarke, Jr., to be his adjutant and Lewis Howland Brown to be squadron quartermaster, and was commissioned on January 26th. Even before that he had to undertake the organization of a new troop to be known as Troop L, to fill one of the vacancies in the 1st Cavalry—another troop, M, being organized in Brooklyn.

By great good fortune Merritt H. Smith, a former captain of Troop I, was prevailed upon to return to the colors, and under his dynamic, genial, and inspiring leadership Troop L jumped fully armed into the midst of the squadron family and made its presence felt from the first singing of "Noah Built Himself an Ark." A christening party was held at the Squadron A Club, at which Captain Smith and Lieutenants Henry Sheldon and Graham Youngs, in nurses' costume, presented the members of the proposed troop, in infants' dress, to Colonel Bridgman and Major Wright; cocktails were served in nursing bottles, and other inspiring drinks in buckets; and Troop L was off to a flying start.

Soon after this, in February, we had the novel experience of our first winter maneuver. Major John F. O'Ryan of the 2nd Battalion of Field Artillery, N.G.N.Y., planned a tactical exercise to be held on February 11th and 12th at the artillery farm at Salem Center, Westchester County, and invited a troop from the squadron to take part. A volunteer troop of thirty-three men was organized under command of Captain Townsend with Robert W. Bush and George O. Redington as lieutenants, and Major Wright, Captain Smith, and Captain Leander H. Shearer (Medical) as military attachés.

Forty horses were assembled at the squadron polo stables at Van Cortlandt Park, and at 5 P.M. on February 9th a horse detail of fourteen men, under command of Sergeant Isham Henderson of Troop F, left the stables for the forty-three-mile march to the farm, the country being covered with deep snow, and the thermometer below zero. After stopping for the night at Valhalla, Sergeant Henderson and his hardy men reached the farm at 4:30 P.M. on Saturday the 10th—forty-three miles in ten and a half hours' traveling time—with men and horses in fine condition.

Giving all a few hours' rest, he met the troop (which had come up by train) at Purdys Station, and all reported at the artillery farm at 9:30 where the horses were put in barns and the men quartered in an unheated farmhouse.

On Monday the 12th, the enemy, represented by silhouettes, was definitely located in position by the patrols of the preceding day, and was attacked by infantry, cavalry, and artillery, all firing live ammunition, and after a final charge was routed with many hits. The men returned to quarters, mess was served, and at 2:30 P.M. the return march was started via Cross River, Bedford, and Armonk to Valhalla (twenty-five miles in five hours) where the horses were left in charge of squadron grooms to be brought back the next day. The men returned to the city by train.

Not long after this, on March 11th, another reorganization hit us. Troops C, H, I, K and M were detached from the 1st Cavalry; our

CAMP AT PONCE, 1898
CAMP AT COAMO, 1898

VOLUNTEER TROOP A ON RETURN FROM PORTO RICO, 1898

former Troop L became Troop C; and the 1st Cavalry was reinforced by Troop H of Rochester and Troop I of Buffalo (the latter under Captain William J. Donovan). Captain Merritt H. Smith was promoted to lieutenant colonel of the 1st Cavalry (vice Debevoise), Lieutenant Henry Sheldon taking his place in command of Troop C; and with Majors Harry S. Richmond of Albany, Wright of New York, and Howard K. Brown of Syracuse in command of squadrons, our regiment (less three troops—K, L and M) was ready to go again.

During the spring, Troops A and F were ordered out as part of the escort to the remains of Major General Philip Kearny, U.S.A., and Troops C and E, for similar duty for the remains of Major General Frederick D. Grant, U.S.A.

About this time we were stunned by the news that the legislature had passed a law retiring all officers at the age of sixty-four and that our beloved General Roe, our first captain and our first major, must retire under the law on May 1st. A dinner was given to him by the Ex-Members' Association at the Hotel Savoy which was attended by ex-members and active members alike. General Roe assured us that the squadron would fill the same place in his thoughts, as a retired general officer, that it had when he was the major general commanding, and we all tried to tell him what we thought of him. It was with a feeling of deep sorrow that we saw him relinquish his active work. His place was filled by the promotion of Major John F. O'Ryan, our recent host at the artillery farm, who was destined to command the New York National Guard on the Mexican border in 1916 and throughout the World War. He promptly appointed Captain Townsend of Troop A to be lieutenant colonel and quartermaster on his staff—First Lieutenant Howard M. Cowperthwait succeeding to the command of Troop A. Later, in September, Captain Olmsted became aide to General O'Ryan, and First Lieutenant Emerson R. Newell took over Troop C.

In the meantime our squadron held two very successful week-end camps at Van Cortlandt Park; Troops C and F on May 11th and 12th and Troops A, E and G on May 25th and 26th. The latter camp was visited informally by President Taft and formally by our new Major General O'Ryan. On May 11th mounted games were held at Van Cortlandt Park resulting in an overwhelming victory for Troop F, largely through the efforts of Sergeant Latham R. Reed, who won four events and was second in another for a total of 23 points.

THE CONNECTICUT MANEUVERS

From August 8th to 19th occurred the Connecticut maneuvers of 1912, both interesting and instructive. While in some respects the prescribed character of the program lessened the reality and left a less vivid impression of the campaign as a whole than in Massachusetts in 1909, still the work steadily increased in interest, until it culminated in the capture and subsequent defense of Newtown Hill on the closing day, where we occupied grandstand seats for as fine a military spectacle as could be staged.

The Blue cavalry was ordered to assemble at Bridgeport, and on Thursday the eighth, having obtained permission to march thereto, the five troops of the 1st Cavalry which were stationed in Manhattan left their armory at 2 o'clock, and with complete wagon train.

Sunday was spent quietly in camp, but on Monday morning we received orders to go to the assistance of the 2d Brigade of New York, about a mile north of Milford, to cover its withdrawal.

On Tuesday, the 13th, we were ordered to cover the retirement of our Blue infantry brigade and, when that was safely accomplished, to destroy all bridges across the Housatonic. Accordingly, with the 2d Cavalry in reserve, our regiment divided into three squadrons—with one troop thrown out in patrols to the north and east—moved by three parallel roads on Naugatuck Junction, halted about a mile from the river, until the infantry crossed, and then followed and (theoretically) blew up the bridge. To our great disgust, the enemy viewed our retirement with indifference, and no contact was secured except by patrols, who reported that the Reds were concentrating on Derby and, thence, crossing to Shelton.

Wednesday was one of our banner days. Orders were received to proceed towards Walnut Tree Hill and support the Blue New Jersey Brigade at that point. Marching via Nichols Farms we reached crossroads 357, about a mile southwest of Huntington, and halted to learn the wishes of the Blue brigade commander. While we were waiting there, a small patrol that had been thrown out to the southeast returned with great speed slightly ahead of a larger Red cavalry patrol. The Reds, in turn, executed "To the rear," when charged by a Blue platoon, and countered with a troop which ran into two troops dismounted and the 1st Cavalry machine gun. In a very few minutes two squadrons of the 1st Cavalry and one of the 2d Cavalry were celebrating their first sight of the Red horsemen, who were attacking us dismounted in full force. Both sides, apparently anxious for close acquaintance, were soon lining opposite sides of the same stone wall, which offended the umpires so greatly that they ordered us all to rest for thirty minutes. While resting, Colonel Parker thought of something much better, and leaving Troops D and E, 1st Cavalry, to stand off the Red cavalry attack, proceeded to "beat it" for Huntington with the rest of his force, where he immediately started to annoy some Red infantry which was perpetrating a "normal attack" at that point. By hard riding the umpires caught him at last, pulled him out of the fight, and sent us all back fifteen miles for "off side" (or something like that) to a point on the Aspetuck River near Flirt Hill, where we went into camp.

Thursday was quiet, operations consisting merely of moving camp to Hattertown, chasing out a Red troop which we found there, and, with the 2d Cavalry looking out for the outpost work, resting up for the final period. On Friday we started on the stroke of seven for Newtown to operate on the left flank of the Blue army which was concentrating between Bethel and Dodgingtown. Nearing Newtown, word was passed back that the Red cavalry was reported and we would charge with the saber. This sounded promising, but the Reds did not show up.

Saturday we were ordered to go back and reoccupy the position we had just left, and preparations were made accordingly. It seemed impossible to believe that it would not be strongly held by the Reds, so Colonel Parker allowed fifteen minutes to get there and to capture it, and announced this in a message to the Blue army commander. On the tick of seven, we left camp at a fast trot which increased to a gallop as we neared the goal, and although the expected Reds wiped out our leading troop, the rest of the brigade swarmed over the hill and occupied it on schedule time. We immediately took position on the crest, dismounted, the 2d Cavalry on the left, one squadron of the 1st Cavalry with the machine gun immediately in front of the Coles house, the balance of the 1st Cavalry on hill 698. During the next three or four hours several attacks were made on us and there was enough action to suit the most critical. The final attack came after eleven o'clock, and every move of the Red infantry—firing line, supports, and reserves—could be seen from the machine gun position at the Coles house. The attack seemed to divide at this point, swinging off to the left and right and affording splendid opportunities for enfilade fire. The machine gun made use of these opportunities to the full and the three troops of that squadron fired over fifty rounds per man, so the constructively dead must have been piled high. While the Reds were still pressing on, we were told that the Blue infantry was in position and that we were to withdraw to the flanks; so letting off the last belt in the machine gun for luck, we mounted our horses and pulled out, expecting more action and plenty of it. However, our march took us back to Hawleyville to camp, and the war was over. The same evening we made camp in the dark at Danbury, and broke it the next morning in a cloudburst.

The balance of the year was quiet and peaceful, marked only by the participation of Troop G in the centennial celebration at Albany on October 5th and by the arrival of Captain David H. Biddle as an additional U.S. instructor and assistant to Captain Andrews.

1913

THE SCHOOL AT MONTAUK POINT, AND ANOTHER REORGANIZATION

Nineteen thirteen was a year of parades. It opened with a review in the armory on January 25th for Major General Thomas H. Barry, U.S.A., commanding what was then known as the Eastern Division. The spectators agreed that the high point of the ceremony was the drill of the machine gun squad commanded by Sergeant Walter C. McClure of Troop C. For this exhibition, the ancient 1898 Colt machine gun carried by Troop A, U.S. Volunteer Cavalry in Puerto Rico, had been resurrected, rechristened "Babbling Bessie" (she was also called many other more impolite names when she refused to function), and fitted with a "muffler" to permit the automatic firing of blanks. The achievement of actually firing the ancient weapon was, however, not enough for its ambitious crew. Snap and speed were their watchwords. The squad would enter at the gallop, its artillery carried on a flying pack horse; at signal the squad would halt in a shower of tanbark; the gun and tripod would be set up in double time; and firing would begin immediately upon the gun being clamped to the tripod.

On February 11th, the first of the competitions for the "Justice" cup for horsemanship was held. This trophy had been presented by Private Alden S. Blodget and named in honor of his horse "Justice," the winner of fifty-three horse-show ribbons. Blodget was a member of the winning team of four men from Troop C.

The squadron also visited Washington to act as escort to Governor Sulzer of New York at the inauguration of Woodrow Wilson as President of the United States; returning to New York, a review was held on May 2nd for Major General Roe and Troop A of the Spanish War of 1898.

On May 10th we escorted General O'Ryan at the unveiling of the Carl Schurz monument, and on May 30th, after the usual Memorial Day parade, Troops A and C assisted at the unveiling of the *Maine* memorial in Columbus Circle.

Meanwhile, two week-end squadron camps had been held at Van Cortlandt Park, and Captain Newell of Troop G had been forced, by pressure of business, to leave his troop and had been succeeded by First Lieutenant Philip T. Stillman.

In the absence of appropriations for more extensive field training, officers' and non-commissioned officers' field schools had been arranged for the summer, and on Saturday morning, June 21st, at 7 A.M., the details of officers and men from the squadron left the armory in a drizzling rain for the cavalry school of application to be established at Montauk Point, Long Island: 16 officers, 30 men (five troop details of 6 men each, practically all of whom were non-commissioned officers), a machine gun platoon with 2 guns and 20 men, and 90 horses for our own use and for assignment to the details from the upper part of the state.

The camp at Montauk Point was pitched on a grassy plain between Fort Pond and the ocean—which are only about two hundred yards apart—and was in the form of a square open at the north, with the troop line (Sibleys, with six men to a tent) on the west; the student officers, two men in each wall tent, facing them on the eastern side, with the administration tents on the south. The machine gun tent line was just back of the troop street, and the picket line, in the form of a square, on the shore of Fort Pond to the north.

The terrain was ideal for cavalry work. Rolling grassland in every direction, with very little wooded country but good cover in the folds of the ground, no fences or cultivated land, several small lakes, some high points from which beautiful views of the Sound and ocean could be had, and fresh air which chased the cobwebs from the brain in a moment. Captain Lincoln C. Andrews, U.S. Cavalry, was in full charge of the camp and of the instruction, with Captain David Biddle, U.S. Cavalry, as assistant. First Lieutenant A. E. Phillips, 10th U.S. Cavalry, was instructor for the machine gun platoon.

After the summer vacation we took up armory drill again. It might be interesting for purposes of comparison to record the average strength and average attendance of the several troops for the training-year ending September 30th: Troop F, average strength 58, average attendance for the year 98.27 per cent; Troop C, 50 and 96.83; Troop A, 54 and 96.65; Troop G, 52 and 93.30; Troop E, 48 and 91.92. Our aggregate strength was at all times up to the figure allowed by Division Headquarters.

In November, the answers to various pointed questions which the Federal government had been asking about our two cavalry regiments, neither of which had its full complement of units, could not be put off any longer. After several conferences betwen Adjutant General Henry DeWitt Hamilton and Major General O'Ryan, orders were issued detaching the Manhattan troops from the 1st Cavalry, designating them as the "1st Separate Squadron" and "1st Separate Machine Gun Troop," and combining the balance of the 1st Cavalry and the entire 2nd Cavalry into one full regiment, the 1st, under command of Colonel Debevoise; Colonel Bridgman remaining in command of the "Cavalry Post" where our squadron troops were quartered. The troops of the squadron were also relettered: A, E, F and G became A, B, C and D, and the former Troop C (born L) became the machine gun troop. Thus our troops took another step in the collection of alphabetical decorations.

1914

A SILVER ANNIVERSARY, A SQUADRON FARM, AND A COUNTY FAIR

The first official event of 1914 was the second competition for the "Justice" cup, and again the machine gun troop was the winner, with a team composed of Sergeant Sullivan, Corporal Young, and Privates Blodget and Thorne. After the competition in horsemanship, a rough-riding contest was held between teams of twelve men representing

Battery A of Massachusetts and Squadron A. The squadron showed more experience and more finish, and was declared the winner; but the Battery team put up a fine show. The team and their "cheering section" were afterwards our guests at a smoker, where the friendship established the preceding year was still further cemented.

On March 5th, we became Squadron A again instead of the 1st Separate Squadron, General O'Ryan having been persuaded that as we were a separate squadron and it would affect no one but ourselves, we might just as well be Squadron A. No change was made in the troop designations.

The proper celebration of the twenty-fifth anniversary of the squadron was intrusted to a committee whose work was so successful that their names should unquestionably be given: William R. Maloney, chairman; Stephen W. Mason, Robert W. Neeser, Durant Rice, and Harley L. Stowell, secretary. "Squadron Week" opened on Monday, April 20th, with a review. General Roe was the reviewing officer and he was escorted by a strong detachment of the original Troop A as mustered in twenty-five years before. Throughout the week, this troop was given the post of honor in all events and turned out in fine strength. Wednesday, a squadron ball was held at the Hotel Biltmore and no one will forget the beauty of the scene with the many brilliant gowns and the full-dress uniforms of the active squadron. The ball lasted until the rising sun warned us that another business day had dawned. Saturday, a dinner was held at Delmonico's to which all who had ever belonged to the organization were invited and to which most of them came; and on Sunday, with General Roe at the head of the column and Troop A, 1889, immediately behind him, we marched to the Church of the Heavenly Rest (at that time at Fifth Avenue and Forty-fifth Street) for a service conducted by our honorary chaplain, the beloved Herbert Shipman.

In connection with the review, a twenty-five-year Squadron Service Medal was presented to Colonel Bridgman, destined to remain the only one to be issued until 1932, when Major Egleston achieved a similar honor. Colonel Bridgman also received from the active squadron a fine bronze of a cavalry trooper as a memento of his long and faithful service.

The next event, and one of great importance, was the purchase and opening of Squadron A farm at New City, Rockland County. The question of having a farm, where our horses could be turned out, forage could be raised, and week-end camps established, had been discussed for over a year; committees had reported favorably and had scouted the county in all directions. Finally Sergeant Isham Henderson located the Verdin property at New City—about one hundred and forty acres with a fine old mansion—and it was agreed that this was the spot. Financial arrangements were completed and we took over the property on June 1st. Charlie Muller was converted from stableforeman to farmer and sent up to manage the new enterprise, which he did in his customary painstaking and competent way until he was killed some years later when a team he was driving bolted into the big barn. Mention should also be made of the assistance that we received during the early days of the farm from "Doc" Wilson, genial host at the "Elms" in New City, and of the many pleasant hours we spent in his hospitable rooms.

We introduced ourselves to our new neighbors at the annual fair of the Rockland County Industrial Association held on the fair grounds in September. An entire afternoon was set aside to give the squadron an opportunity to show what it could do, and everybody in the county packed the grandstand or lined the railings of the track. Flat races, exhibition jumping, hurdle races, Roman races, roughriding, machine gun exhibition, cavalry drills, and, finally, a melee were put on, and were received with great applause. The *Rockland County Press*, the next day, reported that our exhibition "was without doubt the greatest, most exciting and really enjoyable attraction ever presented at a Rockland County fair," and we were firmly established as a bona fide "county family" and as desirable neighbors.

During the year, Major Leander H. Shearer and Captain Reginald H. Sayre had left us, and in their places Lieutenants Harry A. Riley and Frederick W. Wurster, Jr., had been commissioned respectively as assistant surgeon and as inspector of small arms practice. Captain Outerbridge also was forced by business to turn over the welfare of Troop B to Captain A. W. Putnam.

1915

Major changes of 1915 were the loss of Captain Lincoln C. Andrews, our senior instructor, and Lieutenant Thomas B. Clarke, Jr., our squadron adjutant. "Link" Andrews was an ideal instructor and

Tom Clarke was a born adjutant, and their joint loss was a severe one; but Lieutenant William N. Haskell [1] came to help Captain Biddle with our instruction, and Sergeant Major William R. Maloney was promoted to the adjutant's job, so we closed up our ranks and moved forward.

On Washington's Birthday, Troop C started our travels with a winter camp and maneuvers at the squadron farm; a very successful trip in spite of deep snow and extremely cold weather.

The "Justice Cup" was again won by the machine gun troop, and our twenty-first military games were held. As these mounted games have been omitted since this date and their place is now taken by indoor polo, perhaps the following list of events will be of interest and value to posterity. They were making and breaking camp, low reach, rescue race, tug of war (mounted), head cutting with hurdles, saddling race, roughriding, novelty race, and mounted wrestling.

A review was also given to Colonel Daniel Appleton, the commander of the Seventh Regiment, and troop week-end camps were held at Van Cortlandt Park by our recruit squad and by Troops C, D and MG, at the squadron farm by Troop B, and at the United Hunts Club at Belmont Park by Troop A.

During the spring, also, the Squadron Employee Decoration for long and faithful service was established and appropriate bars were presented to Armorer Aber for twenty-five years' service, to Muller, Lange, Quinn, and Seaman for fifteen years' service, and to Stemler, Baker, McTiernan, Effinger, and Archer for ten years' service.

Money was available to send two reinforced brigades to field training camps, the Manhattan regiments in one brigade and those from Brooklyn in another; so on July 17th we boarded the boat to go up the Hudson, disembarked at New Hamburg, and then marched to "Camp Whitman" at Fishkill Plains, near Hopewell Junction, Dutchess County.

The training at Camp Whitman was splendid. Problems were held each day, there was plenty of work for the cavalry, and we were pitted against regular army cavalry of the highest type so that we had to be wide-awake at all times. The Major had evidently decided that if we were to be criticized, it would not be for lack of aggressiveness, so we

---

[1] Now major general, commanding the 27th Division.

were constantly involved in attacks on the enemy's rear—his wagon trains or anything that came handy—in the meantime protecting ourselves as well as we could against a very aggressive regular squadron which was alert to show us up if we neglected any precautions or became entirely too rash. The high spot of the week was our mounted charge against the rear of Major Bandholtz's regular infantry battalion, which was made after riding entirely around the left flank of the enemy army. Think back and recall Dave Biddle, bedecked in the white bands, etc., of an absolutely impartial umpire, meeting us just before the final charge and thereafter riding ahead, calling back, "Come on! Come on! You've got 'em. Come on!" And the infantry umpire who stood in the road and tried to stop us until he saw that we were a through express, and, at the last moment at which it was still possible to save his life, scaled the fence with extreme agility and watched the squadron whiz by. And again, Colonel Dickman—who carried considerable weight—caught in the same road, sheltering himself behind a tree-trunk and laughingly waving to us, as we swept around him. That was a glorious day, and we returned to camp with our buglers lustily blowing the most triumphant quicksteps in their repertory.

The rest of the year was marked by a "Military Tournament and Wild West Show" at the Piping Rock Club, by the combined review of the 1st and 2d Brigades at Van Cortlandt Park, and by a review of the squadron, in the armory, for General Dyer, our brigade commander at Camp Whitman. We also received an issue of the latest model machine guns (the Benet-Mercié) for our Machine Gun Troop and were joined by Sergeant Howard J. Parker, of the 2d U.S. Cavalry, the first of our instructor sergeants.

1916

THE BORDER SERVICE

Affairs in Mexico were approaching a crisis when we started 1916, but several events were to happen before the actual call came for our participation.

In the first place, the squadron reached the highest figure for peace-time strength that it had ever attained. Division Headquarters had authorized an increase of all troops to seventy-one officers, and men and all had been recruited to the limit with a waiting list still maintained. The official figures for the annual inspection were:

	Present	Absent	Percentage
Field and staff	5	0	100.00
Troop A	71	0	100.00
B	71	0	100.00
C	71	0	100.00
D	69	2	97.32
M.G.	70	1	98.59
Aggregate	357	3	99.16

Also another very important step, the full value of which we did not realize until later, had been taken in the organization and muster in of the "Depot Troop" under Captain Latham G. Reed. While we were serving on the border the Depot Troop kept our possessions safe for our return, and they met and escorted us "home" to the armory. Again when we left for Camp Wadsworth and the World War the next year, they took the long walk with us from the armory to the ferry. They returned to become "Squadron A, New York Guard"—first under Major Reed and then successively under Major Barry and Major Wendt—to hold a place for the squadron in the Guard, to insure the building of the new armory, and to preserve and pass on the spirit and traditions of the squadron's life history. And then when the 27th Division came home and the Guard was reorganized, Major Wendt and as many of his officers and men as were not needed stepped quietly down, and gave up their places to the men with war experience whom they felt and said should organize the new squadron; asking no consideration and claiming no honors for their years of effort. That the squadron is alive today is due, in a very great measure, to the devoted services of Majors Reed, Barry, and Wendt, to the other officers and men of the Depot Troop and Depot Squadron, and to the way in which they kept "the home-fires burning." No older member of the squadron will forget those services. No present or future member of the squadron should be uninformed of them.

In connection with our efforts to arouse support for a new armory for our squadron, a review was tendered, this spring, to Mayor John Purroy Mitchel, and shortly thereafter an event occurred which had a direct and immediate effect on that project. One morning General

O'Ryan sent for the squadron commander and on his arrival told him that a number of men who had been in the cavalry troop at the last summer's Citizens' Training Camp at Plattsburg wished to continue their training and desired, if possible, to use the squadron armory. The Major politely stated this was impossible as the armory was in constant use and was already cramped for space and time. General O'Ryan replied that before a final decision was reached he might mention that the personnel of the troop which wished to use the armory included the mayor of the city and the president of the Board of Aldermen. The Major saw the point at once, asked that a representative of the troop call on him to make final arrangements, and offered his service as instructor. Drills were soon started on Thursday afternoons. The troop had a fine personnel from the city government, the police force, and the best of clubs. In its makeup it was very reminiscent of the personnel of Roosevelt's Rough Riders. Alderman Henry H. Curran was first sergeant; Mayor Mitchel was a corporal; J. G. Milburn (brother of Devereux Milburn of polo fame) was a sergeant; State Senator J. Mayhew Wainwright was a corporal; police captains and police lieutenants were sergeants, corporals, and privates; and well known names, too many to mention, filled the ranks. The troop prospered from the start and closed its career in May with a week-end camp at the squadron farm and a dinner at the Yale Club. At the dinner Major Wright was presented with a fine pair of field glasses, suitably inscribed, which is still one of his most treasured possessions; but the high point of the evening was reached when Mayor Mitchel, called upon to speak, stated that personal experience had shown him that the squadron armory was far too small, the squadron deserved a new armory, and he was going to see that it got one, and directed Major Wright to call at his office in the City Hall the next morning to start action. Needless to say, the Major kept that appointment to the minute, and from that time official indifference ceased and the armory moved slowly but steadily to its final construction. It is true that much work had to be done by Major Reed, Major Wendt, and Major Egleston before our present armory became a concrete fact, but until Mayor Mitchel's untimely death he pushed the project vigorously, and to him should go the credit and the thanks for a definite start.

On the retirement for age of Colonel Daniel Appleton, who had commanded the Seventh Regiment for over twenty-five years, arrangements were made by our commanding officer with the adjutant of the Seventh, Captain (now brigadier general, retired) DeWitt Clinton Falls, to give the Colonel a surprise party on the occasion of his Retirement Review at the Seventh Regiment Armory. The plan was kept a profound secret and the squadron assembled and marched out of the armory with only the commanding officer knowing its destination. The Seventh was equally uninformed; and, after they had passed in review before their colonel for the last time, were formed in a hollow square. Then Squadron A, in the blue and gold hussar dress uniform of those days, with colors and guidons, marched into the drill hall, formed in mass facing the retiring Colonel, presented him with a silver loving cup, and passed in review before him in troop front and out of the armory; many to return as individuals for the post-review events of the evening. The contrasting dress uniforms of the Seventh and of the Squadron made a beautiful spectacle. General (as he became) Appleton often referred to this compliment which Squadron A had paid to him, and the Seventh showed their appreciation by a friendship which has lasted to the present day.

In May, retirement and promotion came home to us in the promotion to brigadier general, and in the retirement, at his request, of our own Colonel Bridgman, which closed for a time his cavalry career of twenty-seven years. Of course his active personality could never permit him to retire permanently, and he came back to perform valuable active service at the time of the World War, to succeed General Roe as the perpetual president of the squadron's Ex-Members' Association, and to be, today, as well known a figure in our own and many other National Guard armories as are the respective commanding officers themselves. At a dinner at the Waldorf Astoria, the squadron officers endeavored to express their delight in his promotion—coupled with regret for his retirement. Those who know him today will understand how we felt.

Meanwhile, affairs in Mexico were rapidly "getting no better." The fight at Carrizal had occurred, and Captain Boyd, umpire with the squadron in Connecticut, and Lieutenant Adair, who fought against us at Pine Plains, had been killed. We all knew that it was merely a question of a very short time before we would have to assist the regular army in putting an end to an intolerable situation.

On June 19th, information was received that the President of the United States had called upon the National Guard for mobilization.

The squadron at that time was scattered over the face of the earth—in Switzerland, California, Yellowstone Park and many other places frequented by privates of cavalry when not on active duty—but all started back at once and, at the time ordered, 95 per cent were on hand for assembly; all others coming in to report with a promptness in proportion to their distance.

Major Wright informed the squadron of the President's call, and stated that there was no question of volunteering; we were all obligated to serve. Such definite conclusions proved most unwise, for the War Department, a few days later, produced a perfectly new oath, and we were told that unless we swore thus individually and collectively we could not go to the front—wherever that might be. It naturally developed later that we would have gone anyhow; and during the rest of the year we were kept busy answering why we had taken the oath on June 30th instead of earlier or later (we nearly had to take it all over again on that account), whether having taken it we considered ourselves National Guard or organized Militia (our first answer to this—"Both"—was subsequently found to be a bad guess), and other embarrassing questions. The squadron roster of officers at this time was:

Major William R. Wright; Surgeons Captain Samuel McCullaugh and First Lieutenant Henry A. Riley; Adjutant, First Lieutenant Reune Martin; Inspector of Small Arms Practice, First Lieutenant Frederick W. Wurster, Jr.; Quartermaster, Second Lieutenant Dudley M. Cooper; Troop A: Captain Howard M. Cowperthwait, First Lieutenant Samuel H. Gillespie, Second Lieutenant Reginald E. Wigham; Troop B: Captain Albert W. Putnam, First Lieutenant Robert B. Bartholomew, Second Lieutenant James R. Knapp; Troop C: Captain Robert W. Bush, First Lieutenant Latham R. Reed, Second Lieutenant Ridgley Nicholas; Troop D: Captain Graham Youngs, First Lieutenant Nathaniel H. Egleston, Second Lieutenant Melton D. Cole; Machine Gun Troop: Captain Henry Sheldon, First Lieutenant Stanton Whitney, Second Lieutenant Colgate Hoyt, Jr., and Alfred W. Booraem.

No changes occurred during the border service except that Lieutenant Reed was transferred to the 69th Infantry and promoted to the grade of lieutenant colonel on October 5th, Captain Bush retired on the completion of twenty-years' service on December 2nd, and Lieutenant Knapp of Troop B resigned on December 5th. Troop C returned to New York under the command of Captain Ridgley Nicholas with First Lieutenant Frederick W. Wurster, Jr., and Second Lieutenant Robert H. Leake.

Our armory being cozy instead of spacious, orders were at once issued which were calculated to remove most of us from the premises, and plans were laid for transferring the whole squadron to Van Cortlandt Park under canvas.

During the first week of our service the galleries of the armory were filled with eager cavalrymen, the burden of whose conversation was "A horse, a horse, my kingdom for a horse." The one hundred and thirty horses always on hand would, of course, not go far towards mounting the five hundred eager applicants who, with the troops at war strength, would clamor for something better than shanks' mare. Fortunately, arrangements had already been made to supply the squadron with horses for the proposed summer tour of duty at Camp Whitman, and this contract was transferred to meet the new conditions. On Wednesday, the 20th, therefore, Troops A and B mounted our own horses and rode off to Van Cortlandt to establish camp, while a detail from the other troops departed for the West One Hundred and Thirtieth Street docks to receive the first installment of our new chargers.

In accounts of the doings of the various equine reception committees details vary, but all are unanimous in saying that General Sherman was right. A vast open space with a concrete floor was carefully moistened to the required degrees of slipperiness and filled with a large number of horses from lighters. The horses were then properly excited by black snake whips operated by well trained hostlers, and the game was on. A man who did secure a good horse and got him out of the dock usually had him taken away by the Division Q.M. Department at once and saw his prize given to some other organization; unless the intelligent animal seconded his efforts to dodge around the corner. On the outskirts of the melee hovered the faithful sergeants, setting legs and arms, binding up wounds, administering restoratives and calling, "once more into the breach, dear friends." These scenes were repeated daily during the first ten days of our service, the horses being transferred first to the armory and afterwards to the camp at Van Cortlandt. Our journeys thereto at times partook of all the dash and glamour of a cavalry charge, and at others resembled the retreat from Moscow. Even when our chargers were safely delivered, assigned to troops, and tied on the picket line, troubles did not cease. Devilish ingenuity was shown by stable sergeants who had acquired particularly trying lots, and he was in direct line for promotion who could, day after day, report the same number of horses on the line and yet point with pride to a steady improvement in their appearance and manners. Sorry, indeed, was the fate of the recruit horse guard who found at the end of his tour of duty that he had seven more horses than were present when he was posted, and that all of the seven were kicking seventeen different ways. Stern were the refusals of experienced troopers when loose horses were brought to them, although their captors (from another troop) might even tearfully protest that they just saw those same horses break away from that troop line and had expected thanks for their kindness. With gradual inspection, branding, and identification, these troubles disappeared. Many well known disturbers of the peace were weeded out and rejected by the Horse Board.

Our departure for the front had been delayed by the necessity of securing a full complement of horses. However, on July 5th, everything was ready: all men sworn in, examined, and mustered; a horse, such as he was, for every man; and mules for every wagon and machine gun pack. Moreover, generous relatives and friends had supplied each troop with a 1½-ton motor truck (absolutely invaluable throughout our service), and a delegation of former squadron members and other friends had presented two motor cars for the use of squadron headquarters.

On the morning of Thursday the sixth—a beautiful clear and cool day—we broke camp, packed up, received the colors with ceremony, and in column of twos departed for our entraining point at Yonkers.

Very soon after our arrival at McAllen, Texas, our camp was supposedly drained; dikes and ditches protected all tents and we thought that we were ready for anything. One Sunday, however, Texas favored us with the first of its many weather surprises. A shower, seemingly no more severe than others, visited us, and our beautiful camp disappeared under the waves. Ditches ceased to exist, dikes were submerged and dissolved. With frantic haste, each troop turned out en masse and put forth every effort to dam the water into another troop street before it could be dammed into theirs.

The next day we commenced that rival of the Panama Canal which, for the rest of our period of service, successfully prevented the recurrence of our first tragedy and always brought our camp

SQUADRON A COACH

FULL-DRESS UNIFORM   COVER PICTURE ON DANCE PROGRAM

LOADING AT THE ARMORY FOR BORDER SERVICE, 1916
TRIALS OF MOTOR TRANSPORT, MC ALLEN, 1916

above water before we sank for the third time. During its construction the most popular uniform consisted of that formerly useless but now (with the addition of one safety pin) most useful article, the "abdominal protector." This was for the more highly civilized who could not at once return to the conditions of the Stone Age. Hardy spirits on arising took off all encumbering garments, grabbed a pick or shovel, and went to work secure in the knowledge that within five minutes they would be so covered with mud as to be unrecognizable. Officers modestly wore slickers, but a mounted slicker is so constructed that, when reinforced by no other clothing, the sudden shock of a rear view materially detracts from the dignity of its appearance from the front.

Our military training falls, naturally, into several classes. First, our hikes, which were in many ways actual holidays as they took us out of camp and varied the monotony of existence. On August first, two weeks after our arrival, we were pronounced ready for our first one and, accompanied by the Division Commander, set out to look over the ground for the infantry hikes which later were required of all troops. The first of the Division, we visited Sterling's, La Gloria, McAllen's ranch, Young's ranch, Laguna Seca and Monte Cristo—names strange at first but well known later. 'Tis true that our own motor trucks and those sent to us by the Division quartermaster sank all over the country and had to be pulled out on our return trip. Still, we saw the mesquite country, and to get away from the McAllen mudhole did both men and horses good in spite of hard work and short rations.

Another hike was taken later to Sam Fordyce, where we found the 2nd Texas stationed, and through Penitas and Ojo de Agua where the mercury burst the tube while we were making camp, so that we never knew just how hot it was; and then off for Hidalgo, Donna Pump, and Mercedes. At this point, the well known hurricane stepped in; when we reached the Hidalgo road we turned north instead of south and reached our home camp just in time to catch it as it was blowing away and to pull it back to earth again.

Another hike was planned through the ranches northwest of Sterling's and home by Rio Grande City, but other duties always prevented its start. Many of us, individually, visited the old Mexican town of Rio Grande, and Fort Ringold near it, and regretted that we could not have gone there with the whole squadron.

Drills, of course, were daily necessary evils. Similar in structure to armory drills, but how different; with a whole state to drill in, and with drainage canals into, across, and over which we slid, climbed and jumped—trooper, troop, or squadron. Nor can we omit to speak of the élan attained by the led horses going to the rear in dismounted action—when any supports which were present climbed trees if dismounted, or turned and fled if mounted.

Drills were varied with field problems; and, no matter what decision was given by an umpire, these always furnished food for discussion and mutual recrimination for days afterwards. We also had several larger maneuvers with other troops of the Brigade or Division: the first was made notable by our capture of Hidalgo without firing a shot, owing to our adoption of the safe, though oft neglected, method of approaching via the "Family Entrance" instead of the front door. On another occasion we planned a little problem of our own against a small settlement where some squatters had recently been evicted, and their houses and crops burned by sheriffs. Approaching the supposedly deserted ruins concealed in thick brush, we guarded every avenue of exit, formed cordon of mounted skirmishers, and charged in with raised pistols to discover that our "deserted village" contained about a dozen Texas rangers bristling with weapons, as usual, and somewhat puzzled over our sudden and warlike appearance. A peace without victory was established, and we withdrew.

A particularly pleasant and profitable trip was the field firing at La Gloria. We had had practice before at the short range near Sharyland, but this was different. Not only was it instructive but it was good fun, and we fired with vindictive energy at the sometimes almost invisible silhouettes. When all records were in we learned that the squadron led the Division in battalion scores and that all our troops had finished in the "first ten" companies.

Reviews, possibly unpopular with other troops at McAllen, were no hardship to us. As the line of march to the White House field ran by our camp and our honorable position at such functions was at the tail of the column, we could always breakfast, saddle, and fall in leisurely, while infantry and artillery plodded by, and finally the appearance of the First Cavalry would warn us that our time was approaching. Nor—when we reached the field—was a review lacking in novel features after the introduction of the "extended gallop." We received this innovation coldly at first, and the squadron field and staff beat the rest of the organization by approximately half a mile. Thereafter we woke up to the possibilities of such a maneuver, and on future occasions the staff had to ride for their lives, while machine gun mules were simply towed through the air until the reviewing point was passed.

A pleasant feature of our service, the nearest approach to what we had expected when mobilized, was river patrol. Within a week of our arrival at McAllen a composite troop was ordered to Hidalgo for this duty. How eagerly were places on this detail sought after! What tales were brought back of the lazy brown river, of peaceful Mexico seen close at hand, of willow thickets and steaming heat therein, of Mexican guides, and of the old military road! Later, the entire squadron performed similar duty.

Lieutenant Colonel John D. Hartman, 3rd U.S. Cavalry, joined us in August as instructor. Although he remained only a short time, his fine instruction was very helpful. He returned later with an inquisition, known as an inspection board, and put us through our paces in an unexpected and thorough field inspection. Some time later he told Major Wright, in confidence, that the board (which had inspected all cavalry along the border) had given Squadron A the highest squadron-rating of any National Guard cavalry in Federal service. That confidence has been respected up to the present, when it is believed that it may be broken. A little later Captain Robert C. Foy, 3rd U.S. Cavalry, affectionately and naturally (but to his own great mystification) known as "Eddie," was detailed to us. He introduced us to the "Riley seat"—which caused stiffness and soreness to so many supposedly hardened cavalrymen—grooming by the numbers, and other novel ideas.

One day the Major General appeared approaching from the direction of McAllen. The squadron was at drill. Number 1 gazed in horror, hoping against hope that something would deflect the approaching fate. Hope faded and died. "Turn out the guard, Major General Commanding." One bashful rookie burst from the guard tent blushing at thus being thrust into the limelight. He formed platoon front, counted fours and presented arms. The General appeared interested. He dismounted, inspected the guard in detail, and asked for the commanding officer. For some time after this the guard tent was always crowded: generals, colonels, and privates, who passed, were received with all the honors of war. The entire guard was there in serried ranks. Arms flashed and bugles flourished.

Shortly after this, the guard was faced with a situation which had no precedent in the squadron. Word was received that a prisoner was being brought in. What was the proper thing to do?

While all of these martial duties had been going on, our camp had been gradually changing; in fact, improvements were being made up to the day of our departure. The official camp water system, which never produced more than a gentle perspiration, was replaced by our own well, pump, tank, and pipe lines; the gift of a member of Troop B, anonymous but ever blessed. Watering troughs for the horses and shower baths for the men appeared. Water flowed freely. No longer was it necessary to buy White Rock with which to shave. Not to us applied the daily order which came down from headquarters that "owing to the scarcity of water, baths would be permitted only between the hours of 2:00 and 2:05 A.M."

Canvas-covered horse sheds, screened tent frames, mess shacks, officers' "bird houses" appeared; and through the generosity of the mother of a member of Troop A, our own roomy infirmary and diet kitchen. When once admitted to that haven, even caviar and paté-de-foie-gras were yours for the asking, and methods of faking just the right temperature to prolong the stay were cherished secrets.

The Squadron A Club, "Texas Branch," was built, and made us think of home over our Bevo, because it was so different (both architecturally and alcoholically). Later it was supplied with a large blackboard for football scores and totally erroneous and misleading election returns.

The glee club was formed and flourished; also quartets and banjo clubs. Vaudeville talent sprang up on all sides. At one of our first shows that popular ballad "Christmas at McAllen" was introduced to an appreciative public, followed later by other gems by the same talented but necessarily anonymous author.

More sturdy sports prevented our decadence. We entered the Division "Field and Frontier Day" with enthusiasm. Our magnificent track team of one consistent point-winner (First Sergeant John R. Kilpatrick of Troop B) carried off the point-prize from all of the regiments of the Division, and our mounted athletes also scored the greatest number of points in the mounted part of the program.

Two polo games were played with the army officers at Fort Brown.

Both lacked the vital element of victory, but both were close, fast contests and served to introduce us to the joys of Brownsville. In "intra-mural" sports, baseball (hard and soft), football, soccer, and general roughhouse filled our few daylight hours of leisure, while at night the great American game flourished—with bridge or chess for the highbrows. Several crap shooters of all-American caliber were also discovered.

During the fall months weather conditions materially changed for the better. That is, mud disappeared and dust took its place. "Princeton bugs" apparently migrated to other lands, but tarantulas, scorpions, rattlesnakes, and coyotes seemed to enjoy the fall weather as much as we did. "Northers" from time to time kept us from becoming too enamored with the Texas climate, but overcoats and sweaters had been received and stoves were plentiful. The shortening days brought late reveille but no diminution in the morning schedule, which was condensed but not reduced. Just before one of the shifts of reveille, that celebrated morning report of a squad leader was made to a first sergeant: "I think they're all here, but I can't be sure until the sun comes up."

As the fall season wore on, the glee club introduced a new song which was greeted with thunderous applause at all of the Division entertainments held about semi-monthly in front of General O'Ryan's quarters:

>Now we've been down here six long months,
> On the banks of the Rio Grande,
>We've eaten tons of pork and beans,
> And hiked throughout the land;
>
>We've liked our stay im-men-se-ly,
> And worked hard every day—
>But now, the summer's over,
> The time has come to say:
>
>*Chorus:*
>When do we go home, John—
>When do we go home?
>The girls up North are anxious
>And they miss us.
>The Broadway lights are burning,
>The office needs us back—
>When are those Pullmans coming, General?

Thursday, December 15th, was finally set for our departure. Camp was struck; furniture and personal property were distributed to the less fortunate; the thirty-two horses per troop which we were to take home were picked out and the others sent to San Antonio; tarantulas, wild cats, goats, burros, and other mascots were collected to show we had really been "there"; the train was loaded—and we were ready. We cannot fail to mention the kind send-off given us by the less fortunate organizations which we left at McAllen: the editorial statement in the official Division paper, the *Rio Grande Rattler,* that "nothing has been too difficult for Squadron A to undertake cheerfully, and execute promptly and efficiently"; the luncheon at the 12th Infantry camp; its subsequent parade as our escort to the station; the coffee and chocolate served by the 69th at the train that evening; the turning out of the entire 1st Cavalry mounted, to bid us farewell—all made us feel that the New York Division was something more than a name.

Before the train started, the following letter from General O'Ryan, the division commander, was handed to our C.O.:

Squadron A being under orders to entrain for home station in New York City, the time is appropriate to make acknowledgment to you, and through you to your officers and enlisted men, of the excellence of the service rendered by the squadron during the period of its stay on the border.

That the personnel of your command are of the type in civil life who have important business obligations and responsibilities which have suffered materially by reason of the enforced absence of six months is well known. What therefore is particularly commendable in connection with their service is that their loyalty and zeal were not only above par at all times, but served as an inspiration to the Division. Squadron A, throughout its service, met the unpleasant and the disagreeable details and features of field work with apparently the same zeal and interest that it displayed in performing the most attractive field exercises. The horsemanship and marksmanship of the squadron have set high standards.

Please convey to the officers and men of your command my appreciation of the excellence of their work and of the really remarkable spirit back of it.

About midnight the wheels commenced to turn; we were off at last. The trip home was, of course, marked by the same speed as when outward bound. Getting out of the state of Texas consumed three days. At one place we had to unload and repack all of our wagons because the cars in which they were placed were declared to be too large to go through certain West Virginia tunnels; but this was merely a customary and usual incident to troop travel, and to balance such events are memories of the hospitality of Houston and Louisville. Finally, the first section pulled into Jersey City at 1 A.M. on Saturday, December 23rd, and at daylight we started to unload. Escorted by the Depot Troop of platoons, we marched through to Fifth Avenue, swung into column, and drew saber. Through Christmas streets and Christmas crowds which received us with kindly applause, past friends whose greetings strained "Attention" to the breaking point, past the reviewing stand at the University Club—filled with civic and military dignitaries—we pressed on to the armory, and finally filed through its familiar door. "Retreat" was sounded; and the command was given: "Captains, dismiss your troops." The border service was over.

1917

THE OLD SQUADRON GOES TO PLATTSBURG, AND A NEW SQUADRON PREPARES FOR THE WORLD WAR

Upon its return from the border the squadron was promptly mustered out of Federal service and then given a month's leave until January 29, 1917. Before the month was up we were informed that the annual Federal inspection would be held the first week in February.

Early in March, at the invitation of Governor Whitman, we sent two volunteer troops in service uniform and carrying the A and B troop guidons to escort him during President Wilson's second inauguration.

Events were moving slowly, and the first to affect us occurred when the first officers' training camps were opened and over two hundred of our members started for Plattsburg and other camps to qualify as officers for the proposed National Army.

The squadron's contribution to the officer personnel of our armies in the World War is a glorious page in its history; and the record of the 105th Machine Gun Battalion is one in which we can take a deep and well warranted pride. Our one comparatively small organization furnished over 750 officers; all did their full duty and many performed exceptional services and won high honors. Over sixty Squadron A graduates were in the 77th Division alone; and wherever one went, in France or in the United States, other graduates would always be found doing their bit and anxious for news of other former troopers, of the machine gun battalion, and of the home squadron.

The men sent to the first training camps were followed by details to other camps and by direct promotions, until the squadron that finally went to Spartanburg was an almost entirely new organization, except in the higher grades.

Before our first detachment departed, however, Marshal Joffre paid a visit to New York and we were detailed as his escort during his stay. Especially at the parade on his arrival, when we took him at a steady trot from the Battery to the Frick mansion at Fifth Avenue and Seventy-first Street, the squadron made a fine showing; men and horses seasoned by the recent long months on the border, and the service uniforms adding to, rather than detracting from, the picture. These were the last real pre-war parades of the old cavalry squadron.

Call for service came finally on July 16th, and as our officer personnel was considerably changed from that which took the field only a year ago for service in Texas, it might be well to give the names of the officers who entered the service at this time: field and staff, Major William R. Wright; surgeon, Captain Henry A. Riley; adjutant, First Lieutenant Frederick W. Wurster, Jr.; supply officer, Second Lieutenant Alwyn Ball, III; Troop A: Captain Howard M. Cowperthwait, First Lieutenant Allen C. Smidt, Second Lieutenant Lucius H. Biglow, Jr.; Troop B: Captain Albert W. Putnam, First Lieutenant Theodore Crane, Second Lieutenant Joseph F. Cook; Troop C: Captain Ridgley Nicholas, First Lieutenant Robert H. Leake, Second Lieutenant George W. Vanderhoef; Troop D: Captain Graham Youngs, First Lieutenant Nathaniel H. Egleston, Second Lieutenant John Reynolds; Machine Gun Troop: Captain Stanton Whitney, First Lieutenant Colgate Hoyt, Jr., Second Lieutenant Knowlton Durham.

Our scheme of mobilization was the same as the scheme of the previous year: in the armory at first and then under canvas in Van Cortlandt Park; but our stay in each place was longer.

Early in August the following letter was received from General O'Ryan:

1. Reports just received indicate that your unit, Squadron A, has again reached war strength, after having been down to a minimum through furnishing officers for the new National Army. The record of accomplishment of Squadron A since the declaration of the present war has been quite as remarkable in this way as the excellence of its service on the Mexican border. It is trying to a commanding officer to see his well trained and dependable enlisted men leaving his organization in large numbers and their places taken by untrained recruits. The recognition by the government of the value of

your exceptional personnel for higher and more important duties would seem to amply compensate their loss to you. The government was fortunate to be able to draw so heavily on Squadron A for officers. The high character of the new personnel gives promise that the squadron will continue to be as valuable an asset to the government as it has been in the past.

2. I take this opportunity to commend the squadron for its extraordinary accomplishment along the lines referred to.

Shortly after this, we moved the whole squadron to our old camp ground in Van Cortlandt Park near Jerome Avenue and settled down to real work. There was so much dismounted drill that we feared rumors to the effect that we would not remain cavalry were true.

Early in October the blow fell. We were to leave at once for Camp Wadsworth to join the 27th Division and, on arrival, were to become the 105th Machine Gun Battalion. Captain Cowperthwait (our senior captain) and Captain Nicholas would be transferred to the 27th Division trains. Troops A and B, combined, would become Company A, under Captain Putnam; Troop D would become Company B, under Captain Youngs; and Troops C and M.G. would combine to form company C, under Captain Whitney.

Breaking camp at Van Cortlandt Park, we moved to the armory, and the next day, escorted by the faithful Depot Troop, we marched down Fifth Avenue and entrained for the South. We arrived at Camp Wadsworth, Spartanburg, South Carolina, on October 13th, buried our yellow hat cords for the duration of the war, and settled down to learn from our associates of the former Machine Gun Troop what a machine gun really was and how one should be treated to attain the best results.

When we reached Camp Wadsworth, our first thought (with the memory of McAllen in our minds) was drainage and, with past experience to help us, roadways and sidewalks were constructed in all streets, and officers' shacks (all of one pattern) and a guard house were built. Later, tent floors and sides were delivered to us "F.O.B. Quartermaster Depot"; and many will remember Billy Effinger coming down the long hill towards camp with a four-mule team at the full gallop and an escort wagon loaded with floors and sides—no brakes, and with soldier "ballast" spilling off at every jump. A Roman chariot race was a mild spectacle in comparison. Mention should also be made of the ingenuity, thoroughness, and competitive spirit exhibited in the field of "landscape architecture," both at Van Cortlandt Park and at Camp Wadsworth.

Among the atrocities perpetrated upon us by the War Department during our period of training were singing instructors. One afternoon a musical gentleman called at headquarters and reported that he had been detailed to teach the 105th Machine Gun Battalion how to sing not only in camp but on the march—especially on the march. The Major's pessimistic countenance brightened at these last words. He stated that the battalion was going on a march at once and the first lesson could be given without delay. Now, those "hikes" were really about as tough as they have been pictured. Moreover, the old squadron always sang when it felt like it, and on one of the "hikes" discovered that the Major could not keep step to that classical ditty "They're Wearing Them Higher in Hawaii" and—consequently—became "all hot and bothered." Therefore, this tune had become a sort of national anthem and was sung by the hour. Our new instructor stepped out briskly at first, and bravely started "John Brown's Body," or some similar "cheerful" song; but his voice was drowned in a triumphant roar of "They're wearing them higher in Hawaii." After two hours of that song, at a pace of about five miles per hour, he decided to let someone else teach us to sing, and he dropped out of our lives forever.

One more incident deserves a place on the record. We never did know much about prisoners, and while they were still comparatively scarce in our guardhouse, we had accumulated a few steady customers. The C.O. had his doubts as to whether their treatment in the guardhouse was acting as a deterrent to crime or the reverse, but whenever he endeavored to pay a surprise visit he was spotted by some alert "outpost," so that no just criticism could be made by him upon his arrival for inspection. He determined to learn the truth by other methods and accordingly sent for Lieutenant John Reynolds, who had just completed a tour of duty in charge of the Division prison cage and was, therefore, qualified as an expert. Lieutenant Reynolds was directed to make a quiet and unobtrusive investigation and turn in a report on the real facts of the case. The final paragraph read as follows:

In conclusion I can only say that the relations between guards and prisoners in the 105th Machine Gun Battalion guardhouse can be described as altogether charming. I am sure that the evil-doer who has had the good fortune to be confined in our jail will always look back with the greatest of pleasure upon the good old guardhouse days.

Machine gun drills, schools of all kinds, inspections, and platoon contests filled the closing days of the year. A deep snow storm made our camp look like New York in the days of the 'eighty-eight blizzard; and finally Christmas came and was celebrated in every mess hall, and our first year of preparation for the war was over.

1918

A CURTAIN FALLS

The task assigned to the present historian is completed. While he might write of the incidents of the first three months of 1918, still they consisted only of further and more intensive training and of transfers of officers and men to other organizations, and were overshadowed by the great events of the balance of the year when the battalion, under Major Kenneth Gardner, played its part so well as a unit of an active combat division.[2]

Let us, therefore, ring down the final curtain on our present story. And as that curtain falls and we take a last look at our stage, we see our original squadron, now in the uniform of the 105th Machine Gun Battalion, preparing to sail for France; we see, standing beside it, Squadron A, New York Guard, ready to carry on at home during the war and then, in the post-war reorganization, to become a new squadron of the New York National Guard; and behind these two, outnumbering even their combined strength, we see a great body of "Officers of the Armies of the United States," who will serve in every arm of the service and in nearly every division of those armies—our "graduates," but still—and always—"Squadron A men."

[2] See p. 197.

THE MEXICAN BORDER SERVICE
Knowlton Durham

On the Border by the Rio's hardpan shore.—Squadron Ballad

SQUADRON A Cavalry and Machine Gun Troop departed for Van Cortlandt Park per G.O. 18, AGO, NY, dated June 19, 1916, arriving there June 21, 1916. Mustered into Federal Service June 30, 1916. Left Van Cortlandt Park July 6, 1916, and arrived at McAllen, Texas, July 12, 1916. Left McAllen, Texas, December 15, 1916, and arrived New York City, December 23, 1916. Mustered out of Federal Service December 28, 1916. Strength of Squadron A at muster in, 17 officers and 455 enlisted men. [From the official History of Squadron A as published by the Adjutant General's Office, Albany, New York.]

Monday, June 19, 1916, brought the mobilization order we had been expecting ever since the little affair at Vera Cruz, two years before. For months the men of the squadron had been singing, to the tune of "Hello, Hello, New York Town":

> Hello, hello, Squadron A
> We're going down to Mexico.
> Everything down there is in a mess
> And it's up to Uncle Sam, I guess—
> So put on your breeches and your boots
> Bring along old Bessie [1] if you're sure she shoots,
> Hurry, hurry down this way
> Hello, hello, Squadron A.

---

[1] Bessie was an old Colt machine gun of Spanish War heritage—the special pride and care of the machine gun troop.

So the call had come. The squadron was really to see active service in Mexico. With a very real thrill, that evening the five troops, assembled in the old Ninety-fourth Street armory, listened to Major Bill Wright's brief orders announcing that we were from that moment in the Federal service.

Busy days followed. The mobilization camp was established at Van Cortlandt Park. Recruits began to pour in. The "rookie squad" soon reached and passed the hundred mark. The men were drilled on foot and on horse, taught how to put on a blanket, which part of the horse afforded the safest and easiest approach, how to hold a rifle, and how to keep contact on the skirmish line while advancing through woods. These and many other bits of valuable information were instilled into their willing minds by one of the best of instructors, Latham R. Reed, then a lieutenant in Troop C.

June 24th saw all five troops in camp. Horses began to arrive from the West—green ones, tough ones, old wily ones, mean devilish ones, kickers, buckers, rejects of the Italian government, and—some good ones. Also automobiles rolled in from the South, until the road by the camp looked like the approach to the scene of an international polo match. June 30th we were all assembled, took the Federal oath and were mustered into the service as a squadron of the National Guard of the United States—three years of active duty, three of reserve.

Sunrise, July 6th, saw the tents down as the "General" sounded; and surrounded by a procession of automobiles, the march to Yonkers began and ended. In the heat and dust of the Yonkers freight yard, horses, mules, motor trucks, forage, tentage, and all that goes with a cavalry outfit were loaded on freight cars; and at sundown, with cheers and songs, we bade farewell to old New York for the unknown land of Mexico.

Seven days on train from New York. Stops at Buffalo, Toledo, St. Louis (never-forgotten heat of the East St. Louis stockyards), Dennison, and Houston to unload, feed, water, rest, and reload horses. Crowds at every stop. Welcome and enthusiasm everywhere.

At last, McAllen of the "Magic Valley!" They told us it hadn't rained there for fourteen months. It began the day we arrived and didn't stop for the next three. Mud up to your knees: thick, heavy, sticky mud that cakes your shoes and your horses' legs, and makes grooming the trooper's despair. Work, ye tarriers! Unload that motor truck, empty those dozen cars of horses, lead them down that slippery runway and out through that slough of despond. Load those wagons. Drag the whole business a mile and a half through that swamp. Clear that cactus away. Now, hurry up with the tents. Supper? Wonderful anticlimax to a day of torture. Bed? What can beat the good old loam of Texas?

Uncle Sam presented the squadron with no dude ranch—just a flat clay under foot, covered with mesquite and cactus, kitchen flies, and Sibley tents. With bolos issued to the machine gun troop we attacked the mesquite and cactus, but soon discovered it far more efficient and less blistering to the hands to hire the local "spics," who proved so adept at the business that it became a real delight to watch them. Tent floors came later—purchased out of a common pool. Likewise, canvas covering for the picket lines and even a driven well and gasoline pump—for our camp was located at the end of the only pipe line out from McAllen, which had to supply the 7th and 12th and 1st Cavalry before reaching us, so that except for the hours after midnight all we received was an occasional trickle.

Five months in Texas. Bright days and a blinding sun, with the thermometer climbing to 110 and above in the shade (if you could find any) and no water for washing and precious little for drinking. Wet days, and a camp flooded like a section of Egyptian desert overflowed by the Nile. Dry days, with the Gulf wind sifting sand into your eyes and mouth, filling your tent, and ruining your temper. Hot days, with flies as thick as Jersey mosquitoes, followed by nights when mosquitoes made the Jersey variety look like ministering angels. Cold days, when the wind whipped around and came driving back at sixty miles an hour —Texas Northers, they call them. Lazy days, when there's nothing to do after you've fed, watered, and exercised horses, and cleaned your equipment. Busy days, when you're off at daybreak for a day's maneuvers or a week's hike. Glorious sunrises—we saw every one from July to December. Marvelous moonlight nights, and a good chance that the Major will order a night attack. Then it's saddle up and off at a trot in ten minutes.

A land flat as the ocean bottom, which it once formed; where every bush and tree prick with the sting of a snake; where every bug likes a bite and where you hear the occasional rattle of old diamond-back as you ride across country; where the coyotes come near at midnight, and the pack yelps and snarls as it tears its prey to pieces; where buzzards sail lazily overhead at mid-day, waiting and watching; where doves perched overhead in the moss-hung trees of the river jungle carry on their incessant cooing; where tarantulas and scorpions hide in your blankets and extra breeches, and swarms of flies and "Princeton bugs" infest the camp by day and mosquitoes swarm after sunset; where distance has no bounds and a human being is but an atom in the scheme of things.

A day's work in a cavalry camp begins and ends with care of the horses: reveille at 5:30, then feed horses and police the camp; mess at 6:15; "Boots and saddles" at 7:00; mounted drill at 7:30; recall, 10:30, cleaning equipment, then an hour's grooming, watering, and feeding; mess, 12:30; school, 1:30; stables and water call, 4:00; dismounted drill, 4:30; recall, 5:30; guard mount, 5:40; retreat, 6:00; mess, 6:30; quarters, 9:45; taps and lights out at 10:00.

The mess is fair—the army ration is twenty-eight cents per day per man—bacon, coffee, bread, potatoes, and sugar. We eke out with contributions from each one, add the extras received from home and best girls, and make out fairly well.

The program varies. In July, five men from each of the squadron troops and also four troops of the First Cavalry are assigned to a provisional troop under the command of Captain Bill Putnam, with Stanton Whitney as first lieutenant, Lieutenant Hughes of C Troop, First Cavalry, as second lieutenant, Ray Biglow as first sergeant, and Cort Handy as mess sergeant. (The fame of mess sergeants is usually left unsung, but this one won our undying gratitude by providing us, after one of our tropical hikes, with a huge tub of ice-cold lemonade.) Their task is to scout the trails up and down the Rio Grande on both sides of Hidalgo: learning the crossings under the tutelage of Louis, the bandit guide, who entertains with recitals of the cattle-stealing of Louis de la Rosa, who now, so it is rumored, is planning a raid from just over the river. At Hidalgo is a company of the 28th U.S. Infantry, commanded by Captain Green with a First Lieutenant by the name of Crockett. The officers bunk in the house which Green occupies, the only respectable one in Hidalgo, while the men make themselves at home in their pup tents in the schoolhouse yard. Green and Crockett know of the squadron and are both critical of its discipline, arguing that it really is only a gentleman's agreement on the part of the enlisted men to do what the officers command. Green is known as a stern disciplinarian. His punishments for the slightest infractions of orders are severe, but he is convinced that his method is the only effective one, and implies that we are merely playing soldier. The argument continues night after night between Green and Crockett arguing for their method, and Putnam and Whitney arguing for ours. We return from Hidalgo a few days later; Bill Putnam, riding up the road, meets Crockett, whom he discovers is in search of deserters—about half his company having gone A.W.O.L.—and we learn afterwards that he spent a large part of the summer trying to get back the men who had run away on account of Green's discipline.

In August the squadron escorts the Major General on a week's raid through the ranches north of Mission. Then the squadron gains its border reputation of being the "hardest riding bunch down there." Later there is added, "and the hardest drinking," but that was undeserved, for G.O.7 was in force and Bevo was king. August also brings the first and worst of the Texas Northers, when the whole Division camp came near crossing the International Boundary.

A practice march to Sam Fordyce was on the program. Some time before, the Major decided he would survey the road by automobile, and so started off in his Marmon car, driven by Allie Ball and accompanied by Reune Martin and Captain Putnam. They went up the road by the railroad through Mission as far as Fort Ringgold, and then came back and proceeded down the old military road (the one which Zachary Taylor built and over which he marched his troops to the defeat of the Mexicans a hundred years before) along the river. Every now and then the automobile would get stuck in the mud, but with the help of his three passengers pulling on a rope Allie would be able to work the car out of the mud puddles, until they had gone some four or five miles past Hidalgo and about three miles before reaching Donna Pump, when in a very lonely stretch of road there suddenly appeared a mud puddle larger than any of the others. Allie shouted that he could make it, and put on full speed (estimated at least sixty miles an hour), but the Marmon finally ended up in the very middle of the puddle, fifty yards from shore, the water coming up to the feet of those seated within. The Major thereupon sent Martin and Putnam to walk to Donna Pump and there to telephone back to camp for a truck to pull them out. This was done, and Martin and Putnam thereupon returned and all waited for the truck, which, however, did not appear that night. The mosquitoes were terrible, and in the middle of the night the Major disappeared—but was eventually discovered in the top of a mesquite tree, where, he stated, he had gone to see if he could not get above the

EARLY DAYS AT MCALLEN, 1916

SQUADRON A PICKET LINE, MC ALLEN, 1916
VIEW OF CAMP, MC ALLEN, 1916

mosquito line. No truck having arrived in the morning, Martin and Putnam walked to Donna, and thence returned to camp to find that the relief truck had itself been stuck; but it finally got out and eventually reached the Major, who was pulled out of his predicament.

During the early weeks at McAllen we remained under the delusion that action with the Mexican bandits might be expected at any time. When on duty along the river our patrols were armed with ball cartridge and a real thrill ran down the line when the order came to load, but as time went by we became more and more skeptical about the actuality of war. One amusing incident happened when Troop B was on tour of duty at Mission. The horseshoer was kept at McAllen, so that horses requiring to be shod were sent back under detail. Late one afternoon a detail of four men under a corporal was ordered to take horses back to McAllen. The ride was across country, and as darkness came on the going became more difficult. In attempting to cross a dry irrigation ditch, the Corporal's horse fell and the one he was leading ran away. He was stunned; the others who had been riding ahead missed him but could not find him, and went on to camp. Some time later, when he began to come out of his daze, he pulled out his automatic and fired a number of shots. The reports were heard in camp by the Major, who for a time thought that the camp was about to be attacked. The following morning, when Captain Putnam rode over to McAllen, he was met by the Major with the question as to whether he had heard any firing during the night in the direction of Mission, because he, the Major, had been waked up by very heavy firing. The discreet Captain told him nothing, and in fact did not dare tell him until years later that the "attack on the camp" had been nothing but one of his corporals firing off his revolver at the bottom of an irrigation ditch.

It was eight o'clock one Wednesday morning when the squadron rode west to Sam Fordyce—twenty-one miles of dirt road following close to the one-track railroad. As far as eye can reach, nothing but dead, flat country covered with mesquite and cactus; nothing in sight to relieve monotony except, every four or five miles, a cluster of shacks surrounding one village store—miserably poor dwellings of half-clad Mexicans, adobe walls, thatched roofs, barred or latticed windows. Pigs, hogs, chickens, and other pets enliven the front dooryards, bare flat clay, without trees, bushes, or flowers. As we ride by, the inhabitants flock out to stare stolidly at us: a man, two or three women, six to twelve children. Occasionally a youngster bolder than the others repeats monotonously as we pass, "Hallo, boy"; but as they speak no English, and only a few of us know their lingo, we usually ride by staring with mutual suspicion.

Two o'clock, and the glorious sight of water greets our eyes—a resaca —almost forgotten delight—where once the Rio Grande coursed until it grew tired of the general monotony of the scenery and moved its way southward. Swims (our first in two months), luncheon and rest while the horses grazed and then watered—a slow, difficult process as the banks were steep. On the road again at six, and the end of our march at Sam Fordyce at 6:45—a flat stretch of hard clay. Officers quickly disappeared with those of the 2nd Texas Infantry. (Evening of moonlight, good dinner, no G.O.7, and the music of guitar and mandolin.) Making the camp was left in charge of the first sergeants; and fifteen minutes later, picket lines up, horses unsaddled and fed, shelter tents up and guard posted, the squadron fell in for mess. In the middle of the night the regular officer attached to the company of the 2nd Texas Infantry awakened the Major in his shelter-tent, informing him that he thought there was a raid from Mexico over the river, as a fire was burning brightly some three miles from our camp by the side of the river, and shooting had been heard. A platoon of the 2nd Texas had been sent by motor truck, and he wanted a cavalry platoon to assist it. The Major ordered out a platoon from Troop B, which speedily mounted up and galloped down the road toward the fire, with a regular officer acting as guide. The night was pitch black and the men had a feeling that they might really get into some action, but as they neared the scene of the fire they met the truck with the platoon of the 2nd Texas returning, and the report that there was no raid. A Mexican's house on the river caught fire and the owner had been shooting off his gun to obtain help. Disappointed that there was to be no bloodshed, the platoon returned to camp, "and so to bed."

Five-fifteen A.M. reveille next morning, and on the road at eight. Only ten miles that day—the thermometer hit above 120—and we made an early camp and loafed the long afternoon through. Friday we were off at 7:30 and at Madero by 10:00, passing through Oyo de Agua on the way, where there had been a Mexican raid in the spring and several American soldiers shot. There a "norther" hit us. The Gulf wind shifted to the northeast. Rain came with the wind, then the deluge, then cold. By noon the wind was so strong the Major ordered our return to camp. At two o'clock, when we arrived, it was a gale and the thermometer was below 50. It took every man in the outfit to keep that camp from blowing away, but the only thing that disappeared was G.O.7—and no one died of chills.

By midnight the storm blew itself out, and the Saturday sun ushered in one of the hottest days of our lives, so we dried out and cleaned up and on the seventh day rested from our labors—rested as much as we were allowed to by a pest of flies and midges which were sucked in by the retreating storm.

September brought a week's target practice for the Machine Gun Troop at Penitas, and guard duty for Troops A, C and D at Monte Cristo, and for B at Mission; also the famous Frontier Day and the no less famous review on Whitehouse Field for General (Galloping Jim) Parker. In October, drills became more interesting as the horses rounded into shape. The 1st Cavalry horse show brought a touch of Piping Rock. Squadron and Division maneuvers added interest; and then occurred the thrilling battle of Hidalgo, and the wild cavalry charge through the streets of that sleepy town, ending with the rout of the Red forces. Then occurred also the field firing practice at La Gloria, when the squadron made the high record of any squadron or battalion in the National Guard. November brought river patrol duty —and duck shooting—and for the Machine Gun Troop two weeks at the school at Harlingen, and a record-breaking, forty-mile night ride back to camp. Camp pets became the vogue: dogs, burros, goats, cats, a parrot, a bald-headed eagle, Raymond and Arthur—our beloved ducks —and little "G.O.7"—our six-weeks-old burro—so called because he drank only milk; and at the end, of course, Thanksgiving and turkey. December, best of all, brought the orders—long rumored, long waited, and always doubted.

How, in this brief space, can one make real the thousand experiences of that Texas campaign—the drudgery of the daily routine, or the memorable hours off duty when we followed the river trails or rode across country through the cactus and mesquite? How describe the despair of "stables" the morning after a cloudburst, with the horses over their fetlocks in Texas mud, or the delights of a fast trot by moonlight to Pharr or Madero? How picture the deadly night hours of sentry duty, or the welcome freedom from routine, when they sent us down to guard the river crossings? How tell the monotony of the early days when we watered horses twice a day at the resaca half a mile from camp; or the excitement of an early morning dash to catch the Reds in rear, or take that one controlling position, over east of the irrigation pump; or the thrill of a wild gallop past the Governor at the Divisional review?

Five months from our arrival the song had changed—the same tune but different words.

> Hello, hello, Squadron A
> We're going back to New York town.
> Everything up there is at its best
> And we're going home to take a rest,
> So put away your breeches and your boots,
> Get out your dinner coats and full-dress suits.
> Hurry, hurry up that way;
> The high-balls are rolling along Broadway.

ADJUTANT'S CALL.

THE DEPOT TROOP
LATER, SQUADRON A, NEW YORK GUARD

FOLLOWING the contribution by General Bridgman of the story of the New York Hussars, papers were requested from Major Wright and also from the three officers who successively commanded Squadron A, New York Guard. As the following three papers were prepared without conference there is some repetition; but as they are all brief it is thought best to print them, without change.

GUARD MOUNTING.

THE DEPOT UNITS: ORGANIZATION AND DEVELOPMENT
1916–1917
Latham G. Reed

Back to the Army again, Sergeant.
—KIPLING

No van todos soldados a la guerra.—Spanish Proverb

THE above title has a twofold application at this point in the genesis of Squadron A of today. It opens the account of such depot units as have had their place in our history; and it indexes the legal steps of their establishment.

Depot organizations are formed under the provisions of the military law of New York State. Provisions generally and specifically as to this outfit of ours are set forth in the circular issued by Major Wright to all former members in 1915. Relevant quotations from that circular are given below.

The circular was dated October 6, 1915, and addressed to ex-members of Squadron A.

For some time there has existed in the Squadron . . . what is known as a Depot Battalion, the purpose of which is to have an organization to assist the Squadron in case the latter should be ordered into the U.S. service . . . by securing, training and forwarding recruits and, at the same time, being in readiness to perform the Squadron's home duty of aiding the civil authorities in case of necessity. . . . With the approval of the Major General commanding the Division N.G.N.Y., the Squadron intends to attempt the organization of at least a Depot Troop complete in all grades from officers to privates with a definite length of service. I believe that this plan is in line with the proper system of preparedness and will greatly increase the efficiency and prestige of the Squadron, and will be a decided advance towards a thoroughly complete and proper organization. I trust the Squadron will have the honor of leading the Guard in the formation of the above mentioned Troop and of showing that the idea can be carried out by an organization possessed of a body of ex-members who still retain their interest. Give the matter your very serious consideration and signify your intention of joining, if you find it possible, by mailing the enclosed card at once.

The foregoing was followed on October 18, 1915, by another circular of Major Wright's to ex-members, in which he writes:

The response to the circular of October 6, 1915, has exceeded expectations, and it will be possible to organize a Troop at war strength of 3 officers and 100 enlisted men. It is desired to complete the organization of this Troop at once, and for this purpose all those who have signified intention of joining and any others who are interested are requested to meet in the Assembly Room of the Squadron A Armory at 8.30 P.M. on Friday evening, October 29th. It is expected that the Troop will be officially recognized by the State under the provisions of the Military Law, 1915, Pars. 80, 80a and 120, and application for this organization has already been made to the Adjutant General.

It seems unnecessary to quote from Sections 80 and 80a. Section 120 provides that when a regiment, the companies serving in the coast defense command, the organized battalions of the corps of engineers or a squadron or battalion not part of a regiment shall be in the actual service of the United States, the governor shall organize depot units as follows: a battalion to take the place of a regiment and such number of companies, troops, or batteries as he may determine to take the place of other units. Such depot units shall not be called on for duty outside of the state except in case of emergency, but the members thereof may be transferred by the governor to fill temporary or permanent vacancies or to make up a deficiency in strength of the organization for which the depot unit is formed. The governor from time to time and *in advance* of the entry of the organization into the actual service of the United States may appoint and commission officers necessary for the depot unit or units. The governor *in advance* of an organization entering into the actual service of the United States may authorize the issue for its depot unit or units of such arms, equipment, colors, camp, and garrison equippage as may be necessary for the proper performance of the duty required by this chapter.

Major Wright closed by saying:

I desire to express to the ex-members of the squadron the deep appreciation of the Squadron Commander and the active members of the squadron for the interest exhibited by the ex-members in this project and the hearty and immediate response they have made thereto.

By order of Major Wright, on December 6, 1915, a circular was sent to the volunteers calling a meeting for the purpose of organizing a Depot Troop, Squadron A Cavalry, N.G.N.Y., as authorized by S.O.190, A.G.O., 1915, to be held at the armory on December 20 at 8.30 P.M.

It was stated in the circular that, as 148 men had signified their intention of joining and as the maximum number now authorized is three officers and one hundred enlisted men, precedence in enlistment would be given to men attending the meeting and in the order of their original application.

It was announced that Captain Latham G. Reed had been nominated for the commander of the troop and authorized to nominate other officers and non-commissioned officers.

It is a trait of Major Wright to say the civil thing if possible and, when he wrote as above that the number of responses to the first circular was gratifying, one may suppose that he expected perhaps two-thirds of the number of actual volunteers. In view of the great number of the squadron's discharged and dropped men and what was obviously being prepared for, it does not seem a very tumultuous rush. All the more credit to those who did volunteer! And all the more credit to those who remained to perform their military duty as privates and minor officers with little encouragement or aid from the state until nearly two years elapsed, notwithstanding the duty of the Governor as above stated.

The state's neglect adequately to support us and the inspection to be held in April, referred to below, bring to mind the advertisement —"Mr. and Mrs. Cohen have cast-off clothing of all descriptions and invite inspection."

This is the place to set forth the Muster-in-Roll containing the names of those who came forward; but, as nearly all and some others are in the depot squadron later organized, it is not printed, and the roster of the squadron as later formed will be found below.

Here it should be said that the Muster-in-Roll appears to be the only record of the squadron's depot units to be found at the armory. The names of such men as joined after the formation of the squadron are unknown to the writer; they have the honor of being unknown soldiers if not forgotten men.

The troop was mustered into state service on March 14, 1916.

Two former captains of the regular squadron volunteered, quite content, and entitled, virtually, to appointments as two lieutenancies in the Depot Troop; and so with other volunteers who had been officers or non-commissioned officers in the regular squadron.

After taking command of the Depot Troop in March, orders were issued by the writer requiring the inoculation of the men of the troop against typhoid (with certain exceptions), and appointing the non-commissioned officers and grades, as farriers, cooks, etc.

Notice was given that, under M.R.961, there would be an inspection and muster of the troop at the armory in April. Men were required to be provided with uniform, cap, shirt, breeches, and shoes; N.C.O.'s with proper chevrons. It was stated that a machine gun platoon might be organized and that the project would be given every encouragement.

Rifle and pistol teams were organized, and competitions arranged.

It was also stated in the orders that there had been commendation on the behavior and appearance of the troop on its entrance into the National Guard on March 14.

The men were notified that, at the coming inspection, they might be asked by the inspecting officers concerning their knowledge of "N.Y. Military Law and Military Regulations, Basic Course for Cavalry," by Captain Lincoln C. Andrews, and of a pamphlet called "Fire Control," by Captain Gleaves, U.S.A.; that time given to the study of these books would be worth while; and they would be an essential minimum if there is any real belief that some or all of our men might be called upon to be officers in some new levy of troops.

In June, 1916, by verbal orders of Adjutant General Stotesbury, at Van Cortlandt, the Depot Troop was ordered to reorganize as Depot Squadron A with two troops, and the writer as major thereof. This was followed by regularly printed and filed orders which, presumably, are to be found in the Adjutant General's office.

Subsequent to the order creating the Depot Squadron, under A.O.135, A.G.O., N.Y., July 1, 1916, a third troop—C—was authorized, and First Lieutenant W. R. Maloney and Second Lieutenant Rodman Gilder, transferred from Squadron A, were assigned as its officers.

The writer thereupon issued orders:

No. 1 taking command of the Depot Squadron, dated July 10, 1916.

No. 2 dated July 14, 1916, referred to orders issued by Major Wright on July 4 as of June 29, 1916, dividing the Depot Troop into Troops A and B, forming Depot Squadron A.

SQUADRON A

The roster of the new squadron was as follows:

HEADQUARTERS

Major Latham G. Reed
1st Lieut. Adjutant Howard C. Smith
2nd Lieut. Quartermaster Lewis Rowland Brown
Sergeant Major Alfred Roelker, Jr.
Q.M. Sergeant Abel I. Smith, Jr.

DEPOT TROOP A	DEPOT TROOP B
Captain Herbert Barry	Captain Emerson R. Newell
1st Lieut. Ward, Henry M.	1st Lieut. Hall, James W.
2d Lieut. Hoppin, Gerard B.	2d Lieut. Sullivan, Leonard B.
Sergeant Jones, F. W., Jr.	Sergeant Coleman, C. W.
Corporal Jenny, I. H.	Corporal Danforth, N.
Satterlee, H. S.	Howard, C. W.
Saltus, R. S.	Whitfield, H. D.
Saddler, Heroy, J. H.	Farrier, Stowell, E. E.
Horseshoer, Olney, P. B., Jr.	Cook, Montgomery, H. P. A.
Cook, Holbrook, J. B.	Trumpeter, Peck, H. M.
Trumpeter, Tilt, A.	Private Barrett, G. H.
Wagoner, Martin, E. E. I.	Behr, K. H.
Private Adams, N.	Bottomley, J. F.
Belknap, W. P.	Brooks, C. A.
Bodman, G. M.	Butler, C. S.
Bodman, H. L.	Cairns, Douglas W.
Borden, A.	Cary, E. M.
Bradley, S. R.	Cattus, John V. A.
Chambers, W. R.	Coulson, R. E.
Cheseborough, F. W.	Crocker, G. A., Jr.
Day, H. M.	De Haven, W. B.
Dealy, D. E.	Dickinson, A. G., Jr.
Debevoise, P.	Duer, E. R.
D'Este, J. L.	Fayerweather, C. S.
Edwards, J. A.	Flannigan, H. C.
Edwards-Ficken, H.	Frederick, K. T.
Geer, A.	Hathaway, S. S.
Gould, E.	Hine, F. W.
Haight, S. P.	Howell, L. M.
Herbert, R. L.	Ijams, J. H.
Hollister, G. C.	Keppel, F. P.
Hopkins, L. S. R.	Lee, J. D.

DEPOT TROOP A

Leale, L.
Leech, R.
Libby, W. G.
McKinlay, W. B.
Marshall, R. P.
Maynard, G. W.
Mellen, Clark
Peabody, G. R.
Preston, S. D.
Randolph, R. J., Jr.
Reeve, H. L.
Schwarz, H. F.
Smith, A. C.
Smith, H. B.
Stiger, W. D.
Stone, C. F., Jr.
Sumner, A. C.
Trimble, R. F.
Turner, S.
Walker, A. D.
Weeks, R. F.
Weston, G. S.
White, R. V.
Willis, R. S.
Zinsser, R.

DEPOT TROOP B

Lee, Ronald C.
Lenssen, N. F.
Logan, W. J.
Marston, H. S.
Merrill, C. E., Jr.
Mygatt, G.
Neal, C. T.
Neeser, R. W.
Nicoll, C.
Noyes, D. C.
Orth, C. D., Jr.
Peck, E. J.
Rodgers, F., Jr.
Rolston, R. G.
Sloane, J.
Smith, E. D.
Sutton, R. D.
Thorne, J. N.
Tilton, S.
Travis, A. C.
Van Sinderen, H. B.
Wadhams, W. H.
Ward, A. L.
Wardwell, A.
Wood, W. F.
Wyckoff, C. P.

DEPOT TROOP C

1st Lieut. Maloney, Wm. R.
2nd. Lieut. Gilder, Rodman

It will be seen that there was a large enough personnel in the troop to man a small staff and non-commissioned staff and two troops.

Troop C consisted of two members, both officers; and as Lieutenant Maloney soon resigned, Lieutenant Gilder must have exercised self-command to continue to contemplate the emptiness of mere rank.

It will be remembered that the regular squadron departed for the border in July, 1916. It fell to the lot of the commander of the Depot Squadron to have something to do with the horses gathered at Van Cortlandt Park to mount the departing squadron. With the horses belonging to the squadron, the private horses and those from the bunch collected in the West, the squadron was mounted; but it is doubtful if such a savage lot of brutes was ever gathered together as was collected from the plains of Kansas and other states in the West: hammer-headed, ewe-necked, long-maned horses that had certainly never been under the saddle. Many of them were simply wicked and quite a number of men belonging to the squadron were injured in getting them off the train and bringing them to Van Cortlandt. The pick of them, of course, was taken, but some fifty or sixty horrors were left after the departure of the squadron. It is to be hoped that they were devoured by wild beasts, because that was the only proper end for them. The writer presented to the Ex-Members' Association a Civil War Cavalry bit; a piece of control as savage as were the animals that must have been supplied to the Northern cavalry.

There was little of interest outside drills and instruction at the armory for the depot members to do. One or two detachments from outside of New York were piloted through the intricacies of New York streets from Westchester to some ferry; and finally the Depot Squadron turned out to escort the squadron, on its arrival in New York from the border late in December, from West Twenty-third Street to the armory. The column was reviewed by the Governor of New York at the University Club.

After the return of the regular squadron the Depot Squadron, although its official existence continued, had, of course, little if anything to do. On the declaration of war by the United States, the task of starting the vast machinery for raising, financing, munitioning, feeding, clothing, and transporting a great army of American soldiers was undertaken. Man after man of ours was called to duties doubtless more important than those of a soldier in a train band. Such men applied to be discharged or dropped and, as superior authority in the state's military headquarters was liberal about it, such requests were, almost as a matter of course, granted.

Efforts to get enlistment into the Depot Squadron from within and without the old membership were not encouraging. They were made. Whether, after the writer's declining the majority in the New York Guard, the membership picked up is not known to him, but certainly the home squadron did most worthily hold the fort. Though ready, it had no opportunity to follow the enthusiastic responses of the Irish troop whose commander, on the eve of a fight, turned to his men and, waving his saber, loudly called, "Will yez fight or will yez run?" "We will! we will!" came the glorious shout. "Yez will WHAT?" "We will NOT!"

It is to be remembered that the depot outfits were up to this time part of the National Guard of New York. On August 3, 1917, the propriety of not continuing to designate the home guard as "National" became apparent; and such alterations in the military law were made that the depot units were constituted the New York Guard instead; and the writer was continued in command of Squadron A, New York Guard. On August 17, 1917, Captain Newell resigned, and Captain Alfred Wendt was commissioned Captain and assigned to Troop B.

Later, nominations were sent to headquarters and to the Adjutant General of the state for new commissions in the New York Guard. The writer received the issued written nomination to be major of Squadron A, New York Guard, but declined the nomination and was placed on the reserve. And so ended the second and last edition of his military service in the State of New York.

In view of the foregoing and the long unrecorded and little recognized service which members of the Depot Troop and Squadron gave without financial aid from the state—reach-me-down uniforms, little equipment, no secretarial assistance in headquarters—it must not be considered invidious to any other member if the writer names especially for his assistance and loyalty Lieutenant Rollin S. Saltus, who was adjutant of the squadron under the writer after the resignations of Lieutenant Smith and Lieutenant Maloney, and until long afterwards.

NOTE. On the day I finished the foregoing sketch, one who was mustered in to old Troop A in April, 1889, with me, Oliver B. Bridgman—Lieutenant, Captain, Major, and head of our Ex-Members' Association—died. I believe he and I were two of the three or four surviving original members; and probably I am the only man who had been with him in all such capacities. Orators and fluent writers will with just eloquence tell of the importance of General Bridgman to all the bodies in which he devoted energy and wisdom, but only one or two others now living can be affected in recollection as I am by General Bridgman's death, and in one's seventy-eighth year such events speak pretty plainly. I lay my wreath of praise and appreciation at his grave.

THE DEPOT TROOP, THE DEPOT SQUADRON, AND SQUADRON A, N.Y. GUARD: A SHORT INTERLUDE 1918

Herbert Barry

Bugles blown at morn, the summons comes—R. W. GILDER

IN 1898 Squadron A, N.G.N.Y., was called upon to supply a troop of cavalry for the Spanish-American War. This was done by organizing from the squadron personnel a volunteer troop. The squadron continued to function in New York, supplying extensive replacements to the volunteer Troop A.

In 1916, when the squadron was called into Federal service for duty on the Mexican border, the entire squadron moved out; and in anticipation of this a Depot Troop had been organized, with Captain Latham G. Reed in command, to function in its absence and occupy its quarters. Former members of the squadron, including this writer, formed the personnel. His first commission in this organization is dated March 13, 1916, and designates him "First Lieutenant, Depot Troop, Squadron A Cavalry, National Guard, New York."

A later commission, dated July 7, 1916, designated him Captain, "Depot Cavalry, National Guard, New York," which indicates the formation of the Depot Squadron during the intervening period.

Upon the return of the squadron from duty on the border, the Depot Cavalry suspended activities; but when in 1917 Squadron A was again mustered into Federal service, the Depot Cavalry was reassembled. Official records recite: "Depot units organized," on April 20, 1917; and on August 3, 1917, by order issued from the office of the Adjutant General of the State of New York, the organization was redesignated "Squadron A Cavalry, New York Guard." Major Latham G. Reed continued in command.

It was about twenty years before that Major Reed had been appointed captain of the then newly created Third Troop, and the present writer had with pleasure and enthusiasm collaborated with him in building up that organization. In 1917 he aided, with like interest, in organizing and building up the depot units and Squadron A Cavalry, New York Guard.

Officers and men took up the study and practice of drill formations totally unlike those familiar to them in their earlier service, and with energy and zeal molded into military organization a personnel that had earned honorable discharges, in some instances, twenty or twenty-five years earlier. The roster of these older men returning to service in any capacity open to them is an interesting document.

On one occasion a week-end tour of duty at the squadron farm gave opportunity for combined drill with one of the troops in Federal service, and much emulation resulted. The older men wanted to show that they were still soldier material, and the younger ones wanted to show that they were worthy successors. It was a success all around.

Much to the regret of his associates, Major Reed retired in December, 1917. This threw on the present writer, then senior captain, the burden of responsibility; and the other officers gave him the same cordial cooperation that he had endeavored to give to Major Reed. The tireless and self-effacing activities of our adjutant, First Lieutenant Rollin S. Saltus, will always remain in our memory.

While the present writer had participated in person throughout the period of Major Reed's command, his personal participation during his own tenure as commanding officer was brief. His commission as "Major, Cavalry, New York Guard" is dated December 17, 1917; and on January 17, 1918, on reaching his office in Wall Street, he found an official telegram from the War Department directing him to report for duty at the officers' training school at Spartanburg. Having already been rejected on account of age, when seeking admission to an earlier school, and having made no application for admission to this one, he had misgivings as to the authenticity of the message; but on telephoning Assistant Secretary of War Keppel, who had been a former member of the old Troop 3, he found there was no doubt of its genuineness.

He also had qualms as to whether the authorities at Albany would consent to the newly appointed Major absenting himself so speedily from his command, but this problem was solved by direct application to the Brigade Commander, General George R. Dyer, who wholeheartedly endorsed the project and granted leave of absence.

Within the next forty-eight hours Major Herbert Barry, New York

SQUADRON A CLUB, MC ALLEN, 1916
WATERING HORSES AT A RESACA, MC ALLEN, 1916

SQUADRON A IN REVIEW, ON THE BORDER, 1916
OUTPOST ON THE RIO GRANDE

Guard, became also Private Barry in Federal service at the Officers' Training School, Camp Wadsworth, South Carolina.

This dual position produced at least one quaint episode. The Chief Justice of the Appellate Division for the Second Department desiring to secure a copy of his son's record as a member of the squadron sent a letter to Major Herbert Barry, commanding Squadron A, New York Guard; the communication was transmitted from the armory of Squadron A to headquarters of the 27th Division at Camp Wadsworth, South Carolina, and, through the channel, was passed by endorsement ultimately to Company A, Officers' Training School, where Private Barry received the communication intended for him as Major Barry.

At this period the former Squadron A, N.G.N.Y., had become the 105th Machine Gun Battalion, and its streets were quite near those of the school. It was an odd coincidence that in one of these streets of the machine gun battalion was quartered Sergeant Herbert Barry, Jr., who enlisted in May, 1917.

At the conclusion of the school, Private Barry, with only a small piece of white tape on his sleeve to distinguish him from any other private as a graduate of the school, arrived on furlough in New York, and on May 4, 1918, received telegraphic notification of his commission. A trip to Governors Island followed, where the oath of office was administered by Lieutenant Colonel Thomas B. Clarke, Jr., also formerly of Squadron A; and thereupon automatically Private Barry became Major Barry in the Federal service, and ceased to be Major Barry, Squadron A, New York Guard.

He knew that the responsibility of the latter office had already been capably handled by Captain Wendt, and was gratified that Captain Wendt would no longer be delayed in securing the rank commensurate with his activities.

SQUADRON A CAVALRY, N.Y. GUARD: CARRYING ON AND FULFILLMENT

January, 1918–June 12, 1919

Alfred Wendt

It ain't the individual, nor the army as a whole,
But the everlastin' teamwork of every bloomin' soul.
—J. Mason Knox

A LETTER from Major William R. Wright, commanding Squadron A, N.Y.N.G., to the Association of Ex-Members reads in part as follows:

August 10, 1917

In accordance with orders just published the *Depot Squadron* will hereafter be "Squadron A Cavalry, New York Guard." The law of the state prescribes that a force of organized militia shall be maintained in the State at all times. The Depot Squadron now becomes the squadron as it was before the Dick and Hay Bills. Whatever military organization the federal government may adopt during or after the present war, whatever may happen to the present active squadron, it seems certain that Squadron A, New York Guard, if properly supported by you, will remain in existence, to afford a sure and certain means of carrying on unbroken the life and traditions that have always been ours.

Nothing can better state the aims and purposes of all of us who served in Squadron A, N.Y. Guard, than the above words of Major Wright. To uphold the traditions of the old squadron, now in the field as the 105th Machine Gun Battalion, to build up the new squadron embodying the ideals of the old, was the goal toward which we were striving.

When Squadron A left the armory in the summer of 1917 to be mobilized into the 105th Machine Gun Battalion at Van Cortlandt Park, it took with it all equipment, arms, and horses.

When, having obtained leave of absence to attend the Federal Training Camp, Major Barry, my predecessor, turned over the command of the squadron to me in January, 1918, the squadron was still without horses.

At this time our organization consisted of Troops A and B, in command, respectively, of Captain Melton Douglas Cole and Captain Alfred Wendt (later, First Lieutenant J. W. Hall commanding). The squadron staff was as follows:

Adjutant	First Lieutenant Rollin S. Saltus
Supply Officer	Second Lieutenant Louis Howland Brown
Inspector of Small Arms Practice	First Lieutenant T. Towar Bates
Medical Officer	Captain E. C. Brenner
Honorary Chaplain	Rev. Frank Warfield Crowder, D. D.

The two troops soon grew to full strength (65) and a third troop was mustered in on April 18, 1918, as Troop C, Captain T. Towar Bates commanding. This troop also soon grew to full strength.

In April, 1918, the squadron received from Major Edwin Gould and Mr. John H. Iselin a present of several new Lewis machine guns. These guns were assigned to Troop C under Captain Bates, and the troop thereafter became the Machine Gun Troop and did good work as such.

After Captain Bates assumed command of Troop C the department of small arms practice was assigned to First Lieutenant Karl T. Frederick, a former member of the squadron and winner of the pistol competition in the Olympic Games.

Our recruiting problem was not an easy one. With the draft calling men into National service, and with others of our personnel continuously entering Federal service, the recruiting committee was kept busy. About 100 per cent of the original troop strength in this way passed through our organization into Federal service, but the required full strength of the three troops was kept intact at all times. Sergeant William B. de Haven and his committee deserve praise for their work.

We also owe our appreciation to Sergeant Alpheus Geer, a former member of the squadron, well known in the amateur boxing world, for taking charge of the department of physical training. One-half hour of every drill was devoted to shadow boxing, sparring, and other exercises, which greatly helped to keep up the enthusiasm of the men in their work.

The question of providing horses for the squadron proved an interesting one. Every former squadron mount was taken into Federal service by the organization leaving for the field. We had no longer any state military fund available. The trustees of the civil funds of the former squadron advanced to us six thousand dollars, secured by personal notes of several of our members. With this amount, forty-three horses were purchased by our horse committee and became squadron property.

Owing to the untiring efforts of this committee—First Lieutenant Gurdon M. Maynard, Lieutenant Alfred Borden, and Lieutenant Grimwood—in combing not only the Federal horse markets but every private source possible, the horses purchased were of exceptional quality. This is evidenced by the following list of winnings in both the National and other horse shows: Six cups—1 championship—31 firsts—27 seconds—29 thirds and 28 fourths.

A detailed report of the various horses may be found in a pamphlet, "A Report of the Work of Squadron A Cavalry, N.Y. Guard, Dec. 1917 to Dec. 1918," in possession of the Ex-Members' Association at the armory. This success did a great deal to place the squadron before the eyes of the horse world, and incidentally helped recruiting.

Drills were increased from the old twenty-four a year to forty-eight a year.

Under Lieutenant Frederick inter-troop rifle and pistol matches were a great stimulant to small arms efficiency.

Various outdoor troop camps and three squadron camps, and the state officers' training camp in September, 1918 (named Camp Whitman after our War Governor), helped increase the efficiency of our officers and enlisted men.

Our squadron supplied the horses for Camp Whitman. Under command of Captain T. Towar Bates this horse detail left the squadron farm at Nyack, August 30, 1918, at 6:30 A.M., and reached Camp Whitman at midnight on the same day, having marched forty-eight and one-half miles. Horses and men were in excellent condition.

Captain Herbert Barry having successfully completed his training at Spartanburg and been commissioned major, National Army, U.S., I was commissioned Major, Squadron A, N.Y.G., on May 21, 1918.

On March 24, 1919, we had the honor, together with the Ex-Members' Association, of acting as escort to the 105th Machine Gun

Battalion, 27th Division, U.S.A., on their return home. We met them at their arrival at East Thirty-fourth Street, and the march home, escorting the war organization of about seven hundred strong, was one of the events of our squadron history.

As already mentioned, it had always been the purpose of all our officers to enter the state service during the war, not only to organize a cavalry organization for use of the state but to continue the squadron as a cavalry organization until the end of the war, when a return home of our war organization would make a merging possible. In this way the history of the squadron would remain unbroken.

This spirit was well expressed at a dinner given to the officers of the 105th Machine Gun Battalion by the officers of Squadron A, N.Y.G. One of the overseas officers said, in substance, "Although of course we were officially the 105th Machine Gun Battalion, we always felt that we were Squadron A in the field." With such a feeling of comradeship between field and home troops the future of Squadron A was assured.

In the spring of 1919 Captain Bates resigned from the New York Guard, owing to pressure of business, and Captain John Reynolds, a former member of Squadron A and subsequently a captain in the 105th Machine Gun Battalion, was commissioned a Captain of Cavalry, New York Guard, and took command of Troop C, N.Y.G. Captain Reynolds was the first "overseas" officer to come back into our organization—the first to reestablish the link between our home and the overseas command so vital for our future success.

On Memorial Day, May, 1919, all Manhattan units of the New York Guard paraded and were reviewed by Major General O'Ryan, Division Commander of the 27th Division, A.E.F., and his staff. Our squadron passed the reviewing stand, well mounted, well uniformed, and armed. We had a full corps of buglers sounding the cavalry marches as we passed the stand, with a squadron composed of staff, headquarters-detachment, and three troops with machine gun detail. Our silk cavalry standards were presented to us by General Oliver B. Bridgman, and we gratefully acknowledge the gift.

When I recall the words of Major Wright, quoted at the beginning of this narrative, I cannot but feel that we "kept the *faith*," as he asked us to do.

Recognizing the great importance of having a commanding officer of war experience and distinguished service overseas take over command of the squadron, we were particularly fortunate in obtaining the consent of Major Nathaniel H. Egleston, U.S.A., a former member of Squadron A, to do so. In taking this step we of Squadron A Cavalry, N.Y.G., felt we had fulfilled our mission and our responsibility toward our overseas comrades, and that our organization would go to further successes and efficiency with an unbroken service record as a cavalry organization.

A review of the squadron was tendered Major Egleston and soon after, upon my request, I was transferred to the state reserve list as a major of cavalry, to take effect June 12, 1919, and Major Egleston assumed command of Squadron A, N.Y.G., on July 14, 1919.

Before ending this report I desire to express to all my comrades of Squadron A Cavalry, N.Y.G., my appreciation of, and thanks for, their loyal cooperation and untiring support during the time of my command. I also beg to express to General George Dyer, our brigade commander, my appreciation of his many helpful suggestions and kindly acts of encouragement which were of great service to us.

1917-1919
THE WORLD WAR PERIOD

Your old men shall dream dreams, your young men shall see visions.
—Joel 2:28.

For the purposes of the narrative this crucial period is considered under the following heads: (1) The Roll of Honor: A tribute to those who died in the service; (2) The Roll of Service of those who had served in Squadron A; (3) The 105th Machine Gun Battalion, and its distinguished record.

The Roll of Honor is the list of our honored dead: those who made the supreme sacrifice. It includes those who died on the battlefield, and those who died of wounds or sickness while still in service. It is the list of those who did not return from the Great Adventure; who, having put on the uniform, never again returned to civilian life. In this recital the list of officers includes those who, having served in the squadron before our entry into the World War, then volunteered and served as officers in other units. The list of those not officers includes both the enlisted men of the 105th Machine Gun Battalion who died in service, and also ex-members who served as enlisted men in other organizations.[1]

[1] An asterisk (*) indicates one who served in another unit than the Machine Gun Battalion.

To Arms.

THE ROLL OF HONOR

Hero and patriot . . . the glory and safety of his country.—RUSKIN

> To you from failing hands we throw
> The torch; be yours to hold it high.
> —McCRAE, "In Flanders Fields"

OFFICERS

John Giraud Agar, Jr.*
Arthur D. Alexander *
Charles D. Baker
Raynal Cawthorne Bolling *
Belvedere Brooks *
Fritz L. Dressler *
John Fine *
Herbert Groesbeck, Jr.*
Thomas Addis Emmet Harris *
Sheldon E. Hoadley *
Frank Wakefield Koch *
Edward Jules Lamarche *
James Ely Miller *
Marshall G. Peabody *
James Jackson Porter *
Gordon L. Rand *
William Bradford Turner *
Russell T. Walker *
Rae Wygant Whidden *
Earl C. Williams *

ENLISTED MEN

KILLED IN ACTION

George O. S. Carr
Harold W. Chestnut
Matthew D. Cleary
Edward A. Day
John J. Doyle
John J. Dunn
Edward J. Durney
George Evans
Fred A. Glasser
Sherman R. Greene
Emil Hubsch
Theodore L. Johnson
Alcan H. Levy
Henry T. Mohr
Arthur S. Moran
Edward H. Munroe
Eugene J. Murphy
William J. O'Connell
James Jellis Page *
William F. Pauly
Charles Pilkington
Louis Roeper, Jr.
Christopher J. Schumacher
Thomas J. Sheilds
Albert L. Simendinger
Lester W. Smith
Emil Tintera
Howard A. Van Dohlen
David I. Westland
Eugene E. Wilson
David Wischer
Charles S. Woodruff
Joseph J. Wynn
Oswald Zinkand

SQUADRON A

DIED OF WOUNDS

Lawrence T. Ballard
Frederick W. Bodamer
George B. Cosgrove
Edward J. Lange
Henry J. Pilger
Harry Reinhold

Henry Montgomery Suckley *

DIED IN SERVICE

Lloyd S. Allen
James J. Bealin, Jr.
Francis W. Clancy
Frank Currie
Frank P. Curry
Stephen H. Dorr, Jr.*
Philip M. Drabble
Harry F. Dulhagen, Jr.
Frank H. Ellis
Ramon J. Kelly
Thomas P. Kenny
Albert H. Lanzer
Harry McGinness
Edward Nord
John A. Osterberg *
Van Horn Peale
Andrew W. Rolff
Henry S. Sherwood

William C. Taylor

* * * * * *

Mort au champ d'honneur

The valiant never taste of death but once.
—SHAKESPEARE, "Julius Caesar"

TAPS.

THE ROLL OF SERVICE

Quit yourselves like men.—I Samuel 4:9

THE history prepared by Colonel Stanton Whitney includes the "Roll of Service" mentioned in our introductory paper. It is a descriptive list of individuals, including those who served in the squadron before it became the Machine Gun Battalion, and later served in the war as officers in other units. A printed pamphlet of the Ex-Members' Association dated March, 1920, shows the number of officers supplied to other units as approximately eight hundred; as already mentioned, Major Egleston in the same year estimated the number as more than eight hundred. This exceeded the entire personnel of the Machine Gun Battalion, at any one period.

The Roll of Service published in Colonel Whitney's history in 1923 is an integral part of the history of Squadron A, and is so referred to; though limits of space preclude its reproduction here with its addendum, it occupies 180 pages of that history, and is an impressive and memorable list.

THE 105th MACHINE GUN BATTALION

> Only the monstrous anger of the guns
> Only the stuttering rifles' rapid rattle
> Can patter out their hasty orisons.
> —DAVENPORT

> Reality surpasses imagination.—GOETHE

> Multitudes, multitudes, in the valley of decision.—Joel 3:14

Both Major Wright and Major Durham in the present volume and Colonel Whitney in his history describe the remarkable contribution to officer personnel for service elsewhere after the return of the squadron from the Mexican border. It returned with ranks practically full, trained, disciplined, and efficient; within a few months almost the entire enlisted personnel had been commissioned or released for training as officers. The ranks were promptly and satisfactorily filled with recruits, who speedily absorbed the ideals and morale of Squadron A; but many of these recruits in turn were lost to the squadron by receiving commissions elsewhere. For example, one corporal, a recruit in May, 1917, under twenty-one years of age, was not eligible for a commission; but he lost nearly all of his original squad by such promotions. The same corporal, after becoming a sergeant, had similar losses in his platoon.

Notwithstanding this great turnover, the squadron entrained for Spartanburg, South Carolina, with ranks filled. On arrival it ceased to be Squadron A and became the 105th Machine Gun Battalion. Its five troops were reorganized as parts of three new companies. To it were added groups from infantry regiments; and later another entire machine gun unit was embodied with it. Ultimately its personnel received additions from more than twenty-five different states. Ohio contributed 41; Pennsylvania and Illinois, 38 each; Georgia, 34; New Jersey, 33; Michigan and Florida, 18 each; Texas contributed 11, and California 7. There were extensive changes in officer personnel also. It was a composite organization, and the personnel derived from Squadron A—both officers and enlisted men—preserved and transmitted to the other elements the ideals, morale and discipline developed in the parent organization through a period of thirty years. In the welding of the personnel these typical qualities of Squadron A became characteristics of the 105th Machine Gun Battalion. The story is told in the published history by Colonel Whitney, and the present series of papers introduced by Major Knowlton Durham.

TO FIGHT ON FOOT.

THE STORY OF THE
105th MACHINE GUN BATTALION

Compiled by Major Knowlton Durham (Then First Lieutenant, Company C)

THE history of the 105th Machine Gun Battalion was written by Major Stanton Whitney, who commanded the battalion from February 19, 1919, to its demobilization on April 1–2, 1919. It was written while the experiences were still fresh in his memory, and gives a vivid picture of that unit. The narrative of the battalion is a part of the volume published by the Squadron A Association in 1923 under the title "Squadron A in the Great War, 1917–1919." In this volume the roll of service of individuals who saw service in Squadron A before the war exceeds in space the narrative, apart from the numerous appendices. The whole is a valuable historical contribution.

We do not intend to duplicate that chronicle, but an account of the battalion is an essential part of the history of the first fifty years of Squadron A. The compilers therefore include a series of sketches in narrative form, descriptive of certain phases of the work of the battalion, and these, prepared by several of the company officers, together with an introductory paper written by the Battalion Commander, are here presented as the story of the battalion. In no sense is this a complete or even a comprehensive history. The limits of space make that impossible. The account of the conversion of Squadron A into the 105th Machine Gun Battalion, of the months of training at Spartanburg, of the final training in France, of the period from the armistice until the homecoming and demobilization at Camp Upton—all this is necessarily omitted. So also is the story of the battalion transport, of the training schools, of the marches, inspections and reviews, of the battalion runners through whom the companies in action were in continuous communication with battalion headquarters, of the company kitchens which throughout the operations at all times kept the men supplied with proper rations. Each would justify a chapter in this book, but all must give way to the requirement of brevity.

But no account of the battalion would be fair to the subject without a word concerning the Commanding Officer. Perhaps I, more than any other officer, can write that word; for throughout the entire period of front-line service I was at his side as his aide—or, as he jocularly expressed it, his "fighting adjutant"; for immediately after returning to the battalion from the machine gun school at Châtillon-sur-Seine he detached me from my own Company C and assigned me to his headquarters, and there I remained until my commission as captain shortly after the armistice resulted in my assignment to the command of Company C.

Major Gardner was one of the most indefatigable leaders it has been my privilege to know, by nature intense, energetic, demanding of his officers and men performance of the best they had to give, quick to appraise and keenly alive to every situation. Both officers and men felt that the Commanding Officer knew his job thoroughly. Sparing himself not at all, ambitious that his battalion should be always the best, keeping himself alert at all times to obtain every bit of information that might be of help, he found, I know, in his new command a loyal response which enabled him to develop and maintain an unusually well trained and functioning machine gun battalion. Assigned to its command from another organization, he contributed substantially to the building up of a very proficient machine gun unit—then a new branch of the military service which at that time had not any established background of esprit such as the cavalry had long enjoyed. It was not altogether an easy task. Many difficult and trying adjustments were necessary. It was accomplished, however; and to Major Gardner should go great credit and honor for the part he played in developing a military unit of outstanding ability.

Squadron A was called into Federal service July 16, 1917, and was trained at the Ninety-fourth Street armory and at Van Cortlandt Park. Twice during that time it granted discharges to any men who wished to enter the training camps for commissioned officers. Twice its strength was depleted and recruited through voluntary enlistments. On October 12th it left for Camp Wadsworth, Spartanburg, South Carolina. On the 13th it detrained as the 105th Machine Gun Battalion, and from then to May 4, 1918, it was encamped and trained at Camp Wadsworth. While there, various changes of personnel occurred. Enlisted men of the 10th New York Infantry, the 47th New York Infantry, and the 71st New York Infantry were transferred to the battalion, and Company A of the 104th Machine Gun Battalion in its entirety was transferred to the battalion and became Company D. Numerous changes of officer personnel occurred, including transfers to other organizations; and on April 18, 1918, the command of the battalion passed to Major Kenneth Gardner, formerly captain of the Machine Gun Company of the 107th Infantry.

On May 4, 1918, the battalion left Camp Wadsworth and entrained for the port of embarkation at Newport News. Arriving there May 5th, it left two weeks later, May 18th, on the transport *Calamares* en route for France. The ship was one of a convoy of eight transports. Off the Azores it was met by a group of destroyers and was then convoyed in two groups: one, including the *Calamares,* went to St. Nazaire, and the other, to Brest. Disembarking at St. Nazaire, the battalion on May 31st moved by rail to Noyelles, close by the English Channel; then marched to St. Firmin, where on June 5th it was equipped with British Vickers machine guns, limbers, general service wagons, water carts, Maltese cart, officers' cart, and 159 draft horses. On June 16th it moved to Sallenelle, continuing its training in the Rest Area, returned to Noyelles on July 3rd and entrained there for Wizernes, and finally arrived at Quelmes, where it continued in training until July 14th. At Quelmes it was rejoined by the advance party of officers and N.C.O.'s who had been sent in advance to the machine gun school at Châtillon-sur-Seine. This training period of more than a month occurred in the Second British army sector, where for more than four years the British had held Ypres against assaults comparable with those resisted by the French at Verdun. Sunday July 14th, in the rain, the battalion proceeded by marching toward what was designated as the East Poperinghe lines, going into camp in pup tents in Beauvorde Woods just beyond Steenvoorde in Belgium. It had then become a part of the Second British army, commanded by General Plumer.

The ensuing service of the battalion in Belgium and in France is graphically recorded in the papers to follow. Appropriately, the story commences with extracts from the notice sent out from Squadron A Headquarters on May 24, 1917, by Major Wright, calling upon the ex-members to share in the work of recruiting the squadron in preparation for its early departure for mobilization camp. There follows a paper by the overseas commander, Lieutenant Colonel Gardner, briefly summarizing the accomplishments of the battalion in its war service; one by Lieutenant Colonel Whitney, which of necessity I have extracted from his narrative as published in the volume "Squadron A in the Great War," descriptive of the preliminary training of the Battalion in Belgium; a paper by Major Molyneux, who commanded Company C, and one by Captain Biglow, who commanded Company A, both recounting the part which the battalion played in the smashing of the Hindenburg Line; and a closing paper by Lieutenant Colonel Reynolds, telling of the final engagement of the battalion in the allied attack at La Selle River.

On October 1st, after the Hindenburg Line "show," the battalion was given a brief rest period at Red Woods. The losses had been severe and all companies had been greatly reduced in effective fighting strength. On the 7th of October it resumed marching toward the east, arriving at Becquenette Farm on the 12th, where it bivouacked in preparation for forthcoming action. The 27th and 30th American divisions were then part of the British Fourth army, engaged in the pursuit of the Germans who had been steadily withdrawing after their defeat at the Hindenburg Line. It was apparent that the enemy intended to stand on the high ground immediately east of La Selle River and to dispute the crossings of the river. A general attack was ordered for the Fourth army, as soon as the Ninth and Thirteenth British Corps could come up on the left and right of the American divisions. Colonel Reynolds' paper was written shortly after the return of the battalion from France, when the events which he has described were still vividly fresh in his mind. It is a part only of his narrative of his own experiences covering

COMPANY STREET IN SPARTANBURG, 1917
SAME STREET, SPARTANBURG, SOME MONTHS LATER, 1918

MACHINE GUN IN POSITION, SPARTANBURG, 1917
CLASSY ROCK RIFLE RANGE NEAR SPARTANBURG, 1918

his entire service with the battalion, but the limits of space have necessarily required the omission of all but this part of his story.

After its final engagement and withdrawal to Vaux, the battalion remained there until November 26th and then, by rail and march, moved to Le Breil in the Le Mans Area, when the Division again became a part of the American army. Its available strength was then 11 officers and 487 enlisted men; and its effective strength, 8 officers and 303 enlisted men.

The routine of the following month was cross-country hikes, drills, athletic games, inspections, and occasional reviews. Without the incentive of the preparation for war, it was difficult to maintain interest and enthusiasm for things military, but in spite of difficulties a high degree of morale was maintained. Extensive maneuvers on December 23rd were engaged in by the Division, but it was difficult to maintain enthusiasm for a game in which there were no machine guns and "in which a single man with a flag represented a company of infantry, a battery of artillery, or some other such unit." Thus Colonel Whitney described the situation in his narrative of the battalion. But at least the marching and maneuvers kept the men's minds away from their speculations as to when sailing orders would be received.

On December 27th the battalion moved a short distance from Le Breil and was billeted in three adjacent towns—the headquarters of Companies A and D at Le Luart, Company B at Vouvray, and Company C at Sceaux—where it remained until February 19, 1919. During this period most of the equipment was taken away and many replacements were received. On January 3rd there was a review and inspection by General O'Ryan; and on January 22nd, a Divisional Review by General Pershing, at which the Congressional Medal of Honor was awarded to six men, among whom was Sergeant Reidar Waaler of Company A. On February 19th, Major Gardner was promoted to Lieutenant Colonel and assigned to the Division staff, and Captain Whitney was promoted to major and assigned to the command of the battalion. On the same day the battalion proceeded, under its new commander, to Champagne and entrained for Brest, arriving there February 20th and proceeding to Camp Pontanezen in a heavy rainstorm.

February 25th the battalion boarded the U.S.S. *Leviathan* with a strength of 18 officers and 770 enlisted men. The ship docked at Hoboken on March 6th and the battalion proceeded to Camp Mills, near Garden City, arriving there late in the evening. On March 24th the battalion proceeded by train to East Thirty-fourth Street, where it was met by Squadron A Cavalry, New York Guard, and by the "Ex-Members of Squadron A," and was escorted by them up Fifth Avenue to the armory at Ninety-fourth Street. The following day it participated in the "Home-Coming Parade of the 27th Division." On the morning of the 26th, it left the armory and proceeded to Camp Upton, Long Island, where the routine work in preparation for discharge occupied the next five days, and was completed on April 2, 1919.

I

CALL TO ARMS

HEADQUARTERS, SQUADRON A, NEW YORK CAVALRY
NATIONAL GUARD
Madison Avenue and 94th Street
New York

May 24, 1917

To the Ex-Members of Squadron A:

Orders have at last been received that the National Guard shall recruit to war strength and prepare to go into the field in July.

I therefore ask the earnest, sincere and *immediate* cooperation of each and every ex-member of the squadron in order that I may report *at the earliest possible moment* that our ranks are filled.

The squadron, as always, has been faced by a double problem. Not only must we maintain an efficient organization, but we must answer all calls made on us for officers for other organizations. Never have these calls been as many and as urgent as during the month just past, and never have they been answered more freely or fully. To the 12th New York Infantry, the 15th, the 69th, the Field Artillery, we have sent over twenty officers in the last four weeks. Others have gone to the Regular Army and the Marine Corps. Officers were needed for the new National Army, and training camps were established for their instruction. To these camps the squadron has sent a number out of all proportion to its size—nearly two hundred—and knowing the spirit in which our men have taken up this new work I am confident that the final list of officers selected from the camps will still further reflect to the credit of the squadron.

Squadron A has lived up to its tradition of service without question or hesitation, but this duty has not been performed without sacrifice. It was felt that this sacrifice was necessary; that it was in fact a duty. It was felt that we owed it to our country to give of our best at its call—to give all and more than all that was asked. We did this in the confident belief that our ranks could and would be filled with others to take the places of those who left to assume these new duties, and that we could and would still go forward, as an organization, to meet the still greater obligations and opportunities which will be offered to us as an organization in the future. . . .

We want you to share with us in this work. We can do it, but we can do it just that much quicker with your help. We want that help for a work in which every past and present member of Squadron A should have a share. . . .

I cannot tell you the exact date of the squadron's departure for mobilization camp, nor where that camp may be. I cannot tell you the date of our landing in France or indeed if France will be where we shall land, but I can say that I believe that with the squadron's record in the past and its standing in the present, it cannot be overlooked. Useful work will be found for it, opportunities will be offered and will be seized. For the man who wants to serve, a place is open, and faithful service will bring him the chance for which he looks. . . .

Send us men and send them at once. Send them to the armory on any Monday or Thursday evening. Send them to the Recruiting Committee, which meets there on those nights, or, if you prefer, to the Commanding Officer or the Captain of your former troop. And send them with a letter telling us all that you know about them, stating that you know that they are of the squadron standard, that they are the kind of men you want to fill your place. In addition, if you can, send us some men for special work, horseshoers, saddlers, cooks; also stenographers and clerks and accountants for the headquarters and supply troops, for we can use some of these also.

We have five weeks in which to accomplish the second half of our task. I want to do it in three or less. We can do it if you will help. As they used to say on the border last summer, "Let's go."

WILLIAM R. WRIGHT, *Major*.

II

SQUADRON A AS A MACHINE GUN BATTALION IN THE WORLD WAR

Lieutenant Colonel Kenneth Gardner

The contribution of the squadron as an organization to the American Expeditionary Force in the World War was the 105th Machine Gun Battalion.

The battalion participated in all engagements in which the 27th

Division was involved. Every member of the battalion was proud of the fact that his battalion was "first in and last out" whenever the Division was called upon for front-line duty.

Almost immediately after arrival in France an officer and several enlisted men were detailed for service with the 18th British Division of the Fourth British army, then holding the front line opposite Albert on the Ancre River. A little later the entire battalion went into the line with the machine gun units of the 6th and 41st British Divisions of the Second British army in Flanders and served with distinction in the Scherpenberg and the Dickebush Lake sectors of the Ypres Salient. In this battle-scarred area the battalion spent the entire summer of 1918. As August ended and September began, the Germans were driven from Vierstraat Ridge and Mont Kemmel; and then the battalion, as part of the 27th Division, was transferred to the Australian Army Corps of the Fourth British army in Picardy and participated in the fierce fighting that led up to and included the breaking of the Hindenburg Line. Two American divisions, the 27th and the 30th, contributed mightily to the success of that undertaking—one of the greatest battles of the World War.

With depleted strength, but as hardened veterans, the battalion continued forward to participate in the fighting along La Selle River, which the battalion crossed one cool morning in mid-October, and went on to plant its machine guns at the farthest point reached by any unit of the British army on that front prior to the armistice.

Those veterans who founded the squadron and those who served in it before the war may well be proud of the contribution of the squadron to America's army in Flanders and in France. The pride of organization which the veterans of that early day instilled into the squadron helped to sustain the members of the machine gun battalion when they were called upon to perform the highest duty of a military organization —"the supplying of dead on the battlefield."

How well the squadron served overseas as a machine gun battalion is testified to by the Commanding General of the 27th Division, who was able to say in a letter to the Commanding Officer of the battalion, "I have never seen in our own Division or in any other Division with which we have been associated, including foreign units, anything to excel the standards of precision and disciplined excellence exhibited by your command."

Following the armistice, the Commander-in-Chief of the American

Expeditionary Force came to inspect the battalion. General Pershing told the Commander of the battalion how he, as a young officer in the army, had considered accepting a commission in Troop A during the Spanish-American War and how proud he was of the splendid service of the squadron of which he, under other circumstances, might have been the commanding officer.

When the 27th Division returned from France, the Division Machine Gun Officer, the Commanding Officer of the 104th Machine Gun Battalion, the Commanding Officer of the 105th Machine Gun Battalion, and the Commanding Officer of the 106th Machine Gun Battalion were all men who went to France as officers of the 105th Machine Gun Battalion.

When a proud city welcomed home its National Guard Division it stretched a silken cord across Fifth Avenue to symbolize the Hindenburg Line, and to symbolically "break that Line," the Commanding General of the Division selected Sergeant Reidar Waaler of the 105th Machine Gun Battalion; he had won the Medal of Honor in France, and his first enlistment was in Squadron A.

III

IN BELGIUM

Lieutenant Colonel Stanton Whitney (then Captain of Company D) [1]

Since July 15, 1918, the Battalion had been learning the Game of War to the accompaniment of the German heavy artillery fire in the vicinity of Mt. Kemmel in Belgium. Right in "The Sector" we were—the Bloody Sector, the devastated salient of Ypres—made famous by the stubborn British defensive of virtually four years' duration. At Verdun the French had said, *"They shall not pass!"* and they did not; at Ypres the British said nothing, but the German never passed. The enemy was able to destroy Ypres with his artillery but no hostile German foot was ever planted in its streets. *"They shall not pass!"*

It was our first experience of the enemy artillery, and day and night the German shells crashed about us. It was most exciting and most disquieting to us "amateurs of war," but to us who did not appreciate the

---

[1] The following story of the Battalion in Belgium is a portion of the late Colonel Whitney's Narrative as published in the volume "Squadron A in the Great War, 1917–1918."

real danger and had not as yet seen our dead, it was not nearly so nerve-racking as it became later when we had more experience. So far we had never seen one of our boys (most of them were boys, though they acted like men) disappear as a human being and reappear as a lump of bloody flesh as the result of one of Jerry's shells. Our first wounded and our first dead were men of Company B. On July 26, two men of this company were slightly wounded by shell fragments, but later rejoined their command and were discharged with the others at Camp Upton. On August 14, two Company B men were killed at Bida Farm by a high explosive shell. One of them was instantly killed, and the other died the next day in the Casualty Clearing Station to which he had been taken. Our first real casualties and we had never actually been in action! It shows the "luck of the game," because the total number of Company B men killed in action was only five and the shelling in the East Poperinghe lines was mere child's play as compared with the shelling in the Hindenburg Line and at La Selle River. Towards the end of hostilities we realized that one lone shell may do more damage than a perfect hail of shells which do not land quite right—or rather quite wrong. . . . At first, under enemy artillery fire we were fidgety, later on we were nervous, and in the end we were frankly and avowedly afraid. All this experience was being gained while we were holding the East Poperinghe defensive line—a line of reserve trenches included in the defence of Ypres located some distance in the rear of the Front Line which was up about Scherpenberg Hill ahead of Dickebush Lake and La Clytte. . . . We were in these positions from July 15 to August 20, with occasional short reliefs.

. . . On July 24th the battalion was relieved in the East Poperinghe lines by the 106th Machine Gun Battalion and was attached to the British in the front line. Company A and Company C were attached to the 6th Divisional Machine Gun Battalion, B.E.F., and Company B and Company D were attached to the 41st Divisional Machine Gun Battalion, B.E.F. The various companies were under the British Captains—not for administration but merely for machine gun training. . . . On July 31, the 106th Machine Gun Battalion came up for its period of training in the Front Line and the Battalion marched to the Oudezeele area where such pleasures as baths and the Division show were enjoyed. . . .

On August 21st, we started on our own. We had graduated from training and were now part of the Allied Army. We were finally a fighting unit. From the East Poperinghe lines we moved forward and took up a position in the Dickebush Lake and Scherpenberg sectors where we were close up to Jerry's front lines, and here we experienced our first taste of machine-gun strafing—and most disagreeable it was. Mt. Kemmel was held by the Germans and Mt. Kemmel dominated everything in sight. From its crest, Jerry could see our every movement; and every movement that he saw was greeted with a deluge of shells. The German was never asleep. Whiz-bangs, high-explosive shells, trench mortars and machine gun fire put an effective stop to any daylight movement of the Allies. . . .

Dominated as we were by the German positions on Mt. Kemmel, all our movements and all reconnaissance had to be made by night—and how dark those nights were! . . . No glow in the sky from some city, no lights along what roads remained, no lights from flickering fires. Utter darkness. The twelve guns of each company were established, more or less, in pairs, and these pairs were sited at some distance apart. As we had been warned that the Germans might launch an attack at any minute, the guns were established in depth—that is to say, in each company, four guns were on a general forward line, four were positioned on an approximate line some two or three hundred yards to the rear, and the remaining four were still further behind. The guns were sited in this way so that if the enemy made good his attack and put the four forward guns out of action, the second line of guns could still operate, as could the guns furthermost to the rear if the second line of guns were overrun by the German attack. . . .

The march forward of Company A and Company D can be taken as an example of the routine. The trip was more or less uneventful because, although the companies moved forward during a time when the Germans were strafing the roads with their artillery, none of the shells fell close enough to them to be dangerous. The British guides, designated for that purpose, met them at Reninghelst, once a village of Belgium and a British Rest Camp, but then merely a mass of ruins which served as a target for the Boche artillery. From that point on to Company Headquarters, Companies A and D wore gas masks because the Germans were amusing themselves by throwing over a flock of gas shells. Very disagreeable people were those Germans. From Company Headquarters, the gun teams had to proceed on foot. Limbers were therefore unpacked, and guns and ammunition and all the other machine-gun paraphernalia had to be transported by carrying. A machine gun is no light load to carry at any time—neither is the tripod—but the ammunition is the load that breaks the hearts of the men. Twenty-one thousand rounds at the least have to go up with each machine gun; and it must be remembered that an ammunition box holds only one belt of two hundred and fifty cartridges. When a gun crew is not up to full strength (and it never seemed to be as long as the Battalion was in action in France) the question of transporting the ammunition up to the gun position meant trip after trip by the machine gunners. Walking in the dark over an unknown bit of terrain, carrying a heart-breaking load, stumbling over all sorts of obstructions, under constant harassing fire by the ever-vigilant enemy—it was not pleasant. And our men did it without complaint.

From Company Headquarters, the various gun teams disappeared off into the darkness on their way to relieve the English machine gunners. The Captain established Company Headquarters in the cellar of a ruined farmhouse situated close to the second platoon of four guns. Maps were taken over from the English, and various routine matters connected with the taking over of Trench Stores and with the identification of the S.O.S. lines were attended to. As the second in command of each company had been over the ground on the previous night, all plans had been made. Guides had been provided for each gun team so that there would be no delay in completing the relief. Then the Company Commander waited for the reports to come that the guns were in position and that the British guns had been withdrawn: he waited for the report of "Relief complete" from each platoon commander. A long wait. . . . Finally the Second Platoon reported "Relief complete"; and he could breathe a bit easier while waiting further news. Another long wait before the First Platoon reported, and a still longer one before the Third Platoon was heard from. The Captain then wrote out his "Relief complete" report for the Company and sent it back by runner to battalion headquarters which were located some distance to the rear. The routine as thus given for one particular company applies, with various minor modifications, equally well to the other companies.

Up to this time, the enlisted men of the battalion had enjoyed a monopoly of hard physical work; but now real work began for the Captain. Moreover, he had to hurry because he had to cover a great deal of ground in a limited period of time. He had to work in the darkness and could not be moving after dawn unless he was willing to have German artillery, German sharpshooters, German machine guns, German trench mortars, and German everything else take pot shots at him. And more than that, vastly more important than any question of his personal safety, he could not give away the positions of the guns so that the enemy could concentrate on them. Therefore no movement could be made under German observation. Officers were fairly easy to replace but enlisted men and machine gunners were scarce. But to return to the C.O. and his routine duties. He had to inspect all of the guns to see that they were properly sited in order to carry out the designated tasks: he had to make sure that each Platoon Commander and each Gun Commander clearly understood his orders, the position of the enemy, the field of fire that each gun was supposed to cover: he was responsible for the S.O.S. lines and all other necessary data. . . .

Having inspected the gun positions, he hurried back to headquarters but could not make very good time, owing to the nature of the ground. This country had been shelled continuously by the Germans for over three years and it was a veritable nightmare. Not a living thing about but the Allied soldiers, and they not at all in evidence. Not a tree, not a blade of grass, and, of course, not an unruined house left standing: the few isolated walls of what used to be buildings could hardly be called houses. It was more than depressing—it was nauseating. The ground was nothing but a series of shell holes, even the trenches being almost obliterated by shell fire so that it was not an easy country to walk over in the pitch darkness. How dark those nights in Belgium could be! And added to it all, the constant CRUUUMP, CRUUUMP, CRUUUMP of the Boche shells was disquieting—to say the least—until it became monotonous. On returning over the route, the officer generally found that the Germans had been busy in that neighborhood as evidenced by fresh shell holes which had not been there when he first had made the trip. As long as no one was hit, it made very little difference. Finally the company Headquarters cellar was reached and, after a bite to eat, all hands rolled up in their blankets and were soon fast asleep. All this happened on the night we Yanks took over from the British and put our machine guns into position.

We were in these positions from August 21 to 30, and, as the routine of each day and of each night was about the same, a typical twenty-four hour schedule will serve as an example. . . .

Working by night and remaining under cover and resting by day made the schedule a bit topsy-turvy. Company Headquarters generally woke up and began to get busy about ten-thirty in the morning, and had some sort of lunch at half-past eleven. Daylight hours were usually taken up in figuring fire-data for harassing fire—that is to say, working out the elevations and compass directions for some specified target so that, at night, we could lay a designated gun on that target (always some important point or locality held by the Boche) and open fire, hoping to do all the damage possible—to morale as well as to personnel. Such tentative targets as possible concentration areas, tracks, crossroads, areas of activity, relief points, and much traveled roads would be chosen. Naturally no target was engaged in this night harassing fire without sanction from Division Headquarters, as our own troops might be engaged in a raid into Jerry's lines at a point where our machine-gun fire might cause them to suffer casualties. The choice of targets depended on such data as was obtained from scout planes, service of information and other such sources, all of which information was carefully correlated and transmitted to us by Division Headquarters. All the figuring for this harassing fire had to be worked out from our available maps (and they were splendid ones), as it was impossible to use direct observation instruments in the terrain involved. It was most interesting to work out these firing problems so that all that had to be done when the proper time for shooting arrived was to lay the gun by compass and by clinometer and be fairly sure that the majority of the bullets fired would hit the designated point: you were absolutely sure that all the bullets would hit in the near vicinity of the target engaged.

At six P.M., Company Headquarters' supper would usually be ready, and Company Headquarters would always be ready for supper. It was surprising how hungry you could get. . . .

Around about nine P.M., Headquarters would be on the lookout for the ration parties from the guns and the ration limber from Rear Headquarters, the limber that came up nightly with the rations for the following twenty-four hours. As soon as possible, these would be unloaded and the limber would hurry away, back to Rear Headquarters, for the vicinity of Company Headquarters was far from safe, as Jerry also indulged in harassing fire and had a nasty habit, every now and then, of shelling us with the utmost vigor and precision. He also took keen enjoyment in smothering us periodically with one of his many obnoxious gases—generally choosing the most inconvenient times, preferably when we were at meals. But to return to the subject of rations. These rations were made up at Rear Headquarters (no fires being possible in the front lines; the rations were cold) and usually consisted of bread, bully beef, jam, and cheese. They were packed in gunny sacks, one sack to each gun team, one sack to each Platoon Headquarters, and one to Company Headquarters. Dominated as we were by the ever-menacing Mt. Kemmel—how we hated that place!—it was impossible to get to the gun positions by daylight. All rations, therefore, had to be distributed at once. Two men from each gun team and two from each Platoon Headquarters would be on hand on the arrival of the ration limber to hurry the arriving rations back to their positions. As there was no water fit for drinking purposes in this part of Belgium—although there was plenty under foot—drinking water had to be brought up with the rations and was transported in five-gallon petrol tins (British for a five-gallon gasoline can), one tin to each ration gunny sack. What we would have done without the English petrol tin, I do not know. We soon learned to acquire any serviceable one we ran across and valued it next to the Vickers machine gun and the ammunition. It was used to carry water, coffee, or tea; it served to bring up the rum ration (when we got it) and, properly altered, it came in useful as a wash basin. In localities where a fire was permitted, punched full of holes and filled with wood embers, it did splendid duty as a brazier. Doubtless, had the War lasted a little longer, it could have been adapted to take the place of the issue uniform; it surely could have been used for auto repairs— maybe it was. The English petrol tin was invaluable and should be celebrated in verse, as a necessary non-combatant, along with the Army mule. The Germans had special soup carriers, special utensils to transport water, special braziers, special things for special purposes, while we had the English petrol tin which served all purposes. Without doubt, the tin helped win the War.

The ration-carrying parties had no easy task: they had to pass over ground torn up by years of constant shellfire, the darkness was intense and the Germans would intermittently cover the terrain thoroughly with their high explosive shells. It was not a task for any man who was not willing to take risks. Immediately after the distribution of rations to the carrying parties, the Company Commanding Officer (accompanied by his Second in Command, if he was lucky enough to have one) would pick his way through the darkness to the guns selected for night harassing fire, see that they were moved to their night-firing positions and give them their firing data: "Such and such a compass bearing, so many degrees and minutes elevation, search and traverse so many degrees, rate of fire so and so, firing to begin at such an hour and to discontinue at such an hour." We never fired these night harassing guns from their daytime positions because Jerry could often locate the position of a machine gun by the flash of its firing—notwithstanding all our precautions to hide it—and once the Boche located a machine gun, that locality was not one to tarry in, as every bit of available Hun artillery seemed to concentrate on that spot. It was always a source of amusement to us to watch a heavy concentration of German shells on a position occupied by a machine gun the night before the Strafe. Also it was a source of thankfulness that we were not there.

After seeing that the guns were firing and that all instructions were understood (the instructions were in writing), the C.O. would either remain with them until it was time to inspect the other guns or would return to Company Headquarters to wait for that time. Jerry was very methodical: if the heaviest firing occurred at a certain time on one night you could be quite sure that it would again occur at that same time on the following night. Very seldom were we fooled. In this particular sector we soon discovered that on an ordinary night, when nothing had happened to "put his wind up," Jerry shelled all areas pretty heavily from dark to one A.M., and would then let up a bit until four A.M., so that, although walking about a terrain devoid of any cover except that afforded by shell holes was not a very safe pastime at any time of the day or night—you ran less risk if you made all necessary visits to the guns between one and four A.M. . . .

About one A.M., the Company C.O., generally accompanied by his Second in Command, would start to make the rounds—to inspect his gun positions. A pistol—very often carried in the trench-coat pocket where it was instantly available—and a cane completed the armament for the tour of duty; and, of the two weapons, the cane was the more useful. The cane was not for swank; it was indispensable. You used it as a blind man uses one, tapping away in front of you to feel out the way and to prevent, if possible, a sudden slip into some shell-hole half-full of slimy malodorous water. It might be that the C.O. had not proceeded far on his way to the first gun position when CRUUUMP, CRUUUMP, CRUUUMP and the Boche had landed a flock of high explosive shells ahead of him. So he promptly changed his mind about continuing to the guns along that special path and decided that it would be wiser to make a detour—better a bit of a longer walk with an even chance of arriving at the destination than a short cut with all chances in favor of walking into a Boche shell and—finis! Slipping and sliding and occasionally falling into a shell hole—lucky for him if it were a dry one—he finally arrived at the gun position and found the gun crew alert. Remember, we were expecting, at any moment, an attack from Prince Rupprecht of Bavaria's group of Armies which was opposing us in that sector, so that none of the men was taking any chances of being caught napping. The gun crews were alert! As there were other guns to be visited and much ground had to be covered before dawn, the C.O. was soon on his way. He might learn that one section had been subjected to gas-shell strafing during the day without any resultant casualties, and maybe at that moment the Hun shells were dropping about him. If none of them hit within thirty yards or so, he did not worry, because the narrow slit in the ground—you could not call it a trench—dug for the shelter and protection of the machine gun and the gun crew, afforded him as much protection as he could get anywhere in Belgium.

Maybe while he was at a gun position: "Sniff, sniff! That's a queer smell! Not cordite! Smells like garlic! Damn it all, Jerry is throwing over some more mustard gas shells! GAS!" On with the gas masks and hold your breath until they are adjusted if you don't want to pay a visit to some hospital with all the chances of coming out with a pair of hopelessly ruined lungs. . . . A test for gas shows that it is still there; later, another test finds no virulent traces of gas. "ALL CLEAR!" and off come all the masks. Eye-pieces are cleaned and masks are put back in the wallets ready for another quick adjustment which may be necessary at any moment.

And so he hurried through the night, visiting all his company guns. Slipping into shell-holes, getting caught in the barbed wire, his feet mixing themselves up in bunches of telephone wires which were laid all over the place, dodging shells and seeing the enemy where there was no enemy, he finally stumbled back into his headquarters. The Company C.O. and the Ration Parties (mentioned before) ran the same risks each and every night. It was about 5:30 A.M. when the C.O. reached his palatial headquarters, so he got a bite to eat, wrapped himself up in his blanket, trench coat, overseas cap and all, prayed that Jerry would not register a direct hit on his shelter (he did hit one of the Headquarters a few days before we "took over" and killed the two English officers who were there) and went to sleep, thoroughly tired out. At 11:00 A.M. he was up again and another day had started.

Some nights were very exciting, others were comparatively tame; but the routine never varied. If Jerry's "wind was up" and he was shelling heavily, any movement outside of headquarters or of a gun position was very risky and you were never quite sure if you were going to get back. If Jerry was contented and just indulging in harassing fire with his artillery and his machine guns, your only danger was from some stray shell which you stood a good chance of dodging—you could hear it coming. However, at no time was it safe to let your brains go wool-gathering. . . .

The twenty-four-hour schedule described so far has mainly applied to the company headquarters routine; the men at the gun positions have scarcely been mentioned. However, the men of the gun crews kept very much the same hours as did company headquarters, resting by day and alert by night. Resting it was called by courtesy, because sitting in a hole in the ground with the rain pouring down, thoroughly soaked and wallowing in particularly clinging mud, could hardly be called resting. Some of the gun crews, to be sure, were in concrete emplacements or pill boxes which afforded some protection from the constant rain, but the majority of the men were not so fortunate: they had protection from view but no protection from the elements. Two guns out of Company A's twelve, four of Company B's dozen, one of the twelve of Company C, and five out of Company D's three platoons were lucky enough to have this shelter—twelve gun crews out of forty-eight, more or less sheltered from the ever-present rain. Thirty-six gun crews with virtually no shelter except from view.

Numerous small routine duties had to be attended to during the daylight hours: ammunition and ammunition belts had to be cleaned, guns had to be overhauled, a constant watch over No Man's Land had to be maintained, note had to be taken of all enemy activities which it was possible to observe, gas shelling had to be noted. There was always plenty to do. At night, ration parties had to be sent out and the particular guns designated for harassing fire had to be carried to their night-firing position, flash screens had to be erected. It was natural that the routine of the enlisted man was more monotonous than that of the commissioned officer, because there is no doubt that added responsibility brings added interests.

The weather was atrocious—continuous rain from August 23 through August 31. . . . On August 31, our infantry patrols reported that the Hun, over toward, and on Mt. Kemmel seemed to be withdrawing; by evening the news was confirmed and the menace of direct German observation from that point was removed for good. Although the Germans, at times, held up the Allied armies, they had started their last and continuous retreat. From that day, they never advanced. Mt. Kemmel was promptly occupied by our own troops and, for the first time since we had been in Belgium, it was safe to move about by daylight. Now that we could see them, the routes from gun position to gun position seemed entirely different and we practically had to learn our way about all over again.

. . . September 1, the order came for Companies B and D to "leap-frog" through Companies C and A, and to follow up our infantry which had advanced during the night of August 31–September 1. . . . The infantry had been pushed forward to confirm the German retreat and the machine guns were temporarily left in position to aid the infantry advance and to form rallying points for the infantry should it be forced to withdraw, and especially to hold up the German advance at all costs. Orders were promptly transmitted to the various gun crews of Companies B and D, and the Captains of these companies immediately moved forward to reconnoiter and to get in touch with the situation. As the shelling was fairly heavy, the reconnoitering parties often had to abandon the roads and move forward across country.

The Wytschaete-Vierstraat Road was certainly being searched by the Boche artillery! By half-past four in the afternoon, the First Platoon of Company B was established well forward on the left and the other two platoons were in readiness to move forward on receipt of definite orders. The Second and Third Platoons of Company D were in position near the Wytschaete-Vierstraat Road just to the westward of Vierstraat Ridge with the First Platoon waiting orders in its former position near Company Headquarters. On the way up, the Battalion did not suffer many casualties. Company B had two men wounded, but neither severely enough to be evacuated; Company D also had two men wounded (near the troublesome Hallebast Corners), both of whom rejoined their gun squads at a later date. Not being able to locate definitely the front lines held by the 105th and 106th Infantry, neither Company B nor Company D could put their guns into action but held them in readiness. Company D did get six guns into action under the following circumstances: while waiting just behind Vierstraat Ridge until dusk—because, once on the Ridge, it would be under direct observation by the enemy—the Company was asked to lay a barrage on a portion of Chinese Trench to facilitate an infantry attack which was to start at five P.M. The map was hastily consulted, positions were selected, firing data calculated, and the six available guns were rushed over the Ridge, set up in the open and put into action. Four belts per gun (1,000 rounds) were fired and the guns were promptly moved to a semi-sunken road to the rear and left of the firing position. They were retired just in time, for almost immediately, with a roar and a crash, scores of Jerry's shells tore up the positions so recently vacated. Not a casualty! But Company D made up for it later when at five o'clock in the morning of September 2, the Germans scored a direct hit and killed five men. In addition, ten men were evacuated to the hospital—one having been wounded by a shell fragment, three suffering from shell-shock and six badly gassed. All but one of these men rejoined the company, but at a much later date. As in the case of every man of the battalion who was killed in action, all bodies were recovered and taken to the rear where they were given proper burials with religious and military services. Meanwhile, Company B had its First and Second Platoons in advanced positions with the platoon headquarters at Captain's Post, which, only a few days before, had served as one of the targets for night harassing fire. We were advancing! September 2 passed without many developments as far as the machine guns were concerned. The guns could not be put into action because the forward position of our infantry was not definitely enough known. In the afternoon we received the welcome news announcing that the Battalion would be relieved in the lines during the night of September 2-3 by the 41st Divisional Battalion, Machine Gun Corps, B.E.F. We were very glad of the relief because, although our casualties had not been particularly heavy, we had served a long apprenticeship in the front lines and needed time to digest the lessons we had learned. Companies A and C were relieved early during the night of September 2-3, Company B was out of the lines by three in the morning of the 3rd, and Company D reported "Relief Complete" at eleven o'clock in the morning of that same day. In the afternoon, the Battalion was again reunited near Grove Farm. That night, further casualties developed when two officers and twenty-three enlisted men were evacuated to the hospital, badly gassed by German gas shells. That last night at Vierstrat Ridge the organization had been smothered with these tokens of Jerry's hate. Of these men, one officer was evacuated to the United States, one returned to the company just before the Battle of the Hindenburg Line, and all of

"FAREWELL PARADE" OF SQUADRON A, 1917
COMPANY STREET, SPARTANBURG, 1917

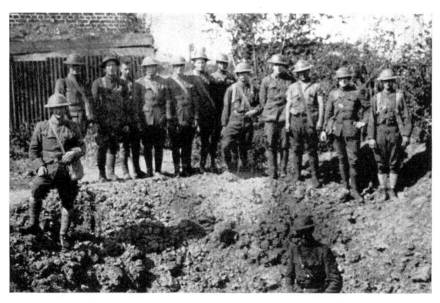

BATTALION HEADQUARTERS IN BELGIUM, AUGUST, 1918
SHELL HOLE JUST OUTSIDE BATTALION HEADQUARTERS, 1918

SQUADRON A

the enlisted men returned at a later date, some, unfortunately, just in time to be killed or wounded in one of the later actions in which the Division participated.

September 4, the Battalion rested, cleaned equipment, and prepared generally for the next move.

Upon the withdrawal from the British lines in Belgium the Battalion underwent a period of special training at Thièvres, near Doullens, France, from September 7th to 23rd. On the 24th, the 27th Division took over the Bellicourt Sector as part of the Fourth British Army (General H. S. Rawlinson, commanding), fronting the Hindenburg Line from Cambrai to St. Quentin, with the center of the line about opposite Bony.

The Battalion established advance headquarters at Ronssoy, with rear headquarters at Lieramont. . . . The 30th Division was on the right of the 27th. The 2nd American Corps covered a front of about five thousand yards. The Ninth British Corps was to the right of the American Corps and the third British Corps occupied a position on the left. This front was the front of the Fourth British Army which had, on its left, the Third British Army and, on its right, the Tenth French Army. The Australian Corps was in reserve behind the front of the Fourth British Army, which meant that they were responsible for the terrain from Cambrai to St. Quentin with the center of the line about opposite Bony. So much for the general positions as they affected the Battalion. With Companies B, C and D moved forward, Company A was temporarily held in reserve at Rear Battalion Headquarters: Advance Battalion Headquarters moved out of Lieramont and established themselves at Ronssoy.

The date set for the breaking of the Hindenburg Line was Sept. 29; but the 27th Division had a preliminary task to accomplish. The Knoll, Guillemont Farm, Quennemont Farm and other strong points of the German outpost line had to be reached and occupied before the main attack could be launched. And bear in mind, that these positions —strongly entrenched and with myriads of concrete machine gun emplacements—had successfully beaten off recent British attacks. So it was that, during the night of the 26-27 September, the Battalion as a part of the 27th Division moved forward to take part in this curtain-raiser scheduled for the early morning of September 27.[2]

[2] Extract from a censored letter: "Then we pulled off the stunt that shattered Hindenburg's notorious system."

IV

COMPANY C AT THE HINDENBURG LINE

Major Robert R. Molyneux (then Captain of Company C)

The battalion left Thièvres at 1:30 A.M. on September 23rd, and marched about four and one-half miles west to Authieule. Here we entrained at 5:00 A.M. and after passing through Doullens, Amiens, Villers-Bretonneux, and Péronne, finally reached Tincourt, where we detrained.

C Company got the jump on the rest of the companies and was ordered up the road away from the station, and awaited the rest of the battalion. From here we marched north through Tincourt Wood and the town of Longavesnes, which was being shelled at the time, and finally arrived at Lieramont, our destination. The men put up pup tents and the officers quartered in "elephant" shelters. The Boche planes bombed in great shape during the night, but no damage was done. The transport arrived, having traveled overland from Thièvres, and the morning of the 24th was spent in changing guns and equipment.

During the afternoon we were told we would go into the line that night. At 6:30 P.M. we were on the road, and marching southeast reached Ste. Emilie, where company headquarters was located. The platoons were here met by British guides. The relief, which was quite difficult because of the advanced positions of the guns, was made in good order without accident or casualties. During the night a sergeant of the Australian Expeditionary Force reported to the company to accompany me during the operations.

At daylight September 25th I went forward with Major Ryder, the British officer, to look over the positions. In Ken Lane, a sunken road running approximately north and south, Lieutenant Flash established First Platoon Headquarters. Four guns of First Platoon were at Doleful Post; Lieutenant Galvin, Third Platoon, had two guns in Ken Lane and two at Coleen Post; and the Second Platoon under Sergeant Werleman had four guns in Thistle Trench.

In the afternoon I received battle maps and verbal information of the attack to be made on September 27th, written orders to follow. While returning to company headquarters, a large shell struck very close, blowing up an ambulance which was being loaded with wounded. We ran around a small ruin, but another shell arrived, knocking us all flat. I thought I was hit, as my left arm and leg had no feeling, and for the moment many things passed through my mind. The others were unharmed and we were soon back at company headquarters. My arm and leg turned black and blue, which may have been from the concussion of the shell-burst.

September 26th was occupied with preparations for the impending attack. At dusk, company headquarters was established in Ken Lane. Lieutenant Flash was placed in charge of the First and Second Platoons, making a battery of eight guns to be placed with his left at Doleful Post, and Lieutenant Galvin's Platoon, four guns, with his right at Duncan Post. Time was growing short. Platoon commanders at once reconnoitered and picked their gun positions while I returned to the relay station to locate the ammunition supply and bring forward the rations.

I soon got back to Lempire Road, where I met a British officer with his transport loaded with S.A.A. and showed him where to locate the dump. Reaching the relay station at 11:10 P.M., the ration parties for the gun squads soon arrived. I did not wait for the rations but with several men started forward with what ammunition we could carry. We also had a large box of medical supplies and more S.A.A. on a stretcher. Four of us carried the stretcher, and as the bulk ammunition was very heavy we frequently had to wait for the others.

We arrived at Ken Lane without losing a man; and the men returned to the relay station for more ammunition and the rations, while I remained in my company headquarters and prepared the firing data for the barrage. When the ration limber arrived at the relay station, the horses were used with pack to bring forward the balance of the ammunition. However, they were unable to pass a trench filled with British and German dead, and from this point the ammunition was carried by hand forward to the guns.

In the meantime, while the officers and non-coms were picking the machine gun positions, the British 18-pounders became quite active, causing the Boche to retaliate with heavy artillery fire.

I gave out the firing data, and after a few final instructions the sergeants started out with their squads and set up the guns in the picked positions. Zero hour was to be at 5:30 A.M.

My company headquarters was a small shelter about eight feet square, cut into the east bank of the road called Ken Lane. It contained two chicken-wire bunks, one above the other, on the north and south sides, and a small table and bench in the center. The doorway, opening on a level with the duckboards in the lane, was covered with a Boche blanket; and all sorts of German food and equipment lay scattered about. The place would have been no protection from a direct hit, but was dry and comfortable. Candles were scarce, and we were very sparing of those on hand.

By 5:00 A.M., Lieutenant Galvin's platoon had reached Duncan Post, and Sergeant Werleman with the Second Platoon had joined Lieutenant Flash in the vicinity of Doleful Post, where the First Platoon guns were already in position.

I was happy, for my guns were in position, we had ammunition, the rations had been distributed, and up to now my company had not received a single casualty.

The artillery had become very quiet, with only an occasional shell burst near by, and now and then the crack of bullets as a burst of machine gun fire passed overhead.

Zero hour arrived, and our artillery opened up a terrific and deafening cannonading. Our machine guns were firing, but their sound was drowned out by the roar of the guns in our rear and the shrieking of the shells. The German counter-barrage now came down and shells burst with great rapidity, with the machine gun bullets seeming to swarm through the air.

In a few moments Sergeant Matthew Casey appeared, leading Acting Corporal McCarrol. The Sergeant seemed to be in a daze and McCarrol was covered with blood. He had three wounds on the head, his eyes were filled with blood, and his right hand was badly shattered, with the bones of his fingers protruding through the flesh. Sergeant Casey was severely shocked and had a piece of shell in his left groin.

McCarrol had been acting as corporal of the third squad, and as he stood there blinded by the blood in his eyes he brought himself to attention and said, "Captain, this does not spoil my corporalcy, does it?" His gun had been located in a shell hole. McCarrol was firing and Private Thomas Shields, a big Irishman and one of the finest soldiers in the outfit, was on his right acting as Number Two. Sergeant Casey was on his left, having just laid the clinometer on the gun, when they were struck by a direct hit. The gun completely disappeared and Shields was killed. Sergeant Casey, although shocked and wounded, succeeded in leading McCarrol through the Boche counter-barrage and brought him to me. The shelling was terrific and it was some time before I could send him to the rear. Realizing it would be a hardship for the men to carry him back, he said that if some one would lead him he could walk back all right. He asked for a drink of liquor but none was available.

The stretcher bearers had just left with him when Corporal Gardner, of the fourth squad, reported his gun had been destroyed by artillery fire. It had jammed; and just as he raised the rear cover the shell struck, a fragment hit the cover and wounded him in the cheek. No doubt the raising of the gun cover had saved his life. Corporal Hunt's gun was the only one left in the First Platoon and remained in action firing the entire barrage. The Second and Third Platoons were intact and after finishing the barrage fire their guns were laid on the German S.O.S.

The infantry wounded now began to appear in large numbers and as we were located well in advance of the rest of the line, many came to us and received first aid. Private Martin, of our Sanitary Department, did great work at Doleful Post. I turned my headquarters into a first-aid station, and as I watched my men bandage the wounded doughboys I felt rewarded for the trouble we had had the night previous in bringing forward that large box of medical supplies.

Things eased up to some extent as the morning passed, and Lieutenant Flash came to talk over the situation.

Shortly after noon two runners came forward from battalion headquarters, and while talking with them we heard heavy machine gun firing. Then in dashed Sergeant McGruder of Lieutenant Flash's Platoon, stating the Boche were making a counter-attack. He had ordered his guns to open fire and then came to notify us.

It was a great surprise and seemed impossible, for we had seen the entire 106th Infantry go forward to the attack over this same ground. It was then that I realized we were holding the position alone. Our operation order had stated that the 106th Infantry would advance to the present post line and select positions to assist consolidation and resist possible counter-attacks, but not an unwounded doughboy was in sight. I immediately sent messages back by the two runners to battalion headquarters requesting infantry support, Lewis guns, and ammunition. Then Lieutenant Flash and I started on the run for Doleful Post. On reaching there I climbed on the top of the trench and with my field glasses took in the situation. As I slid back I could not help noticing that I had been lying on a badly mangled German. Our machine guns had been firing for some time, but small enemy groups could still be seen advancing nearer our position and our guns opened upon them with excellent results. Private Lawrence C. Leonard, who had been wounded in the neck, remained at his gun and wiped out a Boche machine gun platoon advancing towards him. Lieutenant Flash and I each used a British rifle picked up in the trench, and I longed for the old Springfield I used to shoot at home on the Range.

We had lost three machine guns earlier in the day, our ammunition was nearly exhausted, so the men rigged up a light German machine gun and used it to good advantage. The attack seemed slowly to fade away, but the hostile machine gun fire and the artillery fire continued during the day.

The Third Platoon at Duncan Post had a similar experience and, with Major Kincaid and some of the 106th Infantry, successfully repulsed a German counter-attack on that position. I sent another message to battalion headquarters, stressing the seriousness of the situation, which got results; for shortly after, a detachment from Company B brought ammunition forward to our guns. It was a tough assignment for them, but they did not hesitate and came forward under direct observation from the enemy and through considerable shell fire.

Later Lieutenant Matthews came forward to Ken Lane and told me he was bringing up his platoon with four guns at dusk.

During the day three men composing a Lewis gun crew of the 106th Infantry came to Ken Lane, stating that their gun was out of commission. We found another, and using parts of both made one that would function. I sent them to Doleful Post to reinforce that point, but later the gun was destroyed and two of the men were wounded.

In the afternoon I received an order to report to headquarters, Second Battalion, 106th Infantry, at Duncan Post to arrange a defense scheme for Doleful Post, Duncan Post, and Cat Post, so as to form strong points. At 5:00 P.M. I went to Duncan Post and talked with Major Kincaid. It was decided to reinforce Doleful Post, and that night at ten o'clock infantrymen arrived there with two Lewis guns. During the night I moved the Third Platoon from Duncan Post and placed it in Ken Lane.

Just before the barrage had opened in the morning, Privates Desmond, Powers, Munroe, and Duncan, having been relieved from Corporal Hunt's guns, started for Ken Lane, but failed to arrive. They were missing all day but finally reported after dark. They had lost their way and had wandered into German territory where they were caught in the barrage, and had to hide in shell holes all day before they were able to escape. Private Munroe was wounded in the head by a piece of shell that tore through the top of his helmet. They were all very hungry, thirsty, and happy to get back.

I had sent a message to Major Gardner requesting ammunition and rum, and much to my surprise and great joy to the men, a runner arrived during the night with a jug full of issue rum. A drizzly rain had set in, making everything a muddy mess, and everybody, exhausted from lack of rest, greeted that rum as a gift from the gods.

About the same time Lieutenant Matthews' platoon arrived without casualties and was placed in Ken Lane.

The disagreeable weather caused all available shelter to be crowded. My little company headquarters held at least fifteen men. Private Martin, who had done such good work all day at Doleful Post caring for the wounded, came in all fagged out and I put him in a bunk. However, there was little chance for rest; gas shells kept dropping in our vicinity during the entire night, and we spent most of the time wearing our gas masks. The sentries had to be alert for there was no one between us and the Boche lines; but the night passed without any real excitement.

The morning of September 28th was spent in overhauling the equipment and consolidating our position.

Having had no word from the rear for some time I decided to go back to Ronssoy in the afternoon to see what information was at hand. I went through Lempire—being sniped at on the way—and met Captain Ham Andrews and Lieutenant Harry Adsit with the Machine Gun Company of the 107th Infantry on Lempire Road. They had brought their company to this point, ready to go over the top with the regiment next morning.

I went on back to 53rd Brigade Headquarters, reported to Major Gardner, and also had a talk with the brigade commander. Captain Bryant and another machine gun officer had been killed by an H.E.

shell in front of brigade headquarters and their bodies lay at the side of the road. On my return while passing from Y Copse to Z Copse I was again sniped at from the northeast, and remember tilting my helmet over my eyes in the hope that the bullet would glance up instead of down, if one happened to hit my head.

During the evening I received a message that the Boche were active on a road beyond Guillemont Farm, so we did some indirect harassing fire, using a German overcoat to cover the flash from the gun.

C Company's nine machine guns and the platoon from B Company were now concentrated in Ken Lane, which was an excellent position from which to fire a barrage.

On the morning of September 29th the zero hour again arrived and we opened incessant machine gun fire over the heads of the 107th Infantry as they advanced on our front. Again the artillery opened a terrific bombardment and the noise was even more terrible than on the 27th. Again the German counter-barrage came down and the bullets swarmed overhead. It seemed as if you could hold up your helmet and fill it with anything you wanted. However, our guns were so located that we did not have a single casualty during the entire firing of our barrage. The infantry disappeared into the smoke and shell bursts, and then along came the lumbering tanks, many of which were knocked out by artillery fire and land mines very close to our position. I saw one strike a mine and its treads blow up in the air, but there were some brave fellows in that tank, for her gun kept firing through the smoke for quite a time. A mounted British officer rode past and when the smoke cleared a little I saw the horse lying dead. The officer had disappeared.

The Australians began to come along, following our infantry, and the attack on the Hindenburg Line was on in earnest.

About 9:00 A.M. an order was received from battalion headquarters to pack fighting limbers which would report at ration dump, so the company withdrew from Ken Lane to the relay post near Lempire. The equipment was overhauled, belts were loaded, the limbers packed, and I reported with Captain Whitney of D Company to the battalion commander. While awaiting orders a shell landed near the transport, killing Private David Wischer.

Later in the afternoon we were ordered to return to our former positions in the line. Doleful Post was found occupied by four British machine guns, with twenty-four Australian machine guns in the communication trench; so we again took a position in Ken Lane, with the Third Platoon going to Duncan Post.

On the morning of October 1st orders were received that the battalion would retire from the line and would camp that night at Ste. Emilie. On arrival of the limbers at Ken Lane I took the transport sergeant's horse and rode towards Duncan Post, passing the Third Platoon coming from their position. I continued on to Duncan Post to see that all had been cleared and then started back towards Ronssoy.

There was considerable shelling on the road, and through the smoke appeared an automobile. As I approached the car, out stepped Major General John F. O'Ryan and I guided him to Colonel Debevoise's headquarters in Ken Lane.

Once again I started back, and while passing through Ronssoy met our good Chaplain Bass, who presented me with a box of fifty cigars.

When I arrived at Ste. Emilie the men had already pitched camp and were taking a much needed rest. Somewhere I had mysteriously acquired an English canteen full of issue rum; so making a loving cup of the canteen and with the Chaplain's cigars the men once again felt at peace with the world.

V

COMPANY A AT THE HINDENBURG LINE

Captain L. Horatio Biglow

On Wednesday, September 25, 1918, Company A was encamped some miles to the rear of the front line near Lieramont, and was being held in reserve. Two squads had been borrowed from the company and loaned to Company D to make up for losses which Company D had suffered in previous operations. Companies B, C and D had already taken their places in the line, in preparation for the advance which was to be made on the morning of September 27. Company A was taking things easily—not knowing what was ahead—and waiting orders.

On the afternoon of that day, an automobile appeared in which were several officers, including Major Gardner, some Australian officers, and an Australian sergeant. I was requested to join the group in the automobile. It then took the road to the front line and during the ride I was told that Company A would be needed in the push which would take place on the morning of the 27th, that I was being taken to a place where I could see where our guns were to be placed so that they would be ready to assist in the barrage which would start at 5:30 that morning. I was told that, as the place where we were to set our guns was under direct observation of the Germans, it would not be possible to actually fix the positions of the guns until after dark. The plan was for me to view this spot from a distance, go back to the company, get them started for the place, and then to return to the place on horseback and, as soon as it was dark, locate the positions for the guns, figure out the firing data, and set the firing stakes. I began to realize that I was in for a rather feverish twenty-four hours.

In due course we reached the front line, and from a high spot near the positions of B Company, in front of the ruined town of Ronssoy, a flat field, plentifully sprinkled with shell holes, was pointed out to me where we were to set up our guns. A few hundred yards to the rear of this field was Thistle Trench, which we later came to know very well. To the left of the field, which would be on the left of our position, ran Tombois road from Ronssoy directly into the German lines. The Hindenburg Line was directly in front.

As we were under observation from the German lines when looking at the field, our inspection was rather hasty. I was then escorted to Company A camp in the automobile, arriving at about 1 P.M. on September 26th. An Australian sergeant was to remain with me as my advisor. When I got back to the camp I hastily summoned the officers and passed on to them the information I had received, ordered horses to be saddled and, with Lieutenant Cook and a couple of other men, mounted and returned to Ronssoy. The road over which we were traveling was already badly congested with troops and heavy guns.

We got to Ronssoy before dark on the 26th, and Lieutenant Cook and I worked out firing data from the maps which we had with us.

Ronssoy was a completely ruined town, but one could keep out of sight behind the walls of the broken houses. Tombois road was filled with a large number of unburied dead who had evidently lain there for some time.

Things were rather quiet for a while and only an occasional shell came over from the German lines. As soon as it got fairly dark, we attempted to get into the field where our guns were to be set up. Shells were dropping in the field, every now and then Tombois road would be raked by shells and machine gun fire, and Very lights were constantly being sent up by the Germans in an attempt to discover any movements. When the lights went up we had to "freeze" where we were and trust that we had not been seen.

It was about 9 P.M. and dark before we could start work in the field. We selected emplacements for twelve guns and set up stakes to indicate to each gun squad the exact direction and elevations to be used in firing that gun. We lined up the positions for the guns fifty yards apart in the open field. The first platoon was placed on the right; the third, on the left; and the second, in the center—the line of guns running from F 17 A 3:8 almost to the road at 11 C 2:3.

The field was about level, with no buildings, but with a goodly number of shell holes which gave some protection.

We worked in that field until about 1 A.M., getting the stakes set to mark the positions for the guns and the direction of fire, and then went back to Ronssoy to bring the company to the field. It was about 2:30 A.M. before the company arrived. The one road was absolutely jammed with infantry, heavy guns, and lorries. It was a miracle that the company was able to get through at all.

The evening had been fairly quiet as far as shelling was concerned, but by the time we reached the field the shelling had become much heavier, for the Germans were becoming aware that something was impending. It seemed advisable to unload the limbers in Ronssoy under the protection of the ruined buildings and have the men carry the guns and equipment to the gun positions in the field. Each platoon was conducted to the place which had been assigned to it, and started digging. Wherever a shell hole could not be used a small deep slit was made for each gunner and his "Number 1" man. Behind this slit and slightly to one side another larger hole was dug for the use of the remaining men of each squad. These latter holes were belt filling stations when the ammunition belts were to be refilled.

The men had to make numerous trips back to the town to bring up rations, extra ammunition, guns, and other equipment. This meant a hike of 500 yards for the squad on the left gun of our company and of over 1100 yards for those manning the right gun. In addition to the regular allotment of ammunition we carried by hand large extra stores of S.A.A., 1200 rounds per box, a tremendous load for two men under the most favorable conditions, but doubly difficult under the heavy enemy fire. Tombois road was the most feasible track between our positions and the town, and this was the road traveled by the men. It was constantly swept with both artillery and machine gun fire and the Very lights continued to slow up operations. The men dug throughout the remainder of the night, relieving themselves from this duty by changing on and off to the carrying parties.

All of this work, of course, was kept up during incessant firing from the enemy. Every kind and size of shell was dropped in the field and on the road, high explosives were varied with gas, and machine guns raked our positions with their fire. Many of the H.E. shells contained arsenic gas—indicated by low-lying smoke. The enemy was very nervous. We could observe no let-up as we dug and hiked back and forth to the head of Tombois road for supplies, or perhaps helped a wounded man to the company headquarters at Lempire Post. Lempire Post, slightly to the rear of the left of our position and close to Tombois road, was a dugout which we used as an emergency dressing station.

We suffered casualties all during the night, both on the road and in the field. At 5 o'clock Lieutenant Cook notified each platoon commander that "zero" would be at 5:30 A.M.

When the barrage opened at that hour it was still dark and a most awe-inspiring sight. Back of us the heavy guns were placed nearly wheel to wheel. As far as the eye could see there was a continuous blaze of fire in each direction. The previous firing during the night had seemed heavy, but this avalanche of noise was absolutely deafening. In front of us, to right and left, the German lines resembled a gorgeous Fourth of July celebration with all kinds of rockets and signals in the air.

Our own contribution, the machine gun barrage, opened immediately after the artillery and kept up its fire, with brief intervals only, till "zero plus 75 minutes." These short pauses were merely to raise the barrel of the gun increasing the range as the infantry advanced, or to insert fresh belts of cartridges. Our entire battalion fired 48 guns during this barrage, the rate of fire per gun being between 100 and

150 rounds of ammunition per minute. This meant a total of 7,500 rounds per gun for the barrage, about 90,000 rounds for our company alone.

At the beginning of the barrage, the tanks which were to support the infantry came up and passed through us, following the white tapes that had been laid out for them. Many of them were put out of action by the heavy barrage put up by the enemy and by striking land mines laid out in their paths. One of these tanks caught fire from a land mine and burned furiously. Some of its crew were trapped inside, unable, on account of their wounds, to free themselves. It was daylight by now; suddenly our men were amazed to see objects crawling toward our positions. Upon looking more closely they saw that these were three men from the burning tank. They looked as if they had on red underwear, for their clothing and skin had been largely burned off. Sergeant Reidar Waaler of our company made his way to the tank and succeeded in rescuing two, despite the immediate danger of its complete destruction. The possibility of the explosion of its own ammunition from the flames which were consuming it was imminent. German prisoners were starting to come back through our lines; Sergeant Waaler pressed some of them into service as stretcher bearers and managed to get the badly burned men to a dressing station. Later we learned that all the men died soon after their rescue. Sergeant Waaler had his slicker burned off while entering the tank, but was uninjured. Later we were able to examine the tank and could see the burned mummy of the driver still grasping the wheel and peering through the slit in the front of the tank.

For this act Sergeant Waaler received the Congressional Medal of Honor and other medals from the British, French and Montenegrin governments.

As the German prisoners came back, they called out, "Kamerad," incessantly and raised their hands to make sure that we would not shoot.

During the morning one of Sergeant Waaler's guns fired at an enemy plane that hovered over our line, the tripod being completely inverted to obtain a high angle of fire. We received credit for bringing down this plane which crashed to the ground ahead of us.

On the afternoon of the 27th, the company, less the Third Platoon and Number 8 Squad of the Second Platoon, was ordered to retire a short distance to Thistle Trench; this offered a better defensive field of fire and gave the men better protection. We had incurred many casualties before, during, and after the barrage. Some of the gun crews were now so small that they had to make several trips back and forth under heavy artillery and machine gun fire before their entire equipment could be moved to the trench.

We immediately set up the guns in the new positions and prepared for a possible counter-attack by the Germans. Casualties had reduced the number of men on each gun. The belt filling station of Number 11 gun was located in a shell hole. A shell landed directly in the hole, killing four men instantly and wounding one; but the gun was not put out of action. That night, the 27th, we drove a limber to the gun position, wrapped the four in their blankets, laid them on the limber, and sent them to the rear.

The five guns of our company which remained in their original positions were in charge of Lieutenant Downey and were lined on a definite S.O.S. line for use in case of a counter-attack. Despite the casualties suffered by these gun teams, especially Number 11 Squad, Lieutenant Downey was able to keep all guns manned. During the night of September 27th the five squads were ordered to retire to Thistle Trench.

The night of September 27th was spent by the main portion of Company A in Thistle Trench. The guns were set up in vantage points throughout the trench, and two men left on guard at each gun. The remainder of the skeleton squads tried to sleep under a constant bombardment by the enemy, our snatches of slumber being disturbed by gas, shells, and high explosives.

Most of the men were too tired to take notice of the H.E., feeling with a philosophical fatigue that if it would get us, it might do so as well asleep as awake. But the gas was something we could combat and so we were kept more or less alert. Not a few petrol tins of coffee were spoiled for us by the contaminating gas that saturated our entire trench. At night the company transport, under the leadership of Sergeant Charles Paine, would come to the end of the trench, which opened into the Guillemont road, and details would go down for our rations. The transport was very faithful in bringing our food, despite the congestion of the roads and the heavy shelling that it encountered. Our horses were exhausted and it was necessary to shoot one that had been wounded by shell fire. We ate well, too, because enough food for our entire company was sent up to us. Since many of our men had gone back to hospitals wounded, those who remained had the benefit of extra food. The efficiency of the army took care of this very quickly, however, and as soon as the depleted roster of our company was received at headquarters, rations for only the number of men on duty could be drawn.

Private Louis Zimmermann, who procured rations for Lieutenant Cook and me, turned out to be a most ingenious cook. He would make a small fire in the bottom of the trench, using for fuel threads from discarded sand bags and wax scraped from candles, and over this fire would toast crackers and bully beef, putting the bully beef on the cracker, with jam on top. This combination tasted like ambrosia. Lieutenant Cook and I shared a small excavation which we had dug into the side of the trench, above the level of the water in the bottom of the trench; there was small room for number 2 when number 1 went to bed.

Saturday, September 28th, brought more casualties. The protection of the trench undoubtedly saved us from many machine gun wounds and from shell wounds; but the enemy bombarded our gun positions with gas, and several men were sent to the rear for medical treatment.

The operation on the morning of the 27th had not been completely successful in taking and holding all of the objectives assigned to the infantry. The infantry had reached their objectives that day, but were unable to consolidate a new line. We were told that a new attack would be launched on the morning of September 29th, and our guns would occupy their former positions in the field and would again fire a barrage as the infantry advanced.

After dark on September 28th, Company F of the 107th Infantry came to our trench and rested during the night until a short time before zero hour on the 29th, when it set out for its jumping off point.

Just before dawn on the 29th our guns were dismounted and taken from Thistle Trench to the positions from which we had fired the barrage on Friday morning. At 5:50 A.M., Sunday the 29th, the second barrage opened. It was in many respects similar to the one fired two days previously, except that the ranges were different and the gun crews smaller. For this barrage, which opened the attack on the main Hindenburg defense system, we took only a sufficient amount of equipment and loaded belts from the trench to the field. The machine guns fired for twenty minutes. Then the company returned to Thistle Trench. A counter-attack could be repelled even better from the trench than from the field and with far more safety to the machine gunners. No one was hurt before the barrage, the darkness seeming to give us sufficient cover on our way from the trench. Two men, however, were hit on the return trip, one of whom later died.

Once in the trench we put a guard on each gun and awaited developments. Streams of wounded were pouring into the first-aid station on Guillemont road. A tremendous forward movement of soldiers, transport, tanks, armored cars, and ambulances was under way.

We received encouraging news throughout the day; and toward evening the shelling and gas abated somewhat and we were able to enjoy a few hours of real sleep despite the heavy rainfall that set in.

As the shelling had now ceased we walked on the level ground outside the trench. It turned out that this was not a healthy thing to do, as apparently the Germans had snipers concealed in the fields. After one expedition of this kind I happened to take off my coat and was surprised to find the coat sleeve torn under my right arm. I then noticed that my field glasses, which I carried under my shoulder by a strap and which rested under my right arm, holding the arm out from the side, had a bullet crease along the top of the case. A bullet had passed between my arm and my body.

We remained in our positions in Thistle Trench all the next day, Monday, September 30th; and on Tuesday, October 1st, our transport drove up on the top along the trench. The Germans by this time were so far back that our guns were loaded on the limbers and taken to the rear. We were thus able to march back without having to carry equipment of any kind. The march took us to Ste. Emilie, which we had left five days before. When we arrived we learned of still other casualties in the company on September 27th and 28th, while some of our men were on duty with Company D of our battalion. Captain Whitney of Company D gave the squads that had been temporarily part of his company a very fine recommendation for the efficiency and bravery they had displayed while under his command. The killed and wounded in our company from September 27th to September 30th reached a total of 47 casualties, about 50 per cent of our combat strength at the time we entered the line.

BARBWIRE BEFORE HINDENBURG LINE, 1918
THE ST. QUENTIN CANAL

COMPANY OFFICERS NEAR LA SELLE RIVER
MACHINE GUN IN POSITION, LA SELLE

VI

LA SELLE RIVER OPERATIONS

Lieutenant-Colonel John Reynolds (then First Lieutenant of Company B)

On the 16th of October we were informed that the attack had been set for the following day. Our positions were assigned to us, and our company was ordered to fire upon certain German trenches on the far side of the Selle River and located respectively at Sheet 57 B, SE, Q. 35 d. 8035 and Q.35 c.8040.

Captain Egleston and I, with Sergeants O'Keefe, Cox, and Kitching, went up the line to pick out the positions for our guns. We moved over the road we expected to follow that night in order thoroughly to familiarize ourselves with it. Turning to the left before we came to the village of Becquigny, we skirted the town by a dirt road, past a large pond, and then along a dirt road past Le Rond Point until we came to the farm of La Haie Menneresse. Instead of following the high road, which ran along a ridge, we turned to the left along a mere track and took to the fields in a valley which would furnish us with good cover from small-arms fire, bringing us eventually into the high road again not far from the village of St. Souplet. This village was No Man's Land at that time. Patrols of both armies had penetrated and operated there. We picked out a sunken road just below the brow of a hill, on the forward slope of which we intended to place our guns. This road would furnish us with admirable cover for our fighting limbers. A small stream ran alongside the road; and the position we picked out was not over one hundred and fifty yards from our guns. We had determined in this show to apply the theories we had formed of saving the strength of our men for the actual fighting and had agreed that we would run our limbers into this position and keep them there irrespective of the cost in horses.

From our map it was apparent that the other side of the slope was in plain sight of the German lines, which lay not more than a thousand yards across the river from our intended positions. These positions were on the forward slope of the hill, which led by a gradual declivity to the Selle River. On the far side of the river the ground again rose in a steady grade. About four hundred yards from the river, along the opposite slope, ran a railroad embankment (about the height of that of the Pennsylvania Railroad across the Jersey meadows), roughly paralleling the course of the stream. The railroad station of St. Souplet lay across the river, and the road to it passed under the embankment. A train, consisting of an engine and two or three coaches, was standing by the station, but steam was not up in the engine. There were no signs of the Germans, although we thought that we could detect earth thrown up in the fields in various places. Far up the opposite hill we saw groups of farm buildings, which from our maps we identified as Advantage Farm. We were later to spend some exciting moments there.

It was raining steadily and the ground was very wet; it was necessary for us now to do considerable crawling. We threw ourselves on our stomachs before reaching the crest of the hill and, as we wriggled over the top, came into view of the scene I have just described.

About seventy-five yards down the forward slope, we saw two or three shallow detached trenches overgrown with grass, evidently relics of the 1914 fighting. We decided to use these small trenches as a base during the engagement and to locate our reloading station and company headquarters there. We crawled along to these trenches and found them well adapted for the purpose. Egleston and I then crept out twenty yards in advance and staked out the positions to be occupied by the three platoons and our twelve guns. We intended to do a lot of digging that night, so that when we commenced to fire our men might be well protected. All this took about three-quarters of an hour and was immensely tedious and fatiguing because we dared not stand up. We then rejoined our sergeants in the trenches and pointed out to them the plan of operations we had formed for that night.

When we were ready to leave, we were so sick of crawling that we decided to chance it and walk. Egleston was to go first and I was to bring up the rear. He started at a steady walk, reached the brow of the hill without incident, and disappeared. He was followed by Sergeants Kitching and Cox. When O'Keefe stepped out, he was greeted with a burst of machine gun fire, as the enemy was now thoroughly alive to the situation. Crawling was of no use now that the attention of the Germans had been attracted, as the hillside lay in full view. There was nothing for it but speed. Jack made a break for safety. Bullets sent up spurts of dirt all around him but he disappeared over the crest of the hill in safety. It was then my turn to run the gauntlet, and I had no sooner stepped out of the trench than I heard the zip of machine gun bullets striking almost at my heels. I broke into a run. The bullets followed me and played most disconcertingly around my heels, but they all missed. I reached the crest of the hill without mishap and found my friends observing my progress. We all laughed, although it was not much of a joke. I have frequently noticed that laughter is a common reaction to fear.

When we reached camp we found the battalion swallowing hot coffee, with everything packed and everyone under arms. It was nearly six o'clock and already dark. We were tired—having walked about ten miles, not to mention the distance we had crawled—but there was no time to rest. We fell in immediately after mess to march to the positions we had selected.

Our company was first away, under my command, as Egleston had ridden up to speak to the Major. The entrance to our field had been in the direction of Prémont. I intended to save time by cutting straight across the field to the main highroad on which we were to turn right. We marched across the front of Company D who were falling in and I made some joking remark to Stanton Whitney about being late for the party. We were moving in column, each platoon being followed by its fighting limbers, with twenty-five-yard distances between platoons. As the head of our company reached the highroad alongside our field and turned to the right, I received a message from Matthews that telegraph wire was fouled around the wheels of one of his limbers, necessitating a slight delay. Accordingly, I halted, and Company D, which had left the field by the old entrance, came up the road and passed us—Whitney calling out to clear the way for the shock troops. This little delay saved the lives of a number of our fellows that night, my own, perhaps, included.

We followed Company D for about a half-mile, Egleston joining us and riding up and down the column. We then heard very heavy shelling along the road before us at intervals of about thirty seconds, apparently battery fire. At a crossroad just short of Becquigny we were held up by the M.P.'s, who told us that the company ahead had sustained heavy losses. Very soon a number of stretchers bearing wounded came back. We learned from the bearers that two shells had landed squarely in the first platoon of Company D in the village of Becquigny, killing and wounding a number of men.

Sending word to Egleston of what had happened, I entered a hut, beside the road, from which I observed a glimmer of light, in order to consult my map and see whether we could avoid the dangerous corner where I could now hear the shells falling very fast. I found that by taking a slight detour to the left we could strike a narrow road paralleling the course of the road under shell fire and re-enter it beyond the village. I so advised Egleston and he promptly turned the company into the crossroad and we resumed our march. Although we could hear the shells bursting on the highroad not two hundred yards to our right, all was quiet along the track we followed, and we sustained no casualties.

When we turned into one of the roads we had followed in the afternoon, we were stopped by some gunners who told us it was reserved for the artillery. Captain Egleston paid no attention to the remonstrances of the gunners and we marched up the road as we had planned. In this he was wise as it is fatal to change your route at night. As we marched along, machine gun bullets whistled overhead from time to time and one of them went through the jaws of a horse. No other damage was done. We reached our position in the sunken road without having sustained a casualty—the only company in our battalion to escape. I have always attributed our good fortune on this and other occasions to the meticulous care which Egleston took to reconnoiter personally every inch of the ground over which he intended to move his men.

We promptly disposed our limbers along the sunken road and led our platoons to their positions. While we were digging the emplacements, Hillyer figured the firing data for all guns. The data were all rechecked by the platoon commanders. We dug a deep narrow emplacement for each—gunslits, the British called them. These were about four and a half feet in depth, two in width, and about six feet long. The gun was at one end of the slit, protected by the earth which was banked up around the edges. The slits were about twenty yards apart and about ten yards in their rear, and between each pair of guns we dug deep narrow trenches for the section sergeants. The reloading squads and the company headquarters were to be located in the old trenches to which I have already referred. The men took turns at the digging, which was very tedious and which they hated, but which I insisted upon. I believe that the stress we laid on deep slits prevented many casualties next morning.

By three o'clock we had finished our work. We set out the firing stakes along the line of the trajectory of each gun, so that the deflection could be checked. Each corporal, section chief, and platoon commander was given the firing data for his guns. Egleston and I had the firing data for all guns, in case either of us should be killed.

Very slow work, the next two hours. Our orders required us to open fire at twenty minutes past five. Under cover of the artillery and machine guns, our infantry was to cross the river and carry its objectives on the opposite bank. At four-thirty we issued all hands a good stiff dose of some real unadulterated West Indian rum; we all felt ready for anything. Great stuff, that grog. About a minute before zero hour some machine guns commenced to fire from the vicinity of Escaufort, about a thousand yards in our rear. Other guns opened to our right, and the artillery set up a most tremendous barrage. At five-twenty to the second our guns opened and from that moment communication by speech was impossible. This turned out to be one of the biggest machine gun barrages fired during the war, assisted by an unusually heavy concentration of artillery.

The Germans were not surprised. Down came their counter-barrage like a steel curtain. Shells exploded on all sides of us, and the crack of bullets, the hum of projectiles, and the vicious whir of shell fragments was incessant. It was apparent that our guns were sited right on the German S.O.S. line and nothing but our good deep slits saved us from annihilation.

Poor Von Dohlen was hit almost instantly in the back of the head. Hermes and another stretcher-bearer assisted by Lieutenant Matthews dragged him out and carried him through the hail of shell fire to the sunken road, but he was gone before they started. Bodamer was struck in the face by a fragment and subsequently died. In about ten minutes the infantry commenced to pass us in thin lines of combat groups. A battalion of the 107th went first, followed by a battalion of the 105th. One of their sergeants was struck within five feet of me and his hand carried away. He looked at the bloody stump and then jumped into our trench and asked permission to sit there. We bound up his wound and also found he had two machine gun bullets through his leg.

Our barrage lasted forty-five minutes and it seemed an eternity to me. There was nothing for me to do but smoke one cigar after another. As second in command, my job was to wait until Egleston was hit, and then take over and fight the company. The smoke from the guns and shells hung in dense clouds around us, through which I could see the tongues of flame spitting from each of our guns. The ground rocked with the German shells which threw up masses of debris on all sides. The smell of explosives was strangling.

Two of our guns went out of action but the others maintained a steady fire. At the end of forty-five minutes we ceased firing, moved our guns back to the sunken road, and to the credit of our company carried with us every last ammunition box, intrenching tool, and piece of equipment in spite of the fact that this necessitated repeated trips from the firing positions to the limbers under the heavy shelling.

Our orders required us to move forward at seven-thirty and occupy the trenches upon which we had been firing. In the meantime we ate our breakfast of cheese sandwiches and coffee. We had selected an excellent spot as a shelter because, by reason of the steep hill between us and the enemy, only very high-angled fire could reach us. We began to be enfiladed, however, by some long range artillery in the German sector to our left, back of Le Cateau. Sergeant Chubb received a painful blow on the knee from a shell fragment which was almost spent, and I got a smart rap on the thigh. We fed our horses. The beast with the bullet through his jaw ate heartily although two little streams of oats trickled out of the holes.

While we were munching our sandwiches, a battalion of infantry entered our valley and sought shelter under our hill. The battalion commander sent out patrols to the village of St. Souplet and he and some of his officers climbed the hill and took a look at the forward slope from which we had been firing. He returned, remarking that no troops could live there, and his patrols reported that the village of St. Souplet was impassable by reason of the severity of the shell fire. Egleston made no comment, but at seven-thirty ordered Lieutenant Lyon to take his platoon and limbers through St. Souplet, cross the river, and move down the railroad embankment to the right to a small railroad bridge. Lyon and his men fell in without a second's hesitation and started down the road to St. Souplet. In less than a hundred yards they were out of sight in the dust and smoke. George Matthews moved out five minutes later with the first platoon, followed by Lieutenant McCaskey. Their orders required them to pass through St. Souplet, cross the river, advance with their limbers as far as the road was passable, and then cross the railroad embankment and occupy the small trenches on the further slope at which we had been firing. "Goodbye, good luck, give 'em Hell," we shouted. I believed it was the last time I should ever see poor George.

In half an hour a limber drawn by four gray horses at a gallop emerged from the cloud of smoke and dust along the road, and as it approached I recognized my former striker Ocelik driving the lead team and grinning cheerfully. In the limber were O'Neill, with a bad leg wound, and three or four other casualties. Ocelik was driving one of Matthews' limbers and reported that by good luck they had traversed the town safely. There were no troops in St. Souplet. They had been able to cross the bridge which the engineers were repairing as fast as the Germans knocked it down, and had driven their limbers to the railroad embankment. The Germans had blown up the embankment this morning and the road under it was blocked with debris and the wreck of the train we had observed the previous day. The guns and ammunition had been unloaded here and carried forward by hand, and the platoon had occupied the positions to which it had been assigned. While we talked to Ocelik, the other limbers returned in safety and the second and third platoons reported themselves in position.

We reported to battalion and told the infantry that our guns were across the river. They seemed to doubt us, as their patrols reported that no one could live in St. Souplet. We told them we were about to move our headquarters across the river to the railroad embankment, and started off. St. Souplet was under intensive shell fire. The town reeked with gas and the smell of explosives, and was strewn with dead and wounded. I saw no civilians alive, but at the foot of the hill we passed the body of a little shriveled old woman. We laid her on the sidewalk and stood a gun tripod over her body. We were much affected by the cries for help of some wounded, whom we were obliged to pass as no fighting men could be spared to care for them.

The Selle River was narrow, not much over fifteen yards in width. In some places it had been crossed that morning by tanks, but in the sector assigned to us the banks were so steep that it was impossible to get vehicles across except by the bridge. The Germans naturally rained a furious tempest of shells on this bridge and the 102nd Engineers worked steadily under this fire repairing it. They certainly were good men.

After crossing the bridge the road ascended to the railroad embankment. Where it had passed under the embankment we found it piled to the height of twenty feet with every kind of debris. Here we met a lot of German prisoners coming back without any guards, in many cases assuring themselves of a welcome by carrying stretchers containing wounded.

The infantry who had followed us moved to our left into an old abandoned quarry. We established company headquarters on the road beyond the embankment, moving our limbers into the quarry across the road. Egleston and I took turns visiting the platoons.

In the fields to the right of the road were some trenches where the fighting had been very heavy. They were filled with dead Germans. Before them and across the field were strewn the bodies of a number of our infantrymen of the 108th. Almost at the parapet of the trench, with a bullet in his forehead and his pistol in his hand, lay the body of Lieutenant Dick Smith, who had led his men right up to the muzzles of the guns. It was a fine death and from the looks of the trench his men had avenged him. I had traveled with Smith back from that school at Clamecy. When I came home I looked up the girl in Rochester he had desired to have notified in case of his death and wrote her what I had seen. It was the first news she had received of the circumstances of Smith's death.

By three o'clock the German fire had considerably subsided, indicating that the guns were being pulled out to positions further in the rear. At the height of its intensity it had been intended to cover the withdrawal of the German infantry. Our machine gunners were as safe as we could make them. We maintained headquarters at the embankment till dusk and then returned to the sunken road across the river where we spent the night. I lay by the body of poor Von Dohlen and slept the sleep of utter exhaustion.

On the following morning we received orders to advance to the large farm at the crest of the slope across the river, which I have already referred to as Advantage Farm, and to concentrate our company there. The infantry holding the line had been greatly reduced by casualties and it was necessary for the machine guns to step into the gaps at the actual front, thereby violating fundamental tactical principles for the most effective disposition of machine guns. However, *"faute de mieux je couche avec ma femme,"* as our Allies would put it. We sent word to our platoon commanders to move to Advantage Farm and started thither with company headquarters, carrying with us as much ammunition as we could.

The enemy artillery was still shelling St. Souplet and our side of the river. As we walked over the ground from which we had fired our barrage on the previous day we marveled that our company had not been wiped out. The slope of the hill was literally covered with shell craters. We reached the railroad embankment without much difficulty and found that the engineers had made much progress in the removal of the debris, although the road was still very much obstructed and it was impossible for vehicles to pass. We clambered over the pile of bricks, twisted rails, and smashed railway coaches and started on the long, straight road leading up the hill. This was now being shelled very severely by the enemy, so that we moved by the side of the road in column of files at considerable distances. Each of us was carrying spare ammunition. O'Keefe and I undertook to carry two loaded belt boxes in each hand, making a total load of a thousand rounds of cartridges aside from the weight of the metal belt boxes and our equipment. Before I reached the top of that hill I began to feel a great deal of sympathy for ammunition carriers. The day was clear and sunny, quite warm. We were about half-way up the hill when we saw a shell strike almost in the midst of a small group of infantrymen and three of them fall. One was killed and the other two were badly wounded. One of them raised himself on his elbow as we passed and begged us to help him. His mouth was shot away. We could not stop, but promised to send aid, which we did almost immediately, as we met a crowd of German prisoners with some stretcher bearers.

On one of the stretchers was a very attractive looking young officer. He had three machine gun bullets through his chest and I am afraid was in a bad way. He asked us for a cigarette, but one of the bullets must have punctured his lungs, as he could not make it draw. A little further on we met two German officers coming down the road without a guard. They inquired the way to the P.O.W. cage to which we politely directed them. It seemed funny to be talking to them that way.

At the top of the hill we found one of our tanks, which had been wrecked by a direct hit. Avoiding the little town of Arbre Guernon which lay on the crest of the hill, we cut off to the left through the fields and reached Advantage Farm. We found that George Matthews' and McCaskey's platoons had already arrived, as well as Ray Biglow with A Company. Matthews' platoon occupied a hedge on the further side of the road running along the crest of the ridge, upon which Advantage Farm faced. Lyon's platoon came up a few minutes later. This was about ten-thirty in the morning and the enemy's shell fire was very intense. Casualties from Matthews' platoon came in fast. A very good man named Richards was hit quite badly in the leg. Jack Tierney was also wounded, and Matthews while helping tie up his wounds was himself struck in the head by a small shell fragment and his wound bled a good deal. Much against his wishes we sent him to the rear for a shot of antitetanus serum. I took over his platoon and found the men shifting about to avoid the shells. O'Keefe was hit by a fragment and bruised, although not cut. We were finally ordered to fall back into the shelter of the farm buildings which were only a hundred yards from us. In about an hour the shelling ceased.

Egleston and I took a look at the situation, talked with the infantry officers, and made up our minds that it would be a question of hanging onto this position for some time. The infantry was too weak to do much advancing. We determined to bring up our entire transport and park it on the Farm, which was quite large enough to hold it all. We ran a considerable risk of having it wiped out by shelling, but determined that this risk was more than offset by the advantages of having the whole company together and the kitchen available, so that the men could have the best food possible. That night Sergeant Carver brought up the transport and the rest of the company, taking a road through St. Martin's instead of the road by which we had walked.

About three o'clock in the afternoon an English lieutenant with a patrol of about thirty hussars galloped through the gate of our courtyard and dismounted under the shelter of the walls. Almost immediately a sheaf of machine gun bullets whistled through the same gateway, showing we were under observation. The lieutenant had come up in search of information as to the front line. I told him where he could find Egleston, who was the best posted man in that sector, and he started off on foot with his sergeant to look for him. They all crawled to within a few yards of the German position.

Egleston returned shortly afterwards with the information that a large farm known as La Jonquière Farm about seven hundred yards from us was very strongly held by the Germans, who appeared to be massing there for a counter-attack. Our infantry commander believed it would help if we could treat them to some fire. I took seven guns across the road under cover of a hedge, figured the firing data, and blazed away. I watched them for a while and then went back to the farm to report to battalion. Harold Downey of A Company met me and inquired what we had been doing. He was horrified when he heard of our firing on this farm, which, reports to A Company indicated (he said), was held by patrols of the 107th Infantry. I told him Egleston had looked the place over and knew it was German. While we were arguing, a staff officer came up, who was also satisfied the place was within our lines, and to add to the confusion Captain Campbell of the 102nd Engineers arrived with eighty of his men and stated that he had been ordered to march to La Jonquière to reinforce the 107th. He showed me his written orders to that effect. I explained to Captain Campbell what was now going on and that we had personally reconnoitered and knew what we were about. I suggested that he leave his men under cover of our buildings and personally satisfy himself that La Jonquière was held by the Germans. Campbell was a very sensible fellow and started off for a little personal reconnaissance. Egleston had returned by this time, and he and I with Ray Biglow and Fahys Cook proceeded to pick out and establish gun positions for the night, with the object of best helping the infantry and making good the shortages in their ranks.

By dark we had our guns in position and had made the rounds. Our dismay may be imagined when a messenger arrived from battalion with very particular and imperative instructions as to the disposition of the guns of our companies for that night. From the positions selected we were absolutely sure that the orders were based on inaccurate information as to the front line. Egleston and I decided instantly that this was an occasion for disregarding orders and we were perfectly willing to assume the responsibility. Biglow and his officers, however, were very doubtful and were inclined to believe that battalion and brigade were in possession of information which we lacked. While we were debating the question among ourselves and with Captain Campbell, a young second lieutenant of infantry joined our group and sat silently listening to the discussion. Then he inquired who had fired the barrage that afternoon on La Jonquière. He said he had been lying with his platoon within three hundred yards of that farm in plain sight of it when our barrage fell and that the Germans swarmed there like a hive of angry bees.

This convinced Biglow and Downey that we were right in our information. We decided to disregard the battalion order and sent back a message to that effect giving our reasons. Captain Campbell put himself and his engineers at Egleston's disposal, who placed them where they would do the most good that night if we were attacked. The Engineers were a great crowd and Campbell was an unusually fine officer. To complete our feeling of comfort, "Chub" Hancock of the 104th Machine Gun Battalion tramped into our courtyard a few minutes later with his platoon, with orders to place his men at our disposal. We placed his guns in the positions selected by battalion, so that everybody was happy.

The night passed off without an attack or a great deal of sleep on our part. The Germans had apparently decided to withdraw and in the morning we found their positions had been abandoned. There were no trenches to speak of in this country, which had never been fought over since the early days of the war. Both sides took advantage of hedges, sunken roads, and other forms of natural cover. Open warfare prevailed. That morning, which was the 19th of October, Egleston and I devoted to reconnoitering positions.

The fighting on October 16th and 17th had been very severe. The young infantry lieutenant who had witnessed our barrage on La Jonquière told me that he had started out on the morning of the 16th with eighty-four men in his company and that by evening only twelve were left. I believe this was M Company of the 105th, commanded by Captain Whipple. The Germans suffered equally severely. In the course of two or three days we counted over fifty German machine gun nests knocked out by us, in each of which there were at least two bodies. In some of the larger ones there were seven or eight corpses. These German machine gunners did not know the meaning of the word surrender and put up a perfectly magnificent fight. They were evidently the picked men of the German armies and it was because of their heroic self-sacrifice that the German retreat was such a success from a military point of view.

There was one very curious feature connected with our occupation of Advantage Farm, for which I have never found a satisfactory explanation. The buildings were on the edge of an important highroad and were solidly built structures of masonry covering almost an acre. We knew that the German guards had occupied this farm in force, and they must have realized that it was strongly held by our people. Yet in the four days of our occupancy the farm was never hit by a single shell. Repeatedly during the day and night the German guns searched the field across the road, and the shells came right to the edge of the field. This happened again and again. An increase of twenty-five yards in range would have smashed our buildings to smithereens. We never knew to what to attribute our escape, unless the buildings really were mined and they were trying to encourage us to stay in them so that the debacle might be more complete—like the little boy patting a dog to quiet it so that he could hitch a kettle to its tail.

On the 19th of October Colonel True, in command of the infantry, made his plans for an advance. He appeared to have the greatest respect for Egleston, and discussed every move with him and went over the ground with him in the greatest detail. He might well have confidence in Egleston. I never saw a soldier with a cooler head or a surer or quicker grasp of the needs of a military situation. He had the endurance of ten men and simply did not know the meaning of the word fear. I have been told that during the four days fighting on the Selle River Egleston's reports, which went back to battalion with unfailing regularity and were masterly summaries of the situation, were the only accurate sources of information of the situation up the line available to Division. They won Egleston his majority the next month.

That evening we received word that our 30th Division, on the right, was to force its way up the hill and carry the town of Mazinghien. This town lay about fifteen hundred yards to our right front. We were ordered to support the attack and accordingly fired a long barrage on Mazinghien until a runner informed us that the town had been captured. This night firing was very good fun. The fact that we were not interrupted by the German artillery indicated that they had again pulled their guns further to the rear.

Our advance next morning corroborated this inference. We moved up all along the line almost to the Sambre Canal where the Germans once more took up a strong defensive position. I was interested to find a number of dead Germans around La Jonquière Farm, the result of our machine gun barrage when Division believed this farm to be occupied by the 107th. We found here two wounded privates of the 105th Infantry, Cahill and Weir, who had been captured by the Germans and held in La Jonquière when our barrage fell. They told us that there were at least five hundred Germans there who were so demoralized by our fire, which they believed was a prelude to an attack, that they would have surrendered to a corporal's guard.

On the 20th of October we learned that we were to be relieved. We were visited by innumerable British staff officers, all of whom tried to pre-empt our buildings as quarters for their particular general, but sheered off when we spoke of the possibility of mines. All generals are averse to mines. Late that afternoon Company B of the 6th British Machine Gun Battalion, which we had relieved at Dickebush, appeared to take over from us. Major Finlay was in England, and the company was under command of Lieutenant Cochrane whom I had met in Flanders.

To avoid congestion on the roads, we decided to move out of the lines by platoons. I started with the first platoon and its transport shortly after dark. We were delayed for some time on the road down the hill to St. Souplet as an enormous British gun drawn by six horses had stuck. The united efforts of my platoon and of a company of Tommies failed to budge the gun. Traffic was halted all up and down the line to everyone's disgust. Finally I sent Sergeant O'Keefe to try to find a path through the fields which could be traversed by our limbers; he returned in a short while and reported that if we could get the limbers up the steep banks the rest would be easy. We had a hard job but finally hoisted our limbers about nine feet up an almost perpendicular bank and squared away through the fields coming into the main road near the railway embankment. The engineers had cleared the mess and rebuilt the bridge over the river. In St. Souplet the Red Cross had opened a canteen so we halted for a mug of hot cocoa and some cake.

Taking the road from Le Cateau instead of the one we had used the night before the fight, we halted at Escaufort where we were joined by the rest of the company. Hillyer left to report to brigade and I marched the company along at a steady pace, reaching our old camping ground of Becquinette Farm after midnight. We pitched pup tents without any particular stress on alignment and everybody had a hot feed and turned in.

The following day was terribly rainy and unpleasant. Our march took us to Bellicourt, where we were supposed to be billeted, but every house in the town was in ruins. We moved into a large field which was covered by water to a depth of a couple of inches, and the men were ordered to pitch shelter tents. It was of course necessary to unroll the packs and lay the contents on the wet ground exposed to the rain, which fell steadily. The men didn't like it a bit and said so, and I did not blame them much. However, the tents went up. We then sprang a welcome surprise. We still had a petrol tin of the rum which had been issued to us the night before the St. Souplet show and we passed the word for everyone to fall in for a rum ration. This order was certainly obeyed with alacrity and everyone got a good dram in his mess cup. In spite of the conditions I did not hear of anybody catching cold, with the possible exception of poor Ellis and Drabble, and I am confident that the rum saved the situation.

In this field were two or three large captured German cannon, covered by tarpaulins, under guard of a British sentry who was tramping up and down in the mud, dripping from every part of his equipment. Egleston went up and gave him a big drink of rum. He grinned cheerfully and raised his cup. " 'Ere's to your werr' good 'ealth, sir, and I 'opes as 'ow you'll henjoy your houting."

On the following morning we resumed our march, crossing the old Hindenburg Line and having a further opportunity for noting the extraordinary defensive preparations made by the Germans. Their belief that this Line was impregnable would appear to be justified. There was a story current in our Division of a conversation between a British General and General O'Ryan. The Englishman congratulated O'Ryan on our victory but commented on our casualties, which he intimated were unnecessarily high, much greater than the British had suffered earlier in the war in their attacks on the position. "True," said O'Ryan, "but we took the Line."

We spent this night in our old bivvies in the sunken road at Hervilly, where we also rested all the next morning. About noon we received orders to march to the small town of Roisel, ready to entrain at two o'clock. This only necessitated a march of two miles, so that we arrived at Roisel (which was railhead for our sector) in plenty of time. Our train, as usual, was not ready, so we made ourselves comfortable alongside the tracks and waited. Time wore on and about four-thirty we served out mess to the company from the rolling cooker. The railway at the place we were halted consisted of a double track on a three-foot embankment. Fifty yards down the track was a grade crossing. A number of empty freight cars were being shunted up and down the tracks.

I was talking to Egleston, as we sat beside the tracks, when I saw his eyes contract as he stared over my shoulder. I turned in time to see the grade crossing blowing up. A large British water cart, drawn by two horses was six feet in the air, one of the horses with his feet towards the sky. The air was thick with twisted rails and fragments of debris. There was no crash or explosion, just a sort of *woof*. We rushed to the spot and found that the damage had been done by a delayed action mine planted by the Germans before they pulled out. As they had not been in Roisel for more than a month the diabolical nature of the machine is apparent. The crossing might perfectly well have been occupied by women and children when the mine went off, as far as the Germans could tell. As things stood, it had raised havoc with a Chinese labor battalion working along the track. I saw one Chinaman with his skull cut clean in half like a boiled egg, his brain still throbbing as he lay on the ground. About two tons of the debris fell into a lorry which was standing near the crossing, in which were a dozen Tommies. We dug these men out, and found three dead with a good many injured. It was lucky for us that we were not entraining at the time. As we were picking up the wounded, a detachment of German prisoners came along and for a few minutes were pretty roughly handled. It was a relaxation. War is cruel work and humane fighting is an anomalous term, but there are some things which ought not to be done. I did not care for this German practice of spreading delayed action mines through the area they were abandoning. It was too much of a piece with the way they hacked down fruit trees, destroyed private property, and generally made themselves as nasty as they could. In this particular instance the railroad was repaired in twenty-four hours, so that the military damage was negligible.

The explosion, however, caused the battalion discomfort as we were forced to resume our march to pick up our train at Tincourt. This meant a hike of about eight miles through the dark, and the rain had commenced to fall again. We reached Tincourt about ten-thirty that night and sat down by the track and waited. Always this infernal waiting. It was cold and we did our best to scrape together some wood and to light a few fires, at which we warmed ourselves.

Our transport had received orders to proceed by road to our destination, which was a small town about fifteen miles up the Somme from Amiens, called Vaux-sur-Somme. Our train pulled in at 3:00 A.M. About dawn we started on our journey to the back area. It was a cheerless ride. We had no food nor any prospect of procuring any, as the towns through which we passed were in ruins and uninhabited. I shall never forget the desolation of the Somme country—not a house standing, not a tree alive, the whole country strewn with wrecked wagons, gun limbers, pieces of equipment, and thousands upon thousands of soldiers' graves marked by the pathetic white crosses. On the crests of the hills the dead, leafless trees looked like gaunt specters.

OFFICERS OF THE MACHINE GUN BATTALION, LE LUART, FEBRUARY, 1919

SQUADRON A FARM
EX-MEMBERS' ASSOCIATION MEETING ROOM IN ARMORY

About three o'clock in the afternoon we detrained at Corbie. The town had been an Australian base during the big March drive and had been frightfully battered. It lay between Amiens and the furthest point reached by the German advance. We marched through this town, where Division Headquarters was located, and about two miles up the Somme to Vaux. It was rather a pretty walk, as the trees in this part of the country had not been destroyed and were bright with the colors of autumn. The river and the canal also were lovely as they wound through the rich meadow lands. The country was hilly.

We found Vaux a very badly battered town, containing no civilians. It had marked the high tide of the German advance in 1918. Portions of the town had been in the possession of both sides, and the German trenches ran through it. There is a very interesting description of this town and of the unusual situation which existed here by reason of the proximity of the hostile lines, in "Now It Can Be Told." The outposts of both sides lay in the woods along the river, which resulted in a bushwhacking, frontier system of fighting that involved frequent skirmishes.

No house in Vaux was entirely roofed, and there were large gaps in most of the walls. Company B was quartered in three large farmhouses along the Corbie Road. We arrived on October 25th and from that time until November 26th, when we left, I do not recall that the sun ever shone, and the rain seemed to fall incessantly.

On our first Sunday at Vaux we held a memorial service in honor of the men in the battalion who had died. We held it in the little Catholic church, with its smashed windows, gaping roof, and shell-shattered walls. The whole battalion turned out. Chaplain Bass preached a fine sermon and Captain Whitney spoke of our dead. The scene and the circumstances made a profound impression on me. A battalion of Americans in their war-stained uniforms, gathered in a ruined little church on the Somme, listening to MacDonald, a former Princeton Triangle Club man, singing, in his wonderful tenor, "Rock of Ages," accompanied by John Going (George Matthews' striker) on a captured Stradivarius violin. It scarcely seemed that it could be true. There was a sincerity, a genuine reverence to this service which I have never felt before or since.

1919–1939
SQUADRON A AGAIN BECOMES A PART OF THE
NATIONAL GUARD

SQUADRON A AGAIN BECOMES A PART OF THE NATIONAL GUARD

> It is most meet to arm us 'gainst the foe;
> For peace itself should not so dull a kingdom,
> But that defences, musters, preparations,
> Should be maintain'd, assembl'd and collected,
> As were a war in expectation.
> —SHAKESPEARE, "Henry V"

> *Prospicere in pace opportet quod bellum juvet.*
> —PUBLIUS SYRIUS, "Sententiae"

THIS crucial period in the history of Squadron A is dealt with in the narrative of General N. Hillyer Egleston, who as Major commanded the squadron at that time.

The history of the 105th Machine Gun Battalion, including its distinguished service overseas, has already been told, as well as the fact that when mustered out on April 1, 1919, and discharged from service in the Army of the United States, it ceased to exist as a military organization.

The organization and activities of the Depot Squadron, which later became Squadron A, New York Guard, have also been recounted. Upon the demobilization of the machine gun battalion, this cavalry unit of the New York State Guard alone remained as the representative of the old Squadron A. It was the natural aim of all interested in the squadron and its history to make this organization again a part of the National Guard and to put it upon the same plane of responsibility and efficiency that the squadron of former days had held. Nearly two years were necessary to achieve this objective; but it was achieved, and the narrative of the squadron commander modestly tells the tale. The prestige of former members who had served overseas and later rejoined the squadron was a vital factor in this accomplishment. This was particularly true of the squadron commander and the other officers.

SQUADRON A

The first to reenter service as a member of Squadron A was John Reynolds, who was given command of a troop in May, 1919, the month following the demobilization of the machine gun battalion. Two months later N. Hillyer Egleston was appointed to command the squadron, and George Matthews, Jr., was given command of a troop. During the remainder of that year three more overseas veterans rejoined, each with the rank of first lieutenant. They were Carleton S. Cooke, Anthony J. Drexel, Jr., and James C. Fargo. Frederick A. Vietor, the present squadron commander, returned early in the next year. The following is a list of those who rejoined: an asterisk being placed opposite the name of any man who held rank as an officer during the war, and the symbol (†) designating a decoration or citation.

Allen, Morton B.†
Aylward, Thomas
Baker, Charles
Barry, Herbert, Jr.
Beahan, Richard P.
Bossard, Wolfgang D. K.
Carver, Richard M.
Ceballos, Juan M.*
Clapp, Herbert M.
Coe, Colles J.*
Cooke, Carleton S.*
Drexel, Anthony J., Jr.*
Durham, Knowlton * †
Effinger, William E.
Egleston, N. Hillyer * †
Fargo, James C.*
Kingsbury, Slocum *

MacKinlay, Donald A. G.†
Martin, James J.
Matthews, George, Jr.* †
Nack, William J.
Reynolds, John * †
Robinson, Hamilton W.
Robinson, James H.
Schieffelin, John Jay * †
Shaw, Lewis Edward * †
Sheldon, Farrington
Shurtleff, Harold R.*
Simm, David
Stammers, Alfred H.
Taft, William H., 2nd *
Vietor, Frederick A.*
Werleman, Frederick H.†
Zimmermann, Louis

The reputation of the squadron and the outstanding position that it had always held doubtless led to large number of enlistments by men who had served overseas in other units; and it is also significant that many of those who after the war enlisted as privates in the squadron had held rank as officers in their overseas service. These former commissioned officers were prominent in a review for General Clarence A. Edwards at Fort Ethan Allen in 1931, when one troop turned out a guard that included twenty-nine former officers, including a major of marines, a major of infantry, five captains, eleven first lieutenants,

SQUADRON A

one lieutenant commander of naval aviation, and ten second lieutenants. Two of the Guard had been aides to General Edwards in France and had held the rank of captain. The names of those who served during the war in other units and afterwards joined the squadron and aided in its rebuilding are given in the following list, and an asterisk is placed opposite the name of each member who held a commission during the war.

NEW MEMBERS AFTER THE WAR, WITH WAR-SERVICE RECORDS OUTSIDE THE SQUADRON

Abbett, Sheldon *
Allan, Parker B.*
Ames, Charles E.*
Amory, John F.
Arnaud, Leopold
Ashmore, Sidney B.
Austin, Charles D.
Averill, Lloyd B.*
Baldwin, Charles H.
Banks, Charles W.
Banks, Robert F.
Barnes, Charles M.
Barry, Rutledge B.*
Bartow, Charles
Bastine, Wilfrid S.*
Bayliss, Charles E., Jr.
Bearce, Herbert P.
Becket, Robert M.*
Bellinger, Edmund B.*
Bennett, David V.*
Bentley, Edward S.*
Blake, Gilman D.*
Bonnevalle, Richard W. *
Booth, Lewis S.*
Bowen, Edmund J.*
Briggs, William W.
Brinkerhoff, Elbert V.
Brookmire, Samuel K.
Brooks, Sidney *
Brown, Harold L.*
Buffin, Leopold L.*

Burns, Arthur S.
Cairns, Robert E.*
Cannon, Townsend L.
Card, Thomas B.*
Carley, Harry G.*
Carnochan, Gouverneur M.
Carpenter, James J.*
Carrington, John B., Jr.
Carson, Donald A.*
Clapp, Charles E., Jr.*
Clark, Arthur Ludlow
Clark, John H., Jr.
Clayton, Charles E.*
Clement, Roger C.*
Cloutman, Harold J.
Cobb, Andrew L.
Cobb, Francis C.
Coffin, John R.*
Coombe, Reginald G.*
Crim, William D.*
Cross, Jeremiah F.
Cumings, John B.*
Cunningham, Francis de L.*
Curtis, Brian C.*
Curtis, John J.
Daly, Raymond J.*
Darrin, Howard A.*
Davis, Robert J.
Davis, Wendell *
Dean, Arthur H.
DeBevoise, Eli W.

SQUADRON A

Dinkey, Alva C.
Donaldson, Chase *
Doyle, Edward J.
Doyle, Milton D.
Drowne, H. Russell, Jr.*
Dunn, Charles B.
Durham, Charles H., Jr.
Ellis, Roland, Jr.*
Emerson, Willard I.*
Emison, James W.
Fahy, Charles H.
Fahys, Joseph *
Fairhurst, Henry D.
Fanning, William L.
Fansler, Henry D.*
Farr, James McC.*
Field, James B.*
Fisher, Schuyler
Fitzgerald, John H.*
Fitz-Gibbon, William
Fitzhugh, Armistead
Fleming, Wallace *
Fleming, William C.*
Flintom, Lathrop B.*
Foster, Stephen M.
Fox, Andrew J., Jr.*
Franklin, Philip A. S., Jr.*
Franks, Ralph C.
Freeman, Morris de C.*
Frey, Alexander H.
Frugone, James G.
Full, Henry P.*
Gaillard, Edward M.*
Gale, Hollis P.
Gamwell, William W.
Garside, Charles
Gibbs, John E.
Gifford, Isaac C.
Glick, Clifford H.*
Goodspeed, Franklin S.
Goss, Walter D.
Gough, William R.*

Gould, James *
Gould, William T., Jr.*
Graham, Joseph A.
Graves, Justin D.*
Greeff, Charles A.
Halliwell, Roger D.
Hand, Herbert T.*
Haneman, Henry W.
Harrison, John D.*
Hasbrouck, Carl J.
Havell, George
Hawkins, David R.*
Hay, William I.*
Hemingway, Charles S.*
Heminway, James C.*
Hill, Edward A.
Hoag, William K.
Hoggson, Wallace *
Holden, Lansing C., Jr.*
Hole, James W.
Hotchkiss, Edward G.*
Houghtaling, David H.*
Hoyt, James K., Jr.*
Hoyt, John R.*
Hunter, Lawrence M.
Iselin, Henry *
Jamison, D. Stearns, Jr.
Johnson, Tom L.
Johnson, Wallace C.*
Johnstone, George C.
Jordan, Sydney S., Jr.*
Kane, Richmond K.
Keith, Isham
Kennedy, John D.*
Kirkland, Samuel N.*
Kline, William S.
Koenig, Herbert A.
Kondolf, Harold *
Lamarche, Albert H.
Lamarche, Richard F.*
Lamb, Horace R.*
LaMotte, Robert H.

Lane, William R.
Langthorn, Jacob S., Jr.
Lardner, Gilmore A.*
Larner, Robert J.
LaRoche, Chester J.
Lawrence, Malcolm R., Jr.
Lea, Charles Russell
Leisure, George S.*
Lesher, Arthur L., Jr.
Lewis, Halstead H.*
Lewis, Henry C.
Litch, Robert B.
Litt, Willard D.*
Lloyd, Robert A. McA., Jr.*
Lodge, Henry G.
Long, Hamilton A.
Lucas, Russell H.
Lull, Ernest P.*
Lyon, Edward A.
Lyon, William E. B.*
MacInnes, John *
MacRossie, Allan, Jr.*
McCaddon, Joseph T., Jr.*
McClellan, Otey
McHenry, Howard *
McKay, Allan T.
McLanahan, John D.*
McNeile, Hector J.*
Machado, José A., Jr.
Maddox, William J.*
Maitland, James W.*
Maltby, Monroe
Marsh, Allyn J.*
Marsh, Norman J., Jr.*
Marston, Robert H., Jr.
Martin, Matthew S.
Martin, Milward W.*
Mason, Francis Van W.*
Mawby, Alfred W.
Maxwell, Douglas P.
Mehlig, Lloyd G.
Merrill, Edgerton
Minton, Maurice *
Mitchell, Alexander
Moffat, Fraser M., Jr.*
Montgomery, Edward G.*
Montgomery, Rodman B.*
Moran, Lawrence J.
Morrison, Julian K.*
Morton, Alfred H.*
Mylott, Joseph J.
Nicely, James M.*
Noble, Francis O.*
Noyes, Frank E.*
O'Donnell, Joseph A.
O'Gorman, James A., Jr.
O'Neil, James H.
Ordway, Frederick I., Jr.*
Orr, Thornton W.*
Otis, Edward V.
Pantzer, Kurt F.*
Parker, Charles F.
Patterson, Robert M., Jr.*
Percy, Donald B.
Perkins, Frank B.*
Petersen, Louis W.
Philips, Kenneth T.
Philips, Roderick *
Platt, Collier *
Pope, Asa P.*
Post, Regis H., Jr.*
Powers, William T.*
Randall, Darley
Read, Barclay K.
Redfield, Alfred W.*
Redfield, William F.*
Reed, Howard C.
Rees, Louis duB.*
Reimer, Otto B.*
Riis, Roger W.
Roberson, William C.
Roberts, Thomas C.*
Robinson, Fielding S.*
Robinson, James V.

Rockwell, Bertrand *
Romaine, Peirce L.
Rorison, John C.*
Ross, Carl G. R.
Ross, John W.
Rudolph, Harold W.*
Sabin, Charles D., Jr.
Sabin, Henry P.*
Schaefer, Bernhard K.*
Schmitt, William J.*
Semler, George H.*
Severn, Douglas K.
Shaw, Albert, Jr.
Shope, William B.
Shrewsbury, Kenneth O.*
Simmons, Conrad C.*
Simpson, William S.
Slade, Henry L., Jr.*
Smith, Gurney L.*
Smith, Harold L.*
Smith, Howard C.
Smith, Hugh M.
Smith, Joseph A.
Smith, Norman P.
Smith, Winthrop H.*
Smythe, Cyrus F.*
Snow, Elgridge G., 3rd
Spalding, Frederic P.*
Speir, Robert W., Jr.
Sprague, Irvin A., Jr.
Spurr, Gregory W.

Stearns, Kendall *
Stone, Thomas E.*
Stout, Robert P.
Sutherland, Andrew G.*
Sutherland, Paul A.
Swede, Allen G.*
Terrell, Claude M.
Throckmorton, John W.
Thurston, Edward H.*
Tiebout, Todd G.*
Timmerman, Louis F., Jr.*
Toolan, Cyprian *
Townsend, Edward D.
Traylor, Michael G.*
Tuttle, Clarence W.
Van Alstyne, David, Jr.*
Van Cott, John D.*
von Goeben, Roland
Waid, Jesse E.*
Wainwright, Loudon S.*
Warren, James C.
Welch, Herbert A.*
Whittemore, Charles L.
Wickersham, James H.
Wilson, Henry W.
Woodford, William H. J.*
Woodruff, Walter A.
Woolley, John E.*
Wylie, Robert S.
Young, George W., Jr.*

To many Ex-Members there may be difficulty in recognizing the continuity and identity of the organization and its respective troops, owing to the numerous changes of organization and of name that have occurred. The identity exists; but it may not be out of place briefly to trace the changes of designation.

Reference has been made in Major Wright's narrative to what may have been an indoor activity at Albany involving exercises in changing names and tables of organization, with results that seemed unnecessary and undesirable.

Briefly, the changes began in January, 1912, when the name "Squadron A" was changed to 1st Squadron, 1st Cavalry, and the designation of troops was changed from A, B, C and D to A, E, F and G. In the following month a new troop was formed as Troop L, and in the next month its name was changed to Troop C. In 1913 the Squadron was further changed from 1st Squadron, 1st Cavalry, to 1st Squadron Cavalry, and the troops were redesignated A, B, C, D, and Machine Gun Troop. In March, 1914, the squadron was again designated Squadron A.

That these first changes were unnecessary seems demonstrated by the ultimate change back to the designation of Squadron A. That they were undesirable is probably the view of the Ex-Members who served in that period.

After the World War, Squadron A, New York Guard, became "Squadron A, New York National Guard," and in June, 1921, it was designated "51st Machine Gun Squadron, N.Y.N.G.," but its troops continued to be A, B and C. The persistent urge to change tables of organization originating in the rarefied atmosphere of superior headquarters broke out again in 1928 and 1929. In February, 1928, the squadron was redesignated "2nd Squadron, 101st Cavalry," and the names of the troops were changed to E, F and G.

In April, 1929, because of another change in the army tables of organization, Troop C became tactically a part of the 2nd Squadron, 101st Cavalry, and was redesignated Troop K. It was on this last change that "Manhattan Units, 101st Cavalry" came into semi-official use in referring to the squadron. The three troops E, F and K were still "Squadron A" and are the successors of Troops 1, 2 and 3 in the original Squadron A of which Charles F. Roe was the commanding officer; and under these titles they preserve and carry on the history and traditions of the original Troops 1, 2 and 3.

These changes in organization and of name were not sought by the organization: they were imposed on it. To men who have served in the earlier periods they seem a deplorable disregard of association and tradition. It is an evidence of the vitality of traditions and associations that the name "Squadron A" is still preserved and used, and is carved above the entrance of the armory. The name means much to those who have served in the organization, and Squadron A, *"The* Squadron," means something in the history of the city and state.

Major Egleston continued in command of the organization under its various designations until the fall of 1932—a total period of more than thirteen years—when he resigned to turn over the command to Major Frederick A. Vietor.

The paper of General Egleston has unique interest in that it deals with the reestablishment of the squadron in the National Guard, and pictures the difficulties it had to confront in that era, and the triumphal achievement.

The paper of Major Vietor brings the narrative down to the present time, and shows the squadron today vigorously and successfully upholding the traditions that are dear to all the members.

Assembly.

THE SQUADRON

From July 1919 to December 1932

N. Hillyer Egleston

To be prepared for war is one of the most effectual means of preserving peace.—GEORGE WASHINGTON

JULY 1919, the beginning of the period covered by this summary, found the squadron, then designated as "Squadron A Cavalry, New York Guard," still only a state military force. It had been formed from the Depot Squadron in the summer of 1917, after the calling into Federal service for war duty of Squadron A as it existed at the time the United States entered the World War. Its personnel was composed mostly of men who had had prior service in the squadron, many of whom were beyond the age desirable for active National Guard duty. Many of them otherwise qualified felt that the purpose for which they had entered the service had been accomplished. The military forces of the state were about to be reorganized so as to fit them not only into the state scheme but also into the Federal military organization. As a part of this general plan it was General O'Ryan's desire that the squadron be reconstituted so as to be ready for any service that it might be called upon to perform in either Federal or state service, yet with the same high-type personnel which had composed it during the many years of its existence prior to the war. There was at this time a lack of interest in things military and a fairly strong reaction against serious military service. It was almost a year since the armistice and many people had the feeling that, with the war so successfully concluded, there was no real reason for taking military training and service too seriously. It was perhaps a natural reaction, but one which made rebuilding the squadron as desired a task of somewhat doubtful outcome, and one which could not be accomplished immediately. General O'Ryan appreciated the situation thoroughly and told me that no question would be raised as to the strength of the organization for two years, as long as it progressed satisfactorily otherwise. When I took over the command on Major Wendt's retirement, Jack Reynolds was already in command of Troop C, and shortly thereafter George Matthews came back to command Troop A. Both officers had performed conspicuously able service overseas during the war and had also had many years' service in the old squadron.

The change in officer and enlisted personnel was necessarily a gradual one and little difficulty was experienced in getting men who had been in the squadron prior to the war and had had commissioned service during it, to come back as officers in the organization. Among these were Ned Shaw, Jim Fargo, Knowlton Durham, Howard Taft, Juan Ceballos, Fritz Vietor (the present squadron commander), and Carlton Cooke. Many of the other officers in this early period also had had commissioned service during the war.

As to the enlisted personnel, qualifications similar to those which were in force prior to the war were insisted upon, and prospective recruits were carefully considered by the admissions committee. As rapidly as it was possible men who did not appear to fit in the organization scheme were dropped and strenuous efforts were made to obtain new personnel of the desired type.

In the winter of 1919-20, General O'Ryan expressed the desire that the squadron be made a training school for officers in all branches of the service although continuing primarily as a cavalry organization. It was necessary, however, to abandon this plan before it was put into effect, as it did not fit into the Federal scheme of organization and training.

At this time the organization occupied and used only the old

SQUADRON A

Squadron A section of the armory; that is to say, the portion of the armory west of the present riding hall. The ring was then in the space (except for a narrow passageway along the Madison Avenue side) between Madison Avenue and the present riding hall and had access to Ninety-fourth Street where the windows of the present Commanding Officer's reception room are. In area the ring was about one-third that of the present riding hall. The quarters were the same as those which the squadron had used for many years prior to this time. While the present riding hall and stable level had been reconstructed during the war, it was not until February, 1921, that the riding hall was available for use for mounted work.

In January, 1920, by the discharge of members who either could not or did not desire to continue in service under the Federal requirements, the strength of the squadron was reduced to 14 officers and 168 enlisted men. In the summer of that year Troop A was commanded by Captain George Matthews, Jr.; Troop B, by Captain J. W. Hall; Troop C, by Captain John Reynolds; Troop D, by Captain F. A. Vietor; and the Sanitary Detachment, by Captain L. S. Booth. In reorganizing the squadron up to this time, officers had been assigned to troops to fill vacancies—regardless of whether they had any prior association with the troops to which they were assigned. Generally speaking, new men enlisting during the early part of this period had no marked troop preference and were usually placed where needed. There had been developing, however, a desire among certain officers to get back to the troop in which they had served prior to the war. On October 21, 1920, in order that these desires might be fulfilled, there was a shifting of personnel between the troops: Captain Matthews was transferred to Troop C; Captain Reynolds, to Troop D; and Captain Vietor, to Troop A. (Each, prior to the war, had been a member of the troop to which he was now transferred.) With each troop commander there were also transferred approximately twenty enlisted men whom he desired and who desired to be in his command. At the same time additional men were also allotted to Troop D as its Federal recognition was in prospect.

Troop D received Federal recognition on November 11, 1920, under Captain Reynolds; and on April 21, 1921, Troop A under Captain Vietor and Troop C under Captain Matthews were federally recognized. On June 1, 1921, the federalized squadron consisting of Troops A, C and D was reorganized as the 51st Machine Gun Squadron, the troops being redesignated A, C and B, respectively. In the preparation for Federal recognition, Troop B, Squadron A Cavalry, New York Guard, had been used as a clearing organization for men undecided on the question of continuing service and whose enlistments were about to expire. Ultimately, a group from it formed the nucleus of the Headquarters Detachment of the Machine Gun Squadron and the troop as such was mustered out of service April 22, 1922. In May, 1922, the organization of the Machine Gun Squadron was completed with a strength of 276. While the idea of being a Machine Gun Squadron carried some appeal because of its unusual character and armament, the training was arduous, and the personnel not only underwent the same training as other cavalry units but had to spend much time in the mechanical phases of the work; that is, taking apart and putting together the machine guns, learning the operating principles, adjustment of packs, etc. However, the members of the organization tackled the work with the energy and good will characteristic of squadron personnel and eventually became very proficient, although hampered by lack of equipment. The organization continued as the 51st Machine Gun Squadron until February 15, 1928, when, because of the elimination of machine gun squadrons from the cavalry scheme, it became the 2nd Squadron of the 101st Cavalry (the balance of the regiment being in Brooklyn), and Troops A, B and C were redesignated E, F and G, respectively. A little over a year later, April 15, 1929, because of a change in regimental organization from two squadrons of three troops each to three squadrons of two troops each, other changes occurred. Troops E and F continued as the 2nd Squadron, but Troop G became Troop K of the 3rd Squadron, 101st Cavalry, and the 3rd Squadron Headquarters was organized, with Captain Matthews promoted as Major to command that squadron. While this brought about separate squadron commands, for purposes of administration and training at the armory all units continued under my jurisdiction as the senior officer of the post. Shortly after this "Manhattan Units, 101st Cavalry" began to be used when referring to the whole organization, to avoid the necessity of specifically naming the units by their various official military designations.

Reference has been made to the difficulty encountered early in this period in obtaining the desired type of personnel. This difficulty, however, did not persist very long. The fact was noticeable that a large proportion of the men proposed for enlistment had had com-

SQUADRON POLO TEAMS IN ACTION

THE ARMORY

ON THE RANGE, PINE CAMP, 1924
PINE CAMP 1926 PICKET LINE

missioned service during the war. During approximately two years preceding April, 1924, 256 applications were approved by the admissions committee. Of this number, 214 were college graduates; 200 had had previous service in the army, navy, R.O.T.C. or S.A.T.C.; and 115 had served as commissioned officers in every rank from lieutenant colonel down, and in almost every branch of the service. The peak of strength was reached in January, 1925, when the total was 378 officers and men. The reduction in strength thereafter was due mostly to limitations imposed by higher authority and to changes in organization.

May, 1925, after several years' preliminary work in connection with the preparation of plans, releasing of funds by the city, etc., found reconstruction started on the old Squadron A armory section (that portion of the present armory west of the riding hall); and the work continued for approximately a year. During this time that section of the building was in chaos, and for some months a bath was an impossibility. Training work was necessarily interfered with and life was generally pretty uncomfortable. It was with great relief that we saw the last of the construction completed, though it was not until some time later that painting was finished and lighting fixtures and furniture installed. The plans originally called for a recessed balcony opening onto the westerly end of the riding hall, but this part of the reconstruction was abandoned because of shortage of funds. It was a very fortunate circumstance, for the non-construction of the balcony made available the space in which the Ex-Members' Association during the winter of 1926-27 constructed and fitted out their rooms, which have proved such a decided benefit to the squadron.

Outstanding events during the period were the unveiling and dedication of the Memorial Gates presented by the Ex-Members' Association of Squadron A to the active organization, April 7, 1929, and the celebrations of the Thirty-fifth Anniversary in May, 1924, and the fortieth anniversary in April, 1929.

Commencing with 1921, the squadron participated each year in the required fifteen days' field training: going to Fort Ethan Allen, Vermont, in 1921 and 1924; the squadron farm at New City in 1922; Camp Dix, New Jersey, in 1923; and in all other years to Pine Camp, New York. It participated in the customary Memorial Day parades and, in addition, on April 11, 1921, Troop B acted as escort to Envoy Extraordinary Viviani of France; on April 26, 1922, the 51st Machine Gun Squadron acted as escort to Marshal Joffre of France; on November 12, 1927, Troop A participated in the Holland Tunnel opening; and on April 11, 1931, the squadron acted as escort to their Royal Highnesses Prince and Princess Takamatsu of Japan. Various reviews and other functions were held at the armory.

Outdoor polo was being played by the squadron at Gedney Farm (White Plains) in 1919 and 1920. Only a limited number of men participated and, though a successful tournament was held in 1920, outdoor play was given up after that summer. The first appearance of indoor polo was in the winter of 1920-21, and during the next few years it developed at a very fast rate—as adequate mounts were supplied—and continued as a successful and almost necessary part of the squadron's activities.

Participation in horse shows brought successful results even early in the period, and became increasingly successful as better mounts were acquired. The most successful years were 1926 and 1927. Commencing with the National Show in 1925 and ending with the National Show in 1926 the squadron won 76 ribbons; and in the calendar year 1927 won 157 ribbons, 29 trophies, and approximately 4000 dollars in prize money. The outstanding show horses were Oxford, Irish Crystal, Mimic, Messenger, Reckless Lady, and P.D.Q., and their successful performances brought great credit to the organization. The National Horse Show was held in the armory from 1921 to 1925, and contributed to outside interest in the organization although interfering with its normal functioning.

The farm at New City, purchased a short time prior to the war, proved decidedly advantageous to the squadron as a place where horses might be turned out during the summer months or sent at any time of the year for rest or recovery from injuries. For some years breeding of horses was conducted there, but was eventually given up as too costly. The farmhouse was kept open for several summers for the use of active members or ex-members, and though advantage was taken of this over week ends, the idea was abandoned as not justifying the cost. At various times consideration was given to selling the farm and obtaining another in some other location, but no more desirable one within the squadron's means was discovered.

The Ladies' Riding Class, open to members of the family of an active member or ex-member, was started during 1921. It was with some misgivings that the venture was entered into, for it was the first squadron activity—except reviews, games, and other entertainments —opening the sacred portals for participation by the fairer sex. It proved successful from the start and has continued as a very valuable asset of the organization.

Space does not permit the mentioning of all those who contributed so effectively of time, energy, and ability to the rebuilding of the squadron and to its efficiency. Three officers, however, are outstanding in this respect and should be specifically mentioned. Captain Reynolds from the start of the period until he resigned on January 3, 1922, contributed vitally in enthusiasm and leadership to the success of the reorganization. Captain Matthews (later Major) and Captain Vietor (later Major) as troop commanders not only played a large part in the success of the reorganization and built up their troops into very efficient units, but also gave unstintingly of their time and effort to the success of the polo and horse show activities. The squadron owes much to these three men.

THE SQUADRON OF TODAY
Frederick A. Vietor

Futurity is the great concern of mankind.—BURKE

WHEN General Egleston left the squadron in 1932, the great objectives of the post-war period had been accomplished. The personnel had been built up on a sound basis and the great recruiting problems of that time had been solved. Through the General's constant and unremitting supervision, the armory had been successfully rebuilt and the troops were in comfortable quarters.

It would seem, therefore, that little was left for his successor to do except to carry on the routine, uphold the high military standards, and to generally carry on the activities of Squadron A.

However, several factors entered this picture of general tranquillity which may be of interest and have a definite place in the history of the squadron.

The first factor is the tremendous increase in the requirements of officers and enlisted men demanded by higher authority as compared with pre-war and even the earlier post-war period. In the matter of schools the amount of time now spent by an officer is more than doubled: first, there is the post school for all officers which is conducted by the federal instructor and consists of an hour of equitation and a longer session of tactics. This school takes place every two weeks. Besides, every officer must complete twenty hours of army extension courses for the grade one higher than his own. No officer below the grade of colonel can be promoted unless he has successfully completed the course for which he is enrolled. In addition, troop officers conduct N.C.O. schools prior to each drill. These must be prepared, as the subjects required by the existing programs are so varied that an officer must engage in considerable reading and study in order to properly conduct these classes.

Regulations with reference to property accountability have been tightened and more strictly enforced, so that this department of command takes more work and time than ever before. No officer can successfully carry out his duties without devoting at least two and often three nights each week at the armory.

As to drills, so much ground must be covered and N.C.O.'s have to be proficient in so many more subjects than ever before, that little time is left for the mounted games, etc., which were a great source of fun and amusement to the men of previous days.

At field training the program has been extended and intensified. The period is entirely devoted to tactics. The qualifications with arms have been cut to a supplementary rifle record practice season and qualification with light machine guns and mounted pistol. Besides this and the tactical work, troops are required to stand Evening Parade and Retreat even though they may not return to camp from their work until late in the day. This, together with the tremendous amount of work a cavalryman must do in camp itself, such as the care of his horse, arms, and other equipment, together with details, guard duty, stable police, etc., makes the camp period an interesting but strenuous two weeks.

The squadron has cheerfully met the increased requirements and for this reason is a more efficient military organization in spite of an ever increasing turnover in personnel. This turnover is caused by general economic conditions. Jobs are not stable. Incomes of the members are not high. Men try to better themselves, accepting positions which often move them to other parts of the country. Marriage takes a goodly number. With the yearly field-training requirements claiming the only vacation period of the individual, friend wife objects, with the result that reenlistments at the end of the first three-year-period are not what they should be. The requirement that but 20 per cent of the enlisted personnel may be married adds another difficulty.

Nevertheless, the caliber of the personnel is as high as at any time in the history of the squadron and it is my belief that its military efficiency has not been matched in the past.

The second item of interest is the greatly increased non-military activity at Ninety-fourth Street. This has been encouraged by the present Commanding Officer, so as to make the armory a place where our men may enjoy themselves at low cost, to enhance camaraderie and to augment esprit de corps. It might be interesting to list these activities:

>   Polo   Badminton
>   Saturday night dances   Squadron A spring horse show
>   Canteen   Friday evening rides
>   Tap Room

Of these, the Saturday night dances, the tap room, badminton and, last but not least, the Squadron A spring horse show have been added during the writer's term of command. The demand for them, and a major portion of the work and management entailed, come from the enlisted personnel—yet they all add to the duties of various officers under whose supervision these activities fall, for they must be co-ordinated and much labor must be performed by the paid employees of the squadron. In this connection I should like to make special mention of First Lieutenant Edward A. Hill, detailed supply officer of the Manhattan Units, 101st Cavalry (Squadron A). His unremitting efforts, excellent sense of organization, and tireless interest and work have made possible many of the activities undertaken.

The greatest new enterprise was the Squadron A spring horse show in April, 1937. This was an immediate success. It is interesting to note that the demand for the show was so great among officers and men that they underwrote the first show and actually deposited twenty-five hundred dollars cash in a special account to guarantee the squadron against loss. Captain Alfred G. Tuckerman has been chairman of the executive committee for both shows and is again in this position for the 1939 show. Mr. Ned King, manager of the National Horse Show, volunteered his services for our initial effort. This largely contributed to our success. The show made an immediate appeal to horsemen so that our classes were well filled with good entries. The second year saw an improvement, and we believe that 1939 will be even better.

Inter-troop competitions have tended to decline. The Ex-Members Trophy for the best general efficiency in field training, presented in 1930 and finally retired by Troop K (3) in 1935, brought out the fact that the three troops were so nearly on a par that the judging of this competition became very difficult. The three troop commanders were all agreed that there should be no competitions except those which can be judged by actual mathematical scoring, such as shooting and the annual equitation trophy. This policy has been followed, so that at present the only inter-troop competitions are:

51st Cavalry Trophy for Rifle Marksmanship.—Competed for by all the troops of the 51st Cavalry Brigade. In 1936 Troop K won second prize, and in both 1937 and 1938, third prize.

The Captain Carleton S. Cooke Equitation Trophy.—Every spring each troop commander enters sixteen enlisted men in this competition—the Medical Detachment, three. Of this number sixteen are chosen and designated as Class A riders, who can ride throughout the year free of charge. The troop from which the greatest number of Class A riders are chosen wins the trophy for the year. Troop K won this distinction in 1938.

The Colonel William R. Wright Memorial Trophy for Pistol Shooting.—This will be competed for, for the first time in 1939. Teams of fifteen men from each troop will fire a prescribed course in the gallery of the armory commencing February 1, 1939.

The record of the trophy presented by the Ex-Members' Association for the greatest efficiency in field training, commonly known as the Ex-Members' Trophy, follows:

1930 won by Troop E, Captain Frederick A. Vietor, commanding
1931 won by Troop E, Captain Frederick A. Vietor, commanding
1932 won by Troop K, Captain H. Russell Drowne, Jr., commanding
1933 won by Troop F, Captain William C. Roberson, commanding
1934 won by Troop K, Captain Alfred G. Tuckerman, commanding
1935 won by Troop K, Captain Alfred G. Tuckerman, commanding

Dress uniforms have long been a subject of discussion. There is sentiment for their revival. The matter has been thoroughly investigated and was the major topic at the 1937 annual meeting of the Squadron A Association. Expense is the deterring factor.

The squadron must supply itself with horses. Of the 161 animals in our stables, but 41 are owned by the government, 55 are maintained by the government but owned by the squadron, and 65 are owned and maintained by us. To replace horses every year is a drain on our resources, an expense which the infantry need not shoulder. Therefore, the adoption of dress uniforms for the entire command, which would cost about seventeen thousand dollars, is out of the question. However, some steps for their partial revival have been taken.

Because of the generosity of certain ex-members, about sixty dress uniforms have been collected. These are pooled and issued to troops and detachments when detailed to special duties, such as escorting the international jumping teams at the National Horse Show, the massing of the colors, etc.

A social evening dress in the form of a mess jacket has been authorized for the officers. The jacket is the well known blue of our hussar uniform; the trousers, midnight blue.

Efforts were made to have an enlisted man's social evening dress uniform authorized, but the War Department refused.

Although the entire command is not equipped, the dress uniform is not dead and is frequently seen in New York. It is hoped that with better times the entire command may be equipped.

In November, 1934, and every year thereafter, the annual review has been held just prior to the opening of the National Horse Show. At these functions the president and directors of the show, all the foreign officers of the various jumping teams, as well as officers of the Regular Army, National Guard, and Reserve have been our guests. Our connection with the National Horse Show has been very pleasant; and the fact that so many foreign officers not only ride their horses in our riding hall prior to the opening but are our guests under circumstances that permit them to see the entire command has spread the name of Squadron A into many foreign lands.

CHANGES IN OFFICER PERSONNEL SINCE DECEMBER, 1932

Headquarters

Major Frederick A. Vietor transferred to 2nd Squadron and in command of Manhattan Units, December 19, 1932.

1st Lieutenant William C. Roberson, Adjutant, Manhattan Units, was transferred to and in command of Troop F, May 18, 1933.

2nd Lieutenant Herbert Martin was transferred from Troop K, May 18, 1933, to Headquarters, Manhattan Units, as Acting Adjutant. Was promoted 1st Lieutenant, June 9, 1933, and assigned as Adjutant, to date.

SQUADRON A

1st Lieutenant Edward A. Hill was and still is Detailed Supply Officer of Manhattan Units, 101st Cavalry.

2nd Lieutenant Gerald J. Farrelly was commissioned as such June 1, 1937, in Headquarters Troop, 101st Cavalry, and detailed as Assistant Detailed Supply Officer, Manhattan Units. Still on such duty.

Troop E

Captain Frederic C. Thomas, who commanded Troop E, was transferred to Inactive National Guard, December 10, 1934.

1st Lieutenant John S. Wise, Troop E, was honorably discharged May 11, 1934. He was commissioned Captain in command of Troop E, January 12, 1935, and was transferred to Inactive National Guard, October 17, 1938.

2nd Lieutenant Herbert C. Sturhahn, Troop E, was promoted to 1st Lieutenant June 1, 1934, and was honorably discharged, August 4, 1936.

2nd Lieutenant Roy D. Reynolds, Troop E, was commissioned as such, December 21, 1934; promoted 1st Lieutenant, November 2, 1936, and honorably discharged, May 27, 1938.

2nd Lieutenant William F. Clare, Jr., Troop E, was commissioned as such, May 5, 1937, and is still with Troop E.

1st Lieutenant Edgerton Merrill, Troop E, was commissioned as such, June 9, 1938, in command of Troop E, and is still with Troop E.

Troop F

Captain Ernest P. Lull, in command of Troop F, was honorably discharged May 16, 1933.

1st Lieutenant William C. Roberson took command of Troop F, May 18, 1933; promoted Captain, June 9, 1933, and is still in command of Troop F.

2nd Lieutenant George C. Comstock, Jr., Troop F, was promoted 1st Lieutenant June 11, 1932, and is still with Troop F.

2nd Lieutenant Robert F. Kohler, Troop F, died April 3, 1938, while in attendance at Cavalry School, Fort Riley, Kansas.

2nd Lieutenant William C. Reed, Troop F, was commissioned June 9, 1938, and is still with troop.

Troop K

Captain H. Russell Drowne, Jr., commanding Troop K, was transferred to Inactive National Guard, August 23, 1933.

1st Lieutenant Richard F. Lamarche, Troop K, was transferred to Inactive National Guard, March 19, 1934.

2nd Lieutenant Jeremiah F. Cross, Troop K, was commissioned as such, June 21, 1933; promoted 1st Lieutenant, June 1, 1934, and transferred to Inactive National Guard, August 22, 1934.

Captain Alfred G. Tuckerman was commissioned September 20, 1933, and in command of Troop K. Still in command of troop.

2nd Lieutenant Lawrence Larkin, Troop K, was commissioned as such June 1, 1934; promoted 1st Lieutenant, October 24, 1934, and transferred to Inactive National Guard, November 23, 1934.

1st Lieutenant J. Noel Macy was transferred from Headquarters, 101st Cavalry to Troop K, November 27, 1934, and is still with troop.

2nd Lieutenant George N. Burleigh, Troop K, was commissioned October 25, 1934, and is still with troop.

Medical Detachment

1st Lieutenant John R. Twiss was promoted Captain in command of Medical Detachment, June 10, 1933, and was transferred to Inactive National Guard, May 11, 1935.

1st Lieutenant Robert S. MacKellar, Jr., was promoted Captain, May 16, 1933, and assigned as Veterinarian. Is still with detachment.

1st Lieutenant Eilif C. Hanssen was commissioned as such August 16, 1935, in command of Medical Detachment; promoted Captain, June 7, 1938; honorably discharged December 19, 1938.

SQUADRON A IN THE ARMY MANEUVERS

August 13–27, 1939

A Supplement to the History of the First Fifty Years

WHEN the Germans invaded Poland, launching a war of unpredictable length, character and scope, the United States Army had just finished the largest peace-time exercises and maneuvers ever conducted here, and Squadron A had participated with efficiency and credit.

Although the present history was then completed as planned, that is, to cover only the fifty-year period beginning April 2, 1889 (the date of the muster in), the editors feel that the situation as a whole calls for the inclusion of some account of what the active organization did in these maneuvers.

The news reports of the German advances emphasize the power and speed of its mechanized forces, in an area and during weather perhaps peculiarly fitted for them; but little or no comment has yet appeared as to the cavalry of either side. The view sometimes expressed by civilians that the day of horse cavalry has passed will doubtless seem fortified by these reports; but that view is not held by those best qualified to form an opinion. Squadron A will not subscribe to any such doctrine; strategy and tactics have been somewhat modified by modern conditions, but although the rôle of the soldier horseman has changed in some respects its importance continues. This opinion is expressed by the Army Commander himself, General Drum (who attended as civilian observer the last week of the maneuvers), in a letter to the President of the Ex-Members' Association, which is here presented; and this letter is accompanied by a narrative by Major Vietor graphically showing what cavalry can accomplish today, as illustrated by the remarkable achievements of Squadron A in these maneuvers. The story is reminiscent of the arm at its best, with its jaunty élan, precision of training and discipline, and its successful endurance of difficulties and privations; and the story also shows the high efficiency and splendid morale of the present active organization. Major Vietor's modesty belittles his own outstanding and essential contribution in planning and preparation, and one can read between the lines his talent for leadership. In all of this the entire personnel of Squadron A, past and present, can feel a proper pride.

HEADQUARTERS 2ND CORPS AREA
Office of the Commanding General
GOVERNORS ISLAND, NEW YORK

September 1, 1939.

HONORABLE PHILIP J. MCCOOK,
Supreme Court of New York State,
Niantic, Connecticut.

DEAR JUSTICE:

Thanks for your letter and the kind wishes contained therein. It was a great maneuver, and I only hope that some will heed the few words of advice that I endeavored to plant. Certainly with the picture of Europe before us, I do not see why they hesitate.

Reference to your letter, I did not bring up the question of horse cavalry versus mechanized cavalry in my talks because this has been thrashed out so many times that I assumed the answer was clear to most people. There can be no question that both types of cavalry are essential to an army. The close-in reconnaissance and detailed inspection of terrain prior to the arrival of the infantry and artillery will be made in the future, as in the past, by horse cavalry. The protection of flanks will be covered by horse cavalry, and in many theaters of operation it will retain its old rôle of mass formations to clear up situations and to act as decisive forces. No doubt, in terrains suitable for its operations, the mechanized cavalry can and will to a large extent take the place of the large horse cavalry forces of the past.

Squadron A must have had a very interesting training experience. Prior to the two-sided Corps problem and the Army problem, its time was devoted to its own and regimental training. In the two-sided Corps problem it worked with the II Corps, operating south of the Saranac River, whereas in the Army problem Vietor's squadron operated with the I Corps up the valley of the Saranac. In both problems it must have had a fine opportunity to work in advance of the Infantry and carry on the detailed reconnaissance indicated in the preceding paragraph. I know that Squadron A encountered the enemy early in the Saranac, and word came back very promptly which assisted in the solution of the problem. I frequently saw the unit and was much impressed with its conduct—the men and the horses and all. Use whatever you want of the foregoing.

Hope to see you soon. With best wishes, I am,

Faithfully yours,
sgd H. A. DRUM

NARRATIVE BY FREDERICK A. VIETOR

When the Army maneuvers were first announced in the early part of 1939 it was the hope of the entire 101st Cavalry that we would participate. We were not included in the maneuvers held at Pine Camp in 1935, which was a great disappointment to us. For a number of years many articles which appeared in magazines and newspapers stated that the horse cavalry was no longer useful in war. We of the cavalry were anxious to show that this was untrue and to counteract the writings of individuals who evidently were not conversant with military tactics, organization, and the use of our branch. The rôle played by the entire 101st Cavalry, especially by the troops of Squadron A, has proved the great value of cavalry work against, or with, the modern weapons.

Before starting my story I might add that whatever we did accomplish was done with incomplete equipment. Each troop was supposed to have six light machine guns—only four were present. The regiment should be equipped with ten scout cars—only three were available. Motorcycles, which are necessary in modern operations, were entirely lacking. One troop of 50-cal. anti-tank machine guns does not exist. We have a 37-mm. anti-tank gun, which, however, is an infantry model and cannot be carried with us in pack.

It is evident from this that the only defense that we had against mechanized troops was our own mobility and ability to ride across country. In every case where mechanized was encountered we successfully defended ourselves in this manner.

Squadron A left its armory at 3 A.M. August 13th, arriving in the vicinity of Schuyler Falls at 2 P.M. August 13th. The first week was devoted to squadron training under the direction of the regimental commander, Colonel Gilbert Ackerman. This amounted to marches, reconnaissance, counter-reconnaissance, communications, and finally an overnight bivouac, with exercises both going to and coming back from the bivouac.

The week end was spent in preparation for the Corps maneuvers. The Corps maneuver between the 1st and 2nd Corps was a north and south exercise, involving the crossing of the Saranac River. The 1st Corps, consisting of the 26th and 43rd Divisions, and the 2nd, was made up of the 27th and 44th.

The 1st Squadron was detached from the regiment and sent to 1st Corps, while the regiment, less the 1st Squadron, operated with the 2nd Corps.

The 3rd Squadron, consisting of Troop I (Brooklyn) and Troop K (New York) commanded by Major Reginald Brayley, were with the 44th Division and the regimental headquarters, plus the 2nd Squadron, Troops E and F, both New York, commanded by the writer, were with the 27th Division. The regiment, less the 1st Squadron, was operating in conjunction with the 13th Mechanized Cavalry. This was particularly true of the 2nd Squadron as the main effort had been ordered on the left flank by the Corps Commander, and therefore the weight of the mechanized fighting power was operating on this flank.

In telling this story I shall have to give the outline of each squadron as their missions and operations were entirely separate. The 3rd Squadron had as its official objective Hill 400, which was within two miles of our base camp. Troop K was the leading troop and the advance guard, and one platoon was under the command of Lieutenant George M. Burleigh. After marching about one-half mile from camp the Squadron came under the fire of what was estimated to be a platoon of the 182nd Infantry. By taking advantage of excellent cover and moving at a fast gallop it was able to envelop both enemy's flanks, driving them out of their position. Within seventeen minutes it captured Hill 400 from the Blue force, estimated to be one infantry company. It held this hill until relieved by two battalions of the 113th Infantry at 7:20. The squadron then mounted and proceeded around the left flank of the 43rd Division and attacked its second line, dismounted (it was estimated to be a battalion), delaying it more than twenty minutes and then it withdrew to a concealed position at about 9:15 A.M. Shortly thereafter the squadron again attacked, having moved into a favorable position, capturing two machine guns, nineteen privates and a battalion commander, together with his adjutant. Umpires caused the battalion to withdraw three hundred yards and put it out of action for ten minutes. Because of the swiftness of the attack, there were no casualties on our side. The Squadron

Commander then contacted the Commanding Officer of the 113th Infantry, giving him full information regarding the location of enemy flanks, general direction of the attack, and other valuable information. Under cover of this infantry the Squadron Commander was able to water and feed his horses, rest, and allow his men to get their noon rations. During the rest of the afternoon the Squadron Commander operated as a reconnaissance force and participated in other minor skirmishes with the enemy. The squadron was then ordered to rejoin the regiment at its bivouac, where it arrived at about 7:30, having covered approximately thirty-eight miles.

During this time the 2nd Squadron, Troops E and F, jumped off behind the mechanized cavalry from a position on the Salmon River about 2½ miles west of Schuyler Falls, followed the mechanized to the first objective—the high ground—about 2½ miles north of the river. The forward movement of the mechanized at this point was very slow and it seemed to the writer that, if the horse cavalry had been allowed to proceed, we could have taken the high ground at least an hour before it actually was occupied by the mechanized. At this point our Regimental Commander received orders to move northward across country. One platoon of Troop E was left as regimental reserve and another platoon was taken over as squadron reserve. This left but the headquarters and one platoon under the command of Captain Merrill, who proceeded north through very heavy country in the direction of Cadyville. The squadron, consisting of Troop F, plus one platoon of Troop E, plus one section of heavy 30-cal. m. guns, moved north along a road running approximately at the center of the sector, but were again preceded by the mechanized cavalry. We received orders to follow the mechanized to the next high ground, which commanded the approach to the bridges crossing the Saranac. The squadron remained behind the mechanized for about one hour when it received orders to proceed to the north and to cover the bridges at Kent Falls, Woods Mills, and Cadyville. We found good cover just south of the river and sent strong patrols to the bridges. The main body of the squadron by that time was cut down to two sections of heavy machine guns, plus one platoon of Troop F and the squadron reserve. We received news that the bridge at Woods Mills was covered by the mechanized, so for the time being this bridge was not covered by the horse cavalry because constant news from our scouts and friendly aeroplane indicated that there were

Blue forces to the east and I therefor did not want to diminish my strength still further. We were finally driven out of this position by artillery fire and moved the squadron's P.C. to Woods Mills where we reenforced the mechanized detachment at the bridge. We started to feed our horses when word was received that what appeared to be a battalion of infantry was approaching our position from the east. I immediately sent out an officer's patrol and received the information that this battalion was proceeding along the road just south of the river. After consultation with the detachment of the mechanized cavalry I reenforced what was left of Troop F with two sections of machine guns and proceeded into high ground in the direction of the enemy. We took up positions with our horses mobile and well under cover, and waited for the battalion to come into range. It had absolutely no knowledge of our presence. It marched along the road as though no possibility of encountering the enemy existed. We opened fire at about four hundred yards and stopped the battalion in its tracks. This was accomplished by eight riflemen and two machine guns. I had ordered the motorcycle of mechanized cavalry to accompany me to the hill so that he could keep in touch with his organization as the continued advance of the enemy forces threatened to take the control of the bridges out of our hands. The enemy force, which turned out to be one battalion of infantry and one battalion of artillery, was held up by this handful of cavalry for forty-two minutes. We were finally driven out of our position by a company of infantry which came up on our left flank and by three infantry tanks. We were able to stay in our position until the very last minute and until we had had time to send a message to the Major commanding the mechanized squadron, who in turn sent a sufficient force of machine guns to cover our withdrawal and to delay the enemy. We withdrew to high ground to the west of Woods Mills and again opened fire on the infantry so that the ruling of the umpires delayed the enemy force for an additional thirty minutes. In the meantime messengers had been sent to the bridges at Kent Falls, retirement from which had been practically cut off by the enemy, but in spite of this fact, Sergeant Carl Herrhammer was able to make his way along the river bank and rejoin his troop. All these actions were reported to the Regimental Commander and to the headquarters of the 13th Cavalry, commanded by Colonel Scott. The squadron was ordered to withdraw

SQUADRON AT EVENING PARADE, 1938
INSPECTION OF SADDLES, 1938

DISMOUNTED ACTION IN ARMY MANEUVERS, 1939
DETACHMENT IN ARMY MANEUVERS, 1939

and reorganize in the vicinity of Cadyville, and then late in the afternoon was ordered to return to regimental bivouac. All this time, from 4 A.M. to about 6 P.M., there had been no possibility to either feed or water our horses. In returning from Cadyville to the southeast we passed around the left flank of the mechanized and went within about two miles of the bivouac. We were held in reserve by Colonel Scott, who was fighting in action with what amounted to more than a brigade of the enemy. While in reserve we were able to water our horses. As darkness approached Colonel Scott ordered the 2nd Squadron to take over this position, because the nature of mechanized cavalry does not permit it to hold ground or operate successfully after dark. We then took over his position, which was more than 1000 yards in width. At about 8 P.M. we had been advised that a battalion of the 107th Infantry would relieve us at 10 P.M., but this battalion never made its appearance. At 12:10 A.M. I received word that a battalion of the 105th had arrived directly behind our position, and I was ordered to return to bivouac where we arrived at about 12:30 A.M.

It was twenty-one hours since my men had had a hot meal, and our horses had had no feed in the same length of time. At 1:30 the squadron lay down on its horse blankets and slept for about one hour and a half until 3:00 A.M., when we again were on our feet, having breakfast, saddling up, and making ready for this day's action.

As we were saddling up in the dark I made it my business to pass around among the men and to listen to their conversation. It is with great pride, and a great tribute to the esprit de corps of the squadron, to be able to tell that there was no grumbling of any kind, but hard, efficient work collecting the equipment in the dark and saddling the horses. The work was well carried out under the direction of the non-commissioned officers. There was a good deal of joking, and a general enthusiasm for the coming day's work.

At about daybreak on the morning of the 22nd, the regiment was ordered to take the high ground immediately to the north of our bivouac, but was driven back by an overwhelming force of the enemy. In spite of confusion on the roads because of the rapid withdrawal of the mechanized and the infantry, the 101st straightened out very rapidly and proceeded across country in good order. After defending itself by rifle fire against some patrols of the enemy which had penetrated to the south, it made a wide encircling movement of about five miles and was in position to go through a gap in the enemy's line with excellent opportunity to attack it in the rear, when the Corps maneuvers were called off in the middle of the morning.

The Army maneuvers, an east and west engagement between the 1st and 2nd Corps, all in the vicinity of Plattsburg, against a divisional corps consisting of the 18th Infantry Brigade, the 1st Division and the 7th Mechanized Cavalry, started at 11 A.M. on Thursday, August 24th. In this exercise the 2nd Squadron, Troops E and F, operated with the 1st Corps on the north flank and the regiment, less the 2nd Squadron, operated on the south flank with the 2nd Corps. The 2nd Squadron was reenforced by one section of heavy 30-cal. m. guns.

As Troop K was with the regiment operating in the south, I will tell their story first and then that of the remainder of the squadron.

The regiment had orders to drive rapidly to the west and to take and hold the town of Peasleeville, as well as the high ground to its north and south. However, because of the rapid advance of the enemy it was driven back. The Regimental Commander ordered the 3rd Squadron to make an encircling movement to the south by crossing the Salmon River, some marshland, and then to climb the steep eastern slope of Terry Mountain. The terrain crossed by this squadron was so difficult that no other troops but horse cavalry could have performed this mission so expeditiously. So rapid was the advance that the squadron penetrated well behind the enemy lines and was able to capture ten supply trucks, and surprise and overwhelm by mounted action a battery of field artillery protected by a platoon of infantry. This operation was well carried out over difficult terrain, which had to be covered in a mounted charge. Our men charged steeply down hill and from a concealed position jumped a stone wall, and so surprised the enemy that it scattered and ran without firing a shot. To cap the climax Troop K captured Brigadier General Walter C. Short, commanding general of the First Regular Army Division. The General was ruled out of action for three hours by the umpires. The squadron then reorganized in safe terrain but soon was in action again as a battalion of the enemy reserve was brought forward against it. The squadron was able to fight a dismounted action against this superior force for some time but finally was forced to mount up and withdraw to the east for a distance of about two miles. Here it learned that it was well within the enemy lines as our forces had retired because of the swift attack of the regulars and the Mechanized Cavalry Brigade. An umpire told the Squadron Commander that although he was in a perfectly safe position and had been granted all the successes, the cavalry's presence in this position was delaying the general scheme of the entire maneuver on the south front. The umpire therefore led the squadron back about four miles and then one-half mile behind its own lines. Here the squadron was ordered to retire for the night in regimental bivouac. At this point Captain Alfred G. Tuckerman, commanding Troop K, Squadron A, took command of the 3rd Squadron, owing to the illness of Major Brayley.

The next day, the 3rd Squadron did general reconnaissance work on the south flank until relieved by the Corps Commander and ordered to return to its base camp preparatory to returning to home station.

The 2nd Squadron was ordered to take and hold high ground about seven miles to the northwest, just south of the Saranac River, and to hold its ground until relieved by the 26th Division. These orders were received at 3 minutes to 11 o'clock. As there was no time to lose, the squadron moved out and covered these seven miles in a little less than an hour, although the major portion of this march was uphill through heavily wooded terrain. We occupied the high ground with Troop E on the left and Troop F well to the right, so that we could cover critical road junctions. We had no sooner sent our elements to their position than we were met by a heavy infantry attack which caused me to withdraw after about an hour's fighting to a second position and also to pull Troop F, less one platoon, in from my right flank as I had not sufficient strength to withstand the ever-increasing numbers of the enemy. The second position was excellent ground which we organized very rapidly. Troop F, which had also been under heavy fire, withdrew from its position, proceeded across country under cover, and joined me on my right flank. At this point a lucky incident occurred in that the scout car operating with the regiment suddenly arrived from the rear in our position. This was sorely needed at this time as we were hard pressed. The car, under the command of First Lieutenant Pierce Hurley, went into very effective action and, because of its mobility, was used in several locations during the long fire fight which ensued. One platoon from the 1st Squadron, under the command of Second Lieutenant Charles K. Graydon, which had been operating on the right of the regiment, also joined my command. As I had lost two platoons of Troop F, this help was more than welcome. The fight continued for a period of four hours, with the enemy ever bringing up more reserves to drive us out of our position. During this time I was making constant radio contact with G3 of the 1st Corps, advising him of the situation and requesting immediate help as I had determined through patrolling that a brigade was in my front. It turned out to be the 18th Infantry Brigade of the regular army. I also tried to learn from Corps Headquarters what the general situation was so that I might have a safe method of withdrawal. However, neither the reinforcements nor the information were forthcoming.

The squadron was finally driven out of its position by artillery fire which first struck us in our left flank and directly in the center of our position. All during the fight I had ordered means of withdrawal prepared by the troop commanders so that we might pull out rapidly. This necessitated cutting wire fences and to find ways through the thick woods which were in the rear of us. Finally after four hours we retired in good order for about $2\frac{1}{2}$ miles to a position where we found a stream in which we could water and feed our horses. Again we contacted Corps asking them for directions as to how to proceed and finally received orders to move to Beckwith School and there cover the front of our forces.

From the position in which we found ourselves it was impossible to proceed towards Beckwith School cross country inasmuch as the entire terrain was thick second growth, interspersed with marshes which would have been impassable. We therefore tried to circle to the south but were met by a battalion of infantry and were driven to cover by three infantry tanks.

I might point out here the great mobility of cavalry. Had those tanks struck the head of our squadron there would not have been any question as to the outcome, for as I have stated we did not have any anti-tank weapons. However, the squadron immediately galloped to its right flank across rough country into the thick woods and was out of sight at a moment's notice. Our advance guard had been captured by the tanks; so we used the scout car for further reconnaissance as to route and our radio car to contact Corps. Corps gave us a route towards Beckwith School which again proved impassable so that finally it was left to my judgment as to how to proceed. As I had no information as to enemy units except those directly in our front, which had been reported, and not knowing anything of the situation to the south, I moved in a southeasterly direction toward the Salmon River valley. Upon reaching a point about a mile north of the river I again ran into trouble with a battalion of the 16th Infantry Regular Army and a battalion of field artillery. I withdrew from this, again without loss, into some thick woods where, fortunately, my command car could follow, and again contacted Corps, reporting the position of the enemy and asking for further directions. It was then 10 P.M. The men had had nothing to eat except two sandwiches, and because of the very hot weather the squadron was entirely without water and all men were extremely thirsty. During this period constant small patrols were sent out by the 16th Infantry but we captured every one of them and held them behind our position. Because of the condition of the men and horses my orders from Corps were to proceed to my base camp regardless of the fact that I would be theoretically captured. This happened soon after leaving our position and was not accomplished by the enemy until it had brought two 75's into action at point blank range.

The next morning we were ordered to the left flank of the Corps and to maintain contact between the 1st and 2nd Corps. We proceeded to our position without incident and upon arrival I found that the 101st Infantry on the left flank of the 1st Corps had already made contact with the 113th on the right side of the 2nd Corps. This fact was reported to Corps Headquarters but we kept patrols out to see that this contact was maintained. It is interesting to note that later patrols were sent out at the request of the infantry commanders and that two patrols, consisting of a corporal and two men each, who were sent out to do this important work, reached their objective, performed their mission, reported to the Infantry Commander and back to the Squadron Commander. Later in the day the squadron was ordered to the right flank of the Corps and was proceeding on its mission when orders were received to return to its camp because of the early departure of Squadron A from the maneuver area to home station.

There are many stories of individual work on the part of officers and non-commissioned officers which might be recounted, all of them redounding to the credit of the organization, and all of them receiving recognition by the umpires and higher authority.

The action of the Cavalry throughout was aggressive. All ranks learned a great deal but most important of all everyone is reimbued with the cavalry spirit and has great confidence in the capabilities of our arm. After two weeks of work, which were as strenuous as any that the squadron has ever had in peace times, especially the second week, the men came home to the armory in high spirits, in fact, were singing as they detrained. The general feeling was that we had done a good job and that the horse cavalry as a whole had not suffered because of our operations.

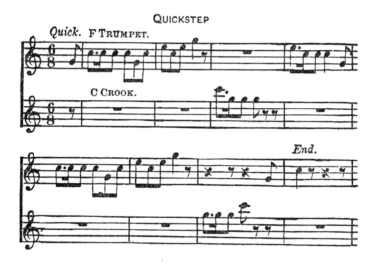

ADDITIONAL PAPERS

Supplementing the narrative of the half-century of Squadron A's career, the compilers present some additional papers which appropriately accompany this history. They are:

>Address upon Dedication of Memorial Tablet
>   to General Roe
>Chronology of Squadron A
>The Armory
>The Association of Ex-Members
>Riding in the Squadron
>Reminiscences of John D. Kilpatrick
>Some Verses and Songs of the Squadron
>List of Former and Present Members

IN MEMORY OF
CHARLES FRANCIS ROE
MAJOR-GENERAL N·G·N·Y·
1848 — 1922
A graduate of U·S·Military Academy and officer of U·S·Cavalry in Indian Campaigns he organized and commanded Troop A and then Squadron A N·G·N·Y· He served as Major-General in the War with Spain and later commanded the National Guard of this State. With his wife Katherine Bogert he worshiped in this Church of which he was for many years Senior Warden. *This Tablet is erected by the Veterans of Squadron A*

ADDRESS UPON DEDICATION OF MEMORIAL TABLET TO GENERAL ROE AT HIGHLAND FALLS CHURCH
November 11, 1936

Herbert Barry

> Once more your Captain calls to you;
> Come to his last review!
> —RICHARD WATSON GILDER

IT SOMETIMES happens that an incident which seems of small consequence at the time is destined to affect one's whole future life and career. Such an incident occurred to me in the spring of 1891, when I accompanied a friend to see the drill of Troop A at Dickel's Riding Academy in West Fifty-sixth Street. This promptly led to my meeting the commanding officer, Captain Charles F. Roe, and being enlisted under him in Troop A; and with the other members of that troop I became subject to the influence of that fine personality.

The modern school of thought considers character development as the basic feature of any educational system, and as an example and guide and as an incentive toward fine ideals, General Roe takes a high place in the ranks of educators. This is not a mere individual experience; the spirit was infused into all the members of the troop, and it spread and developed with the growth of the organization itself. From the outset the typical quality of the membership was its loyalty, enthusiasm, and devotion to the work, and absolute faith and reliance on Captain Roe as the commanding officer. The spirit which he inspired has lived on through the years, and it is no accident that the organization which he developed became a feature not only of local but of national life and took its place as one of the finest of cavalry units. Energy, untiring effort, enthusiasm, and devotion have been exhibited in every member.

Captain Charles F. Roe—afterwards major—commanded the troop, and then the squadron only nine years; but it was he who laid the foundations, created the discipline, and set the ideals which have now become traditional; and it is because of his vital personality, his ability, and patient devotion to the building up of the organization that the original troop and its successor bodies have attained their enviable position.

General Roe was born in 1848. He entered the Military Academy at the age of sixteen, and graduated in 1868. His first assignment as second lieutenant in the First Cavalry was to frontier duty in the northwest, and his next twenty years was practically all frontier duty at different posts, including the hard school of Indian campaigning. In 1876 it was a column under his command that arrived in the valley of the Little Big Horn just after the disastrous defeat of Custer.

Promotion in those days was so slow as to be almost negligible, and after nearly twenty years Roe was still a first lieutenant in the Second Cavalry. He then resigned from the army to enter civil life.

In that same year, however, members of a civilian organization, known as the First Hussars, persuaded Lieutenant Roe to join them, and promptly made him their commanding officer, and at his suggestion changed their name to First Dragoons. Captain Roe, of course, saw at once the inadequacy of a voluntary organization and soon developed the desire for a really military one. This bore fruit on April 2, 1889.

The necessary 51 members were with some effort assembled, when the mustering in of Troop A became an accomplished fact. It was as Captain Roe, of Troop A, that I first met him. But the fervent enthusiasm of the members did not permit it to remain a troop—it grew, and in

1895 became a squadron, with Charles F. Roe as major; and although it has had different nomenclatures at various times, the name Squadron A is always affectionately cherished, as are the memories of the happy associations in that organization.

In 1898 Major Roe was called to a higher command and became commanding officer of the New York National Guard, with the rank of major general. This he held until his retirement fourteen years later; but at all times, even after his retirement, the members of the organization always took pride in him as one of themselves.

Having not only had acquaintance with General Roe in a military capacity, but also been favored with his personal friendship and enjoyed his delightful hospitality, I look back with gratitude on those years and the associations which they have built up. My own experience was that of very many others who certainly have the same feelings. The influence of Captain, Major, and General Roe on the young manhood of the city then and always was a definite and conspicuous one. While we were serving under him he was an inspiration and an ideal. In after years those ideals and inspirations became an established tradition. The best memorial to General Roe is the fine loyalty, devotion, and efficiency of the squadron, and of the whole National Guard; it is a living memorial to him. This tablet is a silent but eloquent expression of the affection in which he is held, a testimonial to his splendid qualities and enduring achievement.

RETREAT.

CHRONOLOGY OF SQUADRON A

History insures to youth the understanding of the ancients.—PLINY

THE FIRST FIVE YEARS

In 1894 Captain Charles F. Roe signed and issued a pamphlet beginning: "Five years ago, April 2nd, 1889, Troop A was mustered into the National Guard of the State of New York with two officers and fifty enlisted men." It then lists the original members—eighteen in all —who were still members of the Troop on the fifth anniversary, with other data as to transfers, discharges and deaths, and adds: "In the five years there have been 212 men in the Troop." The remainder of this pamphlet is quoted in full.

As before stated the troop was mustered in on April 2, 1889; was provided with uniforms and made its first parade April 29, 1889, fully armed and equipped.

The services of the troop, in addition to the regular drills from the 1st of October to the 1st of May each year, were as follows:

1889

April 29: Troop escorted Cleveland City Troop from Dickel's to City Hall and President Harrison from City Hall to Vice President Morton's house on Fifth Avenue, after which it entertained the Cleveland Troop at Jaeger's on Fifty-ninth Street and Madison Avenue, about 5 P.M.

April 30: Took part in the centennial parade as escort to Commander-in-Chief, Governor Hill, first escorting him from Hoffman House to Vesey Street.

May 1: Members of Troop acted as aides to General Butterfield on occasion of civic parade.

May 30: Decoration Day Parade; as escort to Brigade Commander, General Fitzgerald.

Oct. 17: First muster and inspection, dismounted, by General Barber, at the Forty-fifth Street Armory; eighty-one men in Troop.

Oct. 30: Took part in parade at Brooklyn at the laying of the cornerstone of the Soldiers' and Sailors' Arch at entrance to Prospect Park; a sergeant and two corporals carried and escorted the First Brigade flag. Troop also on that occasion escorted General Sherman from the house of Mayor Chapin to the grandstand. Troop marched to and from Brooklyn.

Dec. 10: Troop numbered one hundred and four.

1890

April 24: Troop marched to and from Inwood Park; held a troop drill.

May 27: Annual muster and inspection, mounted, held at Morris Park Race Course by General Barber; total distance marched, twenty-five miles; returned to armory 9:30 P.M.

May 30: Decoration Day parade; escort to Brigade Commander General Fitzgerald.

May 31: Field maneuvers at Van Cortlandt Park; Troop divided into two parts, one with eastern and one with western force. Total distance marched, thirty miles.

July 5: Began march to state camp at Peekskill via old post road to Albany; camped at Tarrytown, bivouacked near hotel; reached camp about 8 P.M.; men groomed horses for the first time about 9 P.M.

July 6: Continued the march, arriving at the camp of instruction at 1 P.M. where met the 9th Regiment.

July 7-11: In camp.

July 12: Left camp of instruction at 2 P.M.; marched to Dobbs Ferry, arriving at 10 P.M. at Mr. Cyrus Field's place, where bivouacked until 4 A.M., July 13, when march was resumed; arrived at armory at 10 A.M. Total distance marched to and from camp, one hundred miles.

Sept. 23: Regular troop day at Creedmoor.

1891

Feb. 19: Troop acted with regular army as part of the military escort to the remains of General W. T. Sherman, reporting to Colonel Langdon, 1st U.S. Artillery at Seventy-first Street and Eighth Avenue, and marched thence at the head of the column to Broadway, Fifty-seventh Street, Fifth Avenue, Waverly Place, Broadway, Canal Street, and Worth Street. Received a letter from General O. O. Howard, U.S. Army, thanking troop for its services and praising the soldierly bearing of the troop.

May 6: Annual muster and inspection at Claremont Park, mounted, by Inspector General Barber. Total distance marched, twelve miles.

May 26: Annual troop carbine practice at Creedmoor.

May 30: Decoration Day parade as part of escort to the Grand Army of the Republic.

June 6: Troop marched to Prospect Park, Brooklyn, and there took part with 1st U.S. Artillery and 23rd Regiment, N.G.S.N.Y., in field maneuvers, under command of Colonel Langdon, 1st Artillery. Distance marched, twenty-five miles.

July 18: Part of troop proceeded to Washington, D.C., and with Troop A, D.C.N.G., marched through portions of Maryland and Virginia. Distance, two hundred miles. Returned to New York, August 1, 1891.

Oct. 8: Took part in Governor's review at Van Cortlandt Park; also acted as escort to Governor Hill of New York and Governor Abbott of New Jersey. Left armory at 7:50 A.M., returned at 8:10 P.M. Distance marched, thirty miles.

1892

April 12: Gave a mounted exhibition drill in the ring of the Brooklyn Riding and Driving Club and was entertained at the Montauk Club.

April 27: Paraded as escort to the President of the United States, Mr. Harrison, from the Fifth Avenue Hotel to the Grant Tomb, at the ceremonies incident to laying the cornerstone of the Grant monument. Later on the same day was mustered and inspected, mounted, by Inspector General McGrath, on the boulevard near 124th Street.

May 28: Annual troop carbine practice at Creedmoor, L. I.

May 30: Decoration Day Parade, as part of escort to the Grand Army of the Republic.

June 18: Commenced march to camp of instruction at Peekskill; camped on Mr. Jay Gould's property.

June 19: Resumed march; reached camp of instruction at 11:30 A.M., met 69th Regiment.

June 20–24: In camp.

June 25: Left camp of instruction 10 A.M., receiving a most enthusiastic send-off from the 69th Regiment; marched to Mr. Gould's property.

June 26: Resumed march, arriving at armory 11 A.M., and was received by a contingent of the 69th Regiment with cheers.

Aug. 18: Received orders to proceed to Buffalo and report to General Doyle, commanding 3rd Brigade, for riot duty.

Aug. 19: Left armory at 12:30 A.M., took passenger and horse cars at West Sixty-second Street, started en route to Buffalo by special train. Arrived at Buffalo at 5:30 P.M.; was stationed in New York Central Stock Yards, East Buffalo, for permanent camp.

SQUADRON A

Aug. 20: Left camp at 8 A.M., proceeded to Black Rock, West Buffalo, returned to camp at 9:30 P.M. Distance marched, seventeen miles.

Aug. 21: Acted as escort to Adjutant-General Porter and General Doyle visiting outlying camps. Distance marched, twenty miles.

Aug. 22: Troop proceeded to the "Island" on Lake Erie, returned to camp at 6:30 P.M. Distance marched, twelve miles.

Aug. 23: Remained in camp.

Aug. 24: Troop was ordered to guard Del., Lack. & Western R.R.; left camp 9 A.M., returned 6:30 P.M. Distance marched, ten miles.

Aug. 25: In camp. Received orders to return to New York; left at 3:30 P.M. via Niagara Falls.

Aug. 26: Troop arrived in New York 9 A.M., unloaded cars, dismissed at 10:30 A.M. Five mounted orderlies reported to General Doyle each day while at Buffalo. Of the one hundred and four men in the troop ninety-eight reported for duty at Buffalo, four being absent in Europe and the West, and two ill in bed.

Oct. 12: Troop acted as escort to General McMahon, Grand Marshal of the parade to commemorate the discovery of America; afterward entertained Essex Troop and Philadelphia City Troop at armory.

Oct. 18: Troop with eighty-two men and horses left about midnight by special train for Chicago, Ill., to act as escort to Governor Flower at the formal opening of the World's Fair, going via Niagara Falls and Michigan Central Railroad.

Oct. 19: En route to Chicago.

Oct. 20: Arrived at Chicago about eight A.M. Established camp just outside of World's Fair grounds, having brought camp equipage, provisions, and forage. Name of camp, Flower; in honor of Governor of New York.

Oct. 21: Marched to Auditorium Hotel, Chicago, reported for duty and escorted Governor Flower and Staff to the World's Fair buildings. The Governor and Staff visited the camp and took dinner. Distance marched, eighteen miles.

Oct. 22: Marched to Auditorium Hotel; escorted Governor Flower and Staff, Vice-President Morton, of the U.S., Hon. Whitelaw Reid and Hon. Chauncey M. Depew to New York State Building. About 5 P.M. camp was broken, camp equipage and horses loaded on cars, and at 6:30 P.M. troop started on return trip to New York.

Oct. 23: En route.

Oct. 24: Arrived in New York about 7 A.M.

1893

March 2-5: Troop acted as escort to Governor Flower at the inauguration of President Cleveland. Left New York night of March 2nd, arrived at Washington morning March 3rd. Took part in the inaugural parade March 4th, returned to New York, night of March 5th.

April 19: Acted as escort to the Duke of Veragua, from Hotel Waldorf to City Hall and return.

April 28: Acted as escort to Governor Flower on occasion of land parade of the foreign navies of the world, from Windsor Hotel to City Hall and return.

May 25: Acted as escort to the Infanta Eulalia of Spain, from foot of West Thirty-fourth Street to the Hotel Savoy.

May 27: Turned out as escort to Infanta, but was dismissed.

May 30: Acted as escort to the Grand Army of the Republic on Decoration Day Parade.

June 5: Acted as escort to Infanta Eulalia from Hotel Savoy to foot of West Thirty-fourth Street on occasion of her departure for Chicago.

June 24: The annual troop carbine practice at Creedmoor.

Oct. 19: Eighty-two men and horses proceeded to Trenton, N.J., by cars. Acted as escort to Governor Flower, on occasion of unveiling of Trenton Battle Monument, returning to armory at 11:50 P.M.

Oct. 21: Took part in drill and review at Van Cortlandt Park, and also acted as escort to Governor Flower to and from the field. Distance marched, thirty miles.

Oct. 27: Annual inspection and muster, dismounted, by Inspector-General McGrath.

The troop gave an exhibition drill and reception in 1891, and has also held three annual athletic exhibitions.

By Act of Legislature passed in 1893, troop was increased by two lieutenants, one veterinary sergeant and four artificers, making the maximum strength one hundred and twelve.

It is my great pleasure to state that the city is building a troop armory which will be the finest thing of the kind in the world. Much has been accomplished in the five years of our troop life, and we can most certainly feel that we have a record that any organization might be proud of, and that record is an excellent incentive, for all of us in the future, to live up to the troop motto—*Boutez en avant* (Push to the front).

CHAS. F. ROE, *Captain*

April 2, 1894

DETAIL IN ARMY MANEUVERS, 1939
SQUADRON COMMANDER AT HEAD OF COLUMN IN ARMY MANEUVERS, 1939

THE MEMORIAL GATE

(The list of names appears on the Roll of Honor beginning on p. 187.)

The foregoing recital mentions an exhibition drill and reception in 1891, and from other data we find that this occurred on January 16. The three annual athletic exhibitions referred to were the early competitive mounted games, which later became an outstanding feature each year. The first of these (according to the printed program) was held on December 19, 1891, and was featured in the public press the next day.

The record does not include the annual church parades, which were held on April 20, 1890, May 10, 1891, May 1, 1892, and May 7, 1893.

CHRONOLOGY OF LATER YEARS

The souvenir issued by the squadron on the occasion of its tenth anniversary, April 2, 1899, supplies a chronology of the second five-year period. The pamphlet of the Ex-Members' Association published in 1911 carries the record to that period; and the Year Book of the squadron for 1916 gives a chronology, somewhat abridged, for the entire period up to that year. For the subsequent years other sources have supplied the data, unfortunately not altogether complete.

1894

Feb. 16: Annual mounted games.

April 29: Annual Church Parade, dismounted, to Church of the Heavenly Rest, Fifth Avenue and Forty-fifth Street.

May 5: Carbine practice day at Creedmoor.

May 15: Inspection and Muster, dismounted, by General McGrath, at 136 West Fifty-sixth Street.

May 30: Memorial Day Parade; escorted the Grand Marshal.

July 10: Cornerstone of Armory, Ninety-fourth Street and Madison Avenue, laid by Mayor Gilroy.

July 16–23: Duty at Camp of Instruction, Peekskill, marching both ways, camping overnight at White Plains on each march.

Sept. 27: Assigned to temporary quarters in 8th Regiment Armory, Park Avenue and Ninety-fourth Street.

Oct. 20: Maneuvers 1st Brigade, Van Cortlandt Park.

Dec. 15: Escort to remains of Major General Josiah Porter, Adjutant General, S.N.Y.

1895

Jan. 21–28: On duty in Brooklyn during street railway riots.

Feb. 9: Troop A was divided into two troops, Troop 1 under command of Captain Oliver B. Bridgman and Troop 2 under command of Captain Howard G. Badgley, thus forming Squadron A, commanded by Major Charles F. Roe.

May 4: Paraded as escort to Governor Levi P. Morton at the ceremonies incidental to the dedication of the Washington Arch.

May 9: Annual Inspection and Muster, dismounted, at 8th Regiment Armory, by General McElwee.

May 11: Carbine practice day at Creedmoor.

June 7: Took possession of new armory at Madison Avenue and Ninety-fourth Street, in accordance with S.O. 32, Headquarters First Brigade.

Nov. 21–27: Atlanta, Georgia, as escort to Mayor William L. Strong attending the Industrial Exposition in that city. While in Atlanta held public exhibition of mounted athletic games.

1896

Jan. 31: Formal opening of armory with reception and ball.

April 26: Annual Church Parade, dismounted, to the Church of the Heavenly Rest, Fifth Avenue and Forty-fifth Street.

May 22: Preparatory inspection of the squadron, dismounted, at armory, in evening. Distinctive dress uniform adopted.

May 23: Inspection and Muster at Van Cortlandt Park by General Barber.

June 27–July 5: Tour of Duty at Camp of Instruction, Peekskill, going and returning by special train.

Sept. 1: Squadron paraded as escort to His Excellency Li Hung Chang, Chinese Viceroy.

Dec. 5: Troop 3 formed from men on the "waiting list" of the squadron, and transfers from Troop 1 and 2, under command of Captain Latham G. Reed.

1897

April 20: Review and Inspection, dismounted, and presentation of Marksmen's badges at armory by Major Roe.

April 26: Paraded as escort to the President of the United States, Benjamin Harrison, upon his arrival in New York to attend the Grant Memorial Parade.

April 27: Paraded as escort to President Harrison at the dedication of the Grant Monument.

May 2: Annual Church Parade, dismounted, to Church of the Heavenly Rest, Fifth Avenue and Forty-fifth Street.

May 8: Carbine practice day at Creedmoor.

June 11: Inspection and Muster at Van Cortlandt Park by General Hoffman.

Oct. 8-11: Camp established at Van Cortlandt Park, the Squadron taking part in the Field maneuvers of the First Brigade, Saturday, October 9th, and returning to armory, Monday morning, October 11th.

1898

Feb. 11: Major Roe relinquished command of the Squadron, having been appointed Major General commanding the National Guard, State of New York.

March 17: Review, dismounted, and presentation of marksmen's badges by Major General Roe, at armory in evening.

March 23: Major Avery D. Andrews took command of the squadron.

April 25: Volunteers for the war with Spain having been called for, the squadron met at armory and tendered its services.

April 29: Troop A was formed from the three troops of Squadron A to represent it in the field during the war with Spain; Captain Badgley in command.

May 2: The Volunteer Troop left armory at 10 A.M. for Camp Black, Hempstead, L.I.

June 9: Annual Church Parade, dismounted, to Church of the Heavenly Rest, Fifth Avenue and Forty-fifth Street.

Sept. 10: The squadron paraded as escort to the Volunteer Troop on its return from Puerto Rico. Reception at armory followed.

Sept. 21: Carbine practice day at Creedmoor.

Dec. 31: Albany, New York, upon inauguration of Governor Theodore Roosevelt. Quartered in 10th Battalion Armory. Tendered reception in evening by friends of the squadron in Albany.
Major Avery D. Andrews relinquished command of the squadron to accept the position of adjutant-general of the state.

1899

Jan. 1: Paraded, dismounted, to All Saints' Protestant Episcopal Cathedral, Albany, where special services were held by the bishop of the diocese.

Jan. 2: Paraded as special escort to the Governor-elect, escorting him from the executive mansion to the Capitol, where the inaugural ceremonies were held.

Jan. 3: Left Albany by special train at 1 A.M., arriving in New York at 7 A.M.

Jan. 5: Review, dismounted, and presentation of marksmen's badges by Brigadier General Avery D. Andrews, Adjutant General, in evening.

Jan. 12: Major Oliver B. Bridgman took command of the squadron.

Jan. 13: Review at armory by General Avery D. Andrews.

April 7: Anniversary dinner.

April 30: Church Parade.

June 2: March to state camp at Peekskill, accompanied by Governor Roosevelt, Major General Roe, Adjutant General Andrews, and Major Lee of the British Service.

June 3-10: Tour of duty at Camp of Instruction, Peekskill.

1900

Jan. 19: Parade and Review at armory as compliment to newly appointed Adjutant General.

Feb. 14: Polo club formed.

March 9: Annual games at armory.

April 16-27: Strike duty at Croton Dam, New York.

May 5: Practice day at Creedmoor.

May 6: Annual Church Parade.

May 30: Escort to Major General at Memorial Day Parade.

Oct. 27: Annual Muster and Inspection at Van Cortlandt Park.

1901

Feb. 26: Annual games.

March 2: Trip to Washington to take part in inauguration ceremonies of President McKinley on March 4th and as personal escort to Vice President Roosevelt.

April 13: Annual dinner at armory.

May 28: Annual Church Parade.

May 30: Escort to Major General at Memorial Day Parade.

May 31: Start for camp at Peekskill.

June 1-8: Tour of Duty at State Camp of Instruction.

Oct. 2: Polo club disbanded, and polo taken up under auspices of squadron.

Nov. 2: Annual Inspection and Muster at the armory.

Dec. 20: Morse Cup games.

1902

Jan. 13: Review by Major General Charles F. Roe.

SQUADRON A

Feb. 23–25: Escort to Prince Henry of Germany during his stay in New York.

March 17: Annual games.

April 19: Escort of President Roosevelt to attend inauguration of President Butler of Columbia University.

May 4: Annual Church Parade.

May 31–June 2: Camp at Van Cortlandt Park.

Oct. 20: Annual Muster and Inspection at armory.

Nov. 15: Troop I attended unveiling of monument to General Josiah Porter at Van Cortlandt Park.

Dec. 22: Parade and Review at armory for Colonel Mills, Commandant U.S. Army Post at West Point, and mounted exercises afterward.

1903

Jan. 23: "Smoker" at armory; talks on military subjects by distinguished U.S. Army officers.

March 28: Annual games.

April 18: Annual dinner at Waldorf.

April 27–May 3: Trip to St. Louis to take part in Louisiana Purchase Exhibition ceremonies.

May 2: Carbine practice at Creedmoor, L.I.

May 10: Annual Church Parade.

May 15: Inspection by U.S. Army Officers at armory.

May 30: Escort to Major General at dedication ceremonies of statue of General Sherman, Fifty-ninth Street and Fifth Avenue.

Dec. 19: Parade of squadron at opening of Williamsburg Bridge.

1904

Jan. 20: Parade and Review of squadron by Major General Henry L. Corbin, U.S.A.

March 3: Inspection of the squadron by Major W. F. Wood, U.S.A.

May 7: Squadron at Creedmoor Pistol and Carbine Practice.

May 8: Church Parade of the Squadron.

Sept. 2–12: Composite Troop of the squadron with Commanding Officer and four members of Non-commissioned Staff, as part of provisional Squadron A, N.G.N.Y., at Manassas, Virginia.

1905

Jan. 17: Review of the squadron by the Mayor of Greater New York.

March 3–6: Squadron at the inauguration of President Roosevelt, Washington, D.C.

April 3: Annual Muster and Inspection of squadron.

May 7: Annual Church Parade.

May 13: Small Arms Practice Day at Creedmoor

May 27–29: Squadron in camp at Van Cortlandt Park.

May 30: The squadron as escort to the Major General Commanding in the Memorial Day Parade.

1906

Jan. 16: Squadron reviewed by Colonel Daniel Appleton, 7th Regiment, N.G.N.Y.

April 2: Annual muster and inspection of squadron.

April 29: Annual church parade.

May 5: Squadron at small arms practice at Creedmoor.

May 30: Squadron as escort to the Major General Commanding, Memorial Day parade.

June 1–11: Tour of duty at state camp of instruction, Peekskill, New York, marching both ways.

Nov. 26: Review and evening parade of squadron, by Adjutant General Nelson H. Henry, State of New York.

Dec. 31–Jan. 2: Escort to Governor Charles E. Hughes at inaugural ceremonies, Albany.

1907

Feb. 20: Review and evening parade of the squadron by Lieutenant Colonel Robert Howze, U.S.A.

April 3: Annual muster and inspection of squadron.

April 28: Annual church parade.

May 4: Annual small arms practice at Creedmoor, L.I.

May 10: Squadron organized into a squadron of four troops, new troop designated "Troop 4".

May 30: Escort to Major General Roe in Memorial Day Parade.

May 30–June 3: Squadron camps at Van Cortlandt Park.

Oct. 8–12: Squadron as escort to His Excellency, the Governor of the State, at the Jamestown Exposition.

Oct. 19: Squadron as escort to the Major General Commanding at the unveiling of the Monument to the late Major General Franz Siegel.

SQUADRON A

1908

Jan. 3: Evening parade of squadron, dismounted, followed by review, mounted, by Colonel H. L. Scott, U.S.A.

Feb. 26: Evening parade of the squadron, dismounted, followed by review, by the Major General Commanding.

April 8: Annual muster and inspection of the squadron.

April 29: Review of the squadron by Lieutenant Colonel Edward F. Glenn, U.S.A.

May 30: Memorial Day parade; escort to Major General Roe.

June 14–25: Tour of duty, Pine Camp, N.Y.

Nov. 14: Squadron paraded at unveiling of monument to Prison Ship Martyrs, in Brooklyn, N.Y.; escort to Major General Roe.

1909

Jan. 1: The squadron as escort to Governor Hughes, at his inauguration, Albany, N.Y.

Feb. 27: Review by Major General Leonard Wood, U.S.A.

April 18: Church parade, to the Church of Heavenly Rest.

April 28: Annual muster and inspection of the squadron.

April 30: Review at Armory by Major General Roe.

May 30: Memorial Day parade; escort to Major General Roe.

June 12: The squadron paraded at the opening of the Queensboro Bridge (escort to Major General Roe, grand marshal).

Aug. 14–21: Field Maneuvers in Massachusetts.

Sept. 30: The squadron paraded at the Hudson-Fulton Celebration. Escort to Governor Hughes and Major General Roe.

Oct. 20: General small arms practice, Sea Girt, N.J.

Dec. 22: Review by Lieutenant Colonel F. F. W. Sibley, U.S.A.

1910

April 3: Annual church parade.

April 13, 14: Annual muster and inspection (at which the squadron paraded 100 per cent present).

May 30: Memorial Day parade; escort to the Major General Commanding.

July 4: Independence Day parade; escort to the Major General Commanding.

July 31–Aug. 11: Tour of duty at Pine Camp, N.Y.

Oct. 8: General small arms practice, Blauvelt, N.Y.

Dec. 14: Review by the Adjutant General, State of New York.

1911

March 25: Review at armory by Governor John A. Dix.

May 30: Escort to Major General Roe in Memorial Day parade.

Oct. 12: Escort to Major General Roe in Columbus Day parade.

Dec. 6: Review at armory by Hon. Henry L. Stimson, Secretary of War.

Dec. 27: First Regiment Cavalry, N.G.N.Y., formed. Major Oliver B. Bridgman appointed colonel.

1912

Jan. 18: Designation of Squadron A changed to First Squadron, First Cavalry, and of Troops 1, 2, 3 and 4 to Troops A, E, F and G, respectively.

Jan. 29: Major William R. Wright took command of First Squadron.

Feb. 2: Troop L, later C, formed under command of Captain Merritt H. Smith.

Feb. 11, 12: Provisional troop, in connection with 1st Battery, F.A. and Company of the 12th Regiment, N.G.N.Y., took part in field-firing problem at Salem Center, N.Y.

April 11: Troops A and F formed part of escort to remains of Major General Philip Kearny, U.S.A.

April 26: Troops C and E formed part of escort to remains of Major General Frederick D. Grant, U.S.A.

May 1: Major General Roe retired under the age limit.

May 11: Mounted games at Van Cortlandt Park.

May 11-12: Troops C and F in camp at Van Cortlandt Park.

May 25-26: Troops A, E, and G in camp at Van Cortlandt Park. Camp visited by President William H. Taft and Major General O'Ryan.

May 30: Escort to Major General John F. O'Ryan, N.G.N.Y., in Memorial Day parade.

Aug. 8-19: Connecticut maneuver campaign.

Oct. 5: Troop G took part in centennial celebration, Albany.

1913

Jan. 24: Review at armory by Major General Thomas H. Barry, U.S.A.

Feb. 11: Competition for the "Justice" cup.

Mar. 1-4: Escort to Governor of New York at inaugural ceremonies of President Wilson, Washington, D.C.

May 2: Review at armory by Major General John F. O'Ryan, N.G.N.Y. Members of Troop A, N.Y. Cavalry, U.S.A., 1898, acted as escort to reviewing officer.

SQUADRON A

May 10: Escort to Major General O'Ryan at unveiling of monument to Carl Schurz.

May 10-11, 24-25: Squadron camps at Van Cortlandt Park.

May 30: Memorial Day parade. Troops A and C took part in ceremonies incidental to unveiling of *Maine* Monument, New York City.

June 21-28: Cavalry School of Instruction at Montauk Point, L.I.

Nov. 15: Squadron detached from 1st Cavalry and designated 1st Squadron, Cavalry, N.G.N.Y., Troop C designated Machine Gun Troop, Cavalry, N.G.N.Y.

Dec. 10: Troops A, E, F and G designated, respectively, Troops A, B, C and D, 1st Squadron Cavalry, N.G.N.Y.

1914

March 5: Designation of 1st Squadron Cavalry changed to Squadron A Cavalry.

April 20: Review at armory by Major General Charles F. Roe, N.G.N.Y., retired, the members of Troop A, N.G.N.Y., as mustered in on April 2nd, 1889, acting as escort to the reviewing officer, in celebration of the twenty-fifth anniversary of the mustering in of Troop A Cavalry, N.G.N.Y.

April 22: Squadron ball as part of celebration.

April 25: Squadron dinner as part of celebration.

April 26: Church parade as part of celebration. Rev. Herbert Shipman, honorary chaplain.

May 30: Escort to the Grand Army of the Republic in Memorial Day parade.

June 21: Squadron A farm bought at New City, N.Y.

Sept. : Mounted Games and Exhibition at Rockland County Fair Grounds.

1915

Feb. 20-22: Camp and field practice at squadron farm by detail from Troop C.

Twenty-first annual mounted games; also "Justice" cup competition.

May 1-2: Recruit squad camp at Van Cortlandt Park.

May 8: Review at armory by Colonel Daniel Appleton, 7th Infantry, N.G.N.Y.

May 15-16: Troop D camp at Van Cortlandt Park.

May 21-23: Troop A camp at United Hunts Club, Belmont Park.

May 29-30: Troop C camp at Van Cortlandt Park.

May 31: Memorial Day parade.

June 5–6: M.G. Troop camp at Van Cortlandt Park.

June 12, 19: Troop B camp at squadron farm.

July 17–24: Tour of field duty at Camp Whitman, Fishkill Plains, N. Y., with 1st Brigade, N.G.N.Y.

Military tournament and wild west show at Piping Rock Club.

Sept. 25: Mobilization and field exercises with 1st and 2nd Brigades, N.G.N.Y., at Van Cortlandt Park.

Nov. 26: Review at armory by Brigadier General George R. Dyer, 1st Brigade, N.G.N.Y.

1916

Review by Mayor John Purroy Mitchel.

Provisional troop of Plattsburg graduates, including Mayor Mitchel and other city officials, given the use of the armory for drills.

Squadron participated in review by Colonel Appleton of the 7th Regiment, upon his retirement.

June 19: Squadron called into Federal service.

June 20: Squadron went into camp at Van Cortlandt Park, preliminary to service on the Mexican border.

July 6: Entrained for Texas.

July 18: Arrived at McAllen, Texas, and established camp.

July 18–Dec. 14: On duty in border service. Drills, reviews, hikes and other duties, interspersed with polo matches with army officers; participation in Field and Frontier Day, including track team and mounted athletic competitions, baseball, football and soccer. Texas branch of the Squadron A Club established.

Dec. 15: Entrained for New York.

Dec. 23: Arrived at New York. Escorted to armory by Depot Squadron and mustered out of the Federal service.

1917

March 4: Two composite volunteer troops acted as escort to Governor Whitman at President Wilson's second inaugural, Washington, D.C.

Acted as escort to Marshal Joffre of France.

May 4: Old Home-Week in the armory.

July 16: Squadron A called into Federal service for the World War.

Aug. 17–Oct. 11: Squadron A training at camp in Van Cortlandt Park.

Aug. 29: Division Farewell Parade in New York.

Oct. 12: Entrained for Camp Wadsworth, Spartanburg, South Carolina.

Oct. 13: Arrived at Camp Wadsworth and reorganized as 105th Machine Gun Battalion, with Headquarters, Company A (formerly Troops A and B), Company B (formerly Troop D), and Company C (formerly Troop C and M. G. Troop).

The subsequent war service is narrated in the history entitled, "Squadron A in the Great War, 1917-1918."

THE DEPOT TROOP AND ITS SUCCESSOR ORGANIZATIONS

1915

Dec. 6: Meeting of volunteers called December 20 by Major Wright for the purpose of organizing a Depot Troop under authority S.O. 190 A.G.O.

1916

March 14: Depot Troop mustered into service under command of Captain Latham G. Reed.

June : Reorganized as Depot Squadron of two troops under Major Latham G. Reed.

July 1: A third troop authorized.

Depot Squadron A entered service with headquarters at the armory.

Dec. 23: Upon return of Squadron A from Federal service, escorted it to armory.

1917

April 20: Depot units again assembled.

Aug. 3: Reorganized as Squadron A Cavalry, New York Guard.

Dec. 17: Herbert Barry commissioned Major in lieu of Major Reed, who had resigned.

Throughout the last six months of 1917, the whole of 1918, and until federalized in June 1, 1921, Squadron A, New York Guard, continued to perform the functions which had been performed by Squadron A, N.G.N.Y., prior to its entry into the Federal service.

1918

Jan.-May 4: Major Barry on leave of absence at Officers Training School, Spartanburg, S.C.; Captain Alfred Wendt assumed command.

May 21: Captain Alfred Wendt commissioned major and continued in command.

July 12-14: Headquarters and Troop A in camp, Jerome Avenue and Two Hundred and Thirty-third Street.

July 19–21: Troop B in camp.

July 26–28: Troop C in camp.

Aug. 30–Sept. 8: Detachment marched from squadron farm, 48½ miles to Camp Whitman.

Sept. 1–9: Detachment at Camp Whitman.

Sept. 7–8: Detachment marched to squadron farm.

Nov. 1: Review; presentation of cavalry standards by General Bridgman.

1919

March 24: Squadron A, New York Guard, together with the Ex-Members' Association, acted as escort to the 105th Machine Gun Battalion on return from overseas, parading with them to the armory.

April 1: Machine Gun Battalion mustered out and discharged from U.S. service.

May 30: Squadron A, N. Y. Guard, paraded in Memorial Day parade, and was reviewed by Major General O'Ryan.

June 12: Major Wendt resigned.

July 14: Major Egleston took command of the organization. Polo matches held at Gedney Farm, White Plains, N.Y.

1920

May 21: Review at armory by Lieutenant Colonel Edward Olmsted, Acting Chief of Staff, 27th Division.

May 30: Squadron took part in Memorial Day parade.

July 6: Squadron fired record rifle practice at state camp, Peekskill, N.Y.

Oct. 1–3: Camp at squadron farm, New City, N.Y.

Nov. 11: Troop B federalized.

Nov. 14: Squadron participated in Armistice Day parade. Indoor polo initiated.

1921

April 11: Troop B escorted Envoy Extraordinary Viviani.

April 21: Troop A and Troop C federalized.

May 12: Squadron attended annual rifle practice at Peekskill.

May 30: Squadron participated in Memorial Day parade. National Horse Show held in armory. Squadron attended annual Church Parade.

June 1: Squadron A federalized and redesignated 51st Machine Gun Squadron, with Troops A, B and C.

July 1–Aug. 14: Annual field service at Fort Ethan Allen, Vermont.

SQUADRON A

1922

January 28: Troop B, Squadron A Cavalry, N.Y.G., demobilized.

April 26: Squadron acted as escort to Marshal Joffre of France.

April : Annual church parade.

May 25: Review at armory by Brigadier General Mortimer D. Bryant, commanding 51st Cavalry Brigade.

May 30: Squadron participated in Memorial Day parade.

August 6–20: Squadron attended annual field training at Squadron A farm, New City, N.Y.

Nov. 10–20: National Horse Show held in the armory.

1923

April : Annual church parade.

May 24: Review at armory by Major General Charles W. Barry, Commanding General, New York National Guard.
Squadron attended annual rifle practice at Peekskill.

May 30: Squadron participated in Memorial Day parade.

July 15–29: Squadron attended annual field training at Camp Dix, N.J.

Nov. 9–19: National Horse Show held in the armory.

1924

May 6–10: Commemoration of thirty-fifth anniversary of Squadron A, including dinner, military ball, and church parade. Review at armory by Brigadier General Oliver B. Bridgman.

May 29: Squadron fired record rifle practice at Camp Smith, Peekskill, N.Y.

May 30: Squadron participated in Memorial Day parade.

July 6–20: Squadron attended annual field training at Fort Ethan Allen, Vermont.

September 12: Entire squadron assembled at armory for test mobilization (National Defense Test Day).

Oct. 10–20: National Horse Show held in armory.

1925

April 5: Annual church parade.

May 5: Reconstruction of armory started.

May 30: Squadron participated in Memorial Day parade. Attended annual rifle practice at Peekskill, N.Y.

July 12–26: Squadron attended annual field training at Fort Ethan Allen, Vermont.

Nov. 20–30: National Horse Show held in armory.

1926

May 16: Annual church parade.

May 26: Squadron fired record rifle practice at Camp Smith, Peekskill, N.Y.

May 30: Squadron participated in Memorial Day parade.

June 15: Reconstruction of armory completed.

June 13-27: Squadron attended annual field training at Pine Camp, N.Y.

June 29: Troop A acted as escort at funeral of First Lieutenant Lewis E. Shaw, Troop A.
(The squadron won many ribbons at National Horse Show in this and the preceding year.)

1927

Feb.   : Reconstruction of armory; construction of rooms of Ex-Members' Association completed.

May 8: Annual church parade.

May 30: Squadron participated in Memorial Day parade.
Annual rifle practice at Peekskill, N.Y.

June 12-26: Squadron attended annual field training at Pine Camp, N.Y.

Oct. 17: Squadron participated in military tournament at Madison Square Garden.

Nov. 12: Troop A participated in opening exercises of Holland Vehicular Tunnel.
(At the National Horse Show, squadron won many ribbons, trophies, and cash prizes.)

1928

Feb. 15: 51st Machine Gun Squadron redesignated 2nd Squadron, 101st Cavalry with the following unit redesignations:

Troop A redesignated Troop E
Troop B   "   Troop F
Troop C   "   Troop G
Medical Detachment disbanded

Annual Rifle practice at Peekskill, N.Y.

April 15: Annual church parade.

May 30: Squadron participated in Memorial Day parade.

June 17-July 1: Squadron attended annual field training at Pine Camp, N.Y.

Oct. 15: Squadron participated in military tournament at Madison Square Garden.

SQUADRON A

1929

April 7: Dedication of memorial gates.

April 7: Annual church parade.

April 15: Headquarters 3rd Squadron, 101st Cavalry, organized with station at this armory with Major George Matthews, Jr., in command.
Troop G redesignated Troop K.

April 23: Review at armory by Brigadier General Oliver B. Bridgman in commemoration of Fortieth anniversary of Squadron A.
Annual rifle practice at Peekskill, N.Y.

May 30: Squadron participated in Memorial Day parade.

June 16-30: Squadron attended annual field training at Pine Camp, N.Y.

1930

March 4: Medical Department Detachment organized and stationed at this armory.

March 12: Review at armory by Major General William N. Haskell, Commanding General, New York National Guard.

April 5: Troop F participated in army day parade.

April 27: Annual church parade.
Annual rifle practice at Peekskill, N.Y.

May 30: Troop K participated in Memorial Day parade.

June 7: Troops E and F paraded as part of N.Y.N.G. at review by Governor Franklin D. Roosevelt at Van Cortlandt Park.

June 15-29: Squadron attended annual field training at Pine Camp, N.Y.

1931

April 11: Provisional squadron of three troops acted as escort to Prince and Princess Takamatsu of Japan on their visit to New York City.

April 12: Annual church parade.
Annual rifle practice at Peekskill, N.Y.

May 14: Review at armory by Brigadier General George R. Dyer, commanding 87th Brigade.

June 14-28: Squadron attended annual field training at Pine Camp, N.Y.

Nov. 10: Troop E acted as escort at National Horse Show to officers of International Jumping Teams.

Dec. 21: Review at armory by Brigadier General Mortimer D. Bryant, commanding 51st Cavalry Brigade.

1932

February 18: Troop K participated in George Washington bicentennial parade.

April 3: Annual rifle practice at Peekskill, N.Y.

April 12: Annual church parade.

May 30: Troop F participated in Memorial Day parade.

June 12–26: Squadron attended annual field training at Pine Camp, N.Y.

December 13: Major N. Hillyer Egleston promoted Lieutenant Colonel, N.Y.N.G., resigned command of Manhattan Units, 101st Cavalry.

December 19: Major Frederick A. Vietor transferred from 3rd Squadron to 2nd Squadron and assumed command of Manhattan Units, 101st Cavalry.

1933

January 21: Troop F acted as guard of honor during funeral of Brigadier General Mortimer D. Bryant, late commander of 51st Cavalry Brigade.

February 15: Manhattan Units, 101st Cavalry, held championship polo and military tournament at armory for the benefit of Emergency Unemployment Relief Committee.

February 28: Review at armory by Brigadier General N. Hillyer Egleston, commanding 51st Cavalry Brigade.

April 8: Troop E participated in army day parade.

April 23: Squadron attended annual church parade and memorial services at Church of the Heavenly Rest.

April 29: Squadron fired record rifle practice at Peekskill, N.Y.

May 30: Troop E participated in Memorial Day parade.

June 11–25: Squadron attended annual field training at Pine Camp, N.Y.

October 22: Squadron attended mounted church parade and memorial services at St. James Lutheran Church on invitation of Chaplain Charles D. Trexler, Regimental Chaplain.

1934

February 21: Review at armory by Colonel William R. Wright, Chief of Staff, New York National Guard.

April 8: Squadron attended annual church parade and memorial services at Church of the Heavenly Rest.

May 2: Manhattan Units, composed of three provisional troops participated in review by Colonel Arthur Poillon, U.S.A. at 101st Cavalry armory, Brooklyn.

SQUADRON A

May 5: Manhattan Units fired record rifle practice at Peekskill, N.Y.

May 30: Manhattan Units participated in Memorial Day parade.

June 10-24: Manhattan Units attended annual field training at Pine Camp, N.Y.

November 13: Troop K acted as escort to officers of International Jumping Teams at National Horse Show, Madison Square Garden.

1935

March 7: Review at armory by Major General Leon B. Kromer, Chief of Cavalry, U.S.A.

April 28: Squadron attended annual Church Parade and Memorial Services at Church of Heavenly Rest.

May 4-5: Manhattan Units fired record rifle practice at Peekskill, N.Y.

May 30: Manhattan Units participated in Memorial Day parade.

June 16-30: Manhattan Units attended annual field training at Pine Camp, N.Y., personnel being transported both to and from camp by motor convoy.

November 4: Review at armory by Major General William N. Haskell, Commanding General, New York National Guard.

November 7, 12: Troop K acted as escort to officers of International Military Jumping Teams at National Horse Show, Madison Square Garden.

1936

April 4: Troops E and K participated in army day parade.

April 19: Squadron attended annual church parade and memorial services at Church of the Heavenly Rest.

May 3: Manhattan Units fired record rifle practice at Peekskill, N.Y.

May 30: Troop F participated in Memorial Day parade.

June 14-28: Manhattan Units attended annual field training at Pine Camp, N.Y.

October 23-24: Body of Colonel William R. Wright, Chief of Staff, N.Y.N.G., also President of Association of Ex-Members of Squadron A, Inc., lay in state in armory.

October 24: Troop K acted as escort at funeral of Colonel William R. Wright from armory to Church of Heavenly Rest.

November 2: Review at armory by Brig. Gen. Guy V. Henry, Commandant, The Cavalry School.

November 4, 10: Troop F acted as escort to officers of International Military Jumping Teams at National Horse Show, Madison Square Garden.

1937

April 4: Squadron attended annual church parade and memorial services at Church of Heavenly Rest.

April 10: Troop F participated in army day parade.

April 16–17: Squadron conducted Squadron A spring horse show.

May 9: Troop K fired record rifle practice at Peekskill, N.Y.

May 16: Troops E and F fired record rifle practice at Peekskill, N.Y.

May 31: Troop E participated in Memorial Day parade.

June 13–27: Manhattan Units attended annual field training at Pine Camp, N.Y.

November 1: Review at armory by Colonel James R. Howlett, commanding 101st Cavalry.

November 3, 10: Troop K acted as escort to officers of International Military Jumping Teams at National Horse Show, Madison Square Garden.

1938

April 9: Troop K participated in army day parade.

April 21–23: Squadron conducted 2nd annual Squadron A spring horse show.

May 1: Squadron attended annual church parade and memorial services at Church of Heavenly Rest.

May 8: Manhattan Units fired record rifle practice at Peekskill, N.Y.

May 30: Troop E participated in Memorial Day parade.

June 12–26: Manhattan Units attended annual field training at Pine Camp, N.Y.

November 3: Review at armory by Major General John K. Herr, Chief of Cavalry, U.S.A.

November 5, 12: Troop E acted as escort to officers of International Military Jumping Teams at National Horse Show, Madison Square Garden.

THE ARMORY

And that dear hut, our home.—COTTEN

IN THE same year that the organization became a squadron it secured its own armory. The inadequacy of the quarters and facilities at Dickel's Riding Academy for the fast-growing active organization had early become apparent, but it was not until June 7, 1895, that the armory was completed. In July, 1894, the cornerstone was laid by Mayor Thomas F. Gilroy, with impressive ceremonies, and the Mayor made a brief address:

> In the name and behalf of the people of the City of New York I now have the honor of laying the cornerstone of the building intended for the use of Troop A. I trust that the organization which this building is to shelter will be as indestructible as the granite of which this stone is made, and that it will always continue in the future to merit as highly as it has in the past the confidence placed in it by our citizens.

In September, 1894, the troop had moved from Dickel's to temporary quarters in a portion of what was then the Eighth Regiment armory, Park Avenue at Ninety-fourth and Ninety-fifth streets, now incorporated in the present armory. The troop used the riding ring of what was then the Fifth Avenue Riding Academy, located on the northeast corner of Fifth Avenue and Ninetieth Street. This building was later replaced by the private residence and grounds of Andrew Carnegie. The troop was in these temporary quarters in January, 1895, when it was called into service to aid in suppressing disorders incident to the Brooklyn trolley strike.

On June 7, 1895, four months after Squadron A was organized from Troop A, the organization took possession of its armory—in which great internal changes were made thirty years later.

The exterior walls are largely unchanged, and the original entrance on Madison Avenue remains, displaying the sculptured insignia of the squadron—the crossed sabers with the "A" above.

The squadron, on January 31, 1896, celebrated the acquisition of its new home. To quote from *The Rider and Driver:*

> The formal opening of the Armory (January 31, 1896) was an event of brilliant military and social importance, being in reality a "house warming." The riding ring had been floored over, and after Gen. Roe and Mrs. Roe had held a reception those present took part in dancing. Gov. Morton had promised to be present but was unavoidably absent. Mayor William L. Strong made a brief speech, as did Mr. Hamilton Fish. Among those present during the evening were former Governor Flower and Mrs. Flower, the Rev. Newland Maynard, General Ruger, commanding the Division of the Atlantic, and his staff; Admiral Sicard and the officers of the Brooklyn Navy Yard, General McAlpin and his staff, Major-General Plume of New Jersey and his staff, Colonel Appleton of the Seventh Regiment and his staff, Colonel Seward, Major Japha, Major Lorigan and Captains Walton and Marks of the Ninth Regiment, Colonel Smith of the Twenty-third Regiment and his staff, Colonel Mitchell of the Thirteenth Regiment and his staff, Tax Commissioner Barker and many other city officials; General Louis Fitzgerald and his staff, General McGrath, Senator Ford and a host of others prominent in military, naval and civic life. The military and naval guests were in full uniform. There were also present the Old Guard and military organizations from neighboring cities, among them being the City Troop of Philadelphia, the Essex Troop of Newark, the Second Troop of Red Bank, N.J., and representatives of Brooklyn regiments, all in full uniform.

The riding ring of the armory in those days was its chief feature and occupied the entire area on the Ninety-fourth Street level, with the exception of a strip, approximately fifteen feet in width, on the Madison Avenue side. In this strip were stairways and passageways, and at each end were offices on the level of the ring. The ring was overlooked by spectators' balconies, and above these were locker rooms, offices, and an assembly room. They were constructed along the sides of the building but did not extend over the central part of the ring; a large skylight over this central portion lighted the ring by day and gas lights furnished the illumination by night. There was an entrance to the ring from Ninety-fourth Street for use in mounted formations, and the runway from the ring to the stables was through the passageway on the Madison Avenue side. The stables were on the Ninety-fifth Street level, with entrance on that street. In this part of the building, on the Ninety-fifth Street level, were also the ranges for carbine and pistol practice, and storage space.

SQUADRON A

The armory aided greatly in the development of the squadron, but as the squadron grew in size, its limited space became increasingly a handicap.

The historical résumé in the program of the Annual Games held in March, 1900, comments:

Owing to our largely increased numbers since our armory was built, at which time we were but *one troop*, whereas now we are *three*, with the staff and non-commissioned staff, forming the Squadron, it can readily be seen that our space is very limited. Every stall in the stables is occupied, and more horses would be provided if we had more facilities for stabling them. More space is necessary for the purpose of drill. It can readily be seen that with only *half of a troop* in the ring, as is the case in the drill this evening, there is very little room to spare, so that in drilling a full troop of 84 men it is very much congested, while full Squadron drills are absolutely impossible. In view of our large increase we hope to be afforded the room necessary for the larger work of the Squadron.

Later in the same year, in connection with the inter-troop athletic competitions for the "Morse Cup," it was necessary to cut down the representation of each troop in the mounted review to the very small numbers designated in Orders of November 30, 1900. From this we quote:

The three troops of the Squadron reduced to twenty troopers each, exclusive of the First Sergeant and Guidon Sergeant, will assemble for review by Major-General Charles F. Roe Friday evening, December 7, immediately following the Inter-Troop Athletic contests. Dress uniform with sabres and white gloves, *not* gauntlets. . . . Boots and Saddles will sound immediately preceding the final athletic event. Adjutant's call five minutes after the Assembly.

When Major Bridgman wanted to impress the city authorities with the inadequacy of the space, he would stage a review for selected officials and somehow get all the troops into the ring and then attempt some drill movements. The formations were closed up until they were hardly distinguishable, and evolutions seemed impossible. The officials marveled at what was accomplished and expressed their admiration at such ability, but seemed to think it showed that no more space was necessary when the outfit could drill so well with things as they were.

The present armory covers the area embraced in the two armories of Squadron A and the 8th Regiment. The present impressive riding ring was acquired in 1921 and is located entirely outside the old Squadron A armory. Five years later the remodeling of the interior of the original armory was completed. The interior changes make the armory more comfortable and well appointed, but have so altered its features that few are recognized by those who use it. The description already given pictures the armory as it was for approximately thirty years, and as the members prior to and during the World War period will remember it. Many will recall Jack Galloway and his fluent and pious speech in an office at the northwest corner—a den crammed with Q.M. stores and equipment; but who can now locate it? Who can identify the exact location of the former squadron headquarters? The present large hall on the first floor, sometimes designated as the squad room, occupies a large part of the space given to the riding ring in the old structure. The beautiful bronze memorial doors in the present squad room were provided by the Ex-Members' Association and form a concrete expression of the common ties and interests of past and present members. The rooms of the Ex-Members' Association are a feature not found in the old-time armory. They occupy approximately the space below that which was the locker room of the Third Troop. They are further described in the ensuing paper, dealing with the Association of Ex-Members of Squadron A.

THE ASSOCIATION OF EX-MEMBERS OF SQUADRON A

Prior to 1903 there was an informal association of honorary members of Squadron A, the requirement for election in which was an honorable discharge upon completing the five-year term of enlistment.

On March 21, 1903, the present Association was formed, with forty members. General Roe was the first president, and continued in that post until his death on December 1, 1932.

According to the constitution its "purpose is to promote friendly intercourse, renew old associations, and encourage the active organization in every way in its power."

The By-Laws do not condition membership upon completion of a full term of enlistment, but upon good and honorable standing of the ex-member during the period of his service. The earlier group of honorary members was incorporated in it, and in 1908, five years after organization, the membership had increased from the original forty to about two hundred and fifty. Six years later, in 1914, the number exceeded three hundred and sixty. Its membership is now more than twelve hundred and forty.

A large reception and supper on March 11, 1905, was made the occasion for presenting to the active squadron a bronze challenge trophy for marks to be competed for annually on the Creedmoor range and to be awarded to the troop having the greatest number of "distinguished experts" in that year.

In 1909 it participated in the celebration of the twentieth anniversary of the mustering in of Troop A; and in May, 1912, a large dinner in honor of General Roe was given on the occasion of his retirement from command of the National Guard of the state.

In 1914 it participated with the active organization in a dinner to celebrate the twenty-fifth anniversary of Troop A; and before this it compiled and published a chronological record of Troop A and Squadron A.

In 1916 the active squadron was called into Federal service on the Mexican border, and the newly formed Depot Troop was organized with personnel of ex-members. Later, when the active squadron again entered Federal service during the World War, the Depot Squadron that succeeded this first unit and received the designation Squadron A, New York Guard, was also in the beginning recruited almost entirely from this source.

During the World War hundreds of ex-members entered service as commissioned officers in various branches of the military and naval service; and after the war the Ex-Members' Association collaborated in assembling data for the record of service of all who had so served and of those who had served in the 105th Machine Gun Battalion. This record of service, as well as Major Stanton Whitney's detailed record of the battalion, is included in "Squadron A in the Great War, 1917–1918," published in 1923 by the Squadron A Association.

Following the demobilization of the 105th Machine Gun Battalion after the war, N. Hillyer Egleston became Major of Squadron A, New York Guard. His immediate objective was to have the organization again become a part of the National Guard. In a letter to the Association, dated January 14, 1920, he said:

> We are going to make an active campaign for the right kind of men. Our colleges send New York every year hundreds of young graduates of the type we want—men to whom the Squadron offers, as it has in the past, opportunities for military training of a character to fit them later to become officers, for agreeable friendship and for exercise. We are going after these men.
>
> It is in this connection especially that we appeal to you. If you want to see the Squadron carried on by men with whom you will not only be proud but want to associate, you must do your bit in helping us to get them. It is from your sons or younger brothers, their friends, and the young men with whom you come in contact that we must draw our recruits. We want you to help us individually and collectively constituting yourselves a recruiting committee for the present Squadron. On your loyal help depends very largely our chances of success. You have never failed the Squadron in time of need—stand by us now in this critical period of reconstruction.

On March 8, 1920, General Roe, as President of the Association, sent a circular to the members, enclosing a copy of the communication from the Squadron Commander and urging members to join in the effort.

In addition, a call was issued over the signature of General Roe as President, for a meeting of the members to be held on April 28, 1920; this meeting had a large and enthusiastic attendance; the greatest cordiality being evidenced towards the building up of the squadron. Among other matters considered, a significant question was raised: Should membership in the Ex-Members' Association be opened only to those who had served with Squadron A—the cavalry organization—or should it be open as well to all members of the 105th Machine Gun Battalion who were assigned to it by draft or otherwise. Discussion ended when General Roe impressively stated that no distinction should be made that would separate those who had served with the colors in the World War from full membership in any ex-members' association of Squadron A; and this view was sustained by acclamation.

In February of the following year a reunion dinner of ex-members was arranged, and was attended in a big way. A photograph of General Roe was on the cover of the program, and the printed seating arrangements show, in addition to the guest table, sixty-two tables and the names of nearly six hundred members who were present. Those who attended may recall that it was not a calm and deliberative occasion. The entertainment committee subsequently issued a circular which stated that as many members had expressed the desire for another reunion, a smoker was arranged for October 26th.

The executive committee of the association also issued a circular on April 25, 1921, calling attention to the prevailing custom of offering a trophy for competition in the active squadron, and while this custom had been interrupted by service on the border, followed by the World War, it was thought desirable to reestablish it. Those who approved the plan were invited to send in their contributions and their suggestions. Contributions from 270 ex-members amounting to $2,644.50 were received to be used for the purchase of one or more show horses to be donated to the squadron. This was in 1923. During the same year a dinner was held at the Hotel Biltmore, when members of the British polo teams were guests of the association, and a smoker held at the Army and Navy Club brought together over three hundred old friends and comrades.

The year 1924 was the occasion of the thirty-fifth anniversary of the birth of Troop A. In addition to a review by General Bridgman on May 6th, the anniversary was celebrated with a Church Parade and memorial service on May 4th, a military ball on May 8th, and a dinner on Saturday, May 10th; in all three the Association participated.

During this period the Association had no home of its own. The armory, originally designed for a single troop, had for years housed from three to five troops, and the clubhouse of the Squadron A Club had been given up during the war. In 1925, however, the remodeling of the armory presented the opportunity for acquiring a permanent home for the Association.

March 24, 1925, at a meeting of the Board of Governors, Captain Matthews announced that the contract had been given out for remodeling the armory, and the Association was requested to take up the question of arranging for a room for ex-members of the squadron. A committee was accordingly appointed, consisting of Thomas B. Clarke, Jr., John Reynolds, Latham R. Reed, Stowe Phelps, and A. R. Whitney, Jr.

At the annual meeting of the members, Colonel Clarke reported that an ideal location had been found on the west side of the old armory at sufficient height so that with the addition of a balcony constructed overlooking the new ring and communicating through the wall with the space above mentioned, the ex-members would have very comfortable and very attractive quarters. The report was received with enthusiasm. A letter from Major Egleston, commanding the active squadron, was read in which he requested that a committee of the association be appointed to consider the design and the placing of an appropriate memorial to the members of the squadron who lost their lives in the World War.

In June, 1926, at a special meeting of the association, a report was received that the war memorial was to take the form of a pair of bronze gates to be placed at the east side of the large room on the first floor covering most of the space formerly occupied by the old riding ring and which was called the "new squad room"; also a report that for the quarters of the Ex-Members' Association it was proposed to adopt the location suggested at the meeting in January, which would occupy in effect the undeveloped portion of the old building below the former locker room of the Third Troop. The cost of the memorial and the rooms was estimated at $46,000; and a letter was read from an ex-member who offered to assume the entire cost of the war memorial and of the ex-members' rooms. By his own request, his name was withheld, as he desired the gift to be anonymous; but the offer was accepted with an expression of appreciation for his great generosity and splendid example of continuing interest. The donor was an ex-member who had served in the very early days of Troop A, had later served for a time as an officer in another organization, and had promptly returned to service in the Depot Troop when it was organized, where he rendered highly efficient service. As donor he remained anonymous during his lifetime, but upon his death, his widow consented, at the request of the Association, to have his name announced in order that an expression of appreciation in the form of a tablet might be placed in the quarters of the Association. The tablet to Edwin Gould was accordingly so placed.

The annual meeting of the Association in January, 1927, was held in the reconstructed armory in the large hall, sometimes termed the squad room. There were about three hundred members present, and reports were received as to the war memorial and the ex-members' rooms. On request of General Bridgman, then president of the Association, Augustus D. Shepard, one of the members, as the architect of the work, designed and supervised the construction of the new quarters that would be the home of the Association. In February, 1927, the new rooms were completed, and for the following twelve years they have been its home. The large windows and the private gallery looking out over the riding ring afford members opportunity to see drills, polo practice, and other activities in one of the largest riding rings of the country. The locker rooms accommodate the needs of those who wish to keep riding clothes there, and the squadron restaurant provides meals. The clubrooms are most comfortable and furnish a repository for trophies, portraits, and other memorabilia.

The Association also enjoys the use of other portions of the armory, including the riding ring. Its well attended annual meetings are customarily held in what is known as the tap room—one part of the old armory that remains intact, formerly the assembly room. The governors, fifty in number, usually have their annual dinner also in this room. The Association also holds frequent gatherings with able speakers on military and other subjects of interest to the cavalryman. These are well attended; sometimes they are held in the clubrooms of the Association and at other times in the tap room. For still larger gatherings the squad room is used, particularly for receptions at which large numbers of guests of the members are invited. This room provides an attractive setting and has been used when the entertainment was supplied by courtesy of the University Glee Club. Many gatherings are held in the clubrooms, which can accommodate as many as one hundred members.

General Roe, the first president, continued in that office until his death on December 1, 1922, and was succeeded by General Bridgman, who in turn occupied that office until his death on June 23, 1933. His successors have been Thomas B. Clarke, Jr., Graham Youngs, William R. Wright, Herbert Barry, and Philip J. McCook.

RIDING IN THE SQUADRON
RECOLLECTIONS AND COMMENTS OF A TROOP COMMANDER

Carleton S. Cooke

A good rider on a good horse is as much above himself as the world can make him.—LORD HERBRT OF CHERBURY

We'll fill our glasses up again and drink to equitation.
—Squadron Ballad

ON MARCH 4, 1910, I, for the first time, trod the deep tanbark of the old gas-lighted ring, part of which is now the squad room on the east side of the armory. A debutant cavalryman, of no very great proficiency as a rider, and accustomed only to a flat saddle and to what was miscalled an "English" seat, I hoisted myself with deep misgivings aboard a hard-gaited animal equipped with a blanket and a watering bridle, and immediately started on about forty minutes of trot and gallop, involving painful speculation as to whether I could possibly survive it. The ensuing lameness and abrasions too numerous and intimate to mention were a common result of the hard-boiled methods of the pre-war cavalry, which did not meet my personal approval at the time; nor has subsequent experience changed the opinion then formed.

The McClellan saddle later vouchsafed did not help much at first; it hurt in new and unaccustomed places. However, to a recruit who had not acquired the relaxation, balance, and confidence necessary to riding at the faster gaits on a blanket without stirrups, it soon became very acceptable. Like our sabers, the cavalry seat then in vogue dated back to the Civil War anyway and probably long before that. It was a "long" or modified cowboy seat, not very different from the position of the mediaeval knight on horseback and not much of an improvement on it. With back and knees practically straight, the long stirrups affording insufficient support, and the legs forward of the perpendicular, so as often to throw the rider's weight back on the cantle, it accounted for sore-tailed riders and sore-backed horses, especially when field duty added the weight of the essential drygoods, hardware, cutlery, and shootlery.

In those days, posting to the trot was taboo. The jiggling shoulders and the pounding bottoms of those who drew hard-gaited horses used to make one recruit (who invariably got the most frightfully rough animals in the troop—or so he thought) wonder whether there wasn't some better way to do it. Then as now, the better riders preferred the English saddle when out of ranks, and posted well and truly—and highly, with plenty of daylight between breeches and saddle.

Hard falls were the inevitable result of combining greenhorns with horses rigged only with blankets and surcingles. The teaching of riding, both practical and theoretic, was substantially confined to the obsolete "mounted exercises" (which were fun for those who could do them well, but discouraging to those who couldn't) and to plenty of work at fast gaits, and to bellowing at some puzzled rookie, "RIDE YOUR HORSE!" To which the unspoken reply was, "Well, what the infernal regions am I doing? Or is the divinely condemned horse riding me?" Or the equally intelligible admonition might be, "MAKE THAT HORSE GALLOP (WALK) (TROT)!" Orders and commands were shouted at bewildered beginners by well intentioned young men who rode well after their kind, but one had to work out one's own equestrian salvation—or damnation—as the case might be. Memory recalls only a few instances where the amateur instructors of the recruit squad (or for that matter in the troop) advised their victims on producing any given action by their horses—what to do, or when to do it, or why.

Though some fell by the wayside—both literally and figuratively—most of us survived this Spartan training. I finally overcame an urge to join the Navy. After a year or so, and a tour of field duty, we could stay aboard in any reasonable conditions and induce our steeds to proceed in approximately the desired direction at the indicated gait, especially in armory formations, where our routined mounts sometimes knew the drill better than their riders. Although no more than "horse-backers," being unaware that we were afflicted with some very awkward habits, we labored under the delusion that we really could ride. Horse management was well taught and practiced, but as riders we were hard on our horses, not from lack of good will, but from ignorance. There were a few really accomplished riders, but somehow they did not make their influence felt. I used to wonder how they did it and why I couldn't.

Rebus sic stantibus (as Gen. C. J. Caesar used to say) with respect to the general equestrian accomplishment, Mr. De Souza, a civilian instructor skilled in European methods and a born teacher, came to Ninety-fourth Street to coach the Fourth Troop team for the Justice Cup competition. This cup, named for a trooper's distinguished mount, was awarded to the troop team adjudged most proficient in equitation, then called horsemanship. For several years this teacher coached unofficial classes and individuals, teaching the French seat and his own marvelous methods of horse-training. The old-timers would have none of him and stuck to their old-fashioned ways, but many others profited by his instruction. He was the first instructor of the Ladies' Riding Class, an institution established only by dint of long and vigorous combating of ancient prejudice and inertia, which became one of our most valuable extracurricular activities. I remember what the Chief of Staff of the 61st Cavalry Division said about it: "No military organization can function in time of peace unless it has its womenfolks behind it!"

At the very first ride with Mr. De Souza one of the members of the Fourth Troop team realized that the new instructor knew a lot more about the subject than himself. Then commenced a series of lessons in riding and schooling horses and a vast deal of reading and research upon the subject of EQUITATION (a word almost unknown in the early days), which may be roughly defined as the art of riding, controlling, and improving the horse—and likewise the rider—with a view to the greater efficiency, comfort, safety, and durability of both parties concerned in the operation. When one gets to the point of forgetting his own troubles and finding his enjoyment in the performance and the improvement of his mount (an animal which is far more than a sort of semi-automatic apparatus on which to enjoy scenery, exercise, or sundry sports) he travels beyond the "horsebacking," which is the be-all and end-all of the great majority, into a new field of unlimited interest and resource.

As a result of the episodes mentioned, having once radically altered my equestrian position from the inexcusable "English" seat to the slightly better "long" seat, I again changed it into something approaching what was to be called the "Saumur" or "Fort Riley" seat. Soon after, the squadron began its long tour of duty of 1916 on the Mexican border. It seemed to me that the wet and hot weather of southern Texas intensified the defects of the old position. Hard on troopers, the climate was horrible for our northern horses; in spite of incessant care, the weather and the insects made surgical cases of what would have been trifling sores in cool weather, and the sick-list of our mounts was appalling.

To the relief of both horses and troopers, Captain "Eddie" Foy (his correct name, if I ever knew it, has escaped me), an officer of the regular cavalry and a graduate of the Cavalry School, was assigned to us as inspector-instructor. The Army was then, I believe, in the process of altering the old mounted position into nearly the present one. Captain Foy was enthusiastic about it. He instilled its principles with vigor and persistence. It took hold, in spite of the Bourbons who, down on anything they were not up to, damned the new seat from reveille to taps. We used to speak of a "Riley" instead of a ride.

From that time it seems to me that there was a steady improvement in the average riding of the squadron. Seen from the worm's-eye view of the enlisted man, Captain Foy was not without his humorous aspects, but it is my belief that the squadron owed him debts of gratitude.

It was the application of what had been learned and studied in and out of the squadron that enabled me in the winter of 1917 to combine one hundred fifty men who could not ride and one hundred forty-four horses who had seldom been ridden into a mounted organization whose drill would have stood comparison with any of the old four troops and whose riding did credit to the principles and methods of the squadron. A further experience during the winter and spring of 1919 at the headquarters, Third Army, A.E.F., School of Equitation at Coblenz confirmed the conviction that a reasonably skillful instructor using the seat and system of the Cavalry School can teach beginners to ride, to control and improve themselves and their mounts with relative safety, comfort, and speed and far more efficiently than by the hard-boiled pre-war methods. During my post-war service in the squadron I continually strove to apply the modern ideas in the troop and in the recruit squad, with results which were, at least to me, very satisfactory.

Since the war, the various inspector-instructors assigned to us from the army have been skilled cavalrymen trained in the modern system. The schools of equitation conducted by them and by the sergeant-instructors confirmed and still confirm the seat and principles now embodied in training regulations, which we as a squadron encountered for the first time in the outer suburbs of McAllen, Texas. If the judgment of one who has given some time and study to the subject amounts to anything, the average riding of the squadron of today is a large improvement both in methods and in results over what we learned in the good old times. The idea in early recruit training mounted is to get the subject to enjoy riding, instead of rather dreading it. The roughneck ways of the past, including the painful lameness and soreness of the pre-border recruit squad, have been largely eliminated. So has the probability of heavy falls which may ruin a prospective horseman—for a recruit who has been painfully injured may never regain confidence on horseback. No rider escapes falls; but they should be avoided as far as possible in early training. The squadron has progressed to a point where, though there are few *accomplished* riders there are many good ones and the general average is creditable. The relative uniformity of position, the better rein manipulation, the improved relaxation, and the remarkable improvement in jumping brought about by the "forward" seat, all compare most favorably with the varying positions, the stiff backs, the hard hands, and tight reins of many riders of twenty-five years ago.

It is not to be thought that the old days have left any painful memories. They were good days and good times, when the general efficiency of the squadron was what it was, is, and always will be. If our riding and riding instruction were not what they might have been, it was the fault of the condition of the art. The officers and non-coms of the old four troops could only give what they had. Their zeal and energy were plentiful—even excessive, we recruits thought. When all but a very few professional riding masters are ignorant persons unable to impart to others what they know even when they really know it, it cannot be expected that amateurs will be highly proficient instructors. Nevertheless, it is thought that now-a-days most of the amateur riding teachers at Ninety-fourth Street try to do what any successful teacher must do; that is, know and like his subject from the practical side, and equally the theoretical aspects of it as found in books—of which we had very few thirty years ago, and those inadequate. Thus equipped, he will try to get over his knowledge to his squad, platoon, or troop, not so much by ejaculating orders or commands, as by patient explanation of what to do, and how and why and when to do it, with incessant correction, criticism, and commendation. Thus he may realize the satisfaction that comes to one who sees, so to speak, his young plants bearing fruit. The best part of the years on the tanbark at Ninety-fourth Street was my work with the recruit squad. There, unlike the never-completed work of troop training, the progressive result of one's efforts with men and minds new to the work, ignorant of it for the most part, but intelligent, willing, and eager to learn whether afoot or on horseback, was actually visible and apparent from drill to drill and from week to week.

REMINISCENCES OF
COLONEL JOHN D. KILPATRICK, U.S.A., *Retired*

THESE inconsequential tales about a necessarily limited number of individuals are submitted to the ex-members with the hope that they may bring back memories of the squadron as it was in the early nineteen hundreds. To be a corporal in the squadron was, we felt, at least equal to being a lieutenant in the —— Heavy Foot; and a sergeant was as important as a major in the —— Infantry, N.G.N.Y. (Numerals to fit these blanks will be furnished without malice by the author.) Furthermore, we believed that the squadron was just about the best club in New York City.

From time to time there will appear in these paragraphs the names of those who have joined the Caravan of the Black Camel and gone West. To the memory of all these men let it be said that they were members of a great organization. And let us keep in our hearts the memory of what fine and valiant souls they were and think of them as being still with us and merely for the time being out of town somewhere.

I have a very vivid recollection of the first time that I saw any of Squadron A in formation. It was at Fifth Avenue and Twenty-third Street in the fall of 'Ninety-eight when I saw Troop A, U.S.V., on their return from Puerto Rico parading up the Avenue to the armory; with old blue shirts, sleeves rolled up or cut off at the elbow, and most of the men wearing beards. There was something in the jaunty, careless way they rode that showed the true cavalry spirit and made the heart come up in one's throat.

In January, 1900, my name was put up for membership by Hobey Betts; never shall I forget my appearance before the committee on admissions down in Bill Maloney's office on Wall Street after sundown, and meeting Howland Brown, Freddie Keppel, and Richard W. G. Welling. The committee were in the dark of the office with the light under a reflector shining full in the face of the candidate who sat in a chair answering questions propounded by those in the darkness. The question that had us all stumped and to which we gave faltering answers was: "Do you know how to ride a horse?" or "Have you ridden a great deal?" To this we all replied, "No, not much, but we can learn." Then, after the election some time later, I reported for recruit drill on Tuesday and Friday nights with Morty Ward as drillmaster. Why I always succeeded in getting No. 13, Old Satan, which was the drum horse in the band, I never knew. Several years later one recruit was thrown so many times by Old Satan that he resigned; then to his mortification and chagrin he saw Memorial Day Parade about a month later, and there was No. 13—the big kettle drums strapped on his shoulders—with the German drummer beating lustily with the sticks and guiding the reins fastened to the stirrups. The horse was striding along shaking his head and ears and paying no attention to what was going on on his back.

Morty Ward was a great drillmaster. In taking the hurdles I fell off so many times that I could land on my head and rotate to either the left or right upon command. This went on until one night Morty made a dirty crack about my inability to sit the blankety-blanketed horse which made me so angry that I sat back in proper position and never had any further trouble.

We went out that spring for a bivouac or three-day field exercise in Van Cortlandt Park, and then and there I was detailed as assistant to the Quartermaster Sergeant and my life career in the Quartermaster Corps was fixed. Chick Childs was the quartermaster sergeant of the Third Troop, and I will tell the interested world that he was the best of them all, or anyway as good as "Able Eye" Smith. Another skill he had, was to play the "Maple Leaf Rag," by Scott Joplin until he could make the old piano in the assembly room shake down to its last caster. Dick Welling, in those days a husky lad, was also assigned to the quartermaster detail. I still hold, however, the undisputed championship and record for having shoveled more manure than any man who was ever in the National Guard of New York. In fact, I wrote a book on the "Use and Abuse of Manure" for the Service Schools. There were two interpolated chapters which had little bearing on the subject at issue. One was a chapter on "Pleasure Cries of All Nations," by Rod Gilder; the other was "Fingers Were Made Before Forks," by Lathrop (Jake) Brown, sometime Congressman from the First District of New York. This chapter was based upon an afternoon's experience at Pine Camp, when Jake was in the quartermaster detail, and stable police was in order. Everything had been taken care of except a little pile of stuff that was too fine to be lifted with pitchforks, whereupon Mr. Brown took off his gloves and carefully gathered the remainder in his own fair hands and tenderly placed it in the four-mule wagon driven by a negro soldier. He was asked why he handled it with his bare hands, and indignantly replied: "I did not care to spoil a perfectly good pair of Government gauntlets"; showing by this action how jealous he was of the protection of Government property and what a splendid training this was for a Congressman-to-be, looking after the interest of the tax-payer.

In those days we went to Creedmoor, Long Island, for rifle practice. This was all right as long as we were shooting the old single-action Springfield .45 carbines with black powder which had a range of about 700 yards if you tilted up the barrel about 40 degrees from the horizontal. Then we got an issue of Krags; and, with smokeless powder and jacketed bullets, the range was increased to about 1500 yards. Stray bullets from Creedmoor range then began to fall all over Queens County and part of Nassau, which led to the abandonment of Creedmoor. It was some years later that a rifle range was bought near New City, and that too had to be abandoned because the stray bullets were landing in Haverstraw.

The maneuver at Manassas in 1904 was the first effort under the National Defense Act of 1903 to train the National Guard alongside of the regulars. There must have been 60,000 troops engaged—and what a sensation it was, and how full the newspapers were of General Fred Grant (looking more than ever like his father) in command of the Blues, and old General Joe Wheeler in command of the Browns! The squadron sent one provisional troop with Captain Badgley in command, Bill Judson as First Lieutenant, and Bill Wright as Second Lieutenant. We left New York at night and got to Manassas early the next afternoon. It took us an hour or two to unload the horses, get the picket lines set up and the horses fed. By this time the tents were up and everybody got inside and lay down for a nap or at least kept out of sight; and that was where the squadron made a great hit with the 15th Cavalry. Troop C of Brooklyn next to us was fairly quiet; but Troop A of Hartford, Connecticut, was staging a riot—tossing recruits in blankets, pouring water over each other, and making a terrific racket. We noticed, that night and the next day, that the regulars of the 15th Cavalry were coming around and helping us out, teaching us little tricks of how to do things easier, and incidentally cadging a few drinks.

Next winter I met Granville Swope of Baltimore, who at that time was top Sergeant of G Troop of the 15th, and asked him why it was that his outfit seemed to be so friendly with us while they ignored the Hartford outfit? He said: "Why, you fellows acted like old soldiers—as if you knew the game. You no sooner had your horses taken care of and your tents up than you kept out of sight of the First Sergeant, who always, after camp is established, is out looking for details to do odd jobs, and spots the unwary recruit who wanders around."

Once we left camp late in the afternoon after chow, going off into the woods somewhere about five miles. Reveille sounded at 11 P.M., followed by breakfast, which consisted of hard bread with a couple of slabs of issue bacon and some coffee. We lay quiet in the woods until dawn and then got into one grand sham battle, dismounted, which kept up until one o'clock the next afternoon. We captured one poor regular's canteen, cartridge belt, and haversack. We got back to camp about four o'clock in the afternoon, having had nothing to eat since eleven o'clock the night before; but Quartermaster Sergeant "Able Eye" Smith had gone ahead, and we had a grand repast of good roast ribs of beef and ice cream.

Harry Stimson, who was a Sergeant at Manassas, sometime during 1905 became First Lieutenant of the Second Troop; then in May, 1911, he was in Washington as Secretary of War. It seems that later in that year, when it got warm, some of the high-ranking officers attached to the War Department asked him if he would like to visit a camp of the garrison of Fort Myer that had gone into the field for several days' training. At Fort Myer they had assigned him a placid cart horse as a mount; but he started off, and of course everyone in the War Department who could rate a mount attached himself to the party, so that, as Harry said, there must have been twenty or twenty-five officers and an equal number of orderlies—quite a cavalcade. When they arrived at the campsite, some three or four miles from Fort Myer, they ran up the Secretary of War's flag and gave him the guns and lined up for inspection. After he had looked them all over, front and rear, and the parade was dismissed by the Major in command of the Squadron of the 15th Cavalry, they went into the Major's tent to have a drink; after the toast was proposed and drunk to the Secretary of War, he turned to the Major and said that he was very pleased with the reception they had given him that afternoon, and that there was much more hospitality than had been shown him the last time he had called upon this selfsame Major. The Squadron Commander was aghast, and said, "Mr. Secretary, I don't know what you mean." "All right," said Harry, "I will tell you. The last time I saw you was at the Manassas maneuvers, when I came with Captain Badgley, who wanted to pay his respects to you. You left me outside holding horses, and did not ask me to have a drink then." Not often in our history has a National Guard Sergeant been jumped to Secretary of War.

Here is another Manassas tale. Freddie Keppel (Assistant Secretary of War, 1917–1918) and Nichols got separated from the troop one day and reported to the Commanding Officer of the 15th Cavalry for duty. They were with that outfit for two days, and then reported back to us. After we returned to New York, Major Bridgman received a letter from the Squadron Commander of the 15th to the effect that he had had with him at Manassas for two days Privates Keppel and Nichols, and he desired to remark that their horsemanship and ability to transmit messages were such that he could well understand, if the rest of the outfit measured up to these two privates, how it was that the squadron had such a great reputation as a National Guard outfit. This, of course, was "nuts" for Major Bridgman, who replied that as for ability to understand and repeat messages, he need only state that Keppel was Secretary of Columbia University and, as for horsemanship, Nichols had a 6-goal rating as a polo player.

Tom Crimmins in 1916 went to the border as lieutenant in the old 23rd Engineers and resigned when he got back to New York. When we entered the World War and the 23rd was called into service Tom came back as a buck private and landed in Spartanburg as such. As soon as the Constructing Quartermaster found out, he asked that Tom be made his assistant in preparing certain areas as campsites. Tom was sent out to take charge of the work and as he refused to be made a non-com., it was necessary that only privates be sent to work in his detail. Many a day you would see Tom in charge of work with as many as two hundred buck privates working for him and every last one of them calling him "Mr. Crimmins." Tom was made Lieutenant before he got to France, was then promoted to major for bravery on the field of battle, and when the 27th Division was ordered home, was a full colonel. Very few know this. When the 27th Division parade took place on Fifth Avenue, Tom quietly lost himself in General O'Ryan's staff and allowed Lieutenant Colonel Conrow to lead the regiment up Fifth Avenue, because Conrow had been with the regiment as lieutenant colonel all the way through the war.

At Pine Camp in 1908 we were visited by several regular officers from Fort Ethan Allen who were with us on an inspection tour or joy ride for several days, and one night we gave a drinking party in one of the larger tents, in their honor. In the fall of 1920, when I was stationed at Sam Houston, I had to go to Fort Bliss at El Paso and while there went to the General Depot on the post and called on Julian Benjamin who, I think, at one time had been a member of Troop A and was then lieutenant colonel, cavalry and executive officer of the depot. The commanding officer was Colonel Guy Preston (who devised the Preston system of branding army horses and mules on the neck and also invented the Preston mess kit). I did not go in to see Colonel Preston but talked to Benjamin in the next room. In about a fortnight I returned and again went to see Benjamin, and had started to visit with him when a roar came from Colonel Preston in the next room to come in to see him. His first remark to me was, "Kilpatrick, what were you in before the war?" I said, "Squadron A, National Guard of New York and a staff officer in New Jersey." "Were you in Pine Camp in 1908?" I said, "Yes, sir." "What were you, a buck?" "Yes, sir." "Do you remember one time when Major Glenn, Major Dickman, and I came over from Ethan Allen?" "Yes, I remember the occasion, but I did not know any of your names." "Well," he said, "were you in a party in a tent one night, and did you tell stories about some animals?" "Yes, you mean the old panorama stories?" He said then, "I particularly remember one about the Walla Walla horse." "Yes, that was my story and I told it that night." "Well," he said, "ever since I heard you talking with Benjamin here two weeks ago, I have bothered my soul thinking where I had heard your voice before, and it just came to me this afternoon."

After General O'Ryan went to France in the fall of 1917 on the preliminary trip of inspection, the command of the 27th Division was turned over to Brigadier General Charles J. Phillips, who was in command of the artillery brigade. He was a very dignified "Old File" from the Coast Artillery, to whom the unusual character of the commissioned and enlisted personnel of the Division was a matter of constant amazement.

SQUADRON A

One night at the Cleveland Hotel, in company with the Constructing Quartermaster, he met Colonel Mayhew Wainwright, who was inspector general of the Division. The General said, "Colonel Wainwright, there is one thing about this Division that I do not understand. I inquire regarding the standing or reputation or ability of some officer, and every once in a while the reply is, 'Oh, he is all right, General, he was in Squadron A,' and they never do give me any other information. I know that Squadron A was a unit in the National Guard of New York, but how does it happen that everyone seems to take it for granted that after the statement is made that the individual has been a member of Squadron A, no other recommendation is necessary?" Colonel Wainwright replied, "That's all right, General, because as long as I have known the outfit—and I have been many years in the National Guard of New York—I have never known anyone in Squadron A that wasn't all right." I thought this was pretty swell coming from Colonel Wainwright, even though he was Herbert Barry's law partner. Colonel Wainwright's accurate appreciation of relative values helped him to become Congressman from Westchester County, and then Assistant Secretary of War.

* * *

The compilers, having "lifted" from John Kilpatrick's narrative an entertaining paragraph and transferred it to an early part of this volume, partial reparation is attempted by now adding an incident supplementing his own story as to former Sergeant Stimson. To avoid error, the former sergeant was asked to outline what occurred, and did so in the following letter:

Dear Herbert:

I have been delayed in answering your inquiry of December 15th. The incident about which you inquire took place in January 1902 when I had gone to Washington to attend a dinner of the Boone and Crockett Club.

I was riding in Rock Creek Park with a friend. There had been a long continued rainstorm of several days and the creek was in high flood. I was a stranger in Washington and was therefore greatly surprised when I heard my name called by one of a group of four men who seemed to be clambering along the wooded hill or cliff on the opposite side of the creek. The voice, which I at last recognized as that of Theodore Roosevelt, said: "Why don't you come over here?" Then the second voice which I recognized as that of Mr. Root said: "The President of the United States directs Sergeant Stimson of Squadron A to cross the stream and come to his assistance, by order of the Secretary of War." To make the order apropos, it happened to be at about the time when Congress was taking steps, on Mr. Root's recommendation, to reorganize the National Guard and to bring it more effectively under Federal jurisdiction. I said to my companion, half laughingly: "Why, that's an order," and turned the horse towards the stream. It was a silly thing to do, for the bank on the opposite side was precipitous and could not be climbed by a horse. I half hoped that my horse would refuse the low barrier which divided the road we were on from the stream; but he didn't. He jumped in and was at once caught by the current and swept off his feet down stream. It was almost of swimming depth. By the time I had got him on to his feet again, Roosevelt and Root had rushed down to the edge of the bank on their side and Roosevelt was waving his hands at me, saying: "Go back; go back." I dismounted (the water was about breast deep) and found a place where I could lead my horse up the bank again on my side; then I remounted, rode down to a bridge which was some distance below, and came back, meeting Roosevelt and Root who were running towards me. They were quite excited and I was considerably cooler than they—both mentally and physically, for the water was icy. I dismounted, saluted, and told the President I had come to his assistance. For a minute or two he was quite embarrassed and said to me: "That was a fine thing for you to do, but to tell the truth, when I heard the order given, I did not think it would be obeyed. I thought you could see that the bank on this side was quite impassable." I saluted again and said: "Mr. President, when a soldier hears an order given, it isn't for him to say that it is impossible of execution." He laughed and said: "Well, it was a fine thing for you to do. Now go home and drink a whole bottle of whisky."

And that evening when we met again at the Boone and Crockett Club dinner (of which he had been the founder), he greeted me with one of his characteristic shouts, calling me "Young Lochinvar." Of course I was not in uniform, and I do not remember what rank I had in the Squadron—whether quartermaster sergeant or duty sergeant. It was one or the other.

I hope that this is a sufficient description of a rather amusing and possibly absurd incident.

Very sincerely yours,
HENRY L. STIMSON

SOME VERSES AND SONGS OF THE SQUADRON

> Strike the concertina's melancholy string,
> Slow the spirit-stirring harp like anything,
> Let the piano's martial blast
> Rouse the echoes of the past . . .
> —Gilbert, "Bab Ballads"

> We'll sing the songs of fellowship.—Squadron Song

In the early years of Troop A and of the squadron the popular songs of the day were generally sung. Some original songs were written to cover certain occasions, and others may have flourished for a season of drill or a tour of duty; but much research has discovered that few originating before 1909 have been preserved. In the period following the Brooklyn Strike and the organization of the squadron were a number of dinner gatherings of the troops and of the platoons, resulting in songs and verses, two of which are here reproduced. In later years, more appeared. Limitations of space preclude the inclusion of many, and also compel the elimination of those sung by the squadron, which are not of squadron origin. Still other limitations debar numerous excellent songs—original and popular—for which troopers must rely upon memory. Where authors have been ascertained, credit has been given. Many variations of the text were found. The verses are, so far as possible, arranged chronologically, and effort has been made to reproduce them as originally composed.

The first in order here pictured a revolt by constituents of the Sheriff; and while not here published in full, its lyric appeal is shown in the following verses:

THE BATTLE OF MASPETH

Air, "We'll Rant and We'll Roar." A Platoon song after the Brooklyn street-car strike, 1895.

One day his dear subjects broke into rebellion;
    They rose up in arms and they captured the place;
They marched into Maspeth and took a strong position
    With a dozen stiff gin mills protecting their base.

Chorus:

Then here's to Troop A and her gallant Commander.
    To Reed [1] and Coudert,[2] boys, now get into tune;
Hurrah for the Corporals and hurrah for the Troopers.
    For the "Third's" gory warriors—the Red Hot Platoon.

Their left wing was a thousand, well-armed with revolvers;
    In the center a hose-cart stood filled up with bricks;
On the right was a regiment of long-whiskered anarchists,
    And the Sheriff had nothing but hickory sticks. [*Chorus*]

Oh, they seized on a trolley car all filled with green motormen,
    And frightened 'em till they had turned lily-white;
And they booted and banged 'em, and threatened to hang 'em
    And showed 'em that life was more real than polite. [*Chorus*]

Oh, the Sheriff he begged and the Sheriff he pleaded,
    But they told him that sheriffs were now in the soup;
Then he rang up the telephone and called for the General,
    And cried out, "For Heaven's sake. Send us the Troop." [*Chorus*]

Through miles of black streets, all astrewn with big boulders,
    Where cats on the trolley lines hung in festoon;
Where the women all swear and the men all throw brickbats,
    Through the thick of the mess rode the Red Hot Platoon. [*Chorus*]

Oh, they came on their bellies and meekly surrendered,
    And the Sheriff was ruler once more of his own.
We had flowers from Beauty and no end of precious booty,
    And they loaned us a trolley car to take the stuff home. [*Chorus*]

THE CHARGE OF TROOP A

With all due respect to Tennyson's memory. By N. A. J. Celebrates Troop A's service during the Brooklyn street-car strike, 1895.

        Half a block, half a block,
        Half a block forward,

---

[1] Captain Latham G. Reed.
[2] Lieutenant Frederic R. Coudert, Jr.

SQUADRON A

All in the City of Spires
  Rode the great horse guard!
"Forward, the cavalcade!
Charge ye, Troop A!" Roe said—
Into a shower of bricks
  Rode the great horse guard.

"Forward, guards tailor-made!"
Was there a man dismayed?
Not on your life—although
  They were the vanguard.
Theirs not to make a kick,
Theirs not to be homesick,
Theirs but to dodge a brick;
Into the howling mob
  Rode the great horse guard.

Trolleys to right of them,
Trolleys to left of them,
Trolleys in front of them
  Couldn't move forward;
Stormed at with bricks and stones,
Fearless of broken bones,
Heedless of shrieks and moans,
Into Third Avenue,
  Rode the great horse guard.

Flashed all their sabres bare,
Flashed in the Brooklyn air,
Whacking the strikers there,
Charging the hoodlums, while
  Motormen hollered—
Plunged down the muddy street,
Right through stiff hats they beat;
Idlers and rioters
Reeled back in full retreat,
  Skedaddling homeward.
Then they rode back, but not,
  Not such a great guard.

Trolleys to right of them,
Trolleys to left of them,
Trolleys behind them,
  Running haphazard;

Stormed at in language vile,
Hooted and curs'd the while,
Still they kept up their style
As they rode back again,
Each with a haughty smile;
No mob was left for them—
    Left for the great guard.

When can their glory fade?
O, the wild charge they made!
    Under Roe's standard!
Honor the charge they made;
Fill them with marmalade—
    Brave, noble horse guard!

THE RED HOT THIRD

Probably by Lloyd M. Garrison. Read at a banquet, at Muschenheim's, in 1895, after Troop A's tour of riot duty, during the Brooklyn street-car strike.

Brothers in arms, we meet again
Safe from the terrible campaign.
With deep emotion now we grasp
Each spared right hand with tightening clasp,
While past our misty eyes there fleets
A memory of those bloody streets.
Ah, well! Peace comes; no more shall worry
Make all our meals a horrid Hurry,
Nor shall the sleepless striker get rash
And drive us from the café Petrasch,
Nor longer shall our hard earned slumber
Hear wheels revolving without number.
Peace makes us vain, their proudest vaunts,
Confirmed by scribes and débutantes,
Made themes for public commendation.
The pampered darlings of the nation
Must not forget that life is real;
That deeds are wrought with stubborn steel;
That, though this festal life be more
Magnificent, *it is not War!*

FOURTH TROOP SONG

Words and air by Henry Clapp Smith. About 1909.

>Comrades, draw your sabers,
>Touch stirrups with your neighbors—
>We'll sing the songs of fellowship,
>   As we have sung before.
>Look to every leather,
>As we ride forth together,
>   And come what may, we'll rule the day,
>And fight for old Troop Four.

THE HORSES

Air, "The Ladies." After Kipling, by Rodman Gilder. 1909.

>I've taken my mounts where I've found them,
>   I've cantered and run in my time;
>I've had my picking of horses,
>   And four of the lot were prime.
>One was a sorrel or buckskin,
>   I never could make out which;
>Two were regular riding school skates
>   And one was an Irish witch.

>The buckskin I had as a rookie,
>   I bought from a man getting out;
>I parted with two hundred dollars,
>   Not knowing what I was about.
>His body was fat and topheavy
>   And his legs unaccountably slim.
>I have figured since then he was worth at least ten—
>   And I learned about horses from him.

>Then I dropped into an auction
>   And purchased a rangy old hack.
>His gaits in the ring were unequalled,
>   But the next time I got on his back
>He broke up like raw macaroni;
>   He hadn't a single sound limb.
>So I gave him away to a groom the next day—
>   And I learned about horses from him.

A black and white cayuse at Durland's
    Caught my experienced eye;
I gave him a thirty-day trial
    And then I decided to buy.
But after he'd rolled over backward
    They told me his name, Loco Jim.
Though I hated to squeal, I went back on that deal—
    And I learned about horses from him.

Then I got Kathleen, a "hunter,"
    From a man who was going abroad.
With nobody up she was languid;
    When I cinched her she merely looked bored.
But she kicked and she bit and she struggled
    At the very first touch of my spur,
And the Captain, of course, shouted out, "*Ride* your horse!"
    And I learned about horses from her.

I've taken my mounts where I found them
    And what have I got for my pains?
Three fractures and four dislocations
    And dozens of bruises and sprains;
And the end of it's walking or driving
    And dodging each horse that you see.
Yet all this, it's true, need not happen to you—
    For you've learned about horses from me.

ALL HAIL TO OLD TROOP A

Air, "Princeton Cannon Song." About 1910.

All hail to old Troop A,
    We pledge our hearts unto thy name,
Shoulder to shoulder stand
    For thy glory and thy fame,
    Old Troop A.
Our hearts shall turn to thee
    In after years where'er we stray,
And we'll sing and we'll cheer
    While we're still comrades here,
    For old Troop A.

DOCTOR LANCE

Air, "Rings on Your Fingers." Words by Rodman Gilder, 1910.

"Now, Doctor Lance, I fear my chance of having kids is slim,
  So please suggest just what is best." The doctor answered him:
"To stimulate virility, enlist in that Third Troop
You'll soon have three or four,
  And then you'll have some more, until there are a score,
    a-creeping round the floor!"

Chorus:

For—he—has—rings on his busby, and bells on his boots;
He knocks out a bullseye, every time he shoots;
The highest form of animal life, biologists all say,
Is the trooper of the Third Troop, Squadron A—Hooray!

RISE UP EARLY

Air, "The Merry Widow Waltz." 1910.

Rise up early, in the morning,
  Groom your horse;
Eat a little, rotten breakfast—
  Tired, of course.
Fight your daily battle,
  Who wins, none can tell.
Brothers of the G.A.R.,
  War—is—hell!

THIRD TROOP SONG

Air by G. J. S. White. Words by Rodman Gilder. 1911.

Now the Gov'nor he said
To the Gen'ral in command,
"I want you to speak frankly as I told yer,
Throughout the Empire State
The voter he is great—
But *tell* me what you think about the soldier."

"There's just one State establishment—
  N.G.N.Y., and that's no lie.
The arm of it that always lands the punch
  It is the cavalree.
The best of New York Cavalry
  Inspectors say, is Squadron A,
And in the Squadron there is just a single troop—
  And that is, by heck! Troop Three!"

RECRUIT SONG

Air, "When You Wore a Tulip." Author unknown. Probably before 1912.

I'm a recruit, sir, a green one to boot, sir,
  I'm all black and blue beside;
I ride on my cantle and eat off the mantel,
  For I've just commenced to ride.
When I'm a-straddle, I rock in my saddle,
  I certainly have no style;
But I'll bet you a cookie, when you were a rookie,
  You only touched once in a while.

THE FIVE TROOPS OF THE SQUADRON

Words of chorus and first four verses by Prentice Strong. About 1912. Numerous variations of the words have been found.

Captain Townsend's[1] troop is grand,
It always rides behind the band,
That's why no horse will ever stand
  For Troop One of the Squadron.

Chorus:
Hooray, Hooray, here we come,
Going some, chuck full of rum,
Looking for someone to put on the bum,
  The Five Troops of the Squadron.

Captain Outerbridge's[2] social lights,
  They sometimes drill on Thursday nights;

---

[1] Captain Arthur F. Townsend.
[2] Captain Frank R. Outerbridge.

They'd rather skirmish at pink tea fights,
  That Troop Two of the Squadron. [*Chorus*]

Captain Wright [3] could not get tight
Although his Troop would drink all night,
They're always up in the morning bright,
  The Third Troop of the Squadron. [*Chorus*]

Captain Olmsted's [4] baby Troop
He found one night on Stowe Phelps' stoop,
He nursed it through measles and the croup
  The Fourth Troop of the Squadron. [*Chorus*]

Captain Merritt's [5] Troop has come.
Their food is concentrated rum,
She'll make you boys sit up, by gum,
  The Machine Gun Troop of the Squadron. [*Chorus*]

Captain Merritt's [5] bunch of drunks,
They carry machine guns in their trunks,
They'll never be taken for holy monks,
  The Gun Troop of the Squadron. [*Chorus*]

HOME, BOYS, HOME

Air, "The Old Countree." Besides the 1898 verses, not of Squadron origin, many topical verses were sung at gatherings of the Third Troop and others—among them the following by Rodman Gilder, 1904–1915. The final verse, of unknown authorship, was sung by the squadron, on the border, 1916.

This message from the Gov'ner shows at last that we can boast
That we have practically got an Armory (almost).
But the thing is confidential, you must promise not to tell;
It says, "We'll build your Armory with blocks of ice from hell."

Chorus:

Home, boys, home, it's home we ought to be,
Home, boys, home, in the Old Countree,
Where the ash and the oak and the weeping willer tree
They all grow so pretty *up* in North Amerikee.

[3] Captain Wm. R. Wright.
[4] Captain Edward Olmsted.
[5] Captain Merritt H. Smith.

We all woke up one morning with a feeling very strange,
To hear on good authority we'd lost the Creedmoor range.
But at the gods in Albany we mustn't take a fling,
For a land improvement project is a very sacred thing. [*Chorus*]

One night I met Ridg. Nicholas of our Troop wrestling team,
At "The Merry Widow," sitting in a kind of hazy dream,
"No, no," said Nick, "I do not like this sort of thing, it's false;
I'm studying the clinches of the Merry Widow Waltz." [*Chorus*]

Said Captain Bill,[1] "Each man has got the silver expert bar,
Our general efficiency has just got up to par.
Now this is pretty good, but we mustn't be content
Until the Troop's efficiency is a—hundred and ten per cent."
[*Chorus*]

When I get back from Mexico, when I get back from war,
The National Guard may go to hell, I won't come out any more;
I'll take a bath and change my clothes, and then, before the Lord,
I will hop a car and go downtown and vote for Henry Ford![2]
[*Chorus*]

TROOP A JOY SONG

Air, "Yip-i-addy, i-ay." About 1912.

Yip-i-addy, Troop A, Troop A,
   Yip-i-addy, Troop A!
Out for a frolic or out for a fight,
Out for all day and then out for all night.
   Yip-i-addy, Troop A, Troop A—
We just want to holler Hooray!
   For water's our drink—
   Yes it is—I don't think.
   Yip-i-addy, Troop A!

IN THE CAVALRY

The composer and the author of this widely popular cavalry song are not known. It may have originated in Buffalo, about 1915, in Troop I, 1st

---

[1] Captain William R. Wright.   [2] Financed the "Peace Ship."

Cavalry, N.G.N.Y., as this Troop was formed by several graduates of the squadron.

> In the Cavalry, in the Cavalry,
> There's where I would be.
> In the Cavalry, in the Cavalry,
> That's the place for me-e-e—
> With a good old scout beside me,
> I care not what betide me;
> And I don't give a damn
> For any old man
> Who is *not* in the Cavalry!

ROE, ROE, ROE

Air, "Row, Row, Row." Words by Rodman Gilder, 1913, for an Armory dinner to Major General Charles F. Roe.

> Way back in '89 there came to this old town
> A fine young cavalryman, husky and brown.
> But a horseman you can't cure—
> He missed the smell of horse manure.
> We had a bunch of Hussars, he had been told
> (Troop A had just been foaled).
> They made him Captain of Hussars—
> On his shoulders now are golden stars!
>
> *Chorus:*
> For it was Roe, Roe, Roe,
> The best we ever had was Roe, Roe, Roe.
> When hell was popping and the jamboree began,
> He was in the van—
> A fighter and a horseman and a double-fisted man.
> For it was Roe, Roe, Roe—
> There never was a boy like Roe, Roe, Roe, Roe, Oh!
> So the guard we'll turn out
> For that bully old scout—
> For General Roe, Roe, Roe.

TROOP D SONG

Air, "As the Backs Go Tearing By." Words by Wilder Goodwin. 1916.

> As Troop D goes riding by,
> All the senoritas sigh—
> A hundred troopers knee to knee,
> Pride of all the cavalry,
> As Troop D goes riding by.
> In the camp or in the field
> There are none to whom we yield—
> At the gallop, walk or trot,
> We can show them all what's what—
> As Troop D goes riding by.

HELLO, HELLO, SQUADRON A

Air, "Hello, New York Town." Words by Knowlton Durham. 1916.

> Hello, Hello, Squadron A,
> We're going down to Mexico.
> Everything down there is in a mess
> And it's up to Uncle Sam, I guess.
> So put on your breeches and your boots,
> Bring along old Bessie,[1] if you're sure she shoots.
> Hurry, hurry, down this way—
> Hello, Hello, Squadron A.

Additional verse, composed on the Mexican border, by several authors.

> Hello, Hello, Squadron A,
> We're going back to New York Town—
> Everything up there is at its best
> And we're going back to have a rest.
> So take off your breeches and your boots,
> Get out your dinner coats and old dress suits—
> Hurry, hurry, up this way—
> Highballs—rolling—on Broadway.

[1] "Constipated Betsy" was the name appropriately applied to the first machine gun ever issued to the Squadron.

THE GRINGO GRENADIERS

Air and words by Edward H. Putnam, during Mexican border service, 1916. A Machine Gun Troop song.

> O list to us, we're tough young fellows,
>   We're cavalry from New York,
> You can tell we're Army broken,
>   For we eat the Army pork.
> We've come down to the Border
>   To lend a willing hand
> And keep the folks in order
>   Along the Rio Grande.
>
> Our machine guns never jam and we do not give a damn,
> We ride like the devil on the rough and the level,
>   For we ride for Uncle Sam.
> And the girls, the pretty dears,
> Are in love up to their ears;
>   They say, "Hooray for Squadron A
>   And the Gringo Grenadiers."
>
> Our machine guns roar as we go to war
> And the other four troops are awful sore,
>   For they envy the punch of the Gun Troop bunch
>   And the Gringo—Grenadiers!

[*The following is usually substituted for the last verse.*]

> Our machine guns roar as we go to war
> And the infantry are awful sore,
>   And they envy the punch of the Squadron bunch
>   And the Gringo—Grenadiers!

GOOD NIGHT, CARRANZA

Air, "Good Night, Poor Harvard." Words by Wilder Goodwin, during Mexican border service. 1916.

> Good Night, Carranza; Carranza, Good Night—
>   We've got your number,
> We're not too proud to fight;
>   For we are five hundred troopers, all roaring tight—
>   When Squadron A gets after you,
>   Carranza, *good* NIGHT!

WHEN ARE THOSE PULLMANS COMING, GENERAL?

Air, "Aguinaldo." Words by Philip J. Meany, during Mexican border service. 1916.

When we were ordered out to fight
We donned our boots and hats;
But instead of fighting Mexicans
We swatted flies and gnats.
We came down to the Border
Where the Rio Grande flows;
But instead of shooting greasers
We had them wash our clothes.

Chorus:

When do we go home, John? [1]
When do we return?
The girls back home are anxious
And they miss us.
The Broadway lights are burning
And Healy's needs us back—
When are those Pullmans coming, General?

We've soldiered down here six long months
On the banks of the Rio Grande;
We've eaten lots of pork and beans
And hiked all over the land;
We've enjoyed our stay immensely
And drilled hard every day,
But now the summer's over,
The time has come to say—

Chorus:

When do we go home, John?
When do we return?
The girls are getting lonely
And they miss us;
The Broadway lights are burning;
The office needs us back—
When are those Pullmans coming, General?

[1] Major General John F. O'Ryan, C.O., 27th Division. This song, produced at a Division Headquarters entertainment, was based on a rumor that cars were on the way to take the squadron home. It was sung by a quartet—Phil Meany, Zack Taylor, Nat Holmes, and Spike Steele. The General is reported to have been highly amused.

We honor our dear President,
He's sure to win our vote;
He's waited long and watchfully
And writes a bully note.
But we down here have waited
As patiently as he
For the greatest note he'll ever write,
The one that sets us free.

Chorus:

When do we go home, John?
When do we return?
These Texas plains are awful
And they bore us;
We've had enough of cactus,
McAllen leaves us flat.
When are those Pullmans coming, General?

THE BORDER—A MEXICAN PEON

By Roger Burlingame. 1916.

Out beyond the Mississippi, down below the Mason-Dixon,
In a spot that no topographer could ever justly fix on,
In a land of open spaces, void of beauties, joys or graces
Down where one hell meets another and the human kills his brother
And the ranger knows no danger from a fatuous law and order,
Where the cactus grows and pricks, where the white and Peon mix,
There's a Styx they call the Rio—muddy yellow-livered Rio;
There's a Styx they call the Rio and a land they call the Border.

O the Border, Merry Border, we're its far-flung Desert warder,
And we post our lonely outposts 'gainst the grizzly Mex marauder,
And the Rio goes on rippling,
And the gun troop goes on tippling,
Till the stars all sing like Shakespeare and the dawn comes up like Kipling;
Merry land with the brand of the Devil in its sand,
On the Border by the ditch that's dubbed the Grande.

In the thirsty tropic night, when the coyote howls his blight,
When the sentries stalk their watches in the stars' uncertain light,
There's a lonely figure crouching with his seven bandoliers—
It's the Sergeant stalking Greasers and he's weaponed to the ears;

Fourteen thousand strong Villistas have assembled at Reynosa
And they won't attack the Squadron—not if he can help it—no, sir!
There's a person on the picket line with mystery about him—
It's a trooper gone to tell his horse he cannot sleep without him;
In the night, gloomy night, while the soldiers dream in sorrow
Of the ditches and the sinks and the wagons of tomorrow.

> On the Border, on the Border, where the land is always broader,
> Where the shrilly Captain's whistle thrills the prelude to each order
> And we climb the seventh heaven
> Through the breach of Number Seven
> With our flask of roaring red-eye 'neath the cactus bush at even,
> Till the fighting Irish roar words we never heard before,
> On the Border by the Rio's hardpan shore.

On the glorious Sabbath morning there's a blessed relaxation
In the undiluted prospect of a day of pure vacation,
When the military lapses and the dull routine collapses,
When the day is soft and warming and the ducks and doves are swarming;
Then it's nice to hear the sergeant
Running, singing down the street,
Merry foremost topping sergeant
With the Lazo at his feet.
And you know it's you he's paging
And there's nothing can resist him,
For he's got his old enraging
Reeking, roaring, roster system,
And it's stable guard all day while the gay palomas play
And you shovel it and shower it and breathe it and devour it
Till the picket line is bare from Carranza to the Mare,
Save one beast who had an afterthought and dropped another there.

> O the Border, Texas Border, with its icy Texas Norder,
> And its Mexicabs and Texicabs and thieving sheriff hoarder,
> Where mañana means forever
> And the vainest pun is clever,
> And to be the Major's orderly's the goal of our endeavor;
> With the barrel in your hand 'mongst the bucking band you stand,
> On the Border clept in mockery the Grande.

When the sun has sought its rest in the crimson-pillowed West,
And the Desert whispers starward of the secrets in its breast;
Then it's sweet to sit and ponder on the easternmost latrine,
While the taran*tula*s sport about upon your buttocks lean;

Down below, a mile or so, all the tissue has departed
And you wail to wake the stable guard in accents broken hearted.
"There's a loose man in the latrine, tell the Curtis [1] he must come"
But the stable guard is dreaming of his porcelain one at home.

> On the Border, Merry Border, we're its safety and its warder
> And we guard the helpless Peon from the ranger's brute disorder
> And the height of our ambition
> Is a trip to Pharr or Mission,
> Where we sip our foaming teapot under M. P. supervision
> Till we're owly-eyed and pickly and we spend our last fond nickly
> For a taxi to the Border and the snaky Rio Grande.

Get your distance in that second four and keep 'em at the walk!
Get your back into that grooming and restrain your wanton talk!
Belly, back, hot and wet—where's the dock? I forget!
Then it's skirmishers—guide right—at those bushes out of sight,
Through the cactus brush you trudge it and unless your name is Blodgett,[2]
It's impossible to dodge it from the break of day till night.
But when quarters dreams its melody in Louis' [3] tremolo
And silence hushes down the street and lights are dimming low,
Then it's fair to see the flower of their country wrapt in slumbers—
Young men seeing visions, dreaming dreams—and snoring by the numbers.

> O the Border, Merry Border, we're its far-flung Desert warder,
> And we post our lonely outposts 'gainst the grizzly Mex marauder,
> And the Rio goes on rippling,
> And the gun troop goes on tippling,
> Till the stars all sing like Shakespeare and the dawn comes up like Kipling,
> Merry land with the brand of the Devil in its sand
> On the Border by the ditch that's dubbed the Grande.

THE DUST CLOUD

Air, "John Peel." Words by Carleton S. Cooke. About 1921.
(*"A high, thin cloud of dust indicates cavalry."*—Field Service Regulations)

> Have you seen Troop D, by the sunrise red,
> When Squadron A rides out ahead
> With saddles packed and horses fed,
>   As they take the road in the morning?

---

[1] Ronald E. Curtis, Supply Sergeant.   [2] Alden S. Blodgett.
[3] Trumpeter Louis Lorenson.

Chorus:

At the trumpet's call, at the break of day,
Form troop and mount, and ride away,
And the dust is high and thin and gray
   Above Troop D in the morning.

For when that high dust cloud you see,
Then—look—out for the cavalry,
When the horses tramp and the road is free
   As they take the road in the morning.

So here's to the horse and the saber true,
And the cracking Colt and the Springfield blue,
And here, Troop D, is luck to you
   When you take the road in the morning.

     [*Last verse softly*]
And you'll find four troops at the end of the day,
When the tents are pitched in the evening gray,
The old Four Troops of Squadron A,
   By the road they took in the morning.

TROOP K SONG

By Armistead Fitzhugh. Date uncertain.

  Fall in! Saddles and bridles.
    Fours left! Down to the line.
  Covers off! Saddle, you wobblies.
    Don't take that bridle of mine.

  Mount up! Hard riding troopers.
    Form troop! (See that brass shine.)
  Eyes front! Here comes the Skipper.
    Third Troop first off the line!

  Forward ho! Follow the Skipper.
    Trot ho! Gather those reins.
  Gallop ho! Ride out, you wobblies.
    Hold back there, use your brains.

  Lead on! K Troop guidon.
    Stand out! Wave in the breeze.
  Follow on! K Troopers.
    Gallop through! Ride at ease.

THE HARLEM HUSSARS, OR RIOT DUTY

Air, "Bonnie Dundee." Words by Carleton S. Cooke. 1925.

To the troopers of D Troop 'twas Reynolds [1] that spoke,
"There's a garment strike on and it's got to be broke,
So ye lawyers and bankers and salesmen so free,
Turn out—you're Hussars of the N.Y.N.G."

Chorus:
Come borrow a saber and spurs and a gun,
Come saddle some horses, come up on the run,
Come open the Armory, let me ride free
With the Hell-roaring Harlem Hussars of Troop D!

The worried lieutenants they form their platoons,
Of lancers, chasseurs, cuirassiers and dragoons;
The enraged garment workers they pale at the look
Of the Uhlans of Cumings [2] and Cossacks of Cooke! [3] [*Chorus*]

As along Ninety-fourth Street the cavaliers ride
The horses all shimmy and toddle and slide—
There are wild garment-workers three thousand times three,
With scissors and clubs for to welcome Troop D. [*Chorus*]

The strikers are gathered in Washington Square,
Their war-cry, *"Oi, oi, Gewalt!"* pierces the air;
But engagements prevent their remaining to see
The terrible charge of Hussars of Troop D. [*Chorus*]

He waves his proud hand, and the horses all cough,
The spurs are dug in and the warriors fall off—
To the clang of the Madison Avenue cars,
Die away the wild notes of the Harlem Hussars. [*Chorus*]

FOUR FEET FROM HEAD TO CROUP

Air, U.S. Marine song. Date recent.

There is one thing in the Cavalry
   That every trooper knows;
He hears it every morning, noon and night,
   It follows him where'er he goes.

---

[1] Captain John Reynolds.   [2] Second Lieutenant John B. Cumings.
[3] First Lieutenant Carleton S. Cooke.

For when he's marching on the road
  In squad, platoon or troop,
Every mile or so some bird will crow,
  "Four feet from head to croup!"

Now he hears that same thing every day
  Until he knows the words by heart.
Even when he's walking with his girl,
  They make them keep four feet apart.
And when they seek those pearly gates,
  And up the golden stairs they troop,
Just as sure as hell Saint Pete will yell,
  "Four feet from head to croup!"

TWENTY YEARS

By Roger Burlingame. For the 1936 reunion of Border Troop D.

Time leads us onward year by year,
  It spurs us and it checks us,
It wrinkles us and fills with fear
  Our growing solar plexus;
Yet twenty years ago our brave
Young thoughts were not upon the grave...
'Twas twenty years ago we gave
  The Border back to Texas.

And in those gay and careless days
  Our arches had not fallen
And no one yet had sung the praise
  Of Hitler or of Stalin;
Then Kings still ruled by godly right
And met their commoners at night,
When Mexico gave up the fight,
  And we gave up McAllen.

Van Cortlandt Park no longer rings
  With voices young, seraphic,
Singing the songs the trooper sings
  When slightly pornographic;
Where, once, wild mustangs scaled the heights,
Belching exhausts now foul the nights
And all night long the traffic lights
  Go winking at the traffic.

SQUADRON A

Where is the pomp of yesterday,
    The march we used to ride on,
The desert where we held our sway,
    The sand we almost died on?
Where is the sharp and cadenced beat
Of all the countless sand-cracked feet
That dressed along the hardpan street,
    On Cooke's[1] relentless guidon?

Time hath conspired with palsied hands
    To anger and enwrath me;
Say, hath it changed the desert sands
    As deeply as it hath me?
They tell me it is green and rich
Along the irrigation ditch
Where once the mare we called "The Bitch"
    Drank deep and rolled on Gwathmey.[2]

Yet as I look on D Troop's own—
    On hair which should be grayer
And waistlines only slightly grown,
    It makes me somewhat gayer.
On Hilyer,[3] Wilder,[4] Ronnie,[5] Steve,[6]
Old age is absent without leave;
I see no reason yet to grieve
    The Deity with prayer.

They say time alters man and thought,
    The 'scutcheon and the motto,
It dims the dream for which we fought
    And turns the whole world blotto;
Yet, while on grim, relentless wings,
Over the settled scheme of things
It scoffs at dynasties and kings,
    It does not change Hank Otto.[7]

On Russian steppes and Roman plains
    Dictators twist and addle
The thought of proletarian brains
    With unremitting twaddle.

---

[1] Carleton S. Cooke.
[2] Archie B. Gwathmey, 2nd.
[3] N. H. Egleston.
[4] Wilder Goodwin.
[5] Ronald E. Curtis.
[6] Stephen W. Mason.
[7] Henry S. Otto.

Yet, while the tyrants herd their sheep
And liberty is put to sleep,
We do not care if we can keep
   Jack Reynolds [8] in the saddle!

So let the empires wax and wane
   Under their strange dictation;
We'll fill our glasses up again
   And drink to equitation.
But if there ever comes the day
When there is no more Squadron A,
I'll pack my boots and spurs away
   And sign my abdication.

[8] John Reynolds.

THE MEMBERSHIP ROLL OF FORMER AND PRESENT MEMBERS OF SQUADRON A

> Let the scroll
> Fill as it may, as years unroll;
> But when again she calls her youth
> To serve her in the ranks of Truth,
> May she find all one heart, one soul—
> At home or on some distant shore—
> "All present or accounted for!"
>
> —Edward Everett Hale

The Roll of Members compiled by Major George Matthews, Jr., is a valuable record. The bound volume, which rests in the rooms of the Ex-Members' Association and is the basis of what is here presented, lists the names alphabetically for each successive year—a method that allows for the continuation of the record in like manner in subsequent years. For the purposes of this history a rearrangement has been made, so that for the fifty-year period all names are presented in alphabetical order.

In accordance with the system adopted in the membership list prepared by Major Matthews, it has been attempted to classify the membership by Troops, by placing a number opposite each name, which indicates the Troop in conformity with the following table.

No. 1 signifies membership in the following:

Troop A   N.G.S.N.Y., 1889–1895
Troop 1   Squadron A, N.G.N.Y., 1895–1912
Troop A   1st Cavalry, N.G.N.Y., 1912–1913
Troop A   1st Squadron Cavalry, N.G.N.Y., 1913–1914
Troop A   Squadron A, N.G.N.Y., 1914–1921
Troop A   51st Machine Gun Squadron, N.Y.N.G., 1921–1928
Troop E   101st Cavalry, N.Y.N.G., 1928–1939

No. 2 signifies membership in the following:

Troop 2   Squadron A, N.G.N.Y., 1895–1912
Troop E   1st Cavalry, N.G.N.Y., 1912–1913
Troop B   1st Squadron, Cavalry, N.G.N.Y., 1913–1914
Troop B   Squadron A, N.G.N.Y., 1914–1920
Troop B   51st Machine Gun Squadron, N.Y.N.G., 1920–1928
Troop F   101st Cavalry, N.Y.N.G., 1928–1939

No. 3 signifies membership in the following:

Troop 3   Squadron A, N.G.N.Y., 1896–1912
Troop F   1st Cavalry, N.G.N.Y., 1912–1913
Troop C   1st Squadron, Cavalry, N.G.N.Y., 1913–1914
Troop C   Squadron A, N.G.N.Y., 1914–1921
Troop C   51st Machine Gun Squadron, N.Y.N.G., 1921–1928
Troop G   101st Cavalry, N.Y.N.G., 1928–1929
Troop K   101st Cavalry, N.Y.N.G., 1928–1939

No. 4 signifies membership in the following:

Troop 4   Squadron A, N.G.N.Y., 1907–1912
Troop G   1st Cavalry, N.G.N.Y., 1912–1913
Troop D   1st Squadron, Cavalry, N.G.N.Y., 1913–1914
Troop D   Squadron A, N.G.N.Y., 1914–1920

M.G. signifies membership in the following:

Troop C   1st Cavalry, N.G.N.Y., 1912–1914
M.G. Troop Squadron A, N.G.N.Y., 1914–1917

The present list is intended to cover all those who served at any period in Squadron A as such. Those who became members of the Machine Gun Battalion without previous service in the squadron are not here included; the "History of Squadron A in the Great War" provides that record.

> From mere oblivion I reclaim
> The soldier's name, the soldier's name,
> And write it on the scroll of fame—
> The Muse of Fame am I.

—W. S. Gilbert

FORMER AND PRESENT MEMBERS OF SQUADRON A

Name	Troop or Detachment Served	Date of Enlistment and Final Discharge	Name	Troop or Detachment Served	Date of Enlistment and Final Discharge
Abbett, Sheldon	3	1921–1924	Ambler, John G.	1	1889–1890
Abernathy, Samuel	2	1918–1920	Ames, Azel, Jr.	3	1926–1932
Achelis, John Fritz	1	1914–1917	Ames, Charles E.	1	1921–1923
Achilies, Paul S.	2	1915–1917	Amory, Copley, Jr.	2	1913–1917
Ackerman, Arthur F.	Med	1926–1929	Amory, John F.	3	1924–1925
Adams, Clinton*	1	1889–1890	Amy, Louis H.		1917–1919
Adams, Crittenden H.	3	1915–1917	Anable, Harry M.	1	1924–1924
Adams, James B., Jr.	3	1930–1931	Anderson, Carl G.	1-2	1918–1920
Adams, John Fairchild	4	1913–1916	Anderson, Clarence M.	2	1933–1936
Adams, Julius L.	1	1893–1894	Anderson, Frederick		1917–1919
Adams, Newton	1	1903–1917	Anderson, Frederick H.	3	1932–1935
Adams, Stuart Corlies	1	1906–1907	Anderson, Henry B.	1	1890–1891
Adams, Stuart L.	1	1936–1937	Anderson, James B.	1	1938–
Adams, Thatcher M.	1	1895–1900	Anderson, Leroy	2	1938–
Adams, Thomas S., Jr.	3	1936–	Anderson, Merrill	Hd	1927–1929
Adams, Welles, McK.	1	1924–1928	Anderson, Roulhac	3	1929–1933
Adams, William	1	1895–1898	Andrade, Eduardo	3	1932–1935
Adams, William Crittenden	2	1898–1904	Andrews, Arthur G.	3	1935–1936
Adee, Charles S.	3	1898–1898	Andrews, Avery D.	Hd	1898–1899
Adee, George T.	3	1898–1898	Andrews, John G.	3	1928–1928
Adler, Frederick A.	2	1917–1919	Andrews, Joseph, Jr.	2	1920–1921
Ador, Robert	3	1933–1934	Andrews, Joseph L.	3	1918–1920
Agar, John G., Jr.*	3	1914–1917	Andrus, Craig	3	1937–
Agather, Victor N.	1	1937–	Annerstedt, James	1	1934–1936
Agnew, Cornelius	2	1895–1906	Anthony, Richard A., Jr.	2	1923–1926
Agnew, Cornelius R., Jr.	1	1930–1937	Aplington, Horace Thurber	2-4	1908–1910
Agnew, George B.	1-2	1892–1902	Appleton, William H.	3	1909–1912
Ahern, Jas. M.	3	1925–1926	Armfelt, Waldemar	3	1928–1937
Albrecht, Ralph G.	2	1924–1930	Armstrong, Thomas E.	3	1929–1932
Alcott, Delafield S.	1	1899–1890	Armstrong, William C.	1	1915–1917
Alden, Frederick A.	3	1917–1920	Arnaud, Leopold	1	1925–1928
Aldrich, Richard S.	4	1910–1911	Arnold, Francis X.	2	1917–1919
Alexander, Arthur D.	2	1914–1917	Arnold, Ripley*	1	1891–1891
Alexander, Brooke	3	1936–	Arthur, William H.	2	1937–
Alexander, Walter*	1	1893–1898	Ashburner, James E.	3	1925–1925
Alexandre, Jas. Henry, Jr.	2	1906–1911	Ashmore, Sidney B.	2	1932–1935
Alexandre, Jerome*	3-MG	1907–1917	Aspegren, John B.	3	1932–1933
Alfke, Harry G.		1917–1919	Aspinwall, Breck	3-2-1	1918–1921
Allan, Parker B.	1	1921–1921	Aspinwall, J. Lawrence	1	1889–1891
Allen, Harry S.	1	1889–1890	Atherton, Henry Francis	1	1910–1911
Allen, Henry Butler	1	1913–1914	Atterbury, Grosvenor	3	1896–1903
Allen, Horace R.	MG	1916–1917	Auchincloss, Reginald	2	1915–1917
Allen, John Appleton	2-1	1900–1905	Auerbach, John Hone	3	1906–1911
Allen, Lloyd S.	1	1915–1917	Ausberg, Alex. T.	1-2	1919–1921
Allen, Morton B.	1-3	1917–1926	Austin, Charles D.	3	1925–1926
Allen, Morton Bogue		1917–1919	Averill, Lloyd B.	2	1926–1929
Allen, Thomas H.*	1	1889–1899	Aycrigg, George B.	3	1916–1917
Allen, Walter Best	1	1909–1910	Ayers, Edward L.	2	1920–1923
Alley, Rayford W.	4	1916–1916	Aylward, Thomas	MG	1916–1933
Almy, Henry	2	1898–1904	Aylward, Wm. R.	2	1920–1923
Alsop, Samuel	3	1918–1920	Ayres, Bartow N.	2	1921–1922

357

SQUADRON A

Name	Troop or Detachment Served	Date of Enlistment and Final Discharge	Name	Troop or Detachment Served	Date of Enlistment and Final Discharge
Babcock, Edward D.	4	1916–1917	Barker, Stephen	4	1907–1919
Babcock, Fred Huntington	1	1910–1913	Barker, William E., Jr	3	1925–1927
Babcock, Harry S.	4	1916–1917	Barkley, Harry W.	2	1895–1897
Babcock, Sherrill	2	1900–1918	Barlow, Samuel L. M.	3	1916–1916
Babcock, Theodore S.	2	1916–1917	Barmore, George	4	1910–1912
Bacon, Rogers H.	3	1896–1903	Barnard, Allen Gardner		1917–1919
Badgley, Howard G.*	1-2	1889–1905	Barnard, Horace J.	1	1892–1907
Bahnsen, Henry	4	1916–1917	Barnard, Horace, Jr.	1	1933–
Bail, Hamilton V.	2	1923–1925	Barnes, Chas. M.	2	1924–1928
Bailey, Benjamin P., Jr	3	1926–1927	Barnes, J. Sanford	1	1893–1899
Bailey, Ellsworth N.	3	1934–1935	Barnes, John W.	2	1924–1926
Bailey, Theodore L.	1	1900–1913	Barnes, Thomas S.	1	1911–1912
Bainbridge, Wm. W.	Hd	1926–1928	Barnett, Chas. M., Jr.	2	1920–1921
Baird, Alvin V.	1	1908–1912	Barr, Rufus C.	4	1909–1914
Baker, Allan G.	2	1921–1922	Barrett, G. Hinman	4	1912–1917
Baker, Browning	2	1909–1910	Barrett, Harold B.	Hd	1925–1928
Baker, Charles	Band-1	1913–1921	Barrett, John J.	3	1929–1932
Baker, Charles		1917–1919	Barrett, John Joseph		1917–1919
Baker, Charles D.*	3	1914–1917	Barrett, Jos. Russell*	2	1908–1910
Baker, Charles W.	1	1914–1919	Barril, Guyon*	3	1898–1898
Baker, John Whitney	3	1909–1916	Barrows, Elliot A.	1	1938–
Baker, Newton A.		1917–1919	Barry, Herbert	1-3-Hd	1891–1918
Baker, Norman	1	1915–1919	Barry, Herbert, Jr.	3	1917–1925
Baker, Wm. E., Jr.	4	1914–1916	Barry, Robert P., Jr.	2	1897–1902
Bakos, Jules	3	1919–1921	Barry, Rutledge B.	2	1921–1922
Balch, Francis DuPont	1	1905–1906	Bartels, John R.	1	1924–1926
Balch, Henry H.*	1	1889–1894	Bartholomew, George H.*	4	1910–1912
Baldwin, Alfred W.	1	1889–1892	Bartholomew, Robert B.	Med-2	1905–1917
Baldwin, Charles H.	1	1925–1926	Bartlett, Charles G., Jr.	3	1907–1909
Baldwin, Chas. M.	1	1890–1919	Barton, Benjamin B.	2	1918–1918
Baldwin, Charles W.	1	1936–	Barton, John H.	1	1933–1935
Baldwin, Delavan Munson	1	1910–1914	Barton, Randall W.	2	1928–1931
Baldwin, Harry B.	1	1893–1894	Bartow, Charles	1	1924–1925
Baldwin, Joseph C., Jr.*	1	1893–1897	Bascomb, Jas. A.	3	1918–1918
Baldwin, Peter	3	1928–1931	Bass, Jas. G.	2-Hd-2	1920–1930
Baldwin, Roger S.	3	1898–1904	Bastedo, Walter A., Jr.	3	1937–
Ball, Alwyn, 3rd	MG	1912–1919	Bastine, Arthur R.	3	1924–
Ball, George G.*	3	1916–1917	Bastine, Wilfrid S.	3	1922–1924
Ball, John S.	3	1922–1925	Batchelder, Harry B.	3	1924–1926
Ballard, Warren McE.	1	1937–1938	Batcheller, Harry*	1	1896–1901
Ballentine, John H.	2	1918–1918	Bates, Aaron T., Jr.	MG	1916–1917
Ballin, Cyril G.	3	1912–1917	Bates, Grover Cleveland	2	1914–1915
Baltzell, Ernest R.	2	1926–1927	Bates, Joseph R.	MG	1917–1917
Bamford, Walter H.	2	1924–1925	Bates, Putman A.	2	1897–1906
Bancroft, Thomas M.	3	1926–1930	Bates, T. Tower*	2	1895–1918
Bangs, Francis N.	3	1916–1917	Bates, Wm. B.	2	1931–1934
Bangs, Henry McC.	3-4	1906–1907	Bateson, Charles E., 3rd	3	1937–
Banks, Chas. W.	Med	1927–1927	Bateson, E. Farrar	MG	1912–1915
Banks, Harold P.	4	1913–1916	Bateson, Richard H., Jr.	3	1929–1933
Banks, Henry W., 3rd*	3	1916–1917	Battelle, Seavey	2	1900–1903
Banks, Robert F.	1	1921–1924	Battershall, Frederick S.	2-4	1899–1907
Banks, William J.	3	1918–1918	Battle, Thomas Joseph, Jr.	3	1918–1920
Bankson, Philatus C.	1	1918–1918	Bayard, Louis P., 3rd	2	1920–1922
Banta, Cornelius G. F.	3	1925–1926	Baylis, Chester	2	1899–1904
Barber, George H.	4	1916–1917	Baylis, Wm., Jr.	2	1904–1909
Barbour, W. Wm.	2	1908–1913	Bayliss, Charles E., Jr.	2	1924–1927
Barclay, Harold	2	1896–1899	Bayliss, Raymond	3	1912–1914
Barclay, Robert C.	2-3	1896–1901	Bayne, Donald	MG	1912–1917
Barker, Charles D.	3	1928–1930	Bayne, Howard	3	1902–1911
Barker, Francis M.	2	1918–1918	Bayne, Lloyd Moore	1	1917–1919

SQUADRON A 359

Name	Troop or Detachment Served	Date of Enlistment and Final Discharge	Name	Troop or Detachment Served	Date of Enlistment and Final Discharge
Bayne, Ross C.	1	1895–1898	Bethman, Adolf A.	2	1933–1936
Beach, George R., Jr.	3	1927–1929	Betschick, Augustus E.	2	1920–1924
Beach, John A.	2	1924–1927	Betts, Hobart D.*	3	1899–1907
Beadleston, William L.*	3	1896–1901	Biays, John S.	1	1933–1937
Beahan, Richard	1	1916–1930	Biglow, Lucius Horatio, Jr.	1	1909–1919
Beahan, Richard P.	1	1917–1919	Bingham, Arthur W., Jr.	3	1922–1925
Beales, James A. G.	3	1896–1902	Bingham, Frederick C., Jr.	2	1931–1934
Beam, John C.	4	1920–1921	Binkard, Alfred A.	3	1934–1938
Bean, Henry W.	1	1893–1898	Birckhead, Philip	4	1907–1912
Bearce, Herbert P.	2	1930–1936	Bird, Prall	2-Hd	1921–1922
Beard, Alexander H.	4	1919–1919	Bird, S. Hinman	3-4	1907–1912
Beardsley, Henry W.	2	1931–1936	Birdsall, James E.	1	1939–
Beardsley, Randolph H.	3	1929–1931	Birrell, Thomas K.	3	1920–1925
Beatty, John H.	1	1934–1937	Bishop, Heber R.	3	1924–1925
Beaty, Julian B.	MG	1913–1916	Bishop, James D.	3	1928–1931
Beck, George B., Jr.	2	1930–1932	Black, Roger D., Jr.	3	1927–1929
Becker, Frederick W.	1	1897–1907	Black, Wm., M., Jr.	3	1922–1925
Becker, Gilbert B.	2	1922–1925	Blackwell, Hugh B.	Med-2	1916–1916
Becket, Robert M.	Hd	1921–1922	Blake, Arthur M.	1-3	1895–1917
Bedell, Harry P.	2	1925–1926	Blake, Gilman D.	1-Hd	1924–1925
Beebe, Howard W.*	2	1918–1920	Blake, Mason	2	1929–1931
Beebe, John H.	3	1926–1933	Blase, Stanley	3	1920–1921
Beers, Donald	MG	1916–1917	Bleecker, Barclay	2	1920–1921
Beers, Henry N.	3	1930–1932	Block, Irwin S.	3	1935–1936
Behr, Karl H.	1	1907–1917	Blodget, Alden S.	3-MG-4	1909–1916
Belknap, Waldron P.	1-2	1895–1920	Bloodgood, Edward F.	3	1897–1897
Bell, Charles E.	1	1932–	Blydenburgh, Vail	2	1902–1916
Bell, Kenneth A.	1	1932–1933	Blythe, John S.	3	1928–1928
Bellamy, Russell	2-Hd	1895–1907	Boardman, Kenneth	1-MG	1907–1914
Bellinger, Edmund B.	1	1922–1932	Boardman, Sidney S.	1	1899–1901
Bellinger, Frederic C.	1	1922–1925	Bodman, George M.	2-4	1907–1919
Bellinger, Rene DuC.	3	1921–1922	Bodman, Herbert L.	4	1911–1917
Bellows, John Chester	3	1918–1920	Bogert, Chas. H., Jr.*	1	1889–1891
Beltz, Frederick	1	1918–1933	Bogert, Edward O.	MG	1913–1917
Bendelare, Hamilton W.	1	1924–1925	Bollard, Ralph H.	3	1906–1906
Benedict, Frederic P.	2	1918–1918	Bolles, Charles V.	1	1937–
Benedict, Stewart	2	1921–1923	Bolles, Mathew	1	1916–1917
Benjamin, Hamilton F.*	1	1901–1906	Bolling, Raynal C.*	3	1907–1914
Benjamin, Wm. W.*	3	1898–1899	Bolter, Ward H.	2	1932–1937
Benjamin, William W.	1	1925–1928	Bolton-Smith, Carlile	1	1929–1932
Benkard, James G.	2	1896–1898	Bond, Marshall	1	1903–1904
Bennett, David V.	1	1921–1922	Bongard, Wm. J.	3	1919–1919
Bennett, Walter W. K.	3	1932–1933	Bonnell, John Harper	1	1916–1917
Bennett, William R.	1	1933–1935	Bonner, Lionel T.	1	1922–1923
Bentley, Edward S.	1	1922–1925	Bonner, Paul R.	1	1893–1899
Bentley, Jerome H.	2	1932–1934	Bonnevalle, Richard W.	1	1921–1925
Benton, Paul D.	2	1939–	Booraem, Alfred W.	3	1896–1917
Benziger, Xavier N., Jr.	2	1935–	Booraem, J. Francis	3	1896–1903
Berberyan, Chan S.	2	1919–1921	Booth, Lewis S.	Med	1920–1921
Berdich, John E.	1	1923–1932	Bordeau, Chester	3	1935–1938
Berg, Milton E.	Hd	1923–1926	Borden, Alfred	4-2	1902–1919
Berliner, Michael W.	3	1935–1936	Borden, Robert R., Jr.	2	1937–1938
Bernuth, Charles M.	3	1931–	Borkland, Ernest W., Jr.	2	1930–1935
Bernuth, Oscar N.	2	1898–1901	Bornemann, Frederick H.	MG	1913–1916
Berry, Burton J.	2-4	1904–1907	Boss, Herbert L.*	2-Hd	1922–1927
Berry, Harold H.	4	1907–1909	Bossard, Wolfgang, D. K.	2	1915–1921
Berry, John K.	3	1931–1932	Bostwick, Elmore, Jr.	3	1937–
Berry, John M.	1	1928–1931	Botsford, Edward P.	2	1931–1934
Berry, Richard S.	3	1927–1932	Bottomly, John F.	1	1908–1917
Beswick, Samuel F.	Hd	1924–1928	Bougard, Wm. J.	1	1919–1919

SQUADRON A

Name	Troop or Detachment Served	Date of Enlistment and Final Discharge	Name	Troop or Detachment Served	Date of Enlistment and Final Discharge
Boulton, Howard*	4-2	1909–1915	Brousseau, Edward W.	1	1923–1932
Boulton, Howard, Jr.	3	1931–1935	Brower, Burr V.	1	1936–
Boulton, Wm. B., Jr.	4-2	1909–1917	Brown, Arthur F.	3	1898–
Bowditch, John B.	2	1938–1938	Brown, Bache Hamilton	2	1917–1919
Bowen, Edmund J.	1	1921–1923	Brown, Clyde, Jr.	3	1931–1937
Bowers, Joel Foster	3	1917–1919	Brown, Edward V.	2	1925–1926
Bowne, Francis D.*	1-2-3-4	1894–1914	Brown, Gardner	3	1896–1902
Boyer, Philip	2	1906–1909	Brown, Harold L.	2	1922–1923
Brabner–Smith, John W.	1	1930–1930	Brown, Howard K.*	3	1898–1898
Brabner-Smith, Joyce	1	1930–1933	Brown, Hubert R., Jr.	2	1931–1936
Bracken, Barrie	3	1921–1923	Brown, James Crosby*	1	1894–1898
Bradley, John D.*	1	1893–1894	Brown, L. Howland	3-Hd	1902–1922
Bradley, Stephen R., Jr.	1-Hd	1893–1917	Brown, Lathrop	3	1904–1909
Bradley, Wm. C.	3	1897–1903	Brown, Stanley	2	1906–1913
Brady, Philip H.	2	1930–	Brown, T. McKee, Jr.*	1	1894–1897
Brady, Thomas J.	2	1920–1931	Brown, Truman B.	3	1928–1930
Brady, Wm. A., Jr.*	Hd	1922–1924	Brown, Walter D.	3	1929–1930
Brady, William M.	2	1936–	Brown, Warren N.	3	1930–1932
Braithwaite, Albert E.	1	1890–1905	Browne, Curtis N.	3	1916–1918
Brand, Byron A.	Hd	1926–1927	Brownell, Lincoln C.	1	1938–
Breckenridge, Benj. J.	1	1903–1907	Browning, Wm. H.	1	1889–1894
Breckenridge, John C.	1	1897–1899	Bruce, John M.	1	1897–1899
Breed, Nathaniel P.	3	1932–1936	Bruce, Thomas M.	3	1918–1918
Breen, John Taylor	2-4	1918–1919	Brune, Percy J., Jr.	2	1933–1937
Brennan, Peter J.	3	1934–1937	Bryan, Chas. S.	1-Md	1891–1898
Brenner, Edward C.	Med	1918–1920	Bryant, Frederick B.	3	1934–1937
Brereton, Randel	1	1931–1934	Bryce, Peter Cooper	2	1914–1917
Brett, George P.	4	1913–1917	Buck, Gordon M.	3	1899–1906
Breul, Harold G.	1	1921–1921	Budd, Ogden D., Jr.	3	1916–1917
Brewer, Talbot M.	MG	1916–1917	Buechner, Robert	3	1925–1928
Brewster, Robert S.	3	1899–1900	Buffen, David B.	4	1915–1916
Brewster, Wm. Macy	4	1911–1912	Buffin, Leopold L.	3	1930–1932
Bridgman, John C.	1	1937–1937	Bulkley, Francis	3	1933–1936
Bridgman, Oliver B.*	1-Fld	1889–1913	Bulkley, Henry Duncan	3-4	1903–1909
Briggs, Wm. W.	2	1924–1926	Bull, David C.	Med	1916–1917
Brigham, Arthur D.	2	1922–1926	Bullard, Charles K.	1	1934–
Brigham, Frank H.	1	1922–1925	Bullock, Hugh	2	1922–1923
Brinckerhoff, Elbert A.	1-3	1897–1920	Burbank, Walter W.	2	1938–
Brinkerhoff, Elbert V.	2-Hd	1921–1923	Burchard, Russell D.	3	1918–1919
Brinsmade, Charles Lyman	1-3	1895–1917	Burdick, Walter G.	2	1928–1930
Brinsmade, Paul S.	4	1914–1917	Burke, Edmund, Jr.	2	1929–1932
Brinton, Bradford	1	1911–1912	Burke, Frank G., 3rd	3	1937–
Britton, Henry B.*	Med-4	1902–1908	Burke, Gerard A.	2	1933–1937
Brock, Henry J.	3	1935–	Burke, Stanley W., Jr.	3	1938–
Broderick, John R.	Hd	1924–1926	Burke, Thomas C.	3	1925–1932
Bromfield, Arthur W.	1	1938–	Burke, Walter A., Jr.	3	1930–1932
Bromley, Bruce D.	1	1921–1924	Burleigh, George N.	3	1928–
Bronson, Tyler C.*	MG-4	1916–1917	Burlingame, Frederic A.	2	1900–1903
Brookfield, Frank	2	1898–1900	Burlingame, Wm. R.	4	1915–1916
Brookfield, Frank M.	2	1936–1938	Burnap, Clement*	MG-4	1912–1917
Brookfield, Henry M., Jr.	2	1935–	Burns, Arthur S.	1	1926–1927
Brookfield, James H.*	2	1895–1901	Burns, Robert	3	1911–1916
Brookfield, William L.	2	1930–1937	Burr, Winthrop, Jr.	1-2	1919–1921
Brookmire, S. Kennard	3	1925–1928	Burr, Winthrop, Jr.	2	1920–1921
Brooks, Charles A.	1	1914–1916	Burrell, John S.	1	1924–1925
Brooks, George B.	1	1915–1917	Burrell, Norman Macleon*	1	1904–1909
Brooks, Harold W.	1	1910–1911	Burrow, Alan G.	1	1930–1932
Brooks, Sidney	1	1926–1929	Burrows, John B.	3-Hd	1922–1926
Broome, Leslie H.	3	1918–1919	Burton, Crawford	2-3	1908–1916
Broun, Edmund F.	3	1935–1938	Burton, David C.	3	1934–1938

SQUADRON A

Name	Troop or Detachment Served	Date of Enlistment and Final Discharge
Burton, Ernest B.	3	1929–1930
Burton, Frank V.	3	1916–1917
Burton, Van Duzer*	3	1916–1917
Busby, Archibald H., Jr.	2	1933–1936
Bush, Donald F., Jr.	2	1924–1927
Bush, Robert Wilder*	3	1896–1916
Bushman, Stratford St. J.*	3	1916–1917
Butler, Chas. S.	1	1903–1918
Butler, Chas. T.	Med	1912–1916
Butler, George P., 3rd	3	1939–
Butler, Howard G.*	1	1889–1890
Butler, John F.	2	1936–
Butler, Jonathan F.	1	1928–1931
Butler, Walter K.	4	1911–1914
Butler, William M., 2nd	2	1937–1937
Byers, John C.	3	1927–1928
Byrne, Gerald J.	2	1919–1919
Cable, Wm. A.*	1	1889–1890
Cadley, William L.	2	1935–
Caesar, Chas. T.	4	1911–1915
Cahill, E. Hamilton	1	1889–1890
Cahill, John T.	2	1929–1932
Cairns, Douglas W.	3	1915–1917
Cairns, Robert E.	3	1921–1921
Caldecott, Edward D.	2	1925–1925
Caldwell, James H.	2	1895–1897
Calhoun, Charles D.	2	1937–1938
Callahan, Edward P.	3	1916–1917
Callaway, Llewellyn L., Jr.	1	1935–1935
Callaway, Wm. C.	1	1931–1932
Calver, William C.	Hd	1925–1925
Cameron, Alexander		1917–1919
Cameron, Alexander, 3rd	3	1933–1934
Cameron, Arnold G., Jr.	1	1934–1934
Cameron, Gerard G.	3	1934–1937
Cammann, Robert L.	2	1934–1938
Cammann, Wm. C.*	1	1892–1902
Camp, Stuart B.*	3	1902–1907
Campbell, Bruce	1	1931–1934
Campbell, Frederick Barber*	2	1894–1906
Campbell, Harold C. K.	2	1931–1935
Campbell, Henry G., Jr.	1	1898–1900
Camprubi, Augustus A.	3	1916–1917
Candee, Mark C.	1	1930–1932
Candee, Walter M.	MG	1917–1919
Cannon, Chas. M., Jr.	1	1923–1927
Cannon, Charles W.	1-2	1917–1920
Cannon, Henry B.	3	1896–1901
Cannon, Townsend L.	1	1922–1933
Card, Thomas B.	1	1927–1927
Carley, Harry G.*	1	1921–1922
Carmalt, Churchill	3	1924–1926
Carnochan, Gouverneur M.	3-Hd	1921–1923
Carpenter, George W.	3	1907–1913
Carpenter, James J.	2	1920–1926
Carpenter, Richard V.	2	1928–1931
Carr, Joseph P.	3	1921–1921
Carraher, Wallace J.	2	1917–1919
Carrington, John B., Jr.	1	1924–1924
Carroll, Edgar H.	3	1916–1917
Carroll, George Thomas, Jr.	2	1917–1919
Carse, David B., Jr.	Hd	1926–1929
Carson, Donald A.	3	1924–1925
Carson, Joseph	1	1895–1900
Carson, William M., Jr.	4	1914–1917
Carter, David G.	1	1927–1927
Carter, Harry S.	1	1938–
Carter, Herbert P.	2	1931–1934
Carter, Russell J.	4	1916–1917
Carusi, Charles F.*	2	1897–1899
Carvalho, David N.	1	1935–1938
Carvalho, John B.	1	1932–1936
Carver, Richard M.	2-Hd	1920–1925
Cary, Edward M.	3	1897–1919
Case, Clifford P.	2	1927–1929
Case, John D.	1	1936–
Cash, Edwin C.	1	1918–1919
Cassebaum, William H.	Med	1935–1938
Castle, Frederick W.	1	1934–1934
Castle, Karrick M.	4	1916–1917
Caswell, Dwight W.	2	1934–1937
Catlin, Randolph	1	1912–1915
Catoggio, Vincent A., Jr.	1	1929–1934
Cattus, Fenelon C.*	1	1891–1897
Cattus, John C.	3	1917–1917
Cattus, John V. A.	1	1894–1919
Causse, Andrew L., Jr.	3	1913–1914
Ceballos, Juan M.	MG-3	1916–1921
Ceccarelli, Frank E.	2-Hd-2	1925–1930
Chadbourne, William M.	3	1909–1914
Chadwick, George B.	2	1918–1918
Chaffee, Thomas K., Jr.	2	1939–
Chamberlain, Julian I.	1	1898–1900
Chamberlain, Robert Linton, Jr.	4	1917–1919
Chambers, Durno		1917–1919
Chambers, Walter B.	3	1898–1919
Chambers, Walter F.	3	1923–1925
Chandler, Sumner C.*	1	1890–1893
Chapin, Edwin K.	1	1936–1937
Chapin, L. H. Paul*	3	1916–1917
Chapin, Wm. B., Jr.	3	1930–1934
Chapman, Daniel K.	2	1926–1928
Chapman, Henry G.	3	1911–1914
Chapman, John D.*	1	1898–1899
Chapman, John S.	3	1921–1932
Chapman, Page	1	1901–1902
Charles, Alfred C.	2	1901–1914
Charles, Jas. M.	1	1901–1907
Chase, Kenneth F.	3	1930–1931
Chatfield, Sherwood C.	1	1930–1934
Chauncey, A. Wallace	MG	1915–1917
Chauncey, Raymond	3	1915–1917
Chesebrough, Frederic W.	1	1889–1918
Chester, Colby M., Jr.	1	1899–1900
Chew, Philip F.	3	1913–1916
Childs, Andrew L.	Hd	1923–1925
Childs, Herbert H.	3-Hd	1898–1914
Chisholm, Richard S.*	2	1898–1901
Chittenden, George P.	1	1901–1903

SQUADRON A

Name	Troop or Detachment Served	Date of Enlistment and Final Discharge
Choate, Edward A.	2-3	1899–1906
Choate, Stuart K.	3-4-3	1905–1910
Chrystal, Charles H.	1	1918–1920
Chrystie, Thos. W.	3	1925–1928
Church, Theodore W.*	2	1895–1897
Churchill, Lester B.*	1	1895–1898
Claiborne, J. Herbert*	1	1891–1896
Claiborne, John H.	2	1929–1932
Claiborne, John T.	1	1923–1927
Clapp, Charles E., Jr.	1	1920–1923
Clapp, Herbert M.	1-Hd	1920–1927
Clapp, Parmly Scofield, Jr.	1	1917–1919
Clare, Norbert H.	1	1930–1935
Clare, Wm. F., Jr.	1	1930–
Clarey, Louis Hanwalt		1917–1919
Clark, Arthur L.	1	1933–
Clark, David Hatfield	1	1911–1917
Clark, Harold Benjamin	1	1902–1913
Clark, Henry B.	1	1918–1920
Clark, Henry B., Jr.	3	1932–1933
Clark, Hovey C., 2nd	2	1929–1932
Clark, Howard F.	1	1891–1896
Clark, Howard G.	3	1925–1929
Clark, James G., Jr.*	1	1895–1901
Clark, John H., Jr.	1	1925–1926
Clark, Patrick H.	3	1924–1927
Clark, Peter B.	3	1928–1929
Clark, Robert A.	3	1939–
Clark, Robert V.	3	1936–1938
Clark, Walter D.	1	1891–1897
Clark, Warren	3	1925–1926
Clark, William A.	Med	1923–1925
Clark, William N.	2	1923–1926
Clarke, David W.	3	1936–1936
Clarke, Dumont, Jr.	2	1936–
Clarke, Jack W.	3	1937–1937
Clarke, Thomas B., Jr.	1-2-Hd	1901–1915
Clausen, Edgar Y.	1-3	1905–1920
Clausen, George U.	1	1899–1900
Clayton, Chas. E.*	Vet	1924–1930
Cleland, Jas. W. S.*	1	1889–1898
Clement, Roger C.	2-Hd	1920–1927
Clement, Roger C.	Hd	1924–1927
Clerke, Alexander G.*	1	1889–1891
Cless, Wm. E., Jr.	1	1929–1933
Cleveland, Clement, Jr.	3	1901–1906
Clifford, Kenneth P.	1	1933–1935
Clift, Robert J.	3	1939–
Clohesy, John J.	1	1926–1929
Clohesy, Patrick	2	1926–1927
Cloutman, Harold J.	Hd	1922–1923
Cobb, Andrew L.	Hd	1924–1927
Cobb, Clement B. P.	Med	1927–1928
Cobb, Francis C.	2	1921–1922
Coburn, Frank H.	Hd	1925–1928
Cochran, Alexander*	3	1896–1899
Cochran, Edmond W.		1917–1919
Coddington, Clifford	1	1936–
Coddington, Dave H.	3	1908–1916
Coe, Colles J.	2	1915–1922
Coffin, John R.	1	1921–1922
Coghlan, Guede	2	1920–1928
Cohan, John W.	3	1924–1933
Colbron, Paul T.	2	1902–1903
Colburn, Harry	4-1	1916–1925
Colby, Bainbridge	1	1894–1895
Colby, Everett	3	1899–1902
Colby, Francis Thompson	2	1911–1913
Colby, W. Colgate*	1-Hd	1889–1899
Cole, M. Douglas	4	1910–1918
Cole, Newcomb D.	2	1935–
Coleman, Chas. W.	2	1900–1918
Coles, Henry R. R.	3	1896–1902
Colgate, Austin*	1	1889–1899
Colgate, Craig	1	1899–1904
Colgate, Gilbert, Jr.	3	1924–1927
Colgate, Robert B.	3	1927–1927
Colgate, Sidney M.	1	1890–1891
Coll, Walter B.	2	1931–1932
Collier, Leo	1-4	1912–1917
Collier, Miles	3	1938–
Collingwood, Ludlow K.	2	1938–
Collins, Bradley	2	1936–1937
Collins, Herbert C.	2	1925–1926
Collins, Kenneth Benedict	2	1908–1910
Colt, Harris D.	1	1893–1897
Colt, Zenas C.	3	1931–1934
Colton, John	1	1916–1917
Colton, William R.	4	1909–1911
Colvin, Harold R.	3	1938–
Colyer, Chas. M.	2	1922–1924
Comfort, George V.	3	1939–
Comstock, David C.	1	1920–1923
Comstock, George C., Jr.	2	1925–
Conduit, Wentworth S.	2	1896–1897
Congdon, John Hopkins, Jr.	1	1911–1911
Conger, Frederic	MG	1916–1917
Conklin, William R.	1	1934–1937
Connell, Carleton A.	2	1916–1917
Conner, Lewis A.	3	1896–1899
Connolley, Robert E.	Hd-2	1923–1925
Connolly, Patrick	2	1925–1925
Connor, Alonzo G.	1	1930–1931
Connor, Frank H.	1	1929–1932
Connor, James Roswell	3	1917–1919
Connors, Michael	2	1935–
Connors, Philip	3	1924–1927
Conrad, W. Davis*	3	1910–1917
Conrow, Robert W.*	2	1898–1908
Conroy, Eugene J.	3	1929–1935
Consorty, Murrell H.	A	1917–1919
Coogan, Henry P.	2	1937–1938
Coogan, William G., Jr.	1	1938–
Cook, Charles K.	3	1919–1919
Cook, Harry	2	1915–1915
Cook, Howard A.	2	1939–
Cook, John Alden	4	1914–1917
Cook, Joseph Fahys	2	1908–1919
Cook, Richard K.	2-1	1918–1929
Cooke, Carleton S.	4	1910–1930

SQUADRON A

Name	Troop or Detachment Served	Date of Enlistment and Final Discharge
Cooke, Crispin	2	1933–1935
Cooke, Frederick W., Jr.	4	1912–1914
Cooke, Goodwin	2	1926–1931
Cooke, Thomas F.	4	1912–1914
Coolidge, George P.	3	1917–1919
Coombe, Reginald G.	3	1920–1921
Cooper, Dudley M.	4	1908–1917
Cooper, John A.*	Hd	1928–1929
Cooper, John L.	2	1937–
Cooper, John M.*	1	1889–1890
Corbin, Corbin	1	1922–1924
Corlies, Arthur	1	1897–1907
Corlies, Howard	1	1908–1912
Corning, Arthur W.	1	1889–1900
Cornwall, Leon H.	MG	1915–1917
Corrigan, Wm. B.	2	1924–1935
Corthell, Howard C.	1	1917–1918
Cosby, Arthur F.	3	1898–1898
Costello, Ambrose	3	1927–1929
Cotter, Arundel	2	1918–1929
Cotton, Hugh D.	4	1914–1917
Cotton, John M.	3	1932–1935
Cottrell, Arthur M., Jr.	3	1929–1931
Couch, Clifford D., Jr.	1	1924–1925
Coudert, Frederic R., Jr.	1-2	1889–1899
Coulson, Robert E.	4	1915–1917
Coventry, LeRoy	3	1918–1920
Cowdin, John Cheever	2	1908–1909
Cowdin, Winthrop	1	1892–1897
Cowl, Donald Hearn	1	1913–1914
Cowles, Wm. H. F.	4	1921–1921
Cowperthwaite, H. M.*	1	1896–1917
Cox, Duncan B.	1	1928–1931
Cox, Edward V.	1-2	1897–1899
Cox, Edward V., Jr.	1	1936–
Cox, John L.	1	1934–1936
Cox, Rowland, Jr.	2	1897–1900
Coxe, Davis*	1	1891–1892
Coxe, Gerald M.	2	1925–1933
Coyne, George W.*	1	1898–1899
Cragin, Franklin P.	3	1916–1917
Craig, Allen*	1	1918–1919
Craighead, Robert	1	1899–1901
Craigmyle, Ronald M.	1	1926–1929
Cralle, Jefferson B.	3	1926–1927
Cram, Ambrose L., Jr.	1	1936–
Cram, H. Warren	2	1898–1911
Cram, Jacob	1	1889–1890
Cramp, Walter M.	1	1929–1932
Crane, Percy W.	3	1900–1902
Crane, Theodore	2	1906–1919
Cravath, Philip S.	MG	1916–1917
Craven, Thos. J., 2nd	3-Hd-3	1923–1928
Crawford, William, Jr.	2	1929–1931
Crawley, George Edwin	MG	1914–1914
Creel, Robert C.	1	1939–
Creevey, Kennedy	Med	1928–1931
Crenshaw, Richard P., Jr.	3	1931–1935
Crim, Wm. D.	2	1921–1927
Crimmins, Clarence P.*	2	1916–1916
Crimmins, Thomas	2	1900–1907
Crocker, George A., Jr.	2-3	1903–1917
Croll, Joseph D.	3	1926–1930
Crombie, W. Murray	1	1898–1899
Cromwell, Seymour LeG.*	1	1893–1898
Cross, Benjamin F.	1	1890–1895
Cross, Jeremiah F.	3	1925–1934
Cross, William R.	3	1897–1898
Crothers, Joseph	MG	1916–1917
Crouse, David Stowe	MG	1916–1917
Crowe, Philip K.	1	1930–1933
Crowe, Richard H.	1	1932–1933
Crowell, Wm. B.	1	1898–1899
Crowley, John C.	1	1919–1920
Cruger, Frederic H.	2	1916–1916
Cubberly, Oliver W.	1	1918–1919
Culman, Carl W.	4	1914–1916
Cumings, John B.*	2	1920–1922
Cunningham, Edward J.	2	1930–1930
Cunningham, Francis deL.	1	1923–1928
Cunningham, Frank L.	2	1915–1917
Cunningham, Peter	1	1922–1923
Currens, Turner F.	2	1918–1919
Curry, Edgar H.	3	1932–1936
Curtin, Ernest W.	3	1925–1931
Curtis, Brian C.	1	1921–1923
Curtis, Chas. B., Jr.	1	1901–1907
Curtis, Charles C.	2	1921–1921
Curtis, Dean	Med	1934–1937
Curtis, Edward	1	1919–1919
Curtis, George L.	1	1918–1920
Curtis, Herbert P.	2	1928–1929
Curtis, John J.	3-Hd	1921–1923
Curtis, Ronald Eliot	2-4	1904–1917
Cushing, Harry C., 3rd	1	1915–1917
Cushman, Charles V. B.	2	1933–1936
Cushman, James P.	2	1933–1934
Cushman, Paul	3	1913–1916
Cushman, Victor N.*	2	1898–1898
Cuthell, Robert C.	3	1938–
Cutler, Robert F.	2	1922–1925
Cutler, Wm. Frye	2	1911–1917
Daggett, Stanley P.	1-Hd	1923–1925
Dailey, Clarke G.	3	1917–1921
Dailey, Gibson F.	3	1934–1938
Dain, James McL.	2	1913–1913
Dale, Robert G.*	MG	1912–1916
Dall, Charles W., Jr.	2	1939–
Dall, Curtis B.	3	1922–1925
Dallett, John	Hd-2	1923–1924
Dalton, Alexander S.	1	1923–1928
Dalton, Franklin W.	1	1927–1927
Dalton, John B.	2	1918–1920
Daly, Gerald H.	3	1916–1917
Daly, Raymond J.*	1	1924–1927
Damerel, George S.	3	1936–
Dana, Alfred L.	2	1916–1917
Dana, Charles A.	2-3	1903–1913
Dane, John R.	3	1925–1927

SQUADRON A

Name	Troop or Detachment Served	Date of Enlistment and Final Discharge	Name	Troop or Detachment Served	Date of Enlistment and Final Discharge
Danforth, Charles E.	3	1915–1917	Delehanty, John Bradley	1	1916–1917
Danforth, Francis J.	3	1904–1914	Delehanty, Thornton	1	1916–1917
Danforth, Nicholas	3	1909–1918	Delmonica, Lorenzo Crist		1917–1919
Danforth, Nicholas W.	3	1930–1933	de Muralt, Carl Leonard	2–4	1905–1907
Danzig, Samuel V. H.	2	1916–1917	Dennis, George F.	Hd	1924–1925
Darling, William L.	1	1933–1933	Dennis, Rodney G.	3	1921–1927
Darlington, Clinton P.	1	1915–1917	Denny, Cary F.	MG	1916–1917
Darmstadt, Louis J.	2	1928–1938	Denny, Robert C.	3	1930–1933
Darneille, Bladen J.	2	1927–1931	Denny, Thomas, Jr.	3	1925–1927
Darrach, James McA.*	3	1896–1902	De Persia, George	1	1933–
Darrell, George H.	3	1930–1933	Depew, John D.	3	1923–1926
Darrin, Howard A.	1	1922–1923	de Peyster, Frederic A.	1	1934–1938
Dasey, Robert W.	4	1916–1917	de Rham, William	Hd-2	1923–1926
d'Assern, Joseph M.	2	1935–1936	Derrick, Robert O.	MG	1915–1917
Davenport, Frederick M., Jr.	2	1925–1928	Desmond, William H.		1917–1920
Davidson, James E., Jr.	1	1932–1933	Despard, Clement L.	2	1908–1914
Davies, Julian T., Jr.*	1–3	1894–1899	d'Este, Julian Locke	1	1914–1918
Davis, Clinton W., Jr.	2	1937–	Detmer, Jerome V.	Hd	1926–1929
Davis, Gerald	3	1935–1938	Deuel, Harold E.	1	1924–1925
Davis, Horace W.	Hd-3	1923–1926	Devereau, Alvin	3	1915–1917
Davis, John	Hd-1	1923–1927	Devereux, Frederick L., Jr.	1	1936–
Davis, Marvin B.	2	1935–1936	Devereux, Walter B.	1	1934–
Davis, Philip D.	Hd-1	1923–1924	DeVoe, Raymond F.	Hd-1-Med	1921–1923
Davis, Robert J.	Hd	1921–1922	Dibelius, George G.	2	1919–1920
Davis, W. Shippen	4–3	1913–1923	Dick, Fairman R.	3	1908–1914
Davis, Wendell	2	1924–1928	Dickerman, George W.*	1	1889–1891
Davison, George Howard	Vet-Staff	1898–1914	Dickinson, Andrew G.*	1-Hd	1895–1917
Davison, William B.	1	1927–1928	Dickson, Charles L.	1	1928–1932
Day, Arthur M.	1	1897–1897	Dickson, Henry H.*	2	1930–1933
Day, Harry V.	3	1896–1901	Diefendorf, Warren Edwin	1	1917–1919
Day, Henry Mason, Jr.	1	1907–1917	Dielman, Frederick M.	4	1916–1917
Day, Irvin W.	MG	1912–1916	Dillingham, Shepard	4-Hd	1908–1913
Day, Lee Garnet	2	1915–1917	Dillon, Daniel C., Jr.	1	1938–
Day, Sherman	3	1896–1901	Dillon, Frank J.	1	1928–1931
Day, Thomas Mills, 3rd		1917–1918	Dinkey, Alva C.	1	1922–1923
Dazey, Francis M. H.	1	1916–1917	Disorow, Samuel C.	2-Hd	1921–1921
Dealy, Edmund D.*	1	1889–1917	Ditman, Henry W.*	3	1898–1909
Dean, Arthur H.	1	1925–1926	Dix, John A.	2	1902–1907
Dean, Henry F., Jr.	Med	1924–1928	Dixon, Alphonse Arthur		1917–1919
Dearborn, Eustis	2	1938–	Dixon, Walter E.	2	1920–1924
DeBaun, Melville F.	3	1930–1934	Dodd, Edward H., Jr.	3	1930–1933
Debevoise, Eli W.	1	1927–1929	Dodge, Cleveland E.	4	1916–1917
Debevoise, Paul	1	1907–1917	Dodge, Frank T.	1	1906–1906
Debevoise, Robert L.	1	1930–1936	Dodge, Harry E.*	3	1912–1917
DeBevoise, William Edwin		1917–1919	Doherty, Lignon A.	4	1909–1911
deClairville, Raymond	1	1933–1937	Doherty, Vincent M.	4	1917–1919
de Farro, Dimitrie Jean	3	1896–1897	Dominick, Everit	2	1907–1912
DeGarmendia, de Cordova	4	1907–1908	Dominick, Lamont	1	1896–1901
DeGarmendia, Martin J.*	1	1889–1893	Dommerich, Alex L., Jr.	3	1932–1935
DeGarmendia, Spaulding B.	2	1895–1897	Donahue, Marvel B.	Hd	1922–1922
deHaven, Walter T.	3	1928–1932	Donald, Norman H.	3	1906–1913
DeHaven, William B.	3	1915–1921	Donald, Remsen D.	2	1937–
Dehls, Frederick	1	1918–1918	Donald, Wm. H.	3	1906–1909
DeKay, Adrian	3	1916–1917	Donaldson, Chase	2–3	1927–1931
DeKay, William W.	3	1904–1905	Donnelly, Patrick	3	1923–1923
Delafield, Edward H.	2	1902–1904	Donnelly, Peter	1	1923–1924
Delafield, Fred S.	1	1889–1892	Donohoe, Bernard	2	1923–1923
Delamater, Charles H., Jr.	2	1930–1938	Donovan, Richard J.	1	1918–1919
Delamater, Roswell A.*	3	1916–1917	Doolittle, Julius T. A.	2	1916–1917
Delaney, Edmund T.	1	1937–	Dorr, Goldthwaite H., 2nd	2	1922–1925

SQUADRON A

Name	Troop or Detachment Served	Date of Enlistment and Final Discharge	Name	Troop or Detachment Served	Date of Enlistment and Final Discharge
Dorr, Russell H.	3	1930–1933	Durham, Chas. H., Jr.	1	1927–1930
Dorr, Stephen H., Jr.*	MG	1916–1917	Durham, Knowlton	MG	1912–1924
Dossert, Francis	1	1916–1917	Durham, Robert C.	2	1938–1938
Doubleday, James M.	1	1930–1933	Duryea, Frank W.	2	1896–1906
Doudge, Barton T.*	3	1902–1917	Duryea, Wright	MG	1915–1917
Dougan, Wolston C.	2	1934–1937	Duval, George H.	3	1912–1914
Dougherty, James G.	Hd-2	1927–1930	Dwight, Richard E.	3	1898–1898
Doughtey, James W.	3	1918–1918	Dwyer, Geoffrey J.	4	1912–1913
Douglas, F. Kenneth	3	1915–1917	Dyckman, Stewart	3	1937–
Douglas, H. Percy	1	1896–1900	Dyer, George J.	1	1901–1907
Downer, Halsey S.	3	1937–	Dyer, Lyman T.	3	1896–1905
Downer, John T.	3	1938–			
Downey, Edward A.*	2	1904–1908	Eakin, Alexander	2	1912–1916
Downey, Harold L.	2	1913–1919	Earl, Melvin P.	1	1938–
Downing, Augustus C., Jr.	4	1914–1917	Earle, Henry M.	1	1899–1905
Doyle, Edward J.	Hd	1924–1926	Early, Ernest R.	3	1918–1919
Doyle, Francis R.*	1	1929–1930	Eastman, Albert G.	Hd	1925–1929
Doyle, Milton D.	2	1922–1922	Eastman, Henry H.	Hd	1927–1929
Drabble, Philip Marion*		1917–1918	Eastman, Thomas Collyer	1	1910–1917
Drake, Joseph P.	1	1899–1906	Eastmond, Theodore L.	1	1931–
Drake, Wm. Wilson	3	1897–1899	Easton, William R.	3	1934–1935
Draper, Thayer P.	1	1938–	Eaton, Henry B., 2nd	3	1929–1932
Dreier, Harry E.	1	1899–1919	Eaton, Walter B.	3	1913–1917
Dresser, Evans C.	3	1923–1925	Eberstadt, Ferdinand	3	1916–1917
Dressler, Fritz L.	2	1916–1917	Eccleston, John B., Jr.		1917–1919
Drewry, Henry H.	3	1939–	Eckelberry, Niel E.	Med	1932–1935
Drexel, Anthony J., Jr.	2	1917–1921	Ecker, Frederic W.	1	1921–1922
Dreyer, Walter E.	3	1939–	Eckert, Augustus F.		1917–1919
Driscoll, Robert	2	1916–1917	Eckert, Avery P.*	1	1889–1890
Drisler, William A., Jr.	1	1937–	Eckert, Wm. Stanley	1	1889–1890
Driver, Robert B.	2	1924–1925	Eden, John Herman, Jr.	2	1913–1916
Drowne, H. Russell, Jr.	3	1921–1933	Edey, Alfred W.*	3	1901–1906
Duane, Richard B.	MG	1912–1917	Edey, Wm. S.*	1	1889–1894
DuBarry, Frank D.	3	1933–1936	Edson, Franklin, 3rd	2	1929–1930
DuBois, Delafield	MG	1907–1913	Edson, Roger C.	2	1929–1932
DuBois, Floyd R.	1	1902–1903	Edwards, Chas. W.	2	1900–1902
DuBois, Henry D.*	4	1915–1917	Edwards, James Alex.	1	1909–1917
DuBois, John D.	2	1927–1930	Edwards, Wm. H. L.*	2	1897–1909
Dudensing, Richard, 3rd	1	1933–1936	Effinger, William E.	MG-Hq	1916–1931
Duell, Charles H.	3	1929–1932	Egan, John T.	2	1918–1919
Duer, Beverly	2	1924–1926	Eginton, John W., Jr.	4-MG	1910–1917
Duer, Edward R., Jr.	3	1934–1938	Egleston, Nathaniel H.	1-4-Hd	1907–1932
Duer, Edward Rush	3	1899–1917	Ehrgott, Winston W.	2-3	1918–
Duer, Pennington	3	1935–	Eiser, Anthony C.	1	1924–1926
Duffie, Archibald B.	1-Hd	1889–1898	Elder, George R., Jr.	2	1916–1917
Duffy, Frank J.	2	1919–1921	Eldridge, Wm. M. T.	1	1889–1894
Duffy, William L.	3	1938–	Eliot, Douglas F. G.	4	1915–1917
Dufort, Arthur D.	3	1928–1929	Ellard, Chester Baird	2	1917–1919
Dugdale, Henry S.	3	1921–1926	Elliman, Arthur B.	4-G-D	1911–1919
Dun, Douglass Robert G.	3	1899–1906	Ellinger, Carlton D.	2	1918–1921
Duncan, Samuel A.	2	1922–1924	Elliot, Robert, Jr.	3	1924–1926
Duncombe, Herbert, Jr.	3	1922–1928	Elliott, Henry W.	3	1918–1919
Dunham, William P.	3	1938–	Elliott, Howard, Jr.	3	1923–1925
Dunlaevy, James B., Jr.	1	1923–1926	Elliott, John	3	1912–1917
Dunn, Charles B.	1	1924–1926	Ellis, Edward P.	1	1916–1917
Dunn, George	2	1924–1924	Ellis, Frank W.*		1917–1919
Dunn, Rogers C.	1	1921–1922	Ellis, George C.	Hq-2	1923–1925
Dunn, Theodore B.	Med	1929–1930	Ellis, Ronald, Jr.	1	1921–1922
Dunne, Edward	2	1916–1917	Ellsworth, Richard Robinson		1917–1919
Dunning, Archibald R.	2	1931–1933	Elmer, Clarence J.	1	1927–1929

SQUADRON A

Name	Troop or Detachment Served	Date of Enlistment and Final Discharge
Elmer, Robert F.	3	1898–1918
Elsworth, Bradford	1	1916–1917
Elwes, Frederick P., Jr.	2	1924–1927
Ely, Albert H., Jr.	1	1922–1925
Ely, Alfred, Jr.	4	1908–1914
Ely, David J.	2	1911–1915
Ely, Edward Chappell	1	1906–1914
Ely, Horace G.	4	1907–1910
Emerson, Milton K.	3	1927–1927
Emerson, Willard I.	1	1921–1927
Emison, James W.	3	1925–1926
Emmet, Christopher Temple	3	1899–1900
Emmet, Robert	1-2	1894–1899
Emmet, Thomas A., Jr.	2	1898–1899
Emmons, Alfred P.	1	1892–1893
Emmons, Kintzing B.	1	1924–1925
Enos, Alanson Trask	2	1912–1915
Erdman, Seward	Med	1918–1918
Erickson, Julius H.	1	1925–1926
Erskine, Ralph C., Jr.	3	1939–
Ervesun, Placide A.	3	1930–1935
Erving, John L.*	1-3-1	1895–1899
Esquerre, Henri P.	3	1939–
Ethridge, James M., Jr.	MG	1916–1917
Evans, Gordon K.	1	1929–1932
Evans, Wm. W.*	4	1909–1914
Evarts, Prescott, 2nd	1	1922–1925
Everest, Edward	1	1891–1894
Everett, Arthur R.	Med	1938–
Everett, Torrey	1	1894–1896
Everett, Chas. R.	2	1925–1926
Everitt, Robert H.	1	1935–1935
Evins, Samuel H.	2	1897–1900
Ewall, Robert Hall	2	1911–1916
Ewing, J. G. Blaine	3	1905–1908
Ewing, James G. B., Jr.	3	1933–1934
Eyer, George A., Jr.	3	1938–
Eypper, Norman Kohler		1917–1919
Eyre, Francis B., Jr.	4	1915–1917
Fackler, David E.	2	1939–
Fahy, Charles H.	3	1922–1926
Fahys, George E.	2-Hd	1898–1910
Fahys, George E., Jr.	2	1914–1916
Fahys, Joseph*	2-3	1920–1928
Fairbanks, Thomas N., Jr.	2	1938–
Fairchild, Benjamin T.	1	1912–1915
Fairchild, Frederick T.	3	1927–1928
Fairhurst, Henry D.	2	1925–1926
Fanning, Neuville O.	1-2	1920–1921
Fanning, William L.	3	1917–1929
Fansler, Henry D.	2	1921–1922
Fargo, J. Stanley	3	1910–1911
Fargo, James C.	3	1909–1920
Fargo, William Preston	3	1908–1912
Farish, Wm. W., Jr.	1	1928–1930
Farnham, Ward Wellington	2	1917–1919
Farnsworth, Robert P.	3	1927–1929
Farr, James McC.	3	1921–1923
Farrelly, Chas. Clifford	3	1920–1931
Farrelly, Gerald J.	3	1927–
Farrelly, T. Charles*	3	1918–1921
Farrelly, Theo. Slevin	1-A	1908–1919
Farren, Charles*	3	1920–1921
Farwell, Grosvenor	1	1912–1915
Faulkner-O'Brien, Wm. H.	2	1928–1932
Faxon, Herbert W.	2	1938–
Faxon, William O., 2nd	2	1936–
Fay, Henry W.	2	1897–1904
Fayerweather, Chas. S.	4	1911–1914
Feeny, John Lewis*	1	1913–1917
Feitner, Quentin F.*	3	1907–1910
Fennelly, Leo C.	3	1923–1923
Fenner, Ward	3	1927–1930
Fennessy, Edward H.	2	1900–1907
Feraro, Demetre Jeaude	3	1896–1897
Ferris, Morris D., Jr.	2	1937–
Ferry, Ronald M.	Med	1913–1917
Fesser, Edward	1	1891–1892
Ficken, H. Edwards*	1-2-Hd	1889–1900
Fiedler, Robert H.	1	1924–1931
Field, Edward P.	2	1917–1917
Field, James B.	3	1931–1933
Field, Spencer Albert		1917–1919
Field, William B. O.	1	1899–1904
Field, William H.	1	1915–1917
Field, William H.	2	1931–1931
Fiero, Raymond R.	2	1926–1929
Fine, John*	3	1915–1917
Finker, Edward L.	1	1901–1903
Finlay, George D., Jr.	MG	1916–1917
Fish, Albert R.	3	1898–1898
Fish, Rutgers	2	1917–1919
Fish, Stuyvesant, Jr.	2	1909–1918
Fisher, Boudinot	2	1924–1927
Fisher, Harold P.	3	1918–1920
Fisher, Henry J.	3	1896–1907
Fisher, Horace M., Jr.	1	1926–1926
Fisher, Samuel C.	Hq	1923–1927
Fisher, Schuyler	3-Hq	1921–1922
Fitch, Ashbel P., Jr.	1	1899–1904
Fitzgerald, John	1	1921–1926
Fitzgerald, Philip J.	3-1	1926–1929
Fitz-Gibbon, James E.	Hq	1923–1925
Fitz-Gibbon, Robert E.	Hq-3	1923–1930
Fitz-Gibbon, William	Hq	1924–1925
Fitzhugh, Armistead	3	1927–1927
Flagg, John H.	3	1922–1925
Flahiff, Norman J.	3	1933–1936
Flanagan, John Roberts*	3	1908–1916
Flanagan, Michael J.	1	1927–
Flanigan, Horace Claflin	MG	1916–1916
Flash, Edward S.	3	1914–1919
Fleitmann, Henry T.*	2	1910–1916
Fleming, Alphonse Thomas	2	1917–1919
Fleming, Matthew C.	1	1900–1903
Fleming, Wallace	3	1924–1926
Fleming, William C.	2	1922–1922
Fletcher, George A.	3	1934–1935
Flintom, Lathrop B.	2	1931–1936

SQUADRON A

Name	Troop or Detachment Served	Date of Enlistment and Final Discharge
Floete, Franklin T.	1	1926–1931
Flower, Nathan M.*	1	1897–1898
Floyd, Frederic W.	1	1889–1892
Floyd, Nicoll, 2nd	2	1917–1922
Floyd-Jones, Edw. H.*	1	1895–1897
Flynn, Chas. E.	2	1918–1921
Flynn, William	2	1924–1925
Foley, Gifford	1	1936–1938
Follmer, Charles J.	3	1937–
Fooshee, Malcolm	2	1926–1929
Foran, Augustus E.	2	1918–1919
Ford, William Arnold	3	1921–1922
Forkner, Claude E.	2	1928–1929
Forman, George Lisle*	MG	1913–1914
Forrester, Robert R., Jr.	2	1931–1934
Forster, Gardner	3	1921–1922
Forster, Henry	3	1913–1916
Forster, Reginald	3	1921–1922
Forsyth, Alfred S.	2	1935–
Forsyth, Arthur K.	2	1920–1928
Forsyth, Russell K.	2	1928–1929
Foster, Allen E.	4	1910–1917
Foster, Russell T.	2	1937–1938
Foster, Stephen M.	1	1924–1925
Foulis, Harold Blair	3	1918–1921
Fountain, Alfred Egbert	1	1907–1915
Fountain, John C.	2	1931–
Fowler, Albro C.	4	1917–1919
Fowler, Anderson	3	1936–1936
Fowler, Arthur A.	3	1900–1906
Fowler, Edmund P., Jr.	3	1933–1937
Fowler, Harold	3	1908–1912
Fowler, John	4	1918–1920
Fowler, Oswald	1	1916–1917
Fowler, Robert H.	Med-2-4-3	1905–1910
Fox, Alan	4	1910–1915
Fox, Alanson G.	1	1902–1917
Fox, Andrew J., Jr.	3	1921–1926
Fox, Edwin T., Jr.	1	1939–
Fox, Noel Bleecker	1	1907–1917
Fox, Rector K.	1	1898–1905
Fox, Rector K., Jr.	2	1927–1930
Fox, Richard T.*	2	1898–1901
Francis, Arthur W.	1-2	1892–1899
Francis, James D.	3	1923–1924
Francis, John C.	2	1938–
Francke, Louis J., Jr.	1	1925–1928
Frank, Charles A., Jr.	2	1929–1934
Franklin, George S.	3	1921–1924
Franklin, Philip A. S., Jr.	3	1922–1924
Franks, Ralph C.	3	1924–1927
Franks, Robert A., Jr.	3	1924–1926
Fraser, Alexander John	4	1910–1916
Frazell, Edgar L.	2	1939–
Frederick, Karl T.	4-Hd	1912–1922
Freedman, Robert	A	1917–1919
Freeman, Edgar W.	1	1915–1917
Freeman, Howard B.	1	1916–1917
Freeman, Leon S.	4	1907–1908
Freeman, Malcolm T.	1	1931–1934
Freeman, Morris de C.	2	1924–1927
Freeman, William G.	Hq-2	1923–1925
Frelinghuysen, J. S.	1-2-3	1894–1902
French, Cedric C.	2	1922–1925
French, Dexter S.	2	1933–1935
French, George F.	2	1923–1925
Freston, Julian M.	3	1922–1924
Frey, Alexander H.	1	1924–1924
Frieder, Charles	MG-4	1916–1917
Froment, Frank L.	2	1931–1936
Froment, Howard H.	2	1935–
Froment, Louis V.*	2	1898–1908
Frost, Albert C., Jr.	3	1923–1926
Frost, Robert B.	Hd	1925–1926
Frothingham, Donald McL.	Hq-3	1923–1925
Frugone, James G.	Hd	1925–1926
Fruin, John Gibson	4	1917–1919
Full, Henry P.*	1	1921–1921
Fuller, Charles	2	1897–1899
Fuller, Duncan McT.	1-Med	1915–1917
Fuller, Fraser C.*	1	1889–1892
Fullerton, Henry S.	1	1898–1900
Fulton, Elisha M., Jr.*	1	1889–1891
Furlong, Garrett	3	1918–1918
Gaffney, James J.	2	1917–1921
Gage, Samuel E.	2	1901–1915
Gaillard, Edward M.	3-Hq	1921–1922
Gaillard, Henry E.	3	1932–1936
Gaines, Harlow D.	Hq	1925–1928
Gaites, Arthur B.	4	1919–1921
Gale, Hollis P.	1	1921–1924
Gale, Marland	1	1929–1932
Gale, William H., Jr.	1	1893–1894
Gallatin, Goelet	3	1900–1911
Gallaway, John M.*	1-3	1895–1907
Gallaway, Merrill W.	1	1895–1895
Galloway, Robert W.	1	1928–1929
Galston, Clarence E.	2	1934–1937
Gammell, Arthur A.	2	1914–1917
Gamwell, W. W.	3	1925–1929
Garber, Lyman A.	1	1931–
Garcia-Guzman, Raoul	1	1934–1936
Gardiner, Robert D. L.	3	1931–1932
Gardner, Frederick H.	3	1939–
Gardner, Joseph F.	1	1925–1925
Gardner, Lawrence T.	3	1923–1924
Gardner, William R.	2	1933–1936
Garrett, Guy	3	1916–1917
Garrick, Herbert F.	2	1929–1932
Garrigan, Louis G.	4	1916–1917
Garrison, Lloyd McKim*	1-2	1894–1900
Garrison, Robert T.*	1	1899–1904
Garrity, Devin A.	2	1930–
Garside, Charles	1	1925–1926
Gates, Arthur B.	1	1919–1921
Gault, Elmer D.	3	1918–1919
Gause, Ralph W.	3	1939–
Gavin, Michael	3	1898–1905
Gawtry, Lewis B.	1-Hd	1891–1898

SQUADRON A

Name	Troop or Detachment Served	Date of Enlistment and Final Discharge
Geer, Alpheus	1	1889–1919
Geer, Langdon*	3	1902–1908
Geer, Marshall*	3	1900–1905
Gerard, Victor B.	1	1937–
Gervais, Arthur J.	2	1935–
Giacchetta, Tony	1	1921–1922
Gibbons, Brainard F.	Hq-2	1923–1925
Gibbons, George B.*	3	1909–1914
Gibbons, George B., Jr.	2	1934–
Gibbs, Frederick C.	3	1924–1925
Gibbs, John E.	2	1924–1925
Gifford, Isaac C.	Hq-1	1921–1923
Gilbert, Chas. P. M.	1	1889–1890
Gilbert, Roger	1	1928–1931
Gilder, Harwood	3	1925–1927
Gilder, Rodman	3	1904–1916
Gildersleeve, Henry A.*	1	1890–1891
Gildersleeve, Raleigh C.	1	1917–1919
Gile, Harold H.	MG	1916–1917
Gilford, Samuel T.*	1	1889–1894
Gilford, Thomas B., Jr.*	1-2-Hd	1889–1900
Gillespie, John T.	3	1899–1904
Gillespie, Louis P.*	1	1897–1901
Gillespie, S. H.	1	1901–1917
Gillette, Curtenius	3	1934–1935
Gillette, Edward H.	1	1927–1928
Gilmer, Frederick	1	1931–1934
Gilmore, Robert W.	1	1916–1917
Gilmour, Milton J.	1	1918–1920
Glenn, Henry L.	1	1928–1931
Glick, Clifford	1-Hq	1921–1922
Glidden, Arthur L.	2	1928–1931
Glogau, William E.	2	1916–1917
Glover, John LeRoy	4	1916–1917
Glynn, Thomas B.	3	1929–1933
Goadby, Arthur	1-2-Md	1890–1900
Goddard, Bronson	1	1930–1934
Goddard, Frederick A.	2	1918–1919
Goddard, Henry W.	1	1902–1913
Godillot, John R.	1	1889–1890
Godlay, Frederick A.	2	1914–1916
Godley, George McM.	2	1903–1916
Godwin, Charles G. H.	1	1922–1924
Godwin, Frederick M.	2	1911–1916
Goetze, Richard B.	3	1931–1932
Goffe, James R.	1	1889–1891
Goldsborough, Richard F.	2	1898–1905
Good, Charles K.	Med	1935–1936
Good, Donald K.	2	1934–1935
Goodhue, Fisher*	2	1916–1917
Goodnow, David F.	2	1910–1913
Goodridge, Malcolm, Jr.	1	1930–1934
Goodspeed, Franklin S.	2	1921–1929
Goodwin, Richard J.	3	1934–1937
Goodwin, Vincent L.	3	1933–1934
Goodwin, Wilder	4	1910–1917
Gordon, Albert H.	2	1926–1929
Gordon, George A.	3	1916–1917
Gordon, George E.*	4	1908–1908
Gordon, William S.*	1-Med	1892–1903
Gordon, Wm. S., Jr.	1	1915–1917
Gorham, Edwin S., Jr.	3	1916–1917
Goss, Walter D.	2	1924–1926
Gough, R. Sidney	MG	1915–1917
Gough, William R.	3	1921–1922
Gould, Aubrey Van W.	4	1910–1911
Gould, Carl T.	3	1905–1907
Gould, Edward L.*	1	1893–1896
Gould, Edwin*	1	1889–1891
Gould, James	1	1921–1926
Gould, William S., Jr.	3	1928–1931
Gould, William T., Jr.	3	1926–1926
Grace, Frederic J.*	2	1898–1908
Grace, James W.	1	1893–1895
Grace, Morgan H.	2	1902–1904
Grace, Morgan H., Jr.	2	1930–1934
Grady, George F.	3	1918–1920
Graffin, John C.	1	1923–1924
Graham, Frank	1	1889–1894
Graham, John D.	2	1922–1929
Graham, Joseph A.	3	1933–1937
Graham, Sharon	1	1918–1920
Grand, Brooks D.	1	1939–
Grandy, William S.	1	1930–1933
Granger, Sherman M.	1	1899–1899
Grannis, Horace G.	1	1893–1896
Grannis, John H. D.	1	1898–1900
Grant, Havens	2	1914–1916
Grant, Robert M., Jr.	2	1927–1929
Graves, Justin D.	3	1930–1933
Gray, Gerald H.	1	1895–1895
Gray, Julius C.	3-Hq	1922–1926
Gray, Leslie B.	2	1930–1934
Gray, William H.	1	1889–1890
Greeff, Bernard, Jr.	1	1903–1909
Greeff, Charles A.	1	1925–1934
Green, C. Douglass	2	1903–1912
Green, John D.	1	1924–1926
Green, Henry W., Jr.	1	1927–1932
Green, Morris M., Jr.	3	1939–
Green, Thomas M.	3	1934–1937
Green, Walton A.	1	1910–1910
Green, William D.	3	1918–1918
Green, William H., Jr.	3	1936–
Greene, Francis T.	3	1933–1934
Greene, John A., Jr.	MG	1913–1917
Greene, John R.	MG	1914–1917
Greene, Thurston	2	1933–1935
Greene, Waldo W.	1	1934–1937
Greene, William Dolan		1917–1919
Greenhall, Harry A.	2-Hq	1921–1924
Greening, Orlando A.	2	1922–1923
Greenough, Alfred	3	1909–1912
Greer, Louis M.	1-2	1891–1897
Greiner, Ernest C.	2	1918–1920

SQUADRON A

Name	Troop or Detachment Served	Date of Enlistment and Final Discharge	Name	Troop or Detachment Served	Date of Enlistment and Final Discharge
Greis, Emil F.	3	1918–1919	Haneman, John Theodore	3	1913–1916
Grey, John W.	1	1918–1920	Hanemann, Henry W.	Hd	1921–1922
Grieger, Philip R.	Hd	1926–1927	Hanford, Parmly*	1	1910–1911
Griffith, William F. R.	3	1930–1930	Hannah, Miles C.	1	1911–1911
Grim, Basil H.	3	1918–1919	Hansen, Curt Eric	3	1916–1917
Grimwood, Victor R.	2	1918–1919	Hanson, Edward B.	2	1936–1937
Grinnell, Lawrence I.	4	1915–1917	Hanson, Frank R., Jr.	Hd	1925–1928
Grinslade, Kenneth C.	1	1916–1917	Hanson, John D.	2-1	1934–1397
Griswold, H. E.	1	1901–1906	Hanssen, Eilif C.	Med	1930–1938
Groesbeck, Herbert, Jr.*	3	1913–1917	Hanway, William A.	3	1922–1928
Gross, Paul L.	4	1916–1917	Harcourt, Vivian W.	2	1934–1937
Groves, Morris	2	1917–1919	Hard, Anson W.	2	1906–1907
Guedalia, Jules	1	1919–1932	Hard, DeCourcy	2	1910–1915
Guilmette, Dudley	3	1937–	Hardenburgh, Thos. E., Jr.	4	1910–1912
Gullette, Wilmer C.	1	1928–1929	Hardie, Joseph P.	3	1928–1938
Gunn, Robert*	1	1918–1920	Hare, Meredith	2	1898–1899
Gurnee, Walter S., Jr.	1	1928–1931	Hare, William H., Jr.	1	1898–1899
Gutterson, Herbert L.	MG	1913–1913	Harmon, Clifford B.	1	1918–1918
Guy, Loren	3	1930–1936	Harper, J. Henry, Jr.	3	1916–1917
Gwathmey, Archibald, 2nd	4-1	1916–1928	Harrigan, Michael	3	1922–1923
Gwathmey, Gaines	4	1916–1917	Harriman, John	2	1924–1927
Gwynne, A. Evan	1	1925–1928	Harrington, George P.	2	1933–1934
Gwynne, Arthur	1-2	1895–1897	Harrington, John F.	Hd	1926–1926
Gwynne, John T.	3	1933–1937	Harris, Robert	2	1921–1923
			Harris, Thomas A. E.*	3	1915–1917
Hackett, Wm. H. Y.	2	1912–1913	Harrison, Bernard J.	1	1899–1901
Hadden, Harold F., Jr.	2	1908–1909	Harrison, Francis B.	2	1896–1898
Hadlock, Albert E., Jr.	2	1930–1934	Harrison, James L.	Hd-1	1923–1926
Haight, C. Sidney	1-2	1895–1898	Harrison, John D.	2	1921–1922
Haight, Frederick E., 2nd	3	1938–	Harrison, Lewis W.	3	1930–1931
Haight, Sherman P.	1	1914–1916	Hart, Albert E., Jr.	3	1938–
Hall, Isaac D.	3	1930–1934	Hart, Roswell R.	2	1937–1938
Hall, James P.	3	1930–1932	Hartshorne, Edward C.	2	1895–1900
Hall, James Willett*	1-4	1898–1921	Hartshorne, Harold	1	1915–1916
Hall, James Willett, Jr.	3	1924–1924	Hartshorne, Hugh	3	1914–1917
Hall, John F. G.*	3	1924–1927	Hartshorne, Richard	Hd-3	1923–1928
Hall, Robert F.	2	1936–	Hartwell, George V.	4	1915–1917
Hall, Sherman Rogers	1	1896–1898	Harvey, Alexander*	1-Med	1889–1897
Hall, Wm. Claiborne	1	1906–1907	Harvey, Frederick S.	3	1927–1928
Hallett, Norman	1	1905–1910	Harvey, Richard S.	1	1889–1890
Halley, Erskine B.	MG	1916–1916	Harwood, Lee	1	1924–1928
Halliwell, Roger D.	1	1924–1926	Hasbrouck, Carl J.	2	1924–1926
Halpin, Francis*	1	1889–1896	Haskell, Anson G.	2	1930–1934
Hamill, Samuel N.	1	1935–1938	Haskell, Edward Kirk	4	1908–1921
Hamilton, Charles K.	3	1937–	Haskell, Gorham	2	1930–1932
Hamilton, Edward P.	4	1914–1917	Haskell, John H.	Hd-1	1925–1928
Hamilton, Frederick J.	2	1929–1932	Haskell, Wm. N., 3rd*	1	1929–1932
Hamilton, Laurens*	2-1	1896–1897	Hatch, Horace M.	4	1915–1917
Hamilton, Minard	4	1915–1917	Hathaway, Stewart S.	4	1907–1915
Hamilton, Wm. C.	1	1930–1933	Havell, George	3	1930–1932
Hamlin, Bryan C.	1	1921–1928	Havemeyer, J. Craig	1	1895–1900
Hammond, Francis S.	1	1933–1936	Hawes, Emory*	1	1898–1899
Hammond, John H.	1-3	1893–1897	Hawkins, David R.	1	1924–1925
Hammond, John S., Jr.	3	1932–1933	Hawkins, Dudley W. L.	1	1928–1932
Hammond, Paul L.	4-2	1909–1914	Hawley, Arthur L.	MG	1916–1917
Hammond, Roger N.	2	1911–1912	Hawley, Samuel M.	1	1899–1900
Hand, Herbert T.	Hd	1921–1922	Hay, John L., Jr.	2	1920–1921
Hand, Raymond T. B.	2-3	1926–1927	Hay, Wellington Bent	1	1911–1915
Handy, Cortlandt W.	3	1912–1917	Hay, William I.	1	{ 1917–1918 1920–1923
Handy, Truman P.	3	1915–1917			

SQUADRON A

Name	Troop or Detachment Served	Date of Enlistment and Final Discharge
Hayes, Garland H.	1	1933–1936
Hayes, Hoyt E.	4	1915–1916
Hayes, John S.	1	1936–
Hayes, Robert C.	1	1932–1935
Haynes, Raymond Bontecou	4	1917–1919
Hays, Thomas A.	2-1	1918–1920
Hayward, Boynton	1	1922–1925
Hayward, Howard	2	1939–
Hayward, Leland	Hd-1	1923–1924
Haywood, Alfred W.	3	1912–1915
Haywood, William Robert	MG	1917–1918
Hazard, Geoffrey C.	1	1924–1927
Healey, Charles P.	1	1928–1932
Healey, Giles G.	3	1928–1932
Heatley, Selden E.	2	1938–
Heaton, Wm. W.	3-Med	1896–1899
Hebe, John R.	4	1916–1917
Heckmann, Hans W.	1	1932–
Hedden, Stuart	2	1924–1925
Hedlund, Charles O.	1	1921–1923
Heffernan, Joseph V.	1	1937–1937
Hegeman, John G.	2	1918–1920
Heim, Stanley M.	2-Hd-2	1920–1929
Heinsohn, Augereau, Jr.	3	1920–1922
Helier, Frederick	Hd-2	1921–1922
Helmer, Borden	1	1927–1928
Heminway, James C.	1	1921–1925
Hemingway, Charles S.	3	1921–1923
Hemphill, Albert W.	4	1915–1916
Hemphill, Clifford	1	1912–1916
Hemphill, John	1	1921–1923
Hemphill, Meredith	2	1924–1925
Henderson, Alexander I.	3	1916–1917
Henderson, Eliot W.	1	1901–1902
Henderson, Isham*	3	1901–1915
Hendrian, Richard E.	2	1934–1935
Hendrickson, Helmer A.*	Med	1935–1935
Hennessy, Daniel	2	1925–1928
Hennessy, Daniel	2	1931–1937
Henrotin, Martin F.	3	1936–1937
Henry, John	Hd	1926–1926
Henry, John C.	1	1934–1937
Henry, Ryder, 2nd	1	1931–1938
Henry, Samuel J., Jr.	2	1934–
Henry, William Seton	3	1906–1908
Henshaw, Sydney Parker	1	1910–1915
Herbert, Raymond L.	1	1900–1905
Herbert, Wyman D.	MG	1914–1916
Hereford, Robert C.	3	1932–1932
Heroy, James H.	Med-3	1903–1910
Herrhammer, Karl A.	2	1935–
Herrick, Gerardus Post	3	1898–1910
Herrick, Harold A.	3	1916–1917
Hickox, Chas. R., Jr.	2	1897–1903
Hickox, Charles V., Jr.	MG	1913–1916
Higgins, James B.	Med-3	1925–1927
Higgins, Joseph J.	2	1898–1900
Higgins, Thomas, 2nd	1	1935–1938
Hildreth, Philip R. M.*	1	1898–1898
Hilgers, Carl H.	1	1917–1917

Name	Troop or Detachment Served	Date of Enlistment and Final Discharge
Hill, Charles B., Jr.	Med	1926–1926
Hill, Edward A.	Hd-2-Hd	1923–
Hill, Edward K.	MG	1916–1917
Hill, J. Sprunt	2	1895–1898
Hill, Richardson A.	Hd	1928–1928
Hilliard, Joseph C.	2	1926–1929
Hillyer, Clive Nelson	3	1917–1919
Hilton, Theophilus B.	1	1918–1920
Hine, Francis W.	MG	1913–1915
Hinrichs, Emil	2	1917–1920
Hinsdale, F. G.	1	1899–1900
Hinton, Longstreet	1	1925–1929
Hipp, Walter	Med	1937–1938
Hitch, Joseph C. D.	2	1896–1907
Hitchcock, Charles, Jr.	1	1904–1909
Hitchcock, Howard L.	Med-L	1904–1909
Hitchcock, Wm. G.	1-2	1895–1900
Hitt, Hamilton	1	1930–1932
Hlavac, Albert, Jr.	2-1-Hd	1919–1924
Hoadley, Sheldon E.*	3	1915–1917
Hoag, John T.*	1	1890–1897
Hoag, John W.	2	1926–1927
Hoag, W. K.	3-Hd	1917–1923
Hoag, William K.	Hd	1922–1923
Hoagland, Warren E.	1	1930–1931
Hobbs, Edw. D.	3	1925–1928
Hobbs, Joseph M.	2	1918–1920
Hobson, George H.	2	1936–
Hobson, Henry B.	1	1916–1917
Hockenberry, Raymond N., Jr.	3	1938–
Hocking, George H.	1	1917–1919
Hodenpyl, Eugene	3	1920–1926
Hodges, George H.	2-1	1900–1906
Hoeninghaus, Fritz W.*	3	1896–1904
Hoff, Nicholas R.	3	1931–1934
Hoffman, Eugene A.	2	1927–1930
Hoffman, James M.	1	1916–1917
Hoffman, Lefferts S.	1	1930–1931
Hoggson, Wallace	3	1921–1922
Hoguet, George A., Jr.	1	1938–
Hoguet, Henry L.	3	1934–1934
Hoguet, Roland H.	2	1938–
Holbrook, J. Byers*	1	1897–1902
Holbrook, John K., Jr.	1	1925–1930
Holbrook, William	3	1939–
Holden, Arthur C.	MG	1914–1917
Holden, Lansing C., Jr.*	3	1926–1929
Holden, Raymond P.	MG	1916–1917
Holden, Richard S.	2	1930–1933
Holden, William H.	2	1916–1917
Holder, Daniel S.	3	1926–1926
Holder, Frederick D.	3	1898–1902
Hole, James W.	Hd	1922–1923
Hole, Richard	2-1	1918–1920
Holland, Wilfred		1917–1919
Hollister, George C.	3-4	1898–1907
Holly, John I.*	1-Hd	1889–1895
Hollyday, Richard C., Jr.	1-Hd	1922–1925
Holmes, Alfred	1	1918–1919
Holmes, Charles T.	1	1931–

SQUADRON A

Name	Troop or Detachment Served	Date of Enlistment and Final Discharge	Name	Troop or Detachment Served	Date of Enlistment and Final Discharge
Holmes, Lawrence D.	3	1939–	Hoyt, Charles Sherman	2	1906–1911
Holmes, Lester S.	2	1918–1920	Hoyt, Colgate, Jr.	2-MG	1907–1917
Holmes, Nathaniel, 2nd	1	1915–1917	Hoyt, Edwin C.	1-2-3	1894–1899
Holmes, Oliver E.*	1	1925–1928	Hoyt, Everett W.	1	1933–1936
Holt, Henry E.	2	1898–1909	Hoyt, James K., Jr.	1	1921–1922
Holt, Philetus H.	1	1895–1901	Hoyt, John R.	2	1919–1920
Holter, Edwin O.	3	1897–1898	Hoyt, John S.	2	1895–1896
Hone, Frederick de P.	2	1901–1904	Hoyt, Preston S.	MG	1916–1917
Honey, Robertson, Jr.*	3	1934–1937	Hoyt, Sherman	3	1938–1938
Hooker, Henry S.	3	1903–1904	Hubbard, Gardner G.	2	1912–1914
Hooker, Horace W., Jr.	1	1929–1932	Hubbard, George E.	2	1922–1925
Hooker, Kenneth W.	1	1929–1932	Hubbard, Griffith E.	3	1924–1925
Hooker, Roger W.	Hd-1-Hd	1922–1926	Hubbard, Ralph H.	4	1908–1913
Hooper, Horace B.	Med	1923–1924	Hubbell, George W., Jr.	1-MG	1903–1915
Hooper, John N.	Hd-3	1923–1924	Hubbell, William B.	3	1928–1931
Hooven, Clement W.	2	1929–1930	Huber, Frederick C.	3	1938–
Hopkins, Amos Lawrence	3	1913–1914	Huger, Alfred	4	1908–1908
Hopkins, George A., Jr.	1	1938–	Hughes, John C.	3	1915–1917
Hopkins, Leonard S. R.	2	1895–1902	Hulick, Wm. H., Jr.	2	1922–1925
Hopper, Franklin F.	2	1918–1920	Humphrey, Frank J., Jr.	1	1936–1936
Hoppin, Bayard Cushing	1	1908–1912	Humphreys, James B.*	2-3	1896–1898
Hoppin, Frederick S.	3	1902–1907	Humphreys, May	2-1	1895–1899
Hoppin, Gerard B.	1	1895–1898	Hungerford, Victor W.	1	1899–1904
Hoppin, Wm. W., Jr.	3	1901–1903	Hunnewell, Remsen E.	3	1921–1924
Hormel, Charles B.*	4	1909–1913	Hunt, Charles Warren, Jr.	2	1911–1912
Horn, William Casper	1	1906–1906	Hunt, Joseph H.*	1-2-Hd	1893–1909
Hornblower, George S.*	2-4-3	1905–1916	Hunt, Leavitt J.	2	1900–1907
Horner, Leonard S.	2	1898–1903	Hunter, Edward Sherman	2	1917–1919
Horton, Milton Chase	Hd-3	1923–1925	Hunter, Lawrence M.	3	1920–1921
Hosmer, Edward S.	1	1894–1895	Hunter, Robert J.	1	1889–1892
Hotchkiss, Edward G.	2	1920–1921	Hunting, Sinclair T.*	1	1889–1894
Houghtaling, David H.	3	1921–1927	Huntington, Francis C.	1-2	1893–1904
Houghton, Augustus S.	1	1892–1898	Huntington, Wm. R.	2	1928–1931
Hourdequin, Felix S.	1	1926–1931	Hurd, Edward A.	3	1915–1917
House, Meredith J.	1	1921–1922	Hurlbut, Jesse L., 2nd	Med	1928–1931
Houston, David F., Jr.	3	1923–1924	Hurry, Gilford*	1-Hd	1889–1898
Howard, C. Wadsworth	MG	1912–1915	Hurry, Renwick W.	3	1934–1937
Howard, Edgerton McC.	Med	1930–1930	Hussey, John, Jr.*	3	1923–1925
Howard, Edwin L.	Hd-1	1923–1929	Hutchison, Chas. A.*	2-1	1896–1898
Howard, Graeme K.	3	1921–1922	Hutt, Richard H.	2	1925–1928
Howard, Jacob P.	2	1932–1935	Hutton, John L.	3	1914–1917
Howard, Minot A.	1	1933–1934	Huyler, Cleveland C.	4	1915–1917
Howard, Robert R., Jr.	2	1938–	Hyde, Charles L.*	1	1889–1889
Howard, Thomas A.*	2	1930–1935	Hyde, Donald R.	1	1915–1917
Howe, Fisher	2	1937–	Hyde, John B.	3-Hd	1921–1928
Howe, Frank, Jr.	3	1918–1921	Hyde, John James Hindon		1917–1919
Howe, John	2	1928–1930	Hyland, Charles A., Jr.	3	1939–
Howe, Nathaniel S.	3	1927–1930	Hyndman, Bruce	3	1930–1933
Howe, Russell G.	1	1891–1891			
Howe, Wirt	3	1900–1905	Igams, J. Horton	4	1910–1915
Howell, Alfred H.	1	1938–1938	Ikeler, Frank A.	1	1923–1925
Howell, Henry J.	1	1899–1907	Iler, Alexander	2	1924–1926
Howell, Lloyd M.	1-4	1901–1910	Ilinski, Janusz	3	1934–1938
Howells, Henry C.	2	1921–1922	Illischer, Frank L.	4	1916–1917
Howells, Henry C., Jr.*	1	1892–1898	Ingalls, F. Abbot, Jr.	1	1921–1925
Howgate, Henry O.	Hd-2	1923–1925	Ingalls, Melville E., Jr.	2	1898–1900
Howland, Silas W., Jr.	2	1938–	Ingersoll, John Avery	2	1912–1917
Howley, John	1	1935–1938	Ingold, Wm. F.	2	1918–1918
Hoxie, I. Richmond	1	1902–1908	Inman, Hugh M.	1	1898–1903
Hoxie, Timothy W.	3	1904–1912	Ireland, J. de Courcey	1	1892–1893

SQUADRON A

Name	Troop or Detachment Served	Date of Enlistment and Final Discharge	Name	Troop or Detachment Served	Date of Enlistment and Final Discharge
Irving, Roland D.	3	1934–1938	Johnston, Frank Eddy	4	1917–1919
Irwin, Dudley M., Jr.	2	1922–1923	Johnston, Hugh A.	MG	1915–1917
Irwin, James B.	4	1907–1909	Johnstone, George C.	Hd	1926–1927
Irwin, Robert A.	1	1939–	Johnstone, Williard H.	3	1922–1929
Irwin, Wendell J.	Hd	1922–1924	Joice, James P., Jr.	2	1932–1935
Iselin, Edward G.	3	1925–1930	Jones, Alfred W.	2	1927–1929
Iselin, Henry	2	1920–1924	Jones, Charles A.	4	1917–1917
Iselin, Henry S.	1	1889–1893	Jones, Chester L., Jr.	2	1937–1937
Iselin, John H.	3	1896–1899	Jones, Edward Pavis, Jr.	1	1907–1911
Iselin, John H., Jr.	3	1925–1926	Jones, Frederick W., Jr.	1-3	1893–1898
Iselin, William	2	1928–1932	Jones, Russell C.	4	1910–1915
Isham, Edward P.	2	1928–1929	Jones, Rutgers B.	2	1920–1921
Ives, Chauncey B.	3	1931–1934	Jones, Thomas Carlyle	2	1917–1921
Ives, Gerald M.*	3	1898–1898	Jones, Wm. B.	Hd-2	1923–1925
Ives, Kenneth A., Jr.	3	1925–1928	Jones, William S., Jr.*	1	1891–1892
Ives, Leland H.	1	1889–1890	Jordan, Sydney S., Jr.	3-Hd	1921–1922
Ivison, Sterling H.	4	1916–1917	Judson, Cyrus F.	1	1890–1894
Ivory, Percy V. E.	1	1918–1919	Judson, Harold	2	1918–1920
			Judson, William D.	1-2	1894–1910
Jack, Raymond H.	2	1927–1930	Judson, Wm. F.	1	1890–1891
Jackson, Andrew	1	1931–1935	Julian, Thomas		1917–1919
Jackson, Charles	1	1901–1902	Julian, Thomas	3	1916–1922
Jackson, Fielding V.	MG	1916–1917	Julier, Henry V.	4	1912–1917
Jackson, Frederick W.	3	1918–1920			
Jackson, Millard I.	1-2	1918–1921	Kahle, Herman*	MG	1912–1916
Jackson, Wm. Harding	3	1928–1930	Kaiser, Frank R.	3	1935–1936
Jacob, Lawrence, 2nd	2	1925–1926	Kamna, Harry F.		1917–1919
Jacob, Manning	2	1925–1926	Kane, Edwin V.	3	1911–1915
Jacob, Wm. B.	2	1923–1924	Kane, Paul R.	3	1935–1937
Jacobi, Edwin G.	2	1931–1934	Kane, Richmond K.	2	1927–1928
Jacobi, Herbert J.	2	1930–1933	Kane, Theodore F.	2	1930–1933
Jacobs, Sidney B.	3	1918–1918	Kane, Wm. J.	4	1919–1920
Jacobus, Arthur M.*	1	1889–1895	Karr, Edward R.	3	1926–1931
Jallade, John H.	3	1935–	Kauffman, Sanford B.	1	1935–
Jallade, Louis E., Jr.	3	1935–	Kazanjian, Andon	3	1927–1928
James, Carlton	2	1918–1919	Kean, Robert W.	2	1916–1917
James, Newton*	3	1907–1913	Kearny, Philip*	3-4	1896–1905
Jamison, D. Stearns, Jr.	1	1924–1927	Kearny, Philip J.	4	1911–1914
Janeway, Jacob J., 2nd	1	1924–1928	Keat, John	1	1939–
Jarman, George Wallace, Jr.	4	1916–1917	Kederick, Harry C. B.	3	1918–1919
Jefferson, Frank	2	1917–1919	Keebler, Roy C.	1	1918–1919
Jeffrey, Archibald C.	2-1	1918–1921	Keeler, Arthur R.	2	1925–1925
Jenks, Almet F., Jr.	1	1915–1917	Keen, Herbert B.	1	1918–1920
Jenney, Isaac H.	1	1895–1900	Keenan, Ray W.	Hd-1	1926–1929
Jennings, Harry Bogert	MG	1917–1919	Keinan, Robert P.	1	1907–1909
Jensen, William J.	3	1937–	Keiser, David M.	2	1932–1936
Jevons, Ferdinand T. R.	2	1901–1906	Keiser, Garfield O.	MG	1915–1917
Jevons, Reginald*	3	1899–1906	Keith, Isham	2	1928–1928
Jewett, Charles H., Jr.*	1-2-1	1895–1899	Kelley, Don M.	3	1913–1917
Jochum, Clarence C.	2	1935–	Kelley, Reo S.	3	1936–1939
Johnson, Albert G., Jr.	1	1929–1932	Kellog, Morris W.	1	1899–1904
Johnson, Carlisle H.	2	1924–1925	Kellogg, Marion K.	1	1928–1931
Johnson, Chas. C.	1	1913–1913	Kelly, Carlos D.	3	1930–1931
Johnson, Chas. Chouteau	1	1902–1902	Kelly, Frank E.	2	1916–1917
Johnson, Francis E., Jr.	1	1905–1907	Kelly, James Allison	3	1899–1901
Johnson, James F., Jr.	2	1911–1915	Kelly, John J.	2	1897–1908
Johnson, Norman D.	3	1931–1934	Kelly, Joseph H.	2	1916–1919
Johnson, Tom L.	3	1921–1922	Kelly, Orrie R.	3	1919–1921
Johnson, Wallace C.	1	1924–1930	Kelly, Shaun	4	1909–1912
Johnson, William T.	3	1906–1907	Kelly, Thomas A.	2	1930–1933

SQUADRON A 373

Name	Troop or Detachment Served	Date of Enlistment and Final Discharge	Name	Troop or Detachment Served	Date of Enlistment and Final Discharge
Kelly, Thomas M.	Hd	1925–1925	Klausner, Wm. P.*	1	1918–1935
Kemeys, Walter S.	3	1896–1901	Klein, David	2	1926–1926
Kendall, Norman	2	1924–1927	Kleitz, Wm. L.	2	1922–1925
Kendrick, Edward A.*	1	1918–1919	Klepetko, Ernest	2	1914–1915
Kennard, Richmond P.	1	1921–1925	Kline, William S.	1	1932–1934
Kennard, Spencer P.	1	1925–1925	Klots, Allan T.	1	1913–1916
Kennedy, John D.	Hd-3	1921–1924	Klotz, George M.	1	1935–1938
Kennedy, Raymond H.	1	1916–1927	Klugh, Milton C.	2	1936–
Kennedy, Wm. J.	Med	1922–1926	Knapp, Allen	2	1935–1936
Kenworthey, Charles E.	2	1926–1926	Knapp, Edgar A.	1	1902–1908
Keppel, Frederick P.	3	1902–1910	Knapp, James R.*	2	1907–1916
Kernan, Thomas D.	1	1932–1936	Knapp, John M.*	1-2	1889–1895
Kerner, Chas. H., Jr.	2-1	1896–1906	Knapp, Whitman	1	1935–1938
Kerner, Howard S.	2-1	1896–1901	Knapp, Wm. J.	2	1915–1916
Kernochan, Frederick*	1	1899–1904	Knauth, Felix W.	3-Hd	1922–1925
Kernochan, Walton O.*	1	1889–1890	Knevels, A. Lawrence*	1	1889–1892
Kernochan, Whitney	1	1907–1917	Kniffin, Edgar A.	1	1931–
Kerr, Albert B.	4	1910–1913	Knight, Samuel	1	1889–1890
Kerr, Elmer Coe	3	1910–1916	Knoblauch, George W.*	2	1902–1903
Kerr, George K.	Med	1926–1929	Know, Frederick W.	3	1918–1918
Kerr, Harry S.*	1	1890–1895	Knox, Arthur, Jr.	2	1935–
Kerr, Robert B., Jr.	3	1916–1917	Knudsen, Arthur S.	3	1898–1900
Kerr, William M.	Med	1901–1906	Koch, Frank W.*	1	1902–1919
Ketner, David C.	1	1931–1937	Koenig, Herbert A.*	2	1924–1927
Keyes, Dr. Edw. L.	3	1922–1925	Koerner, Arthur J.	2	1920–1928
Keyser, Richard	2	1921–1922	Kohler, Robert F.*	2	1927–1938
Kidder, Henry M.	MG	1912–1917	Kondolf, Harold	3	1921–1922
Kidder, Wellington H.	3	1918–1920	Kormendi, John	3	1931–1934
Kiendl, Theodore	2	1914–1917	Kormendi, Laszlo	3	1930–1934
Kilbreth, James T., Jr.	2	1895–1900	Kraft, George J.	2	1931–1935
Kilner, Ehrick B.	MG	1916–1917	Kraft, Wilson P.	2	1931–1934
Kilpatrick, John D.	3	1902–1909	Kraissl, Cornelius J.	Med	1926–1926
Kilpatrick, John Reed	2	1912–1917	Krech, Shepard	MG	1915–1917
Kimball, Clarence	2	1918–1918	Krock, Thomas P.	3	1931–1932
Kimball, Comer J.	1	1935–1937	Kuhnhard, George F.	2	1916–1917
Kimball, Morton S.	3	1935–1937	Kunhardt, Kingsley	1	1915–1917
Kimbel, Wm. A.	2	1912–1916			
Kinard, James P.	2	1925–1928	Ladd, Carroll W.	3	1906–1908
Kind, Harry Ernst	2	1917–1919	Ladd, Edward H., 3rd	1	1928–1931
Kineon, James P.	MG	1914–1916	Laffert, James Percy		1917–1919
King, David E.	Hd-1	1923–1924	Lakin, Herbert C.	2	1903–1909
King, Hugh P., Jr.	3	1933–1938	Lalley, Harold V.	1	1922–1923
King, Joseph	3	1916–1917	Lamarche, Albert H.	3	1921–1927
King, Rufus F.	1	1916–1917	Lamarche, Edward J.*	3	1916–1917
King, William P.	1	1934–1937	Lamarche, Richard F.	3	1921–1934
Kingsbury, Howard T., Jr.	2	1927–1930	Lamb, Dana S.	1	1925–1930
Kingsbury, Slocum	MG-1	1916–1924	Lamb, George N.	2	1898–1898
Kinnan, Morris E.	1	1918–1918	Lamb, Horace R.	1	1924–1926
Kinnicutt, Francis H.	2	1903–1917	Lambert, Kenneth B.	1	1927–1928
Kinzel, Otto	2	1937–	Lambert, Robert D.	1	1936–
Kinzel, Robert K.	2	1929–1932	Lambiotte, Oscar E.*	1	1889–1891
Kip, Garret P.	3	1903–1903	LaMotte, Robert Hill	3	1925–1928
Kip, Henry S.*	3	1897–1902	Landreth, Robert N.	1	1920–1920
Kirkham, Hall	1	1926–1927	Lane, Francis C.	3	1938–
Kirkland, George R.	1	1928–1930	Lane, John B.	3	1931–1936
Kirkland, Robert Mason		1917–1918	Lane, Wm. R.	3-Hd	1922–1926
Kirkland, Samuel N.	1	1927–1928	Lang, John	2	1920–1922
Kirkland, Wm. R., Jr.	1	1929–1935	Langdon, John	1	1918–1918
Kissel, Lester	1	1934–1937	Lange, Max*	Hd	1916–1919
Kitching, Lawrence James		1917–1919	Langford, Malcolm S.	1	1933–

SQUADRON A

Name	Troop or Detachment Served	Date of Enlistment and Final Discharge	Name	Troop or Detachment Served	Date of Enlistment and Final Discharge
Langford, Thomas Alexander*	4	1916–1917	Leech, Robertson	1-4	1907–1916
Langhorne, John	1	1927–1929	Lefferts, Barent	2	1904–1912
Langthorn, Jacob S.	3	1921–1923	Leggett, Noel B.	3	1932–1938
Lanman, David H.	1	1898–1905	Leigh, Benjamin W.	1-2	1891–1899
Lanman, Ludlow T.*	2	1916–1917	Leigh, Egbert G., 3rd	3	1928–1929
Lannon, John D.*	1-2	1898–1913	Leisure, George S.	1	1921–1924
Lanzer, Albert*		1917–1919	Leitner, James D.	3	1938–
Lapham, John H.	4	1909–1912	Lenssen, Nicholas F.	4-1	1908–1912
Lardner, Gilmore A.	1	1928–1928	Lentilhon, Eugene, Jr.	1	1917–1917
Larkin, James S.	1	1914–1915	Leonard, Wm. H.	1	1891–1892
Larkin, Lawrence	3	1929–1934	Leoser, John	MG	1917–1919
Larkin, Wm. H.	3	1918–1920	Lesher, Arthur L., Jr.	1-Med	1921–1922
Larner, Robert J.	3	1924–1926	Lesher, William Montgomery	2	1917–1919
LaRoche, Chester J.	1	1921–1927	Leslie, George D.	4	1916–1919
Larrabee, George L.	1	1908–1909	Leslie, Williamar	2	1939–
Laurence, E. W.	2	1918–1918	Lester, Joseph W.	1-Hd	1919–1922
Law, Alfred L.	3	1920–1923	Leverich, Henry S.	2	1903–1909
Lawless, Nicholas	3	1924–1924	Lewis, Charles W.	1	1928–1931
Lawlor, Edward L.	3	1923–1924	Lewis, David	3	1916–1917
Lawrence, Augustine N.	3-4	1901–1904	Lewis, Frederic W.	2	1931–1934
Lawrence, Augustus H.	2-4	1906–1910	Lewis, George H. P.	1	1925–1927
Lawrence, Chas. C.	MG	1912–1919	Lewis, Halstead H.	3	1921–1921
Lawrence, James G. K.	2	1916–1917	Lewis, Henry, 3rd	1	1929–1932
Lawrence, Malcolm R., Jr.	3	1924–1925	Lewis, Henry C.	1	1924–1924
Lawrence, Robert C.	2-Hd	1897–1908	Lewis, Frederic W.	2	1931–1934
Lawrence, Townsend	1-2	1896–1899	Lewis, John B.	3	1925–1929
Lawson, Carl, Jr.		1917–1918	Lewis, Raymond W.	Med	1914–1917
Lawson, John D.	2	1918–1920	Libby, Walter G.	2	1898–1904
Lawson, Peter R.	3	1922–1924	Libby, Walter S.	1	1928–1929
Lawton, Henry D.	2	1901–1912	Liddell, Robert P. F.	3	1923–1924
Lawyer, George	1	1889–1890	Liese, Theodore W.	3	1937–
Laylin, John G.	1	1931–1933	Lightner, Milton C.	1	1914–1917
Lazo, Antonio	4	1915–1916	Lilliestrom, T. Leonard		1917–1919
Lazo, Mario		1917–1918	Lincoln, Frederick W., Jr.*	1-2	1892–1897
Lea, Charles R.	2	1924–1929	Lindberg, Harry V.	3	1930–1938
Leake, Robert H.	3	1907–1919	Lindeberg, Harrie T.	1	1909–1914
Leale, Loyal	1-4	1903–1911	Lindeberg, Lytle P.	1	1938–
Leale, Medwin*	1-2-3	1893–1903	Lindsley, Fanshawe	2	1929–1934
Learned, Henry C.	2	1903–1912	Lindsley, Harold*	1	1900–1900
Leary, Fairfax, Jr.	2	1938–	Lindsley, Van Sinderen	3	1898–1901
Lease, Benjamin Murray	1	1919–1920	Lindsley, Van Sinderen, Jr.	3	1926–1930
Leaycraft, Edgar C.	3	1904–1915	Line, Arthur N.*	2	1898–1901
LeBoutillier, Martin*	4	1915–1917	Link, David C., Jr.	1	1916–1917
LeBoutillier, Philip	3-4	1904–1910	Lippincott, Arthur H.	1	1900–1906
LeBoutillier, Thos., 2nd*	1	1904–1909	Lipson, Howard S.	2	1929–
Lederer, Allison M.	2	1917–1919	Litch, Robert B.	1	1928–1931
Ledyard, George S.	3	1896–1900	Litchfield, Edward H.	1	1900–1908
Lee, Albert R., Jr.	3	1930–1935	Litchfield, Stanton G.	3	1928–1931
Lee, Charles O. D.	1	1937–1938	Litt, Willard D.	3	1921–1923
Lee, Franklin Lawrence*	3	1896–1899	Littell, Emlen T.	3	1896–1902
Lee, Frederick H.	1	1890–1894	Little, Arthur W., Jr.	1	1918–1919
Lee, Hampton	3	1910–1915	Little, Everett W.	2-Hd	1918–1927
Lee, Harold	3	1904–1906	Little, George J.*	3	1896–1898
Lee, James G. K.*	2	1896–1899	Little, Henry C.	3	1929–1932
Lee, Joseph Day	2	1906–1912	Livengood, Charles S., Jr.	1	1935–1938
Lee, Robert B.	1	1930–	Livingston, Gerald M.	2	1918–1920
Lee, Robert L.*	1	1889–1891	Lloyd, Francis E., Jr.	2	1927–1927
Lee, Ronald C.	2	1901–1912	Lloyd, Nelson McA.*	3	1896–1903
Lee, Thomas N.*	3	1896–1898	Lloyd, Robert A. McA., Jr.	2	1920–1923
Lee, W. Murray	2	1918–1920	Lloyd, Robert McA.*	1	1895–1900

SQUADRON A

Name	Troop or Detachment Served	Date of Enlistment and Final Discharge	Name	Troop or Detachment Served	Date of Enlistment and Final Discharge
Lobdell, Leighton	3	1910–1914	Mackie, John M.	2	1928–1930
Lockard, Carl H.	1	1937–	MacKinlay, Donald A. G.	1-A	1917–1923
Lockett, Arthur H.	3	1896–1898	Maclay, Alfred B.	1	1889–1899
Lockwood, Preston	Hd-2	1923–1925	MacLaurin, John M.	2	1939–
Lodge, Henry G.	3	1927–1929	MacNair, Pierce	3	1938–1938
Loeb, Louis M.	3	1925–1929	MacNaughton, Wm.	1	1898–1917
Loew, E. Victor, Jr.	1	1896–1901	MacRossie, Allan, Jr.	3	1922–1922
Logan, Sheridan	2	1924–1926	MacWillie, Donald MacG.	3	1931–
Logan, Walter S.	2	1914–1917	Macy, J. Noel	3	1923–
Logan, Wm. J.	3	1916–1917	Macy, Josiah, Jr.	3	1937–
Lomas, Stanley A.	3	1938–	Macy, Josiah N.	3	1923–
Lomasney, Myron A.	1	1930–1937	Macy, Valentine E., Jr.	3	1923–1933
Lombardi, Cornelius E.	2	1914–1917	Maddison, Wm. H.	2	1917–1919
Long, Hamilton A.	1	1925–1929	Maddox, Wm. J.	3	1921–1922
Longua, Paul J.	1	1917–1919	Maddrey, Milner C.	Med	1935–1936
Lonsdale, Whittaker	3	1929–1930	Magowan, Edward	3	1929–1932
Looram, Matthew	2	1916–1917	Magruder, Robertson B.	1	1920–1921
Lorenz, Joseph	3	1918–1918	Mahan, Robert V.	2	1913–1916
Lounsbery, Richard	2	1910–1911	Maher, Edward A., 3rd	3	1926–1929
Loveland, John W.	2	1897–1900	Maher, James J.	1	1918–1920
Lovell, Harry B.	3	1898–1901	Mahoney, Canice P.	1	1934–
Lovenson, Louis H.	4	1913–1917	Mairs, John D.*	3	1897–1902
Lucas, Russell H.	2	1920–1923	Mairs, John D.*	4	1909–1910
Ludington, William H.	1-2	1889–1897	Maitland, James W.	1	1921–1923
Luey, Laurence D.	2	1930–1933	Major, Howard	4	1909–1914
Luke, Chas. W.	MG	1912–1914	Makepeace, David B.	3	1930–1934
Lull, Ernest P.	2	1921–1933	Makepeace, Ernest	3	1934–1934
Lummis, William M.	3	1916–1917	Makepeace, Frank B., Jr.	3-4	1905–1910
Lupton, Frederick T.	2	1929–1932	Makepeace, Paul B.	3	1934–1934
Luria, Alvord N.	2	1919–1921	Makepeace, Russell	2	1926–1930
Luthy, Kenneth Frederick	1	1912–1917	Mallett, Guy C.	MG	1916–1917
Lutschewitz, Willi	2	1939–	Mallory, Stanford C.	3	1932–1937
Lyeth, John M. R.	4	1911–1913	Malone, Edmund Halsey*	1	1913–1914
Lynch, Edmond C.*	1	1918–1918	Malone, Robert H.	3	1930–1930
Lynch, Hampton S.	4	1915–1916	Maloney, Everett McC.	3	1938–
Lynch, James F.	1	1916–1917	Maloney, Wm. R., Jr.	1-Hd	1904–1916
Lynch, Simpson	4	1916–1917	Maltby, Monroe	3	1926–1926
Lynn, Austin*	3	1922–1924	Mandeville, James R. A.	1	1918–1920
Lyon, Cecil*	3-4	1906–1911	Manice, Wm. deF.	2	1911–1915
Lyon, Edward A.	1-Hd	1919–1922	Manierre, Alfred L.	1	1927–1931
Lyon, Wm. D.	3-4	1907–1909	Mann, Allan Newhall	MG	1912–1915
Lyon, William D., Jr.	2	1936–	Mann, Ellery Anderson	3	1909–1912
Lyon, Wm. E. B.	3	1920–1926	Mann, Paul F.	4	1910–1911
			Mann, Robert C. V.	3	1923–1924
Macauley, Frank A.	2	1917–1919	Manning, Richard F.	3	1896–1899
MacCallum, Robert L.	2	1937–	Manny, Walter Roy	2	1915–1917
MacCollum, Alexander*	1	1889–1890	Mar, Edmundo	3	1925–1925
MacCorkle, Robert C.	1	1916–1917	Marcus, Chapin	2	1914–1917
MacDonald, Colin Islin	2	1910–1912	Marckwald, Albert H.	3	1904–1907
MacDonald, James	2	1918–1920	Marden, Nicholas B.	2	1930–1932
MacDonald, Ronald H., Jr.	1	1915–1917	Marks, George E.	2	1919–1921
Macdonald, William K.	3	1936–1937	Marks, Lawrence M.	4	1915–1917
MacDougall, Allan, Jr.	1	1915–1917	Marquand, Russell*	1	1889–1893
MacGuire, Constantine, Jr.	MG	1909–1914	Marsellus, Max deM.*	1	1889–1906
Machado, Jose A., Jr.	1	1922–1927	Marsh, Allyn J.	2	1921–1924
MacInnes, John	2	1924–1925	Marsh, John Bigelow	1	1911–1917
MacKay, Horace A.	2	1931–1934	Marsh, Norman, Jr.	1	1921–1922
MacKellar, Robert S., Jr.	Med	1930–	Marshall, David P. B.	1	1905–1910
MacKenzie, James C., Jr.	4	1909–1917	Marshall, Levin R., Jr.	2	1925–1928
Mackie, David I., Jr.	2	1929–1932	Marshall, Pardee	2	1938–

SQUADRON A

Name	Troop or Detachment Served	Date of Enlistment and Final Discharge
Marshall, Robert P.	4	1911–1916
Marshall, Rufus S.	Hd	1925–1927
Marston, Hunter	3	1910–1917
Marston, Hunter Sylvester		1917–1919
Marston, Robert H., Jr.	2	1922–1923
Marston, Trobridge	1	1912–1915
Martens, William Clarence		1917–1919
Martin, Arthur H.	2	1918–1919
Martin, Aubrey H., Jr.	3	1924–1925
Martin, Charles F.	2	1928–1929
Martin, Clarence C.	3	1004–1904
Martin, Clyde*	1	1915–1917
Martin, Drelincourt	4	1908–1918
Martin, Edwin E. I.	3	1904–1916
Martin, Ernest	3	1934–1934
Martin, George W.	MG	1913–1916
Martin, Herbert	3	1925–
Martin, Howard J.	2	1927–1930
Martin, James J.	3	1917–1925
Martin, Lee G.	1	1938–
Martin, Matthew S.	1	1923–1927
Martin, Milward W.	1	1921–1930
Martin, Paul M.	1	1919–1919
Martin, Reune*	1-Hd	1898–1917
Martin, Rufus*	1	1889–1889
Martin, Shelton Edward	1	1908–1915
Martin, Wm. L.	2	1928–1931
Martinez, Edward L.	MG	1916–1917
Marvin, Alexander B.	3	1934–1937
Marvin, Walter Ramsey*	3	1901–1906
Mason, Francis Van W.	3	1924–1929
Mason, Jerome	1	1925–1925
Mason, Julian J.	1-2	1897–1898
Mason, Lowell	2	1916–1917
Mason, Stephen W.	2-4	1907–1916
Mason, Vernon L.	2	1931–1933
Mason, Wm. P., Jr.	MG	1916–1917
Master, Edward B.	Med	1936–
Masterson, George C.	3	1934–1938
Masterson, Walter J., Jr.	3	1929–1932
Mathews, Edward J.	3	1921–1924
Mathews, Henderson	2	1925–1928
Mathews, Schuyler L.	3	1929–1930
Mathewson, Samuel A.	3	1915–1917
Matthews, Frederick	1	1904–1905
Matthews, George, Jr.	3	1910–1932
Matthews, Wm. H., Jr.	2	1922–1923
Mattison, Graham D.	3	1930–1932
Mattison, Henry*	4-MG	1910–1916
Mattocks, Wm. A.	1-Hd	1919–1934
Maurice, Charles Alfred, Jr.	1	1917–1919
Mawby, Alfred W.	Hd	1922–1923
Maxwell, Douglas P.	1	1926–1928
Maxwell, Robert R.	2	1915–1917
May, Byron B.	2	1924–1927
Mayer, Wm. D.	3	1920–1922
Maynard, Gurdon	2-1-4	1899–1920
Maynes, Milton	1	1918–1919
Mays, Whitefoord S., Jr.	1	1939–
McAleenan, Henry Alvin		1917–1919

Name	Troop or Detachment Served	Date of Enlistment and Final Discharge
McAlpin, Allan H., Jr.	2	1935–
McAlpin, Allan Heyward	3	1907–1908
McAlpin, Kenneth R.	1	1912–1916
McAnerney, Francis B.	3	1899–1905
McAnerney, George G.	3	1937–
McAnerney, Joseph G.	3	1932–1937
McAnneny, Leonard G.	MG	1912–1917
McCabe, Lewis B., Jr.	1	1932–1935
McCaddon, Joseph T., Jr.	1	1921–1923
McCafferty, William	3	1935–
McCampbell, Geo. M.	2	1895–1920
McCampbell, William K.	3	1933–1934
McClellan, Otey	1	1921–1922
McClelland, Henry	1	1916–1916
McClintock, Harvey C.	2	1924–1925
McClure, Walter C.	4-3-MG	1907–1914
McCollom, Dr. R. L.	3	1925–1930
McConnell, Albert R.	1	1922–1928
McConnell, Elisha R.	1	1936–1937
McConnell, John	2	1924–1927
McConnell, Thomas	3	1928–1930
McCook, Daniel B.	1	1937–
McCook, Hon. Philip J.	3	1904–1919
McCord, Charles W.	2	1934–1937
McCormack, Alfred	1	1927–1930
McCouch, Gordon M.	2	1915–1917
McCoun, Robert D.	2	1937–
McCoy, John E.	2	1938–
McCrory, Bernard	3	1925–1925
McCullagh, Samuel	1-Med	1909–1916
McCulloch, Robert F.	2	1939–
McCullough, Paul L.	1	1915–1917
McCutcheon, Norman L.*	1	1907–1909
McDonald, John Ronald	4	1917–1919
McDonnell, Frank R.	1	1932–1935
McDonnell, Herbert	2	1910–1912
McDonnell, Lawrence E.	1	1937–
McElwain, Alexander	2	1926–1927
McGannon, Thomas L.	3	1931–1934
McGibbon, William C., Jr.	3	1902–1907
McGill, John J.	4	1916–1919
McGill, Raymond J.	1	1921–1921
McGiveney, Alexander J.	2	1919–1921
McGlade, Patrick	3	1923–1926
McGovern, Hal E.	1	1939–
McGrath, Gerald T.	Med	1930–1935
McGrath, Raymond D.	1	1922–1925
McGuire, Timothy S.	2	1934–1937
McGuire, Wm. S.	2-1-4	1897–1907
McGushion, Edward J.	2	1919–1921
McGusty, Robert T.	2	1898–1903
McHenry, Howard	2	1930–1933
McHugh, Thos. E.	2	1930–1931
McIsaac, Charles F.	2	1926–1929
McKay, Allan T.	1	1921–1926
McKee, McKee Dun*	3	1897–1900
McKelvey, Augustus J.	Med	1931–1934
McKelvy, Charles W.	1	1900–1903
McKernan, Patrick	2	1926–1926
McKibben, George N.*	1-Hd	1895–1901

SQUADRON A

Name	Troop or Detachment Served	Date of Enlistment and Final Discharge	Name	Troop or Detachment Served	Date of Enlistment and Final Discharge
McKiernan, Michael	3-1	1925–1932	Mickle, John K.	2	1922–1925
McKiernan, Thomas	2	1927–1931	Middleton, Keith T.	2	1935–1938
McKim, Albert V.*	1	1890–1891	Miles, Robert M., Jr.	3	1935–1937
McKinlay, James B.	2	1898–1898	Miller, Albert P.	2	1920–1922
McKinlay, Wm. B.	1-2	1892–1917	Miller, August B.	2	1927–1937
McKinstrey, DeWitt E.	2	1918–1918	Miller, Beverley E.	1	1938–
McLanahan, John D.	1-Hd	1922–1931	Miller, Chas. D.*	2-4	1904–1909
McLaury, John E.	3	1930–1931	Miller, Edward M.	1	1938–
McLean, Arthur	3	1913–1917	Miller, George J.	2	1935–1938
McLean, Walter R.	2	1922–1925	Miller, Henry W.	3-4	1907–1912
McLeran, Allan McL.	3	1925–1930	Miller, James Ely	2	1906–1911
McLester, Judson C., Jr.	2	1934–1937	Miller, LeRoy	2	1918–1924
McLoughlin, Comerford	MG	1916–1917	Miller, Llewellyn	1	1928–1936
McMahon, Edward W.	2	1918–1918	Miller, Rudolph N.	1	1923–1931
McMaugh, Malick	Hd	1925–1925	Miller, Rutger B., Jr.	3	1937–
McNeile, Hector J.	Med	1922–1930	Miller, William G., 3rd	1	1933–1937
McNish, Frederic B.*	4	1920–1922	Millett, James J.	2	1922–1922
McNitt, Charles W.	Med	1934–	Millett, Stephen C., Jr.	3	1931–1934
McNulty, George C.	3	1918–1918	Millette, Walter V.	Hd	1923–1923
McPhail, John D.	Hd	1926–1928	Milligan, Gilbert McK.	2	1938–
McPike, John A.	2-Hd-3	1916–1918	Milliken, Albert E., Jr.	2	1918–1920
McQuade, John C.	2	1918–1919	Milliken, Gerrish H.	1	1900–1906
McRae, Donald F.	1	1939–	Mills, Henry M.	1	1920–1925
McTirnan, James	3	1915–1919	Mills, Herbert Lawrence	3	1909–1916
McTurnan, Lee M.	3	1931–1934	Mills, James L.	2	1912–1913
McVaugh, Keith F.	1	1916–1917	Mills, Robert D.	3-Hd-4	1898–1909
McVickar, Henry W.*	1	1889–1892	Mills, Seward	3	1928–1931
McWilliams, Robert W.	3	1938–1938	Mills, Willis N.	3	1929–1932
Mead, Frank D.	3	1930–1930	Milne, Frederic F.	1	1937–
Mead, George G., 2nd	2	1923–1924	Milton, David M.	3	1921–1921
Meader, Equen B.	3	1935–1938	Miner, Walter J.	Hd	1925–1925
Meany, Philip J.	1	1916–1917	Minnick, Paul W.	1	1918–1918
Meehan, Theodore T.	3	1938–1938	Minor, Charles H.	1	1931–1933
Meeker, Dayton B.	1	1917–1919	Minott, Wm. A.	2	1895–1895
Meeker, John R.	Hd-2	1921–1926	Minton, Maurice	3	1920–1921
Meeker, Lincoln V.	3	1937–1937	Minturn, Hugh*	3	1905–1906
Mehlig, Lloyd G.	Med	1924–1925	Minturn, John W.	4	1903–1908
Mellen, Clark	1	1894–1919	Mitchell, Alexander	3	1924–1925
Mellen, Sydney L.	3	1930–1932	Mitchell, Cornelius von E.	2	1907–1917
Melvin, Henry E.	1	1939–	Mitchell, James S.	3-Hd	1923–1926
Melvin, William O.	2	1931–1936	Mitchell, John P.	3	1927–
Menhardt, Allen Ray	1	1918–1918	Mitchell, Wm. S.	2	1903–1912
Meninchette, Leone	2-Hd	1921–1922	Moen, A. Rene*	1-2	1892–1899
Merle-Smith, Van Santvoord	3	1914–1916	Moen, Edward C.*	1-2	1892–1899
Merrick, Frank H.	2	1933–1933	Moffat, Fraser M., Jr.	2	1921–1924
Merrill, Charles E., Jr.	3	1899–1917	Moffat, George Barclay	1	1917–1919
Merrill, Edgerton	1	1923–	Moffly, Wm. T., Jr.	1	1931–1932
Merrill, Edwin K.	2	1925–1930	Mohlman, George A.	1	1905–1905
Merrill, Oliver B., Jr.	1	1932–1935	Moir, Wm. W.	1	1929–1932
Merriman, James Davis*	3	1902–1916	Moisson, Marcel A.	1	1918–1918
Merritt, Walter Henry	1	1912–1915	Moller, Charles G., 3rd	3	1917–1918
Mertz, Louis W.	MG	1913–1916	Moller, Charles George, Jr.		1917–1919
Meserve, Frederick L.	3	1930–1935	Molyneux, Robert R.		1917–1919
Metcalf, James I.	2	1924–1924	Monahan, Hugh V., Jr.	1	1933–1936
Metcalf, Jesse	4	1912–1915	Monell, Frederick B., Jr.	1	1923–1934
Mettler, John W.	1	1902–1904	Monell, Ralph	2-4	1901–1908
Meyer, Robert B.	MG-2	1915–1917	Moneypenny, Wm.	3	1924–1924
Meyer, Schuyler	4	1911–1914	Monks, John, Jr.	1	1931–1933
Michalis, Clarence G.	4	1914–1915	Montague, Richard J.	4	1911–1913
Mickle, Charles C., Jr.	2	1922–1925	Montant, Lewis	2	1907–1912

Name	Troop or Detachment Served	Date of Enlistment and Final Discharge	Name	Troop or Detachment Served	Date of Enlistment and Final Discharge
Montgomery, Austin P.	3	1912–1914	Murphy, Walter F.	2	1918–1918
Montgomery, Edward G.	3	1927–1928	Murray, Allan K.	1	1927–1927
Montgomery, George P.	1	1916–1917	Murray, Francis W., Jr.	2	1910–1916
Montgomery, H. P. Alan*	3	1897–1910	Murray, Herman S.	2	1918–1919
Montgomery, John Renwick		1917–1919	Murray, Robert D., 2nd	MG	1916–1917
Montgomery, Rodman B.	3	1924–1926	Muser, Curt	2	1934–1937
Montgomery, Walter E.	1	1934–1938	Mustermann, Otto H.	Med	1926–1928
Moody, Virginius W., Jr.	1	1933–1937	Myers, Arthur	3	1912–1912
Moore, Charles B.	Hd-3	1923–1925	Myers, Henry H.	3	1928–1935
Moore, Frank L.	1	1889–1893	Myers, Irving T.	2	1919–1921
Moore, Harvey W., Jr.	2	1939–	Myers, Walter P.	1	1916–1917
Moore, Lawrence	2	1925–1928	Mygatt, Francis Stetson	1	1915–1917
Moore, William D.	3	1898–1918	Mygatt, Gerald	1	1909–1917
Moran, Lawrence J.	3	1928–1929	Mygatt, Royal E.	2	1934–1938
Moran, Leon S.	1	1926–1928	Myles, Robert C., Jr.	3	1921–1922
Morewood, Alfred P.	1	1918–1920	Mylott, Joseph J.	3	1922–1923
Morgan, D. Parker*	Hd	1895–1908			
Morgan, George E.	2	1895–1898	Nack, William J.	2	1915–1934
Morgan, Harry W.	2	1935–	Nash, Arthur Cleveland	3	1905–1914
Morgan, James P.	1	1931–1934	Nash, Franklin G. A.	3	1924–1926
Morgan, Richard J.	2	1927–1930	Nash, J. H.	2	1917–1918
Morgan, Rodney M.	1	1938–	Naul, Arthur L.	1	1933–1936
Morgan, Wm. F.	1-3	1890–1901	Neal, Chester Trenholm	4	1908–1917
Moriarty, Edward Joseph		1917–1919	Neave, Ralph, Jr.	3	1939–
Morrill, Frank Whitney	1-4	1905–1908	Neergaard, Chas. F.	1	1900–1902
Morris, Charles	3	1926–1927	Neeser, Robert W.	2	1911–1917
Morris, Harry H., Jr.	1	1932–1935	Neilson, Louis	2	1904–1911
Morris, John N.	3	1932–1932	Nell, Edward R.	Med	1937–
Morris, McLean F.	3	1909–1915	Nelson, George L.	1	1891–1893
Morris, Patrick	3	1925–	Nelson, Leonard	3	1918–1919
Morris, Thomas	2	1927–1931	Nelson, Richard A.	1	1930–1933
Morrison, Julian K.	1	1924–1926	Nesbitt, Hugh	3	1920–1922
Morrison, Martin A.	4	1916–1917	Nevins, William Everett		1917–1919
Morrison, Putnam M.*	2	1909–1915	Newbury, DeWitt M.		1917–1919
Morriss, Henry Allister	3	1916–1917	Newell, Albert N.*	2-4	1900–1910
Morse, Franklin B.*	1	1899–1904	Newell, Emerson R.*	3-4	1899–1917
Morton, Alfred H.	1	1924–1926	Newell, George S.	3	1932–1937
Morton, Stratford L., Jr.	1	1935–1937	Newton, Elmer	3	1927–1928
Morton, Woolridge B., Jr.			Ney-Illischer, Frank		1917–1917
Mosle, Max A.	1-2	1891–1911	Nicely, James M.	2	1925–1928
Moszkowski, George A.	1	1935–	Nicholas, Ridgely	3	1904–1917
Mount, John L.	2	1917–1920	Nicholls, Walter A.	2	1937–
Moury, Smith, Jr.	2	1926–1929	Nichols, Charles F.	3	1921–1924
Mueller, Alfred G.	1	1932–1936	Nichols, Ericksen N.	1-2	1890–1899
Mugavin, Joseph C.	1	1938–	Nichols, Erickson N.	2	1928–1930
Muir, Peter U.	3	1922–1922	Nichols, Frederick H.	1	1925–1929
Mullaly, Thornall	1	1897–1902	Nichols, J. Osgood	2	1895–1907
Muller, J. Herbert	3	1925–1930	Nichols, Norman D.	3	1925–1927
Mulligan, Ralph P.	3	1934–1938	Nichols, William B.	4	1916–1916
Mumford, George D.	1-2	1893–1898	Nicholson, Lionel	1	1928–1931
Mumford, Thomas D.	2	1930–1935	Nickerson, John, 3rd	3	1932–1935
Munn, Edward*	1	1895–1898	Nicoll, Courtlandt*	3	1905–1918
Munro, William Wallace		1917–1919	Nicolson, John, Jr.	2	1900–1905
Munro, Willis	3	1902–1906	Nikoloric, Artur	2	1918–1920
Munroe, Vernon	2	1897–1902	Noble, Francis O.	3	1924–1927
Murphy, Donald G.	3	1938–	Noble, Herbert	2	1895–1895
Murphy, Francis E.	MG	1916–1917	Noel, August L.	2	1912–1913
Murphy, Henry	2	1917–1929	Nolan, Wm. L.	2	1924–1924
Murphy, Michael	Med	1923–1927	Norman, John A.	3	1923–1926
Murphy, Robert J.	3	1938–1938	Norris, Nathaniel R.	3	1931–1936

SQUADRON A

Name	Troop or Detachment Served	Date of Enlistment and Final Discharge	Name	Troop or Detachment Served	Date of Enlistment and Final Discharge
North, Franklin H.	1	1894–1899	Outerbridge, Kenneth B.	2	1925–1926
Northrop, Claudean B., Jr.	1	1925–1927	Overton, Joseph A.	1	1935–1938
Northrop, James T.	1	1928–1932	Owens, Simon D.	3	1938–
Noyes, DeWitt C.	3	1900–1919	Owsley, Charles H.	1	1935–1936
Noyes, F. Jansen	MG	1913–1916			
Noyes, Frank E.	3-Med	1921–1923	Packard, Frederick A.	1	1923–1926
Noyes, George S., Jr.	2	1916–1917	Packard, John F. R.	MG	1916–1917
Noyes, Haskell	2	1914–1915	Paffrath, Stanley G.	3	1939–
Noyes, Julius Wentworth		1917–1919	Page, Haven B.	3	1924–1926
Noyes, William H.	2	1924–1928	Page, Horatio A. C.	2	1918–1920
Nugent, William R.	1	1939–	Page, James J.*	2	1916–1917
Nyhagen, Paul T.	1	1924–1927	Page, Richard M.	4	1915–1916
			Pagel, Axel J.	1	1918–1920
Oakley, R. Lawrence	MG	1912–1913	Paine, Alexander B.	3	1917–1918
Oakley, Wm. F.	1	1918–1918	Paine, Edward H.	1	1916–1921
Oakley, Wm. H., 2nd	1	1917–1918	Paine, Edward S.	3	1918–1918
Oakman, John	3	1907–1909	Palen, Frederick P.	2	1938–
Obolensky, Alexis, Jr.	2	1934–1934	Pallen, Thomas A.	2	1925–1928
O'Boyle, Edwards C.	1	1937–	Palmedo, Harold	Hd-1	1923–1924
O'Brien, Alvar deC.	3	1908–1908	Palmedo, Roland	Hd-1	1923–1927
O'Brien, Thomas J.	1	1919–1920	Palmer, Clinton*	1	1890–1893
O'Connell, Desmond H.	3	1930–1930	Palmer, Harold C.	2	1909–1912
O'Connell, Patrick	3	1922–1922	Palmer, Henry B.	4	1911–1911
O'Connor, Gerald H.	4	1909–1913	Palmer, William Eagle	3	1915–1917
O'Connor, Thomas	3	1921–1931	Pantzer, Kurt F.	1	1920–1922
O'Donnell, Joseph A.	1	1925–1930	Paret, John J.*	2	1897–1900
O'Donohue, Jos. J., 3rd	MG-Hd	1915–1917	Parish, Edward C.	1-2-3	1894–1900
O'Donohue, Louis V.*	1-Hd	1889–1908	Park, James	2	1909–1910
O'Donovan, Thomas	2	1922–1923	Park, Waring	Med-2	1923–1926
Ogilvie, John S., Jr.	2	1928–1930	Parker, Charles F.	2	1924–1925
O'Gorman, James A., Jr.	3	1927–1929	Parker, Cortlandt B.	2	1925–1926
O'Hara, Benjamin	2	1914–1915	Parker, Grenville*	1	1900–1918
Ohl, Percy C.*	1	1899–1900	Parker, Gurdon S.	1	1909–1910
O'Keefe, John P.*	4	1916–1919	Parker, Morris K.	1	1909–1911
Okie, Reginald W.	2	1916–1917	Parker, William L.	1	1938–
Olds, Irving S.	MG	1912–1916	Parks, George Elton	1	1907–1911
Oleksiw, Nicholas B.	1	1938–	Parmelee, Edward S.	1	1901–1907
Olmstead, Allan S., 2nd	2	1914–1915	Parry, Stuart K.	2	1919–1920
Olmsted, Edward	1-4	1898–1912	Parry, Vernon F.	3	1925–1927
Olmsted, Frank H.	1	1910–1910	Parsons, Charles	2	1916–1917
Olmsted, Joseph N.	3	1932–	Parsons, P. Allen	1	1918–1919
Olney, Peter B., Jr.	2	1907–1921	Parsons, Robert W.	1	1924–1926
Onativia, Jose V., Jr.	2	1920–1921	Parsons, Wm. B., Jr.	Med	1911–1912
O'Neil, James H.	3	1924–1925	Parsons, Wm. H., Jr.	2	1911–1913
O'Neill, Charles R.	2	1922–1923	Parton, John T.	2	1937–
Ordway, Frederick I., Jr.	1	1921–1921	Partridge, Mason, Jr.	3	1920–1923
Orr, Thornton W.	3	1921–1923	Paterson, Edward L.*	1-Hd-2-3	1889–1901
Orth, Charles D., Jr.	3	1915–1917	Paterson, Wm.	1	1897–1900
Orvis, Warner D.	4	1913–1916	Patrick, Edwin H.	1	1923–1926
Osborne, Earl W.	MG	1916–1919	Patterson, Richard C.	4	1915–1916
Osborne, Ernest B.	1	1915–1916	Patterson, Robert A.	2	1925–1925
O'Shea, Robert E.	4	1920–1921	Patterson, Robert M., Jr.	3	1924–1924
Osterberg, John D.*	4	1917–1918	Patterson, Roger W.	1	1925–1929
O'Sullivan, Daniel J.	2	1917–1917	Pattison, Edward H.	2	1923–1925
O'Sullivan, Thomas C.	1	1921–1922	Paul, Robert H., Jr.	3	1929–1933
Otheman, Edward Roe*	3	1896–1904	Paul, William L.	1	1934–1938
Otheman, Roswell C.	3	1907–1917	Paxton, John R., Jr.	1	1900–1902
Otis, Edward V.	Hd-3	1925–1929	Payne, Samuel B.	1	1935–1938
Otto, Henry S.	4	1913–1917	Peabody, Dudley H.	4	1908–1913
Outerbridge, Frank R.	2	1898–1914	Peabody, George R.	1	1906–1917

SQUADRON A

Name	Troop or Detachment Served	Date of Enlistment and Final Discharge
Peabody, Marshall*	3	1916–1917
Peabody, Stuart	2	1918–1921
Peale, Samuel R.	1	1931–1934
Peale, Van Horn*		1917–1918
Pearson, John B.	2	1932–1936
Pease, Arthur	1	1889–1900
Pease, George W.	2	1922–1922
Pease, Maurice H.	4	1911–1912
Pease, W. Albert, Jr.	2	1895–1900
Peck, Edward S.	4-MG	1906–1916
Peck, Everett J.	MG	1914–1916
Peck, Howard M.	3	1899–1917
Peck, Newton T.	1	1927–1931
Peckham, Charles J.	3	1932–1934
Peet, John K.	2	1929–1932
Peetz, Robert E.	2	1921–1922
Peiniger, Anthony G.	3	1937–1937
Peixette, Vernon M.	4-Hd	1920–1923
Pell, Stuyvesant M.	3	1927–1932
Pellew, Charles E. (Rt. Hon. Viscount)	1-2-Hd	1890–1898
Pendergast, Edward S. H., Jr.	2	1939–
Pendleton, David O.	2	1922–1925
Pennypacker, John G.	2	1923–1926
Pentz, Wm. E.*	1	1889–1894
Percy, Donald B.	2	1921–1923
Perkins, Frank B.	Hd	1927–1928
Perkins, George F., Jr.	2	1927–1929
Perkins, John A.	1	1919–1919
Perkins, Maxwell E.	2	1918–1920
Perkins, Richard S.	2	1932–1934
Perrin, Lee James	1	1910–1913
Perry, Alvan Williston*	1-4-MG	1906–1914
Perry, Cornelius, 2nd	3	1930–
Perry, Henry W.	2	1897–1901
Perry, John P. H.	MG	1912–1913
Peters, Churchill C.	3	1921–1922
Peters, Thomas McClure	4	1914–1917
Peters, Wm. R., Jr.*	4	1911–1911
Petersen, Louis W.	Hd-2	1927–1929
Peterson, Andrew	2	1922–1925
Peterson, Arnold H.	1	1929–1933
Peterson, Charles G.	3	1921–1922
Peterson, Frederic	1	1917–1919
Peterson, Milton L.	Hd	1925–1926
Peterson, Walker F.	2	1914–1914
Peterson, Wm. A.	3	1926–1926
Petrasch, Carl S.*	1-2-Hd	1894–1905
Petrie, Edward C.	1	1918–1919
Petroff, Boris	Med	1936–
Petterson, Robert A.	2	1925–1925
Phelps, Ansel	2	1895–1901
Phelps, Stowe	1-3-4	1894–1908
Phelps, Wm. W.	2	1915–1916
Philbin, Ewing R.		1914–1916
Philips, Kenneth T.	3	1920–1924
Philips, Roderick	3	1920–1922
Philips, Wm. F.	3	1914–1917
Phillips, Alexander	2	1935–
Phillips, Edward S., Jr.	2	1914–1916
Phillips, Giles T.	3	1925–1931
Phillips, James A., Jr.	2	1930–1934
Phillips, Loring	Hd-3	1923–1924
Phillips, Thomas G. T.	2	1937–
Phillips, Walter T.	2	1928–
Phillips, William J. S.	1	1921–1930
Phin, Charles H.	1	1919–1922
Phinney, Charles R.	2	1935–1938
Picken, Marshall W.	1	1918–1919
Pickhardt, Otto C.	Med	1910–1914
Pickhardt, Thomas K.	3	1937–
Pickney, Charles C.	1	1918–1920
Piel, William, Jr.	1	1936–
Pieper, Clifford J.	2	1920–1923
Pierce, Dewey L.	2	1930–1931
Pierce, Earl T.	2	1930–1934
Pierce, Reginald C. M.	1-MG	1910–1914
Pierce, Reginald K.*	3	1898–1904
Piercy, Kenneth T.	1	1938–
Pierrepont, Rutherford S.	1	1909–1912
Pierson, John H. G.	3	1931–1932
Pierson, Thomas H.	1-3	1898–1899
Pike, Glenn M.	1	1921–1921
Pinchot, Amos R. E.	3	1898–1899
Pine, Roswell D., Jr.	1	1936–
Pinkerton, Bledsoe C.	3	1930–1933
Pinney, Humphrey	4	1921–1922
Pipitone, Nino	2	1928–1931
Pitkin, George D.	2	1931–1934
Pitkin, Herbert L.	3	1900–1905
Pitou, Eugene	3	1905–1906
Plakias, John N.	1	1936–
Platt, Collier	3	1920–1924
Platt, Daniel F.	2	1897–1900
Platt, Frederick S.	2	1934–
Platt, Philip S.	1	1914–1916
Platt, Sherman Phelps	3	1912–1916
Plummer, Robert S.	2	1927–1929
Pochna, Stavin	1	1936–
Podlesski, Vsevolod N.	2	1933–1935
Poe, John P.	1	1924–1926
Polk, Frank L.	1	1896–1899
Pollard, William A., Jr.	3	1933–1934
Pomeroy, Brenton C.	3	1915–1917
Pomeroy, John R.	3	1938–
Pomeroy, Lawrence	1	1938–
Pond, Ashley*	3	**1897–1898**
Ponvert, Antonio, Jr.	3	1925–1926
Pool, Wm. H.	2	1903–1912
Poor, Alfred E.	3	1923–1925
Pope, Asa P.	Hd	1924–1926
Pope, Henry V.	2	1933–1935
Pope, Kennedy	Hd-2	1923–1925
Pope, Thomas M.	3	1939–
Popham, Lewis Charles		1917–1919
Popham, Robert M.	1	1927–1928
Porter, Hugh C.	2	1924–1925
Porter, James	1	1889–1890
Porter, James J.*	3	1914–1917
Porter, John F.	2	1931–1934

SQUADRON A 381

Name	Troop or Detachment Served	Date of Enlistment and Final Discharge	Name	Troop or Detachment Served	Date of Enlistment and Final Discharge
Post, Albertson V. Z.	1	1889–1890	Putnam, Harrington, Jr.	3	1933–1936
Post, Alfred S., Jr.	1	1898–1902	Putney, William B., 3rd	3	1932–1935
Post, Carol J., Jr.	2	1899–1904	Pyle, Charles McA.	3	1914–1917
Post, Henry B.*	4	1910–1911	Pyle, Edwin	4	1912–1914
Post, James Otis	3	1905–1911			
Post, Regis H., Jr.	1-2	1921–1924	Quackenbush, John, Jr.	2	1917–1919
Potter, Charles R.	4	1916–1917	Quarmby, Hillary	2	1925–1934
Potter, John P.	3-Hd	1922–1925	Quinby, Joseph R., Jr.	3	1896–1900
Potter, Orlando B.*	2	1918–1918	Quinby, Samuel L.*	3	1897–1901
Potts, Frederick A., Jr.	3	1931–1935	Quinn, Thomas	3	1923–1923
Potts, Gilbert R.	1	1896–1899	Quint, Maurice	2	1936–
Potts, J. M.*	1	1918–1919	Quintard, Wm. I.*	1	1890–1891
Potts, John P.	3	1930–1935			
Powell, Irwin A.	3	1929–1932	Radway, Edward M.	1-MG	1912–1913
Powell, Joseph B.	2	1917–1917	Radway, John Oakley	1	1910–1918
Powell, Llewellyn	3	1913–1913	Raff, Herbert A.	2	1936–
Powell, Robert B.	1	1932–1933	Rainsford, Walter K.	3	1905–1913
Powell, Robert I.	3	1927–1932	Ramsey, Robert*	2	1918–1920
Powell, Webster C.	1	1921–1921	Rand, Gordon L.*	3	1915–1917
Powelson, Roger V. N.	3	1933–	Rand, Wm. B.	2	1908–1909
Power, Richard G.	1	1918–1920	Rand, William B., Jr.	3	1937–
Powers, David J.	3	1934–1934	Randall, Darley	Hd	1921–1922
Powers, Walter H.	2	1901–1916	Randall, David J., Jr.	1	1924–1931
Powers, William T.	Hd	1924–1924	Randebrock, Francis W.	3	1923–1926
Prall, John G.*	2	1902–1902	Randolph, Francis F.	2	1914–1917
Pratt, Alexander D. B.	3-4	1905–1911	Randolph, Innes	MG	1914–1917
Pratt, Edward L.	Med	1909–1910	Randolph, Robert J., Jr.	4	1908–1917
Pratt, George C.	MG	1913–1916	Randolph, Robert S.	2	1931–1935
Pratt, Richardson	3	1915–1917	Ranlet, Robert, Jr.	1	1933–
Pratt, Stewart C.	2	1909–1912	Ransom, Norman K.	1	1921–1922
Prentice, Ezra P.	3-4	1898–1909	Rapalyea, Burtis B.	2	1931–1934
Prentice, Paul C.	1	1902–1902	Raphael, Charles G. C.	1	1929–1932
Prentice, R. Kelly	1-2-Hd	1892–1900	Rasch, Roland O.	2	1926–1927
Prentiss, Edmund A.	2	1918–1918	Rauch, Charles E., 2nd	1	1931–1936
Prescott, Wm. B.	2	1917–1919	Rauch, Wm. Paton*	2	1916–1917
Pressprich, Reginald W.	2	1898–1912	Ravenel, Gaillard F.	1	1912–1917
Pressprich, Reginald W., Jr.	2	1925–1929	Rawlins, Wm.	Hd	1926–1926
Preston, Frederick D.	1-3	1902–1912	Raymond, Franklyn T.	2	1910–1912
Preston, Jerome	1	1920–1922	Raymond, Irving E.	1	1898–1903
Preston, Ord	3	1901–1902	Raymond, Richard V.	3	1922–1923
Preston, Stuart D.	3	1907–1917	Raynolds, Samuel H., Jr.	1	1923–1927
Prettyman, George W.	3	1915–1917	Raynor, Edw. F., Jr.	2	1918–1918
Prettyman, Lambert	3	1921–1924	Read, Barclay K.	3	1928–1929
Preusse, Charles F.	1	1930–1933	Ream, Louis M.	4	1910–1910
Price, Walter W.	1	1890–1899	Ream, Norman P.	1	1915–1916
Priest, Daniel B.*	2	1915–1917	Reavis, Charles F.	2	1922–1923
Prime, Edward Gardner	2	1924–1926	Reboul, Jean B.	2	1922–1926
Prime, Peter	3	1937–1937	Reddin, Patrick	1	1921–1935
Proctor, Lawrence B.	1	1918–1919	Redfield, Alfred W.	1	1921–1922
Prout, William W.	3	1938–	Redfield, Wm. F.	3	1922–1922
Prugh, Edwin N., Jr.	1	1928–1929	Redington, George O.	2-3	1897–1915
Pruyn, Francis L.	3	1904–1912	Reed, Charles, Jr.	MG	1914–1914
Pryor, Morris McKim	4	1917–1917	Reed, Charles M.	3	1909–1915
Pugh, Jack W.	3	1931–1931	Reed, David	Hd	1924–1924
Pumpelly, Raphael W.	2	1910–1910	Reed, Ernest	Hd	1924–1924
Punderford, James C., Jr.	1	1937–	Reed, Howard C.	2	1924–1925
Purdy, Frank L.	1	1889–1890	Reed, Latham W.	1-2-3	1889–1917
Putnam, Albert W.	1-2	1898–1917	Reed, Latham R.	3	1904–1916
Putnam, Edmond	2	1901–1903	Reed, Thomas B.	2-Hd	1918–1924
Putnam, Edward H.*	2-MG	1901–1917	Reed, William C.	2	1929–

SQUADRON A

Name	Troop or Detachment Served	Date of Enlistment and Final Discharge	Name	Troop or Detachment Served	Date of Enlistment and Final Discharge
Rees, Louis DuB.	2	1925–1926	Roberson, Wm. C.	1	1923–
Reese, Richard R.	2	1935–1935	Robert, Edmond E.	3	1897–1903
Reese, Thomas H., Jr.	2	1929–1937	Roberts, John A.	1	1930–1933
Reeve, Henry L.	2	1900–1919	Roberts, John K.	2	1929–1932
Rehm, William L.	Hd-1	1921–1926	Roberts, John T.	4	1908–1908
Reichner, Frederic F.	2-Hd	1918–1928	Roberts, Malcolm	3	1938–
Reid, Charles L.	2	1916–1917	Roberts, Ralph	Hd-2	1923–1925
Reiley, George C.	3	1938–	Roberts, Thomas C.	3	1922–1923
Reilley, Ewing W.	3	1934–1937	Robertson, Kenneth D., Jr.	2	1932–1933
Reimer, Otto B.	3	1922–1923	Robinson, Clarence	1	1918–1920
Rennard, John T.	1	1916–1917	Robinson, Charles P.	1	1914–1917
Renshaw, Paul	3	1913–1914	Robinson, D. T. L.*	1	1889–1894
Reynolds, Eugene B., Jr.	2	1924–1927	Robinson, Dwight E.*	2	1899–1907
Reynolds, John	4	1915–1922	Robinson, Fielding S.	1	1924–1926
Reynolds, Julian L.	1	1937–1938	Robinson, Guy	3	1916–1917
Reynolds, Richard S., Jr.	1	1932–1934	Robinson, Hamilton W.*	2-3-Hd	1917–1926
Reynolds, Roy D.	1	1930–1938	Robinson, James H.	Mg-2	1916–1922
Reynolds, Samuel H., Jr.	1	1923–1927	Robinson, James H.	2	1921–1922
Reynolds, Theodore F.	2	1917–1919	Robinson, James V.	2	1921–1922
Rheims, Harry L.	2-4-2	1906–1908	Robinson, John H.	4	1918–1920
Rhett, Douglas W.	3	1935–1937	Robinson, Lewis B.	MG	1913–1913
Rhoads, Robert P.	3	1937–	Robinson, Monroe D.	2	1910–1911
Rice, Durant	3	1911–1916	Robinson, Theodore Douglas	3	1906–1907
Rice, Wm. R.	MG	1916–1917	Rockwell, Bertrand	2	1921–1921
Richard, Auguste	3	1912–1917	Rockwell, Jarvis W., Jr.	1	1918–1920
Richards, Benjamin R.	1	1937–	Rockwood, John P.	2	1918–1920
Richards, Harold M.	4	1909–1918	Rockwood, Nathaniel O.	2	1913–1916
Richards, Ira, Jr.	1	1912–1913	Rockwood, Philip M.	1	1918–1918
Richards, John V., Jr.	2-Hd	1926–1929	Rodenback, Edward T.	Hd-2	1923–1926
Richards, Lloyd*	3	1915–1917	Rodgers, Frederick, Jr.	4-2	1910–1918
Richardson, Enos	2	1929–1932	Roe, Charles F.*	1-Hd	1889–1898
Richardson, Gardner	4	1908–1914	Roelker, Alfred, Jr.	1	1898–1917
Richardson, Wallace C., Jr.	3	1931–1933	Roeser, John M.	3	1934–1935
Richardson, Wm. E.	4	1916–1917	Roessler, Frederick L.	3	1934–
Richmond, Stacey C.	1	1895–1898	Rogers, Bard P.	2	1934–1938
Richmond, William, Jr.	1	1921–1924	Rogers, Ernest R.	1	1889–1889
Richmond, William D.	3	1926–1929	Rogers, Henry Pendleton*	3	1903–1908
Riedell, John W.	2	1917–1918	Rogers, John S.*	3	1898–1903
Riedell, Wallace C.	3	1938–	Rogers, Martin C.	Med	1937–
Riis, Roger W.	2	1921–1923	Rogerson, James C.*	2	1900–1907
Riker, Henry J.*	1-2	1893–1899	Rollins, Frank S.	2	1896–1902
Riker, Herbert L.	4	1903–1908	Rollins, LeRoy	3	1921–1928
Riley, George C.	3	1938–	Rolston, Brown	3	1911–1914
Riley, Henry A.	Med	1909–1918	Rolston, Roswell G.	3	1911–1917
Riley, Wells L.	1	1916–1917	Romaine, Julian C.	3	1923–1927
Ringgold, James R.	3	1933–1936	Romaine, Peirce L.	3	1924–1929
Ripley, Louis A.	1	1898–1899	Romaine, Theodore C.	Hd-3	1921–1923
Ripley, Sidney Dillon	4	1917–1919	Roome, Kenneth A.	3	1920–1925
Ris, Albert I.	2	1934–1937	Rooney, Lawrence	2	1922–1922
Ritter, Louis S., Jr.	3	1939–	Roosevelt, William E.	1	1938–
Rives, Francis B.	2	1912–1917	Root, Elihu, Jr.	1	1909–1912
Rives, Reginald B.	2	1911–1917	Rorison, John C.	1	1922–1923
Rizzo, Charles J.	3	1938–	Rose, Durant	4	1917–1919
Robbins, Allan A.	2-1	1895–1898	Rosenquest, Eugene H.	3	1925–1926
Robbins, Geoffrey W.	1	1934–1937	Rosett, Lee A.	3-Med	1920–1925
Robbins, George P.	1-2	1891–1900	Ross, Carl G. R.	1	1925–1926
Robbins, Henry P.	1-2	1890–1896	Ross, John W.	1	1921–1926
Robbins, Montgomery H.	1	1934–1937	Ross, Leland H.	1	1905–1906
Robbins, Wm. B.	2	1923–1925	Rossiter, Arthur W., Jr.	3	1929–1935
Robbins, Wolcott P.	2	1896–1902	Rothwell, Albert C.	1	1916–1917

SQUADRON A

Name	Troop or Detachment Served	Date of Enlistment and Final Discharge	Name	Troop or Detachment Served	Date of Enlistment and Final Discharge
Rothwell, Austin S.	1	1916–1917	Schieffelin, Bayard	1	1928–1931
Rothwell, Vincent H.*	1	1916–1916	Schieffelin, George R. D.	2	1917–1917
Rotnem, Ralph A.	3	1935–1937	Schieffelin, John J.	2	1916–1923
Rounds, Stowell	2	1929–1933	Schieffelin, Wm. J., Jr.	2	1914–1916
Rowe, Benjamin A.	3	1937–1937	Schlater, Frederick M.	3	1929–1929
Rowland, Jasper M.*	1	1902–1903	Schmidt, Parbury P.	3	1929–1937
Rowland, John T.	2	1915–1917	Schmitt, Walter E.		1917–1919
Rowles, Don F. S.	3	1932–1935	Schmitt, William J.	2-Hd	1921–1923
Royal, Ralph	3	1918–1920	Schmitz, Frederick	3	1918–1919
Ruckgaber, Louis A.	2	1927–1928	Scholl, Thomas F.	1	1933–1936
Rudd, Tracy A.	4	1909–1910	Schoonover, Wm. G., Jr.	2	1926–1929
Rudolph, Harold W.	2	1920–1924	Schroeder, Henry, Jr.	3	1925–1927
Ruggles, Burnet R.	1	1899–1904	Schuchard, Hans J.	3	1936–
Ruland, Irving*	2	1895–1901	Schuff, Eugene J., Jr.	2	1927–1931
Runkle, Daniel*	1	1910–1915	Schuh, Edward R.	1	1936–1938
Runkle, Henry G., 2nd	3	1930–1931	Schulten, Alexander, Jr.	3	1929–1931
Russell, Eugene F.	4-Med	1913–1922	Schultz, Fay	3	1921–1922
Russell, Frank F.	2	1928–1929	Schumacher, Edwin F.	Hd-1	1923–1925
Russell, Frank R.	3	1916–1917	Schurman, George M.	2	1915–1917
Russell, Paris S., Jr.	2	1932–1935	Schussler, Wm. F.	1	1914–1917
Russell, Randolph	3	1913–1916	Schwab, Benjamin W.*	3	1896–1898
Rutherford, Henry L.	1	1889–1889	Schwaiker, M. W.	3	1916–1917
Rutter, Joseph W.	4	1909–1911	Schwaikert, Martin W.		1917–1919
Ryan, Allan A., Jr.	1	1926–1928	Schwarz, Herbert F.	1-3	1905–1921
Ryan, Charles D.	1	1916–1917	Schwarz, Simon	1	1918–1918
Ryan, Henry J.	1	1918–1919	Scott, Ludlow P.	3	1933–1935
Ryan, John P.	2-Hd	1918–1923	Scott, Myron L.	2	1922–1923
Ryan, Leicester	3	1931–1933	Scott, Randolph W.	3	1923–1927
Ryer, George S.*	1	1889–1894	Scott, Rumsey W.	2	1901–1902
Ryerson, Joseph T.	MG	1912–1915	Scott, Stuart, Jr.	2	1934–1938
Ryle, Arthur, Jr†	2	1931–1937	Scott, William R.	3	1924–1924
Ryle, Joseph D., Jr.	3	1934–1935	Sealy, Robert	3	1915–1918
			Seamans, William S., Jr.	3	1915–1917
Sabean, Ernest E.	2	1925–1925	Seamans, Woodbury*	3	1909–1912
Sabin, Charles D., Jr.	MG-2-Hd	1917–1922	Searing, Arthur F.	3	1939–
Sabin, Henry P.	1	1921–1922	Secor, Jay K.	1	1936–1937
Sackett, Henry W.*	1-Hd	1889–1897	Sedgwick, James B.	1	1939–
St. John, Henry W.	3	1901–1906	Sedgwick, Theodore	1-2	1893–1899
Sallmon, Harry T.	1	1927–1928	Sefton, Russell A.	2	1928–1931
Saltus, Rollin*	1-2	1893–1919	Seggerman, Frederick	1	1889–1891
Sampson, Henry, Jr.	1-MG	1901–1914	Seggerman, Frederick T.	MG	1912–1917
Sanders, Benton	2	1912–1918	Seggerman, Kenneth M.	MG	1913–1916
Sanderson, Lloyd B., Jr.	3	1921–1925	Selden, Edward G.	2	1924–1929
Sanderson, Robert M.	3	1922–1925	Selden, Lynde	MG	1915–1917
Sanford, Henry G.*	3	1897–1899	Semken, Henry L.	1	1918–1919
Sanger, Joseph P.	3	1930–1931	Semler, George H.	1	1921–1924
Satterlee, Churchill	1	1932–1934	Sessions, Marion B.	1	1930–1937
Satterlee, Dr. Henry S.	3	1896–1916	Setterlee, Churchill	1	1932–1934
Saunders, Alexander	2	1929–1935	Severance, Frank A. F.	1	1930–1933
Saunders, Reginald A.	3-MG	1912–1917	Severn, Douglas K.	1	1926–1929
Savage, Hugh M.	1	1938–	Seward, Walter M.*	1	1892–1897
Savage, John R.	1	1939–	Sexton, Michael J.	2	1939–
Sawyer, Arthur T.	1	1933–1936	Seymour, Raymond B.	3	1916–1917
Sayles, Alexander	3	1928–1929	Seymour, William W.*	1-2	1894–1900
Sayre, Reginald H.*	1-Hd	1893–1914	Shannonhouse, Renaud C.	2	1939–
Schaefer, Bernhard K.	Hd	1920–1923	Shantz, Howard D.	3	1928–1932
Schaefer, Herbert W.	MG	1912–1916	Sharp, George C.	Hd-1	1923–1926
Scheafe, Charles M., Jr.	2	1906–1912	Sharp, Willoughby, Jr.	3	1921–1924
Schefer, Anton F.	2	1904–1910	Sharretts, Edward P.	4	1909–1915
Schefer, Ernest E.	2	1925–1926	Shattuck, Edwin P	4	1906–1907

SQUADRON A

Name	Troop or Detachment Served	Date of Enlistment and Final Discharge
Shaw, Albert, Jr.	3-Hd	1921–1926
Shaw, Brackley	1	1938–
Shaw, Lewis Edward*	MG-1	1915–1926
Shaw, Munson G.	1-2	1899–1901
Shaw, Munson G., Jr.	3	1927–1930
Shearer, Harold H.	2	1915–1916
Shearer, Leander H.	2-Hd-Med	1906–1914
Shedden, George A.	MG-4	1912–1916
Sheehan, James G.	2	1925–1925
Sheild, Philip B.	3	1920–1920
Sheldon, Farrington	MG-3	1916–1924
Sheldon, Henry	2-1-3-MG	1900–1917
Shepard, Augustus D., Jr.	1-2-3	1894–1908
Shepard, Ruthford*	3	1897–1900
Shepard, William B.	2	1935–1938
Shepherd, William E., Jr.	3	1915–1917
Sheppard, John S., Jr.	2	1896–1901
Sheridan, Lewis C.	1	1921–1924
Sherman, Richard G.	2	1920–1921
Sherman, William B.	3	1935–
Sherwood, Howard C.	3	1897–1902
Shevlin, Gerard T.	1	1930–1934
Shevlin, Mathew Joseph	2	1917–1919
Shiland, Andrew R.	3	1911–1916
Shillaber, William R.	1	1927–
Shipman, Rt. Rev. Herbert*	Hd	1906–1913
Shoemaker, David O.	3	1930–1933
Shope, Wm. B.	2-3	1920–1922
Shrady, Charles D.	1	1917–1918
Shreve, Wickliffe W.	3	1927–1928
Shrewsbury, Kenneth O.	1	1921–1924
Shults, Russell C.	2	1918–1920
Shurtleff, Harold R.	4-2	1916–1925
Sibley, Henry Hastings		1917–1918
Siedenburg, Reinhard A.	3	1931–1934
Sieniawski, Boris M.	3	1935–1938
Silleck, Walter M.	Med	1912–1914
Silliman, Alfred D.	3	1918–1919
Silliman, Halsey E.	3	1918–1920
Silloway, Stuart	2	1932–1935
Silver, Edward V., Jr.	2	1931–1933
Silvey, Wm. H.	2	1918–1919
Simm, David	MG-2	1916–1924
Simmons, Conrad C.	3-Hd	1921–1929
Simon, Theodore	4	1915–1917
Simonson, Charles A.	2	1932–1933
Simonson, Earle M.	2	1926–1929
Simonson, Harrie Sturgis	1	1917–1919
Simpson, Wm. S.	1	1924–1930
Sims, Alfred W.	1	1924–1927
Sinclair, Donald B.	Med-MG	1910–1914
Sinclair, John E.	2	1930–1933
Singer, Aaron	3	1925–1925
Singleton, Edwin L.	3	1924–1927
Sisson, Edgar G., Jr.	Hd	1925–1928
Sizer, Robert R., Jr.	4	1913–1916
Skeen, Ransom H.	1	1928–1930
Skelding, Henry T.*	1	1924–1927
Skelly, William S.	1	1935–1938
Skinner, John P.	3	1934–1935

Name	Troop or Detachment Served	Date of Enlistment and Final Discharge
Slade, Arthur J.	1	1894–1901
Slade, Francis L.	2	1895–1902
Slade, Henry L., Jr.	2	1921–1922
Slade, John*	3	1896–1898
Slade, Lawrence,	3	1905–1912
Slade, Prescott*	1-2	1894–1899
Slee, James N.	MG	1916–1917
Slidell, Thomas	1	1898–1898
Sloan, Robert S.	3	1932–1934
Sloane, George	MG	1914–1917
Sloane, John	4	1907–1917
Sloane, William*	3	1896–1901
Slocum, Herbert	1-Hd	1914–1917
Smalley, Vincent R.	3	1926–1929
Smidt, Allan Campbell*	2-3	1906–1916
Smidt, Wm. F.	2	1924–1925
Smith, Abel I.	1-4	1899–1910
Smith, Abel I., Jr.	2	1937–
Smith, Albert M., 2nd	3	1931–1933
Smith, Augustine C.*	2-3	1895–1918
Smith, Austin L.	3	1925–1926
Smith, Bearns	2	1934–
Smith, Bernard J.	3	1924–1925
Smith, Carl B.	MG	1915–1916
Smith, Caswell M.	3	1921–1922
Smith, DeWitt H.	3	1934–
Smith, E. Everett, Jr.	2	1936–1938
Smith, Edgar	1	1895–1895
Smith, Edgar N.	2-Hd	1921–1924
Smith, Edward C.	2	1927–1930
Smith, Edward H.	2	1933–1934
Smith, Erskine M.	1	1910–1915
Smith, Eugene Dutilh	3	1910–1917
Smith, Eugene T.	1	1889–1889
Smith, Francis Irving	4	1914–1916
Smith, Freeman A.	3	1901–1906
Smith, Granville B.	2	1922–1923
Smith, Gurney L.	3	1921–1922
Smith, Harold L.	1	1922–1923
Smith, Harold L.	2	1926–1930
Smith, Haviland	2	1930–1933
Smith, Henry Clapp	1-4	1903–1915
Smith, Henry Y. T.	1	1893–1899
Smith, Herbert B.	2	1896–1919
Smith, Howard C.	1-2	1894–1917
Smith, Howard C.	1	1920–1921
Smith, Howard Valentine	1	1913–1916
Smith, Hugh M.	2	1921–1923
Smith, James	3	1933–1934
Smith, James H. A.	2	1918–1920
Smith, Joseph Ascher	3	1917–1924
Smith, Leonard B.	3-4	1903–1913
Smith, Letchworth*	1	1898–1898
Smith, Malcolm E.	1-MG	1905–1915
Smith, Marion B.	2	1929–1932
Smith, Maxwell B.	2	1903–1905
Smith, Merrit H.*	1-MG	1896–1912
Smith, Monroe E.	1	1929–1932
Smith, Norman P.	2	1921–1923
Smith, Paul S.	3	1929–1932

SQUADRON A

Name	Troop or Detachment Served	Date of Enlistment and Final Discharge	Name	Troop or Detachment Served	Date of Enlistment and Final Discharge
Smith, Richard B.	3	1936-1937	Starr, Theodore D.	2	1926-1927
Smith, Robert S.	1	1938-	Start, Louis B.	2	1934-
Smith, St. Clair M.	3	1930-1933	Stearns, Douglas B.	2	1939-
Smith, Sidney J.	1	1895-1896	Stearns, Francis U.*	2	1900-1901
Smith, Sydney R.	1	1916-1917	Stearns, Francis U., Jr.	2	1927-1933
Smith, W. Schuyler	1	1903-1914	Stearns, Henry S., Jr.	1	1915-1917
Smith, Wilfred W.	Hd-2	1925-1929	Stearns, John N., Jr.	1-2-3-Hd	1895-1903
Smith, William	Hd	1925-1925	Stearns, John N., 3rd	2	1916-1917
Smith, William Mason	2-3	1900-1904	Stearns, Kendall	Hd	1922-1923
Smith, William Prescott*	3	1900-1901	Stearns, Phillips T.	2	1939-
Smith, Wilson F.*	1	1895-1908	Stebbins, Rowland	1	1909-1912
Smith, Winthrop D.	1	1901-1902	Steel, G. Drexel	3	1926-1929
Smith, Winthrop H.	3	1921-1924	Steele, Leverett	1	1914-1917
Smithers, Austin L.	3	1925-1926	Steele, William, 3rd	1	1937-1938
Smithers, Herbert B.	2	1902-1907	Steen, James	3	1926-1929
Smolianinoff, Andre V.	1	1936-	Steers, Thomas T.	2	1925-1938
Smollen, John J.*	4	1917-1917	Steinacher, Julio M.	3	1918-1920
Smyth, Wm. R.	1	1916-1917	Steinway, Charles G.	1	1936-
Smythe, Cyrus F.	1	1922-1924	Stelling, Adolf C.	3	1932-1936
Snare, Frederick, Jr.	4	1915-1919	Stelling, Frank P.	Sen. Det.	1917-1919
Snider, Leonard	4	1913-1915	Stephens, James B.	3	1927-1929
Snow, Eldridge G., 3rd*	2-3-Hd	1919-1923	Stephens, Thomas G.	2	1936-1938
Snow, George P.	3	1903-1907	Stephenson, Byron P.	1	1892-1893
Snowdon, Arthur W.		1917-1919	Stephenson, Frederick K.	2	1918-1920
Snyder, Eldredge	3	1925-1927	Stephenson, John P.	2	1918-1919
Snyder, Perrin B.	3	1938-	Stetson, Clarence C.	1	1911-1913
Snyder, Philip M.	3	1932-	Stetson, Samuel Cutting	1	1911-1911
Soper, Willard B.	Med	1911-1913	Stetson, Webster W.	1	1905-1917
Soule, Frank L.	2	1916-1917	Stetson, Webster Wagner	1	1917-1919
Southack, John W.	2-4	1907-1908	Stettinius, Wm. C.	4	1916-1917
Southard, George H., Jr.	3	1904-1907	Stevens, Barrett W.	2	1930-1933
Southwick, William F.	3	1925-1926	Stevens, Francis K.	1	1898-1915
Sowdon, John I.	MG	1916-1917	Stevens, Horace N.	2	1900-1905
Spadone, Henry E.	1	1898-1903	Stevens, Oscar Egerton	1	1909-1910
Spalding, Frederic P.	Hd-2	1923-1925	Stevens, W. Lewis	3	1916-1917
Spalding, James W.	1	1938-	Stevens, Weld M., Jr.	3	1937-
Sparkhark, Charles V.	2	1918-1921	Stevenson, Gordon	1	1927-1929
Speiden, John G. F.	3	1923-1925	Stevenson, Harvey	1	1923-1930
Speir, Robert W., Jr.	3	1922-1924	Stevenson, William M.	3	1899-1900
Spencer, Frank A., Jr.	MG	1913-1916	Steward, James B.	Hd-3	1923-1928
Spencer, George F. M.	4	1914-1917	Stewart, Howard T.	Hd	1926-1929
Spencer, James Beaumont	4	1907-1917	Stewart, John H., Jr.	1	1937-1937
Spencer, James Brooks, 2nd	2	1916-1917	Stidham, Shaler	2	1932-1932
Spencer, Lorillard, Jr.*	2	1904-1912	Stiger, W. D.		1898-1918
Speyers, Albert W.	1	1889-1892	Stillman, Leland S.	2	1898-1899
Spitzer, Victor	4	1917-1917	Stillman, Philip T.	1-4	1897-1916
Sprague, Carl O. M.	1	1912-1915	Stilson, Colby	2	1928-1931
Sprague, Irvin A., Jr.	1	1921-1927	Stimson, Henry B.	1	1910-1917
Sproul, Christopher G.	3	1930-1931	Stimson, Henry L.	2	1898-1907
Sproul, Joseph	1	1922-1929	Stires, Harderick	2	1925-1925
Spurr, Gregory W.	3	1924-1927	Stockder, Robert M.	1	1928-1933
Squibb, Charles F.	1	1893-1898	Stockton, Gilbert	1	1915-1915
Squiers, Bard McD.*	MG	1914-1916	Stoddard, Dudley W.	3	1935-1938
Stammers, Alfred Henry	3	1917-1919	Stoddard, Goodwin	3	1931-1934
Stanley, Leonard L.	4	1916-1917	Stokes, Horace W.	MG-4	1914-1917
Stark, Louis B.	2	1934-	Stokes, J. G. Phelps	2-Hd	1896-1901
Starkey, Earle J.	1	1932-1937	Stokes, J. N. Phelps	1	1891-1892
Starr, Howard D.	3	1930-1933	Stone, C. F., Jr.	1-2-3	1890-1919
Starr, Louis	3	1935-	Stone, Dee W.	Hd-1	1923-1926
Starr, Malcolm W.	3	1933-1933	Stone, Delano	3	1928-1937

SQUADRON A

Name	Troop or Detachment Served	Date of Enlistment and Final Discharge
Stone, George H.	3	1938–
Stone, J. K. P.	2-4	1902–1907
Stone, Philip W.	3	1921–1922
Stone, Ralph E.	2	1926–1929
Stone, Robert K.	1	1922–1923
Stone, Thomas E.	3	1921–1922
Stothers, Hilton H.	Med	1931–1934
Stott, Frederick B.	1	1916–1917
Stott, Gordon D.	1	1930–1933
Stout, Robert P.	1	1921–1925
Stover, Jordan H., 3rd	3	1937–
Stowell, Edward Esty	1	1906–1917
Stowell, Harley L.	1	1909–1914
Strachan, Kenneth	Hd-2	1923–1926
Strahler, Wm. O.	3	1918–1920
Strange, Albert B.	1	1896–1919
Straus, Joseph	1-Hd	1925–1928
Streibert, Theodore C.	1	1927–1928
Strong, Edwin A.	Med	1902–1903
Strong, Prentice	3	1906–1912
Strong, Theron R.*	2	1903–1910
Strout, Edwin A., Jr.	Hd	1922–1925
Stuart, David*	1	1898–1917
Stuart, Joseph, Jr.	3	1930–1936
Stubbs, Frank B.	3	1921–1927
Studda, Colen A.	2	1924–1925
Studdiford, Hervey	4-Hd-MG	1908–1914
Stump, Augustine H.	MG	1915–1917
Sturdivant, Greely, Jr.	1	1933–1936
Sturges, John M.	1	1930–1934
Sturgis, Reginald H.	3	1909–1911
Sturhahn, Herbert C.	1	1930–1936
Stursberg, Herbert J.	2	1914–1917
Suckley, Henry M.*	2	1912–1917
Sullivan, Eldon B.	3	1933–1933
Sullivan, Leonard	3	1909–1917
Sully, Winfield P.	1	1889–1893
Sumner, Adams C.*	1	1901–1917
Sunderland, Edwin S. S.	1-2	1916–1917
Sunderland, Thomas E.	1	1932–1935
Sus, Philip C.*	1-Hd-3	1890–1898
Sutherland, Andrew G.	2	1924–1925
Sutherland, Paul A.	2	1926–1928
Sutton, Francis M., Jr.	2	1924–1925
Sutton, Frederick T.	2	1918–1918
Sutton, Richard D.	3	1907–1913
Suydam, Bernard	2-Hd	1921–1924
Swan, Dallas D.	3	1921–1922
Swan, Edward H.	3	1936–1937
Swayne, Alfred H.*	1	1895–1898
Swede, Allen G.	Hq	1927–1928
Sweet, James L.	2	1934–1938
Sweet, Reginald L.	2	1912–1912
Sweet, Stanley A.	2	1908–1917
Swenson, Herbert J.	4	1916–1917
Swett, Gilbert	1	1922–1926
Swift, Edwin E.*	1	1889–1890
Swift, Frederick T.	1	1889–1891
Swift, Lyman	2	1920–1922
Syler, Charles	4	1916–1917
Symes, George Gifford	4	1908–1916
Symes, John Foster	1	1904–1907
Symington, William H.	3-4	1913–1917
Symmes, W. B., Jr.	2	1902–1907
Taft, Walbridge Smith	1	1910–1913
Taft, Wm. H., 2nd	1-MG-3-2	1910–1922
Tailer, Robert W.	3	1921–1932
Talbot, Charles M., Jr.	1	1902–1906
Talbot, H. R.	1-4	1902–1907
Talbot, Harold R.	1	1930–1937
Talbot, John C., Jr.	Hd	1923–1925
Talcott, Hooker	3	1922–1925
Taliaferro, Albert P., Jr.	Hd	1922–1922
Taliaferro, Van B.	1	1931–1934
Tallant, Hugh	2	1900–1908
Talmadge, Henry, 2nd	1	1906–1911
Tameling, Arthur L.	3	1937–
Tameling, Gerard P., Jr.	3	1932–1934
Tanner, Brent McIlvain		1906–1907
Tarbell, George S., Jr.	1	1929–1932
Tarbox, Walter L.	1	1933–1936
Tate, Henry C.	1	1925–1930
Taylor, Alfred K.	1	1916–1917
Taylor, Benjamin I., Jr.	2	1936–1937
Taylor, Donald F.	MG	1915–1917
Taylor, Howard A.	2	1898–1901
Taylor, Lewis M.	1-2	1918–1922
Taylor, Moses*	1	1895–1897
Taylor, Wm. R. K., Jr.	3	1921–1923
Taylor, William T.	2	1939–
Terrell, Claude M.	Hd	1924–1926
Terry, James T.	1	1898–1903
Terry, Ward E.	1	1930–1933
Terry, Wyllys, Jr.	3	1932–
Thain, Charles C.	1-2	1893–1899
Thatcher, John M. P.	4	1911–1915
Thayer, Bert C.	1	1923–1926
Therkildsen, Alfred O.	1	1939–
Thiery, Auguste M.*	1	1895–1895
Thiery, Lewis M.*	1	1895–1899
Thomas, Colin J.	1	1927–1930
Thomas, Edmund E.	2	1922–1927
Thomas, Egbert E.	2	1918–1920
Thomas, Frederic C.	1	1923–1934
Thomas, Harvey A.	3	1919–1919
Thomas, Herman	3	1896–1898
Thomas, Hugh C., Jr.	Med	1929–1932
Thomas, Jules P.	1	1919–1919
Thomas, Luke G.	1	1916–1917
Thomas, Richard R.	2	1931–1934
Thomas, S. Richard	1	1889–1891
Thomas, Seth E., Jr.*	1	1905–1912
Thompson, Henry S.	2	1896–1901
Thompson, Hugh C., Jr.	Med	1929–1932
Thompson, Laurence M.	Med-MG	1910–1914
Thompson, Lyall W.	2	1933–1935
Thomson, Ernest A.	1-2	1889–1889
Thornall, Clarence E.*	1-2	1889–1897
Thornall, Clarence E., Jr.	2	1918–1923

SQUADRON A 387

Name	Troop or Detachment Served	Date of Enlistment and Final Discharge	Name	Troop or Detachment Served	Date of Enlistment and Final Discharge
Thorne, Gilbert G., Jr.	MG	1916–1917	Tracey, John	2	1913–1913
Thorne, J. Norrish	MG	1912–1917	Tracy, Howard C.	1	1889–1891
Thorne, Joel W.*	1-2-3-2	1890–1902	Travis, Albert C.	1	1914–1916
Thornley, John	2	1902–1907	Travis, Luke O.	2	1939–
Thornton, James C.	1	1912–1917	Trawick, Stovall W.	3	1935–1938
Thornton, Patrick	3	1922–1923	Traylor, Michael G.	3	1921–1922
Thorsen, James W.	2	1930–1933	Treat, Hugh P.	MG	1912–1914
Throckmorton, Alwyn C.	Hd-1	1927–1930	Tregenza, John R.	3	1934–1937
Throckmorton, Burton H.		1917–1919	Tregoe, William L.		1917–1918
Throckmorton, Edgerton A.	1	1921–1925	Trimble, Rufus J.	2	1915–1918
Throckmorton, John W.	1	1921–1925	Troescher, Robert F.*	3	1898–1904
Throop, Enos T.*	2	1902–1903	Trowbridge, Samuel B. P.*	1	1890–1894
Throop, Enos T., Jr.	2	1929–1934	Trudeau, Edward S.*	3	1898–1898
Throop, George E.	1-Hd	1889–1898	Trumbull, Allan T.	4	1916–1917
Thrope, Stanley B.	2	1908–1917	Trusdale, Joseph R.	2	1908–1909
Thrower, Frederick M., Jr.	1	1937–	Tryon, Clarke	2	1934–1937
Thurber, Francis B., Jr.	2	1906–1911	Tucker, Allen*	3	1896–1901
Thurber, Francis B., 3rd	1	1933–	Tucker, Russell Evans, Jr.		1917–1919
Thurber, LeGrand	1	1938–1938	Tucker, William L.	Med	1931–1937
Thurman, Isaac B.	1	1889–1889	Tuckerman, Alfred G.	3	1927–1930
Thurston, Edward H.	1	1921–1923	Tuckerman, Eliot	2	1900–1907
Tiebout, Todd G.	2	1924–1929	Tuckerman, Roger	2	1917–1919
Tilney, Thomas J.	1-Hd	1921–1923	Turnbull, Robert J., Jr.	1	1899–1904
Tilt, Albert, Jr.	1	1897–1917	Turner, Arthur E.	1	1918–1920
Tilt, Benjamin B.*	1	1898–1917	Turner, Howard G.	4	1912–1915
Tilt, Rodman K.	3	1929–1932	Turner, John S.	3	1936–
Tilton, Ernest R.*	1	1889–1891	Turner, Spencer*	1-MG	1908–1917
Tilton, McLane, 3rd	1	1928–1931	Turner, W. Bradford	MG	1915–1917
Tilton, Stephen*	3	1903–1909	Turner, Wallis S.	3	1901–1907
Timblin, Louis McF.	1	1933–	Turner, Warren H., Jr.	2	1938–
Timmerman, Louis F., Jr.	3	1920–1926	Tuttle, Clarence W.	2	1927–1928
Tingue, Wm. J.	2	1900–1906	Tuttle, Winthrop M.	1	1895–1900
Tingue, William M.	3	1938–	Tweddell, Francis T.	MG	1916–1917
Tinker, Edward L.	1	1901–1902	Tweedie, Montague S.	1	1889–1894
Tinsley, Frank	2	1920–1932	Twiss, John R.	Med	1925–1935
Titus, James G.	1	1938–	Twyman, Edwin B.	2	1936–
Titus, Warren H.	1-2	1890–1898	Tyng, Sewell T.*	1	1889–1892
Tjader, Richard T.	3	1928–1929	Tyrrell, Leo D.	2	1918–1921
Tobey, Harold	3	1911–1914	Tyssowski, John	1	1915–1917
Todd, James, Jr.	1	1930–1936			
Toler, Henry P.	3	1913–1916	Ulman, Morrison	3	1924–1925
Tompkins, Boylston A.	1	1918–1925	Underhill, Jacob B., Jr.	1	1915–1917
Tompkins, Douglas L.	1	1918–1919	Underwood, Kennard	MG	1912–1914
Tompkins, Frederic P.	2	1935–	Underwood, William A.	2	1934–1937
Tompkins, Joseph G.	2	1934–1936	Upton, Kenneth	MG	1913–1916
Tompkins, Stuart W.	3	1924–1927			
Toolan, Cyprian	1	1921–1923	Vail, Charles St. J.	2	1918–1918
Torr, John M.	1	1918–1918	Vail, John I. B.	Md	1916–1917
Townsend, A. F.	1	1901–1912	Valentine, Donald	3	1925–1930
Townsend, Charles Coe	1-4	1904–1915	Valentine, Langdon B.*	2	1898–1899
Townsend, Donald C.	1	1915–1917	Valkenburgh, Roger R.	3	1937–1938
Townsend, Edward D.	2	1924–1929	Valpy, Edward	2-3	1903–1906
Townsend, Edward H.	1	1913–1914	Van Alstyne, David, Jr.	2	1922–1922
Townsend, Henry P.	3	1913–1916	Van Arsdale, Malcolm G.	1	1918–1918
Townsend, Howard, Jr.	1-Hd-1	1922–1925	Van Benthuysen, Boyd	2	1900–1906
Townsend, John C.*	1	1911–1914	Van Beuren, Frederick T., Jr.	1-Med	1899–1910
Townsend, John W.	1	1907–1908	Van Beuren, Frederick, T., 3rd		1931–1936
Toy, Channing R.	2	1908–1914	Van Brunt, Arthur H., Jr.	2	1930–1934
Toy, Horace L.	3	1931–1935	Van Cott, John D.	1	1921–1922
Toy, Thomas T., Jr.	3	1927–1929	Vandegrift, Wm. B.	3	1930–1931

SQUADRON A

Name	Troop or Detachment Served	Date of Enlistment and Final Discharge
Vanderbilt, Oliver de G.	4-3	1907–1912
Vanderhoff, Francis Bailey	1-3	1907–1912
Vanderhoff, George W., Jr.	3	1909–1917
Vanderhoff, Wm. B.	2	1910–1915
Vanderpoel, S. Oakley, Jr.	2	1903–1905
Vanderpoel, Wm. H.	2	1906–1911
Van Keuren, Wm.	3	1930–1933
Van Meter, Galen	4-2	1920–1926
Van Ness, Wallace K.	2	1922–1925
Van Norden, Max L.	1-MG	1907–1917
Van Rensselaer, Kilisen, Jr.	2	1900–1905
Van Rensselaer, Lyndsay	1-2	1891–1896
Van Schaick, Singleton*	1	1897–1900
Van Siclen, Edward H.	1	1918–1918
Van Sinderen, Adrian, Jr.	2	1934–1937
Van Sinderen, Henry B.	2-4	1911–1917
Van Steenbergh, James Taylor	2	1917–1918
Van Tine, Addison A.	4	1911–1914
Van Vleck, Edgar W.	3-1	1898–1899
Van Winckle, Edgar B., Jr.	3-4	1906–1909
Van Wyck, Henry	2	1922–1925
Varlet, Rene G.	2	1929–1933
Veiller, Frank D.	3	1898–1901
Vermilye, Frederick M.	1	1889–1894
Vermilye, Henry R., Jr.	2	1930–1933
Vietor, Carl*	1	1904–1916
Vietor, Frederick A.	1	1915–
Vietor, John A.	Med-MG	1909–1914
Violett, Lanier J.	1	1929–1934
Vogel, Joseph	3	1924–1925
Von Bermuth, Oscar M.	2	1898–1901
Von Goeben, Roland	2	1924–1928
Von Grimm, Andrus	1	1918–1918
Von Raits, Eric A.	1	1934–1937
Von Saltza, Philip W.	1	1913–1917
Voorhees, Peter V. D.	2	1926–1930
Voorhees, Willard P. V.	2	1939–
Voorhis, Peter A. H.	Hd-3	1923–1925
Vosburgh, Arthur S.	1	1891–1893
Vought, Donald William	1	1917–1918
Waaler, Reidar	1-3	1917–1921
Wacker, Henry E.	1	1922–1929
Wade, Robert B.	1	1897–1897
Wadelton, Willard T.	2	1939–
Wadhams, William H.	3	1899–1917
Wadhams, Wm. H., Jr.	2	1928–1931
Wadsworth, John E.	3	1936–
Wadsworth, Seymour	1	1923–1933
Wagstaff, George B.	2	1908–1913
Waid, Jesse E.	2	1921–1927
Wainwright, Loudon S.	2	1921–1923
Waldecker, Sydney C.	2	1921–1921
Waldo, Maturin F.	1	1938–
Walholm, Roy W.	2	1929–1930
Walker, Alexander D.	2-3	1899–1920
Walker, Edward Washburn	4	1911–1914
Walker, Elisha, Jr.	3	1934–1936
Walker, John L.	2	1921–1922
Walker, John M.	1	1915–1916
Walker, Paul	3	1925–1928
Walker, Roberts*	1	1900–1905
Walker, Russell Tracy	1	1916–1918
Walker, Willard F.	3	1914–1917
Walker, Wm. C.	3	1919–1921
Wallace, Edward S.	2	1920–1921
Wallace, Gustavus	1	1898–1898
Wallace, Lewis G.	1	1913–1917
Wallace, Russell A.	2	1938–
Wallace, Stanley L.	2	1938–
Wallace, Wm. J.	1-2	1892–1899
Wallace, William J.	1	1937–1938
Waller, Lawrence Waite	2	1917–1919
Walsh, Arthur B., Jr.	2	1935–1936
Walsh, James W., Jr.	2	1909–1917
Walsh, Lawrence J.	2	1931–1935
Walsh, Reginald L.	3	1929–1930
Walter, Henry G., Jr.	2	1936–1938
Walthew, Francis G.*	Hd-1	1923–1926
Walton, Davis S., Jr.	2	1898–1900
Walton, Kenneth	4	1920–1921
Walz, George, Jr.		1917–1919
Warburg, Gerald F.	3	1921–1922
Ward, Alexander L.	3	1898–1918
Ward, E. Mortimer	1-Hd-2	1892–1906
Ward, Edgar A., Jr.	2	1933–1936
Ward, Guy A.	1	1889–1893
Ward, Henry M.	1-3	1895–1917
Wardman, Ervin	1	1896–1898
Wardwell, Allen	3	1898–1917
Warfield, Frederic P.	3-1-3	1907–1919
Waring, Arthur B.	2	1927–1928
Warner, Eltinge	2	1918–1920
Warner, Peter R.	4	1918–1920
Warner, Robert W.	1	1918–1919
Warner, Walcott M.	Hd-1	1923–1928
Warren, Charles P.	2	1895–1897
Warren, George E.	1	1914–1916
Warren, Henry M.	1-3	1895–1917
Warren, James C.	3	1921–1923
Warren, Louis B.	2	1928–1931
Warren, Moses Allen	3	1904–1905
Warren, William C.	2	1935–1936
Washburn, Arthur L.	Med	1924–1926
Washburn, John H.	1	1935–
Washburn, Loring	3	1915–1917
Washington, George Augustine	2	1909–1919
Waterman, David H.	Med	1937–
Watjen, Louis F.	3	1931–1934
Watkins, John B.	2	1936–
Watrous, Charles A.*	1	1891–1893
Watson, Archibald R., Jr.	1	1933–1936
Watson, Harold E.	MG	1915–1917
Watson, John J., Jr.	2	1905–1912
Watson, Preston*	3	1897–1906
Watson, Theodore S.	MG	1915–1917
Watt, Robert H.	2	1937–1937
Watterson, James J.	3	1914–1917
Wattles, Gurdon W.	1	1928–1928
Watts, Edward E., Jr.	3	1922–1923

SQUADRON A 389

Name	Troop or Detachment Served	Date of Enlistment and Final Discharge	Name	Troop or Detachment Served	Date of Enlistment and Final Discharge
Watts, John	3	1930–1930	White, Gustave J. S.	3-MG	1910–1914
Watts, Samuel H.	2	1895–1899	White, Harold T.	1	1898–1904
Weaver, William S.	1	1935–1938	White, Nelson L.*	MG	1915–1917
Webb, Charles	3	1898–1901	White, Ralph Lee	MG	1914–1917
Webb, Earl W.	1	1918–1920	White, Robert C.	3	1938–
Webber, Marvelle C.	2	1895–1896	White, Robert D.	1	1896–1902
Webster, Anthony	Hd	1921–1922	White, Robert E.	3-2	1927–1928
Weed, Charles W.	1	1921–1923	White, Robert V.	1	1915–1917
Weeks, Harold H.	3-2	1905–1906	Whitehead, Lyman T.	1	1925–1932
Weeks, Percy S.	2	1906–1913	Whitehead, Oothout Z.*	2	1895–1898
Weeks, Percy S., Jr.	1	1936–	Whitehead, Wm. S., Jr.*	2	1895–1899
Weeks, Richard F.	3	1914–1917	Whitehouse, G. Meredith	1	1933–1938
Weeks, Sylvester Marius	4	1917–1919	Whitehouse, George N.	1	1898–1900
Weidlich, Clifton F.	3	1934–1937	Whitehouse, Guill S.	3-MG	1910–1920
Weigl, George E.	1	1934–1934	Whiteley, George A.	3	1921–1926
Weiler, Charles B.	Hd	1926–1927	Whitfield, Henry D.	1-2-3	1899–1917
Weinman, Morris	3	1926–1926	Whiting, Borden	3	1899–1900
Weisbach, Arthur H.	Hd-2	1923–1925	Whitlock, Bache McE.	3	1913–1915
Weisbrod, Ivan V.	2	1918–1921	Whitlock, George F.	3	1928–1929
Welch, Herbert A.	1	1921–1922	Whitman, Herbert S.	3	1934–1935
Welles, Russell	2	1922–1923	Whitman, John S.	3	1930–1931
Welling, Charles H.	3	1912–1917	Whitman, Robert	3	1931–1936
Welling, Richard W. G.	3	1902–1908	Whitney, Alfred R.	1-4-Hd	1897–1912
Wells, Francis D.	3	1935–	Whitney, Frank	3	1918–1919
Wells, George J.	2	1930–1933	Whitney, Livingston	1	1901–1917
Wells, James L., Jr.	2	1920–1927	Whitney, Robert U., Jr.	2	1939–
Wendt, Alfred*	1-Hd	1895–1919	Whitney, Stanton*	3-MG	1901–1919
Wendt, Charles*	1	1896–1920	Whitney, Steven S.	1	1916–1917
Wenzell, Adolphe H.	2	1923–1927	Whiton, Augustus S.	3-4	1907–1909
Werlemann, Frederic H.	3	1917–1919	Whittaker, Thomas S.	3	1901–1907
Werlemann, Frederic H.	3	1917–1932	Whittemore, Charles L.	2	1925–1926
Werlemann, George E.	3	1921–1927	Whittemore, Howard	1	1889–1890
Werner, Robert G.	2	1934–	Whittlesey, Granville, Jr.	2	1927–1930
West, Randolph	Med	1916–1917	Wickersham, Cornelius W.	2	1915–1916
West, Robert N.	3	1921–1922	Wickersham, Cornelius W., Jr.	2	1935–
Westcote, William T., Jr.	2	1927–1927	Wickersham, James H.	3	1922–1925
Westcott, Franklin H.	Med	1931–1934	Widdifield, John W.	2	1927–1927
Wester, Anthony	Hd	1921–1922	Wiggin, Frank H.*	1	1889–1892
Westerfield, Jason R.	1-4	1907–1908	Wigham, Reginald E.	1	1898–1917
Westerman, John J., Jr.	Med	1916–1916	Wight, Griffith	3	1916–1917
Weston, George S., 2nd	1	1903–1919	Wilcox, Rollin Crawford	4	1917–1919
Wetherell, Alexander*	3	1906–1911	Wilcox, Wm. M.	2	1905–1906
Wetmore, Russell	3	1935–1935	Wilde, Helm G.	1	1936–1937
Wettling, Louis E., Jr.	1	1920–1921	Wilding-White, Alex. M.	3	1930–1934
Whalen, Edward	2	1923–1926	Wilding-White, Henry de Z.	3	1937–1937
Whaley, Charles C.	3	1916–1917	Wildman, Herbert A., Jr.	1	1934–
Whaley, William	1	1930–1934	Wilkes, Franklin J.	3	1936–1937
Wharton, Richard*	1-2	1898–1899	Wilkins, Frederick F.	4	1915–1916
Wheeler, Herbert, Jr.	3	1927–1930	Willard, Henry Bowers	1-4	1906–1911
Wheeler, Millar	1	1937–1939	Willard, James A.	1	1930–1932
Wheeler, Wm. A. S.	1	1925–1925	Willard, LeBaron Sands	1	1904–1908
Whidden, Rae Wygant	4	1914–1916	Willett, George	2	1918–1920
Whitacker, Harry J.	3	1918–1920	Williams, Andrew Murray	1	1906–1907
Whitaker, Henry C.	1	1939–	Williams, Coleman G.*	1	1891–1896
Whitcomb, Ernest M.	1	1907–1912	Williams, E. Winslow	3	1916–1917
White, Alexander M., Jr.	2	1927–1930	Williams, Earl Trumbell*	1	1911–1914
White, Alfred T.	3	1931–1934	Williams, Hadley B.	2	1934–
White, Bernard H.	1	1939–	Williams, Henry W.*	1	1889–1899
White, Charles C.	Med	1910–1910	Williams, Henry W.*	2-4-2	1904–1914
White, Francis D.	MG	1914–1917	Williams, Howard H.	1	1932–1935

SQUADRON A

Name	Troop or Detachment Served	Date of Enlistment and Final Discharge	Name	Troop or Detachment Served	Date of Enlistment and Final Discharge
Williams, Ichabod T.	2	1931–1936	Woodruff, Alonzo D.	4	1916–1918
Williams, Linsly R., Jr.	1	1935–1938	Woodruff, Ernest W.	4	1916–1917
Williams, Paul W.	1	1930–1933	Woodruff, Walter A.	3	1924–1925
Williams, Ramon O.	3	1922–1924	Woodward, Edward P.	3	1934–1936
Williams, Thomas R.	2	1908–1916	Woodworth, Irving	2	1918–1918
Williams, Weston	1	1903–1908	Woolley, John E.	1	1921–1924
Williams, Wiley M.	2	1920–1923	Woolley, Roger M.	1	1924–1929
Williams, William	3	1897–1899	Woolverton, Wm. H., Jr.	2	1914–1917
Williams, Wm. N.	2	1905–1906	Wooster, Thomas T.*	1	1902–1908
Williamson, George DeWitt	3	1896–1909	Worrall, Walter L.	3	1935–1937
Willis, Frederic A.	3	1915–1917	Worth, R. Donald	3	1920–1921
Willis, Harold S.	MG	1916–1917	Worthington, Arthur L.	2	1939–
Willis, Henry H.	1	1932–1935	Wright, Glenn	3	1900–1907
Willis, Joseph G.	2	1903–1906	Wright, Griffith	3	1916–1917
Willis, Reginald S.*	3	1903–1918	Wright, Harrison	1	1914–1917
Wilpan, Charles L.	1	1935–1935	Wright, John A.	1	1921–1922
Wilson, Christopher W.	3	1937–1938	Wright, Joshua B.	2	1901–1906
Wilson, Daniel L.	Hd-3	1928–1931	Wright, Stevens T. M.	2	1937–
Wilson, Edward D.	2	1936–1939	Wright, William A.	1	1938–1938
Wilson, George L.	2	1928–1932	Wright, William P., Jr.	3	1936–1936
Wilson, Henry W.	Hd-1	1921–1922	Wright, William R.*	3-Hd	1896–1918
Wilson, Stanton W.	1	1931–1933	Wright, William R., Jr.	3	1935–1938
Wiltsie, Irving L.	1	1891–1895	Wurster, Frederick, Jr.	1-Hq-3	1903–1918
Wiman, Francis G.*	1	1892–1896	Wurts, Pierre J.	3	1897–1902
Winant, Cornelius*	3	1924–1927	Wyatt, Inzer B.	1	1933–1936
Winant, Frederick, Jr.	MG	1916–1917	Wyckoff, Clarence P.	3	1901–1919
Winants, G. E.	3	1916–1916	Wyeth, Maxwell*	3-2	1899–1902
Winkelhorn, Kai G.	2	1928–1929	Wylie, Robert S.	3	1938–
Winkhaus, John T., Jr.	1	1939–	Wynkoop, Gerardus M.	1	1889–1893
Winslow, Albert F.	1	1937–	Wynne, William	2	1923–1924
Winslow, John C.	1	1935–1936			
Winslow, John S.	1	1916–1917	Yassukovich, Dimitri M.	2	1927–1929
Winslow, Thomas Scudder*	MG	1916–1917	Yearley, Alexander, 4th	1	1932–1932
Winsor, George A.	2	1918–1920	Yearley, Dorsey	3	1939–
Winter, Keyes	2-1	1901–1906	Yedinack, Charles S.	1	1932–1936
Wirth, John E.	Med	1932–1935	Yeomans, Moreau	1	1932–1933
Wise, Henry A., Jr.	1	1934–	Yerkes, Leonard A., Jr.	3	1932–1933
Wise, John S.	1	1928–1938	Young, Benjamin S.	3-MG	1906–1917
Wisner, Charles H.	3	1930–1934	Young, George S.	2	1923–1924
Wittlig, Norman T.	3	1937–	Young, George W., Jr.	3	1923–1929
Wittmer, Edward O.	1	1932–1935	Young, S. Marsh	1	1889–1892
Wolfe, Charles Holmes	2	1917–1919	Youngs, Graham*	3-MG-4	1900–1918
Wolpin, Alfred A.	1	1918–1918	Yung, Bartlett Golden	1	1904–1906
Wood, Cornelius, Jr.	1	1903–1906			
Wood, Edward A.	1	1916–1917	Zabriskie, Kenneth A.	2	1922–1925
Wood, P. Erskine	2	1909–1913	Zachry, Greer	1	1926–1930
Wood, John F.	2	1935–1938	Zimmerman, Charles H.	1	1917–1936
Wood, Ralph S., Jr.	2	1936–1939	Zimmerman, Louis	1	1916–
Wood, Walter F.	3	1896–1918	Zimmerman, Louis Justus	4	1917–1919
Wood, William D.	3	1923–1923	Zimmermann, Charles		1917–1919
Wood, Willis B.	2	1925–1927	Zinsser, Dr. Hans	3	1896–1900
Woodford, Wm. H. J.	3-Hd	1922–1925	Zinsser, Rudolph	4	1912–1917
Woodle, Bernon T., Jr.	2	1939–	Zinsser, Wm. Herman	4	1912–1916

Made in the USA
Charleston, SC
25 June 2010